EXCERPTA MALDIVIANA

EXCERPTA MALDIVIANA

H. C. P. BELL

GYAN

Published by

Gyan Publishing House
5, Ansari Road
Daryaganj, New Delhi-110002
Phone: 011-47034999, 9811692060
E-mail: books@gyanbooks.com

Distribution Network
gyanbooks.com
India, USA, Canada, UK, Australia, France

ISBN : 978-81-212-3373-6 (PB)
First Published, Colombo, 1922-1935

2nd Impression 2020

Printed at: Gyan Press, Delhi.

The book at your disposal is the edition of an old book originally published long back. The Text quality of this book may not be at par as compared to our other books but many readers approached us to reprint this important book so that it could satiate their hunger. We request all the readers of this book to help us to improve its quality by providing the necessary text of those pages which are not properly visible. Your valuable support in this case will be highly appreciated and acknowledged and our future readers will be benefitted immensely.

PLATE I.

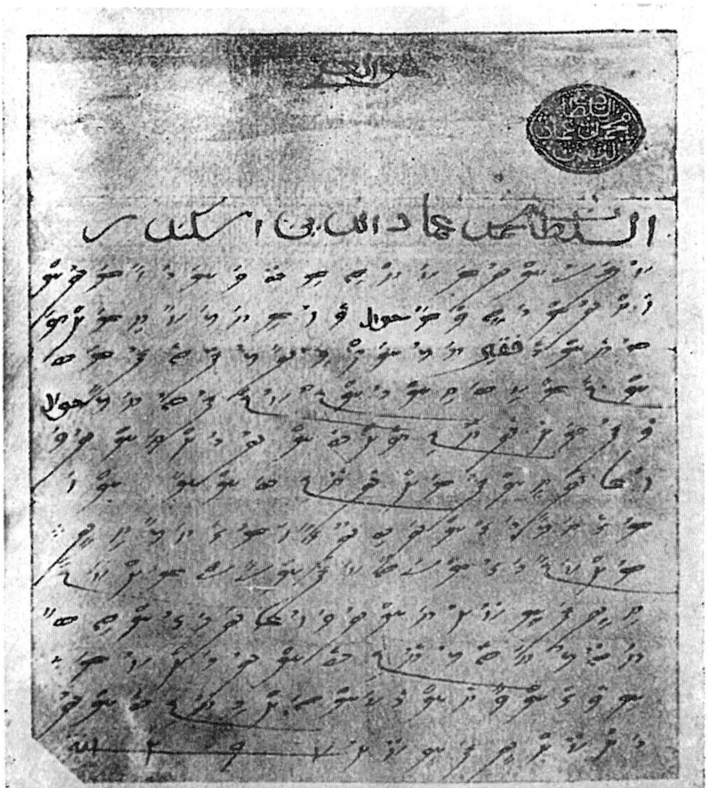

MÁLDIVIAN GOVERNMENT PERMIT:
A. H. 1297 (A. C. 1879-80).

EXCERPTA MALDIVIANA.

BY H. C. P. BELL.

No. 1. Maldivian Government Permit.

The original Máldivian document, reproduced to two thirds size on Plate I, was given to the writer (then attached to H. M. Customs, Galle) by the *Málim*, or Master, of a Máldive *Oḍi*, which had been driven into Weligama Bay by stress of weather in September 1885, nearly forty years ago.

It came to light somewhat recently, when a miscellaneous assortment of Máldivian Papers was being overhauled.

The document is a form of "Permit" issued by the Máldivian Government (at that time under the seal of the Sulṭán, but now-a-days stamped with that of the *Boḍu Baḍérigé*, or Kachcheri) to the *Atoḷuveri*, or Revenue Officer, of Haddummatí Atol, on behalf of an islander named Kuḍa Futu of Munḍú, for the construction of a "*Furedda Oḍi*," or vessel intended for Foreign Trade, at Dambidú, another Island in the same Atol.

Given below are :—(a) Line-for-line Transcript of the *Tána* writing;* with (b) Word-for-word meanings in English underneath†; (c) Notes; and (d) a running Translation.

---

* Like Arabic, read from right to left. The two particular *Tána* letters *avieni* and *ṛavieni* employed with *sukun* for (i) duplication of consonants and (ii) silent termination of words, appear respectively transcribed in brackets thus :—(A), (R).

† Valuable aid towards a better understanding of the document has been kindly rendered by my friends I. Aḥmad Dídí, *Kuḍa Doṛiméná Kilagefánu*, and I. 'Abdul Hamíd Dídí Effendí, Máldivian Government Representative at Colombo, both sons of A. Ibráhím Dídí, *Boḍu Doṛiméná Kilagefánu*, the present aged Prime Minister at Málé.

Transcript[1]

HUWA'L GHANÍ

As-Sulṭán Muḥammad 'Imád-ud-dín[2]

He (God) is richest in bounty.

(1) *AS-SULṬÁN* *MUḤAMMAD* *'IMÁD-UD-DÍN*
The Sulṭán Muḥammad 'Imád-ud-dín[3]
ISKANDAR[4]
. Iskandar.

(2) KULA SUNDURA KA(Ḍ)TIRI BOVANA
of pure race a Kshatriya of the World
MAHÁ RADUN[5]
Great King

(3) HA(Ḍ)DUNMATÍ[6] VÁRÁ *HAVÁLA*VE
of Haddummatí (Atol) the revenue in charge of
HURI AḶAKÁI RA(Ṛ)YA-
(who) is to the servant and to the inhabit-

(4) -TU ENME *FAQÍR*[7] AḶUNA(Ṛ) VIDÁḶU
ants all poor servants (this is) the expressed
FATE[8] FURA BA-
Order (Paper). The Ancient

(5) -NḌÁRA[9] KIBAIN MUNḌÚ[10] KUḌA FUTU
Government from of Munḍú Kuḍa Futu
AḶÁ *HAVÁLA*-
servant authorised

(6) -VE FURA(Ṛ)DE OḌIYE(R)[11] BENDUMA(Ṛ)
is (for) Foreign (trade) an Oḍi for the building
AN DUVA-
(of) former days

(7) -HU *'Á*DAIN FURA(Ṛ)DE
according to the (usual practice) (for) Foreign (trade)
OḌI BANNÁN HA-
an Oḍi to build

(8) -RUGE AḶA MAGUN
a shed of putting up in the (usual) manner
DABIDÚ-GA[12] HARUGE AḶÁI DÍ
at Dambidú a shed (you should) erect (and) give.

(9) RU(Ṛ) KAḌÁ MAGUN[13]
Coconut trees of cutting in the (customary) manner
SATÉKA FANSÁS RU(Ṛ) KAḌÁ-
100 50 coconut trees (you) must get cut

(10) -I DÍFANÍ KOṚU AN DUVAHU ÁDA
and give (of) former days according to

MAGUN TIBÁ
the custom (throughout) the (*lit.* your)

(11) ATOḶU ATOḶU OḌI BENDUMA(Ṛ)
Atoḷs (of an) Oḍi for the construction

KURA-
done

(12) -NI VEGENVA ENME KANTA(Ṛ) MI
in the usual way all work (of) this

OḌI BENDU-
Oḍi (for) the building

(13) -MA(Ṛ) KO(Ṛ)DÍFANÍ KOṚU[14] 1297[15] *Sanat.*
(you must) get done 1297 (Ḥijra) year.

Notes

1. *Transcript*:—Words or parts of words in Máldivian *Tána*, are printed in small capitals; words or parts in *Arabic*, in italic larger capitals; the word for word meanings and the running translation in ordinary type, with italics where necessary.

2. *Sulṭán's Seal*:—Sulṭáns' Seals (variously shaped) appear at the top of the Annual Missives to the Dutch and English Governments in Ceylon; as well as on Máldivian *fatkoḷu*, or grants, etc., issued by the Sulṭáns' direct orders.

3. *Sulṭán Muḥammad 'Imád-ud-dín IV*. (*A. C. 1835-1882*):—Great grandson, in direct line, through Sulṭáns Haṣan Núr-ud-dín (A. C. 1778) and Muḥammad Mú'ín-ud-dín I (A. C. 1799), from Sulṭán Haṣan 'Izz-ud-dín (A. C. 1759-1767), the founder of the Mulí Dynasty.

His long reign of 47 years was politically uneventful, with one important exception—the British Admiralty Survey of the Máldive Archipelago (carried out in the earliest years of his rule), an undertaking of International moment.

He was succeeded by his second son, S. 'Ibráhím Núr-ud-dín—the elder son being ineligible owing to blindness—whose eldest son S. Muḥammad Shams-ud-dín III (after some revolutionary vicissitudes, terminating with the deposition of his cousin S. Muḥammad 'Imád-ud-dín VI) ascended the throne, for the second time, in A. C. 1903. See Sessional Paper, XV., 1921, pp. 20-22.

4. *Iskandar*:—" The Máldive Sulṭáns have assumed the fulsome cognomen *Iskandar*—applied by Arab and Persian writers to Alexander the Great (*Iskandar-al Rumí*)—

perhaps by virtue of supposed descent from the wide-ruling *Iskandar Dhul'lkarnein* ('the two-horned'), a traditional Persian King of the First Race, contemporary of Abraham, and tenth descendant from Noah". (*Bell: The Máldive Islands*, 1882, p. 76).

5. *Birudas:*—Honorific Sanskritic-Siṇhalese epithets, sometimes lengthy, were attached to each Sulṭán, or Sulṭána, from the first Sulṭán Muḥammad-ul-Ádíl (A. C. 1153-4). Variants occur in extant Annual Missives of the 18th Century. These *birudas* have been curtailed since the 19th Century to the stereotyped phraseology "*Kula Sundura Kattiri Bovana Mahá Radun.*" On their coins Máldive Rulers have long styled themselves in Arabic *As-Sulṭán ul bar va'l baḥr* "Sulṭán of Land and Sea, *i.e.*, World". *Loc. cit.* p. 63.

6. *Haddummati Atol:*— Shaped like a ham from N.E. to S.W. Lies between 73°.14′ and 73°.36′, longitude; 2°.7′ and 1°.45′ North latitude, it stretches approximately 17½ miles both from North to South and from East to West at broadest. Separated from Huvadú Atol on the South by the One and Half Degree Channel, and on the North from Koḷumaḍuḷu Atol by the Veimandú Kaḍu Channel.

The inhabited islands (13 in all) lie along the Eastern reef, and round that to South as far as Mávaru on the South-West.

A very thriving Atol. Historically, too, much in evidence; *inter alia* its largest Island, Isdú, having added one, if short-lived (A. C. 1701-1704), dynasty, to those of more than eighty Máldive Sulṭáns; and another Island, Gan, being the birth-place of two of the compilers of the *Tárikh*, or Chronicle of the Máldive Sulṭáns, viz: the *Kázis*, Ḥájí Ḥasan Táj-ud-dín and his grandson Ḥájí Íbráhím Shiráj-ud-dín.

Buddhist Ruins, reported to exist on Gan and Mundú Islands, were explored by the writer in March, 1922.

7. *Faqír:*—"Poor"; used in the sense of "helpless", "commiserated", the Sulṭán standing to his "poor subjects" *in loco parentis*

8. *Fate:*—Orders, grants, etc., under Sulṭáns' seals are styled *Fat* (pronounced *Fai*)-*koḷu* (royal suffix). *Fate*=Siṇhalese *pata*. *Vidáḷu fate*=*vadáḷa panata* of Siṇhalese *Sannas*.

9. *Fura Banḍára:*—The regular term in documents for the Máldivian Government. *Fura:* "Ancient" (Siṇ: *purána*), or "preeminent" (Siṇ: *para*). *Banḍára:* Used of the "Sulṭán" as well as the "Government" (Siṇ: *Banḍára*).

10 *Mundú* :—The fifth island with inhabitants on the Eastern reef of Haddummatí Atol, having Máíbaidú, Huliyandú, Dambidú, and Isdú in succession to north of it.

A dágaba mound (long ago exploíted by the Muslim islanders to build their Mosque, and now in complete ruin), and other traces of Buddhist occupation were examined here on March 20th-21st, 1922. The mound (standing by itself on the right of houses) in Plate II A is the ruined dágaba.

11. *Furedda Odí* :—Máldivian vessels are usually classed, as follows :— (i) *Furedda Odi* (length 36 to 45 ft.) ; (ii) *Bandu Odi* (22 to 32 ft.) ; (iii) *Daturu Odi* (16 to 18 ft.) ; (iv) *Mas Odi* ; (v) *Mas Dóni* (both 14 to 20 ft.).

Formerly *Furedda Odi-faharu* traded as far as Aden (West) and Achin (East). Nowadays No. (i) trade to Calcutta with coconuts ; No. (ii) to Cochin and Colombo with dry fish (M. *kummala mas* ; Sin. *umbala kada*) chiefly ; No. (iii) are used for coastwise trade within the Atols ; (iv) and (v) are fishing boats.

See Plate II. B, for a *Daturu Odi* entering Málé Harbour.

12. *Dabidú* (pronounced *Dambidú*) :—Immediately to south of Isdú, at N.E. end of the reef ; and from early days one of the chief islands of the Atol. The present active old *Atoluveri* (Headman), Hájí 'Ali Fulu Koyá, resides here. This island is exceptional in possessing a *Furedda Odi*.

13. *Ru(r) kadá magun* :—Will also bear the meaning " in the Coconut-cutting-Street ". There are said to be such " streets " for this purpose in some islands

14. *Ko(r)dífaní koru* :—Archaic expression found in documents : the modern equivalent is *ko(r)dífati*.

15. *A. H. 1297* = A. C. December 15th, 1879—December 4th. 1880.

Translation

The Order vouchsafed by (His Highness) Sultán Muhammad 'Imád-ud-dín Iskandar, a Kshatriya of pure race, Great Monarch of the World, to the person in charge of Revenue (Collection) at Haddummatí (Atol), and to all (Our) poor subjects.

(Our) servant Kuda Futu of Mundú (island) is (hereby) authorised by the Máldivian Government to build a *Furedda Odi*.

(You should, therefore,) have a shed put up, according to the usual practice at Dambidú (island); and, (further), have one hundred and fifty coconut trees cut down following the customary method.*

(You must forthwith) get everything done† for the construction of this vessel in accordance with the usage observed throughout the‡ Atols for the building of such vessels.

(Granted, *Anno Ḥijrae*) 1297 year.

---

* Or "from the Coconut-cutting Street". At the present day probably but few islands could spare such a drain on their trees.

† Pois aquillo, que os Reis já tem mandado,
Não pode ser por outrem derogado (Camoens, viii, 82).

‡ Literally "your" (*tibá*).

PLATE II.

A.

HADDUMMATÍ ATOL: MUNḌÚ ISLAND.

B.

MÁLDIVIAN DATURU OḌI

EXCERPTA MÁLDIVIANA.

By H. C. P. BELL, C.C.S. (Retired).

No. 2. SULTANS' MISSIVES: A.C. 1713; 1819.*

The Annual Embassy from the Sultán of the Máldive Islands to the Ceylon Government usually arrives at Colombo in the course of the last three months of the year.

During the Dutch occupation of the seaboard of the Island—and even in British times up to 1844 at least—a complimentary letter was sent yearly to the the "*Govorunadóru,*"[1] or Governor at Colombo.

This affords striking proof of the conservatism and ignorance of events, outside "their own little world," formerly displayed by the Máldive Islanders, loath to break through a custom initiated at least as early as the Embassy in 1649 to Galle; then, and until Colombo was captured from the Portuguese in 1656, the chief seat of the Dutch Power in Ceylon.

The Sultáns' Missives have contained ordinarily request for the continuance of the friendship and favour of the Dutch and British Government in turn; for protection against enemies; and for aid to any Máldivian subjects who may chance to be wrecked on Ceylon shores; concluding—for a long period at least—with an apology for His Highness's Ambassadors, and the regular tender of presents.

These Letters clung so closely to a virtually stereotyped form, as to differ but little during the course of more than two and a half centuries.

* Indispensable help in the translation of the Máldivian texts and the notes has been generously afforded the writer by Ahmad Didí Effendí *Kuda Doriméná Kilaqefánu*, and 'Abdul Hamid Didí Effendí, Máldivian Government Representative.

This applies almost equally to the replies of Dutch and British Rulers alike. The Colombo Governors (and Commanders at Galle no less) have studiously promised to do everything in their power to promote the good understanding subsisting with the Sulṭans; undertaken to succour shipwrecked Máldivians, whilst stipulating for the same friendly office on the part of the Sulṭáns towards British subjects castaway on the Máldive Atols; closing their communications with expression of approval of the conduct of the Ambassadors; and finally specifying the return presents.

In the late Seventies of last Century, the writer, when serving as a Ceylon Civil Servant in Colombo, was enabled, by express permission, to examine the Dutch and English Archives at the Record Office; with the more special object of unearthing all available information regarding the Máldive Islands.

He was fortunate enough to reap a rich harvest; particularly in historical research touching Ceylon's Dependency, "*Divehi Rájje*" or "the Máldive Kingdom".[2]

More than 120 original Missives received from the Máldives came to light,[3] covering the reigns, in whole or in part, of nine Sulṭáns, from S. Muzaffar Muḥammad 'Imád-ud-dín II., of the Diyamigili Dynasty (accession, A.C. 1704) to S. Muḥammad 'Imád-ud-dín IV. (accession, A.C. 1835), the fifth Ruler of the Mulí Dynasty; which still claims the throne, in the person of his grandson, Sulṭán Muḥammad Shams-ud-dín III. (first accession, A.C. 1893; second, A.C. 1903).

These Missives, or a representative selection, may possibly some day be given to the world by the Ceylon Government. Meanwhile, it will not be amiss to publish, from time to time, in the Journal of the Ceylon Asiatic Society some of the Letters of more than formal interest from the long series.

Towards this end, as a start, two Missives are being dealt with in the present Paper. These have been selected, advisedly, for four main reasons:—

(i.) The first Letter is the oldest known actual Missive extant, albeit written in *Tána* the present-day Máldivian script.[4]

(ii.) A century separates it in age from the other Letter.

(iii.) The evolution in the form of the current Máldivian characters is, thereby, the more clearly marked.[5]

(iv.) The contents of the two Missives differ wholly.

Transcripts, with word for word meanings in English, are followed by explanatory Notes, and rounded off by running Translations.

A. SULTAN'S MISSIVE: A.C. 1713.

This, the earliest original Letter from any Máldive Sulṭan discovered in the Dutch Archives,[6] is of much historical value. It confirms the "*Tárikh*," and "*Ṛádavali*", or Chronicles of the Sultáns of the Máldive Islands, as to the particular Sulṭán reigning at the commencement of the 18th Century.[7]

By A.C. 1713 Sulṭán Muzaffar Muhammad 'Imád-ud-dín II., had become firmly seated on the throne. He had secured the Sovereignty nine years previously (A.C. 1704) owing to fortuitous circumstances.

In that year, his predecessor, Sultan Íbráhím Muzhir-ud-dín, of the short-lived Isdú Dynasty, (who had ousted his own cousin, Sulṭán Hasan X., a boy), went the *Ḥajj*; and was confidently reported to have perished at sea on the return voyage.

Persuaded of their Sultán's death, the stronger party's influence at Málé, over-riding the claims of his nephew, raised to the *Masnad* the Chief Vazír,

Muḥammad *Dorimèná Takurufánu*, a distant relative, whom the departing Sulṭán had named as Regent during his pilgrimage.

In reality Sulṭán Íbráhím Muzhir-ud-dín had made landfall somewhere on the coast of India.

Three bold, but fruitless, efforts (the last and nearly successful in A.C. 1711, or only two years before the present Missive was penned) were made by the adventurous ex-Sulṭán—the "Boḍu Kilagefánu" of story—to recover the throne, with aid obtained on the Indian Continent.[8]

Sulṭán Muḥammad 'Imád-ud-dín II. died in A.C. 1721; and was succeeded by his son, the able Ruler Sulṭán Íbráhím Iskandar II.

At the latter's demise in 1750, the Dynasty passed from disaster to disaster; first by the capture and deportation of Sultán Mukarram Muḥammed 'Imád-ud-dín III. in 1752;[9] finally coming to an end, in the third generation, with the murder of Sulṭán Íbráhím Iskandar's only son, Sulṭán Muḥammad Ghiyás-ud-dín, in 1774.[10]

The Letter now published is the Annual Missive of the year (A.C. 1713) it bears on its face;[11] and is couched in a strain humbler than are those of a later date. The fear of renewed attempts by his persistent rival to regain the throne may well account for the earnest, almost pathetic, appeal to the Dutch Governor not to deprive the Sulṭán of his "sheltering care."

In style, the Missive affects, in the phraseology of the day, that simplicity which all Máldivian correspondence, official or private, has always assumed.

The type of the *Tána*-writing will be seen to be both bolder and more stilted, than that in vogue a Century later.

Archaic word and letter forms prevail;[12] the peculiar "J" and "T" are at this day obsolete; "Ṛ" and "N," for (*a*) silent termination and (*b*) re-duplication of succeeding consonant, by far out-number *avieni* (Λ), so freely used in the Letter of A.H. 1235[13] (A.C. 1819); whilst palatal "Ñ" and cerebral "N" (and these, strangely, combined with dental "N") find no place in the later Missives.

The Sultán's seal, name, and the era are alone here written in Arabic: later Missives contain many words both Arabic in language and script.

The use of the honorific plural (*e.g.* AḶUGAḌUMEN, MANIKUFÁNUMEN) was customary.

Very noticeable is the employment of the Christian Era, bespeaking the influence, at the period, of European traders to Málé. Letters of later years exhibit general preference for years *Anno Ḥijrae*, with occasional lapses to *Anno Christi* dating.

Transcript

SEAL[14]

AL MA'UN BIL MALIKIL MUBÍN AN-NÁSIR SHARI'AT MUḤAMMAD UL AMIN AS-SULTÁN MUHAMMAD 'IMÁD-UD-DÍN. LATÍF ALLÁH IBÁDAT AMÍN.

LETTER

1. KOḶUBU / At Colombo — RASKAMUGAI / the Kingly rule — VAḌAIGEN / occupying — INNAVÁ / who is — GOVORUNADÓRU / to the Governor

2. RASGEFÁNA(Ṛ) / Ruler — DIVEHI RÁ(A)JE / of the Máldive Kingdom — *AS-SULṬÁN* / (We) Sultán — *MUḤAMMAD* / Muḥammad — *'IMÁD-UD-DÍN* / 'Imád-ud-dín

3. RASGEFÁNU / King — LA(Ṛ)KA / lakhs — HÁS / thousand — FAṚU / fold — VEDUN[15] / salutation — DENNEVÍMU / make known — AḶUGAḌUMEI[16] / We

4. KO(N)ME IRAKU VIAS KOḶUBU INNAVÁ
whatever time be it at Colombo (who) is
RASKALAKUGE HEU DEKE
of the Ruler kindness (who) have seen

5. E BEI KALUGE VÁGI VERIKAN LIBI TIBE
(and) of that person aid [*lit.* strength] (who) receive
MÍHÍMU AḶUGAḌUMEN-
are the men. With Us

6. ÑÁI HUNNA SUHUBA(Ṛ)TERIKAN KAḌU(N)VAI
existing the friendship break
NU(Ṛ)FAVANI MAṆIKU-
do not Your

7. FÁNÍ AḶUGAḌUMENÑA(N) HIAO AḶAIGEN
Honour to Us shade affording
HUNNA GEHEN FADA SÁHIBÍ VÉ AḶU-
(which) is a tree like the Lord (You) are.

8. -GAḌUMENÑA(N)GE HAI KANTAKAI AḶUGAḌMENÑA(N) VÁ
To Us any matters to Us
TURÁOTAKÁI
and difficulties

9. MAṆIKUFÁNUMENÑA(N) EGI HUNNAṆÍ MIHÉNÍ
to Your Honour are known. This is because
AḶUGAḌUMENGE E(N)ME HAIKAN-
of Our all affairs

10. -TA(N) MAṆIKUFÁNUMEN KABARU ANGÁ
to Your Honour news (who) inform
MÍHÍMU MAṆIKUFÁNUNGE FARUVÁ HIAO
(We) are the men. Of Your Honour's care the shade
DAṚU(N)
(who are) under

11. AḶUGAḌUMEN BÉRU NUKURA(Ṛ)VANÍ
from Us separate do not
AḶUGAḌUMENÍ MAṆIKUFÁNU HEU HÁLU-KOḶU GA-
We Your Honour in good health

12. -DAVE RAFUTUGAI VAḌAIGEN INNAVÁ
vigour and happiness of the continuing
KAMA(N) EDI • DUVÁ KURA MÍHÍMU
in the state (who) prayer make are the men.

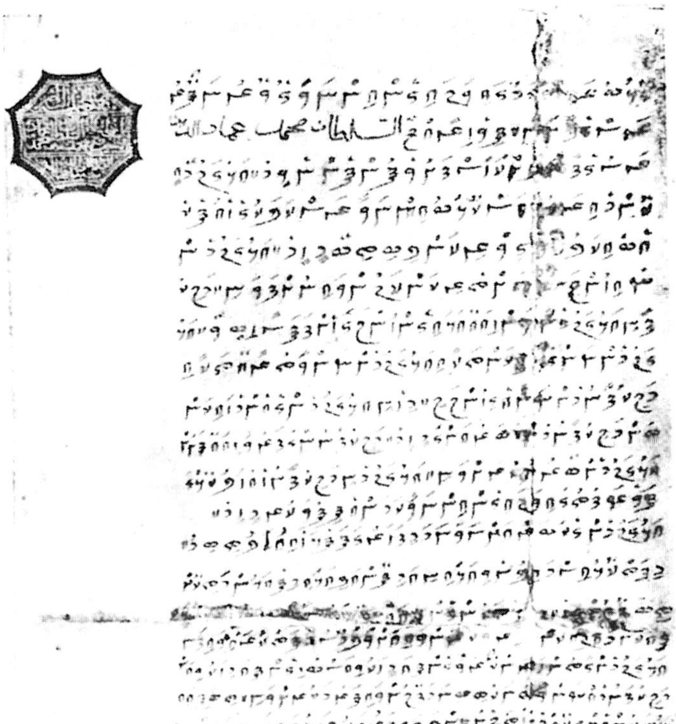

SULTAN'S MISSIVE : A. C. 1713.

Scale : One-third (approx.)

13. AḶUGADUMENGE KABARU A(Ṛ)SAVA NAMA
Of Us news (You) enquire if

MIFAHARU GADA DULAHEI UHALU TIBÍMU
now in sound health (and) happiness (We) are.

14. MI FAṬ-KOḶU ISMAILU NEVI[17] AḶÁI
This missive Ism'á'il Nevi. (Our) servant (and)

NIAMI[17] DON ALI AḶÁI MI DE
Niami Don Ali (Our) servant these two

AḶUN MATIKO(Ṛ)
(Our) servants in charge

15. TIBÁ FONU(N)VÍME (A) MI AḶUTAKUN
placing (We) send. To these (Our) servants

GENDIA ETI KOLAKU VIÁFÁRIKAN
(which) they have taken few things for trading

KURA(Ṛ)VAI
cause (help)

16. DIAKANA MAADIAKANA (.) RAVA[18] KARA(N)VAI
.... cause.

A (Ṛ) VALU MUSUMU DATU[18]
In the early monsoon (their return) voyage

KURA(A)VAIFANI
cause (despatch of).

17. AḶUGAḌUMEN GÁTUN HARÁN-KÓRU[19] VEGEN
Us towards rebel becoming

DIA MÍHAKU VIAS BEHIGEN[20]
has gone (any) man if driven out of course

DIA MÍHAKU VIAS
has gone (any) man if

18. MAṆIKUFÁNUMENNA(N)VA TANAKU TIBI NAMA
(where) Your Honour is to the place (it) be if

FONU(N)VAI DARUMA KURA(Ṛ)VANI TIBA
having sent the kindness do Us. To Your (country)

DIA A-
(who) have gone (Our)

19. ḶUTAKUN ENGI KO(A)ME MUHUTÁJEN[21]
servants make known whatever wants

FIN(N)LAVAI DARUMA KURA(Ṛ)VAIFANI
having satisfied the kindness do.

FAIBÉI A-
In the past

20. -HARU DO(Ṛ)ṬAḌAFI[22] KALÓGE ATU MAṆIKUFÁNU
year by Doṭṭaḍafi Kalóge's hand Your Honour
FOṆUVI FAT-KOḶÁI HADIÁ-KOḶÁI[23] HA(Ṛ)DUVI
(which) sent Missive and presents (We) received.
AḶUGAḌU-
Our

21. -MENGE BOḌU VE HU(A)NA MUHUTÁDÍ KO(N)ME
great (which) are wants in whatever
AHARAKU DANNAVÁ MUHUTÁJU[21]
year made known (those are) the wants.
MI FAT LIUNÍ 1713
This Missive is written 1713

22. MI VANA JANÍRU[24] OITENBARU(N) 16
of this being January October 16
MITA(N) VI HOMA
this (which) is Monday.

Notes

1. *Govurunudoru*:—Corruption, doubtless through Portuguese, of the Latin *Gubernator*. The transliteration of the word greatly exercised the Máldivian State Secretaries: the first part appears in Sulṭáns' Missives under a variety of forms more or less close, e.g., *Govorana-*, *Goruna-*, *Gorna-*, *Govan-*, *Goun-*, *dóru*.

Of the "Commander" at Galle, they made *Kubudóru*.

2. Partially embodied in "Report on the Máldive Islands," Sessional Paper, XLIII., 1881.

3. *Sulṭáns' Missives*:—All the original Missives of the Sulṭáns which had survived between A.C. 1713 and A.C. 1880, were, with the consent of the Government, photographed and lithographed, or both, at the writer's charges.

These comprise Letters of S. Muzaffar Muḥammad 'Imád-ud-dín II. (Máldivian *Tána*, 2) 2: S. Ibráhím Iskandar II. (*Tána*, 9; Arabic, 2; Portugese, 3; French, 1) 15: S. Mukarram Muḥammad 'Imád-ud-dín III. (*Tána*, 8) 8: S. Haṣan 'Izz-ud-dín (*Tána*, 6; Arabic, 1) 7: S. Muḥammad Ghiyás-ud-dín (*Tána*, 8; Arabic 1: French 1) 10: S. Muḥammad Mu'izz-ud-dín (*Tána*, 3) 3: S. Haṣan Núr-ud-dín (*Tána*, 19) 19: S. Muḥammad Mu'ín-ud-dín I. (*Tána*, 11; Arabic, 4) 15: S. Muḥammad 'Imád-ud-dín IV. (Arabic, 44) 44.

Some of the Missives are choice specimens of calligraphy, written in red and black characters; one (A.H. 1208) of S. Haṣan Núr-ud-dín has an ornamental border in gold foliation.

4. The earliest original Missive in *Tána* known is dated A.C. 1713; the latest A.H. 1241 (A.C. 1825) Thereafter all have been in Arabic.

5. The oldest form of Máldivian script yet discovered, (i) *Evéla Akuru*, is that of copper-plate grants (*Lómáfánu*) which have survived to this day. This type, strikingly resembling medieval Sinhalese, gradually developed into (ii) *Dives Akuru* characters: which, though no longer employed, are known to a limited number of Máldivians on the Group.

Both (i) and (ii) read from left to right, the former approximating to the lithic script of Ceylon inscriptions much more closely.

The third form of character, (iii) *Tána*—based on Arabic and Persian elements, and, like them, read from right to left—seems to have been in concurrent use with (ii) *Dives Akuru* from the 17th Century at least, if not earlier.

For detailed information regarding the *Dives Akuru* and *Tána* Alphabets, reference may be made to C.A.S. Journal, Vol. XXVII., Extra Number, 1919, Appendix C.

6. The Dutch Archives contain an Arabic copy of Governor Laurens Van Pyl's reply, in A.C. 1688, to a Missive from "Muḥammad Íbráhím," the Sulṭán then reigning, viz., S. Iskandar Íbráhím I., son of S. Shujáy Muḥammad 'Imád-ud-dín I.

7. See "The Máldive Islands," Sessional Paper, XV., 1921, p. 17.

8. *S. Íbráhím Muzhir-ud-dín*:—He made the first attempt to re-land at Málé within a month of his successor's accession (A.D. 1704). On this occasion he was seized, and banished to Fua Mulaku; his cousin Sulṭán Haṣan being sent to Hitadú Island in Aḍḍu Atol, where he lived in exile until his death in A.C. 1758.

The former, after five or six year's captivity, managed to escape to Ceylon, and thence reached India: where, obtaining substantial aid, he again essayed to capture Málé, but had to retire ingloriously (A.C. 1711).

Towards the end of the same year he repeated his twice abortive efforts with a larger expedition; and by a night assault nearly succeeded in carrying Málé by storm.

The reigning Sulṭán notified the Dutch Governor H. Becker (October 19th, 1711) that Providence had intervened to repel his enemy: *Nu heeft God gementioneerd vyand weder van heer verdreven* (Dutch translation).

9. *S. Mukarram Muḥammad 'Imád-ud-dín III.* :—Betrayed by the Máldivian Kázi, Muḥammad Shams-ud-dín, and his brother Ahmad Muhuy-ud-dín, Khatíb, to Ali Rája of Kannannúr in A.C. 1752.

Those of the Malabars who remained at Málé incontinently put the traitors to death; but were themselves overwhelmed within a few months by a rising of the Máldivians led by Don Maniku, son of *Muhammad Famudéri* Vazír who met his Sulṭán's fate.

He was raised to the throne, as S. Haṣan 'Izz-ud-dín, in A.C. 1759 by a grateful people, after the ex-Sultán's death in captivity.

10. *S. Muḥammad Ghiyás-ud-dín* :—Shared the captivity in India of his uncle, the deported Sulṭán; but some years later escaped and returned to Málé; where he was given royal honour. On the death of S. Haṣan 'Izz-ud-dín in A.C. 1767 he succeeded to the throne, the latter's sons being then minors. Sailing in A. C. 1773 on a pilgrimage to Mekka, he was refused landing on his return to Málé the following year, and murdered by adherents of the late Sulṭán whose wife and children he had banished.

De male quaesitis vix gaudet tertius heros. See Sessional Paper, XV., 1921, p. 19.

11. The writing on Missive of A.C. 1713 measures 11¼″ × 7″, and runs to 22 lines. The photograph (Plate I) shows the old creases in the letter as found folded.

12. Cf: the old *Tána* writing on the *Pandanus* booklet of Máldive "Charms" *(Fadita Fot)* in C.A.S. Journal, Vol. XXVII., Extra Number, 1919.

13. See Sulṭán Haṣan Núr-ud-dín's Missive of A.H. 1210 (A.C.1795), reproduced in Sessional Paper XLIII., 1881; as well as C.A.S. Journal Vol. XXXVII., Extra Number, 1919, where specimens of the present writing are given for comparison.

14. *Sultán's Seal* :—Octagonal; 1 9/10 in.; slightly cusped. This was the favourite shape up to the reign of S. Muhammad Mu'izz-ud-dín; though S. Hasan 'Izz-ud-dín used only smaller seals, round or oval. S. Hasan Núr-ud-dín changed from octagonal (one seal only), and large oval, to smaller horizontal *vesica piscis*. S. Muhammad Mu'ín-dìn I usually preferred a bold circular seal to the latter; but the pointed-oval has been re-adopted since invariably.

15. *Vedun*.—"Has two meanings, (*a*) 'present,' (*b*) 'salutation.' Inferiors use *Salám* (Arabic) in the latter sense" (A.H. Dídí).

16. Read *Alugadumeni* (line 3); *daturu* (line 16).

17. *Nevi*; *Niami* :—*Nevi* was the Chief Máldive Agent and Senior Official in charge of Government or private goods shipped; *Niyami*, the Captain, or Tindal, responsible for the vessel's safety and navigation.

18. "The passage seems unintelligible as it stands: perhaps there is something omitted" (A.H. Dídí).

19. *Harán kóru* :—"*Haram* (Arabic) 'opponent' or 'rebel' *Kóru* here is meaningless" (A.H. Dídí).

20. *Behiyen* or *Behigen gos* (Pyrard: *behigue*, "sailing with the wind and current"). Cf. Drake's (old English) "spooming along before the sea."

21. *Muhutájen* :—"*Muhutáju* should be *mutádu* (Arabic, *muhtaj*)" (A.H. Dídí).

22. *Dottadafi* :—One of the many honorific titles (*kangati nam*), now virtually obsolete, such as *Dánná*, *Fenná*, *Kánná*, *Oliginá*, *Kavalanná*, *Wata Baderi*, &c.

23. *Hadiá* :—Arabic "present". "*Hadiá* presents are exchangeable between equals only; *Vedun* offered to a superior, or *vice versá*." (A. H. Dídí).

24. *Janíru* :—"January". "This term is still employed to denote the Christian Era; but *Isagefánu* ('Jesus Christ') is more usual." (A. H. Dídí).

Translation

SEAL.

The Noble Muhammad, who seeks help from God of the Universe the Imparter of action (motives), by His knowledge of good and bad, and the

Grantor of happiness; Whose laws he (*i.e.*, the Sulṭán) upholds, *viz.* the Sulṭán Amín Muḥammad 'Imád-ud-dín. O God, to that (His) Highness show kindness and mercy, overlooking his shortcomings. Amen.*

LETTER

To the Governor ruling at Colombo, (We), Muḥammad 'Imád-ud-dín, the Sulṭán of the Máldive Islands, offer countless (*lit.* lakhs and thousand-fold) salutations.

We have experienced at all times the goodwill of the Rulers at Colombo, and assistance from them. Be pleased not to (*lit.* do not) break the friendship which exists between Us. (Your Honour is) the Lord (*Sáhib*) who, like the shadow of a tree, doth protect Us. Everything that befalls Us, and the difficulties which beset Us, are known to Your Honour, by reason of Our (*lit.* being the persons) ever keeping (Your Honour) informed regarding all Our affairs. Do not, (We beg), deprive Us of Your Honour's sheltering care, under which We abide.

We (*lit.* are persons who) offer prayers that (Your Honour) may continue in perfect health, vigour, and happiness. Should Your Honour desire to enquire regarding Our health, We are now in the enjoyment of sound health and happiness.

This Missive is sent (to Your Honour) in charge of (Our) two subjects Ismá'il *Nevi* and Don 'Ali *Niyami*. (Graciously) help them to dispose of the few commodities they have taken to trade withal; and (kindly) despatch them early in the monsoon.

Should any persons either inimical towards Us have gone, or (any other persons) been driven out of their course (*behigen*), to any place belonging to Your Honour, (kindly) send them back to Us.

---

* The writer is indebted to I. 'Abdul Hamid Dídí Effendi for transcript and translation of the Sultán's Seal.

Whatever requests Our servants who went to Your (domain) make, (be pleased to) satisfy.

The Missive and presents sent by Your Honour last year, in the hands of *Doṭṭaḍafi Kalóge*, were (duly) received.

Our chief wants are those which (We) make known every year.

This Missive is written on Monday, the 16th October, of this Christian Year, 1713.

B. SULTAN'S MISSIVE: A. C. 1819.[1]

In 1819, the "Hayston," a British vessel, outward bound, with a cargo of metals, wines, glassware and spices, was driven by the S.W. Monsoon on to a reef then uncharted, of the Northern Máldive Atols.

The officers, passengers, and crew took to the ship's two boats and a raft; but owing to the violence of the sea, the larger boat was lost, with all on board.

The other boat and raft, which held the Captain and twenty-nine men, after four days battling with the waves, were fortunately observed by some Islanders; who rescued all the surviving ship's company.

Taken first to Makunudú Island,[2] the Captain and other survivers were (in accordance with strict Máldivian regulation) conveyed subsequently in the Islanders' boats to Málé, the seat of Government.

From here the whole party was transported to Ceylon and India—fourteen men, with the Captain, to Galle; the remaining fifteen to Chittagong.

The Captain, with the first batch of castaways, reached Galle during the last week of August.

On August 28th, the Collector, Galle, reported to the Chief Secretary to Government:—

"I called upon Captain Sartorius, who informed me that every possible attention was shown himself, passengers, and crew during their residence at Málé.

Good houses were allotted them, plenty of the best food the Island afforded furnished, and as much clothing as they required. The boat in which they arrived here was furnished expressly to convey them; and all payment by bills on the shipowners at Calcutta, or other remuneration, refused. They all speak with gratitude of the kind treatment they received at Málé." *

The present Missive of Sulṭán Muhammad Mu'ín-ud-dín I. is one of many similar communications received by Dutch and British Governors in Ceylon testifying to numerous instances which stand to the infinite credit of the Máldivians and their Rulers; wherein, for centuries past, like humane conduct has been displayed by the Islanders towards persons shipwrecked on their Atols.[3]

By former Máldivian Law, or long standing usage, all wrecks were invariably held to be royalty, the property of the Sultan.

This custom, mentioned by Pyrard (French captive at Málé, A.C. 1602-1607,[4]) also ruled in other sea-board States of India, *e.g.*, Kálastri, Sáwantwári, &c.

Under different Treaties with the East India Company, Indian Princes consented to waive their right to wrecks; but no such agreement would appear to have ever been contracted with the Máldive Sulṭáns.[5]

The Máldivians may lay claim to the proud distinction of being probably the only race, similarly situated on the face of the globe, who have not required to be taught by special contract, or legal enactment, the duty they owe their fellow men who have fallen into "troubles by shipwreck" on their "tempest-haunted" Atols.

"*Homines enim ad deos nullâ re proprius accedunt quam salutem hominibus dando.*" (The Maldive Islands. Sess: Pap. XLIII., 1881).

---

* This communication from Galle was kindly supplied by Mr. E. Reimers, Government Archivist.

The "*Europa*" had been wrecked on the Máldives in 1812; in 1815 a Galle Dhoney was also driven ashore there; to be followed, within four years, by the "Hayston."[6]

In the first case the Governor of Ceylon, Sir R. Brownrigg, notified, the Sultán (S. Muḥammad Mu'ín-ud-dín I.) that he had expressed more than once his "sense of the kindness afforded" by His Highness similarly: on the second occasion the cargo of cinnamon from the Dhoney was presented to the Sulṭán in acknowledgment of his "humanity and care."

The third wreck, that of the "Hayston," called forth further hearty testimony to the same Ruler's enlightened action:—

"I have had," wrote the Governor (September 6th, 1819), "with great satisfaction the Letter which Your Highness' Messenger, who lately arrived at Galle, brought to the Collector of the District, containing the particulars of the loss of an English ship off the Máldive Islands, and of the humane treatment the officers, passengers, and crew who were so fortunate as to survive the wreck received from Your Highness during the period of their detention within Your dominions. The vessels in which they were despatched to Ceylon arrived in safety

"I am most happy to learn that the conduct of the unfortunate sufferers gave Your Highness so much satisfaction while they remained under Your protection, and thereby rendered themselves worthy of the kind and benevolent care Your Highness was pleased to take of them.

"I have sent a present* similar to the Annual one usually made to you from this Government, together with

* The present shipped to the Sulṭán on September 22nd, 1819 comprised:—One bale of cinnamon; one ream of Europe paper; one quarter pound each of cloves, mace, nutmegs and cardamons; five pieces of sealing-wax; and five pounds of pepper.

a bale of cinnamon, which I request Your Highness to accept as a mark of my friendship and esteem.

"I shall always be most happy to assist the vessels belonging to my good friends, Your Highness' subjects, whenever such assistance is required.

"May Your Highness continue to enjoy a long, happy, and prosperous reign."

The sharp and pleasing contrast between the courteous behaviour of Captain Sartorius of the "Hayston," and the disgraceful proceedings of Captain Alwayn and the crew of the "Europa"—conduct so outrageous as finally to necessitate the temporary incarceration, and subsequent surveillance, of Captain and Pilot at Málé[7]—doubtless induced the happy eulogy of the former so quaintly expressed in an unsophisticated paragraph of the Sulṭán's Missive.

Transcript

Seal

AS-SULṬÁN MUḤAMMAD MU'ÍN-UD-DÍN

Letter*

1. *AS-SULṬÁN* / The Sulṭán — *MUḤAMMAD* / Muḥammad — *MU'ÍN-UD-DÍN* / Mu'ín-ud-dín

   ISKANDAR / Iskandar — KULA / of pure — SUNDURA / race — KA(A)-

2. -TIRI / a Kshatriya — BOVANA / of the Universe — MAHA / Great — RADUN / King.

   GÁLÍ / Of Galle — KÓṬÉ / Fort — BOḌÁ / to the Great — SÁHÍBA(A) / Lord — MITA(N) / these — LA(A) / lakhs

3. -KA HÁS / thousand — FAṘUN / fold — *DUVÁ SALÁM* / prayers (and) salutations.

   MANIKUFÁNUMENGE / Of Your Honour — IGERÉZÍGE / an English — TIN / three.

4. -KUBU / masted — NAVE(A) / a ship — MI / at this — DIVEHI RÁ(A)JEYA(N) / Máldivian Kingdom

   URINJE EVE / grounded. — MI / This — NAVU / ship's — KA(A)FITÁ- / Captain

---

* Headed by HU'AL GHANI "He (God) is most bountiful."

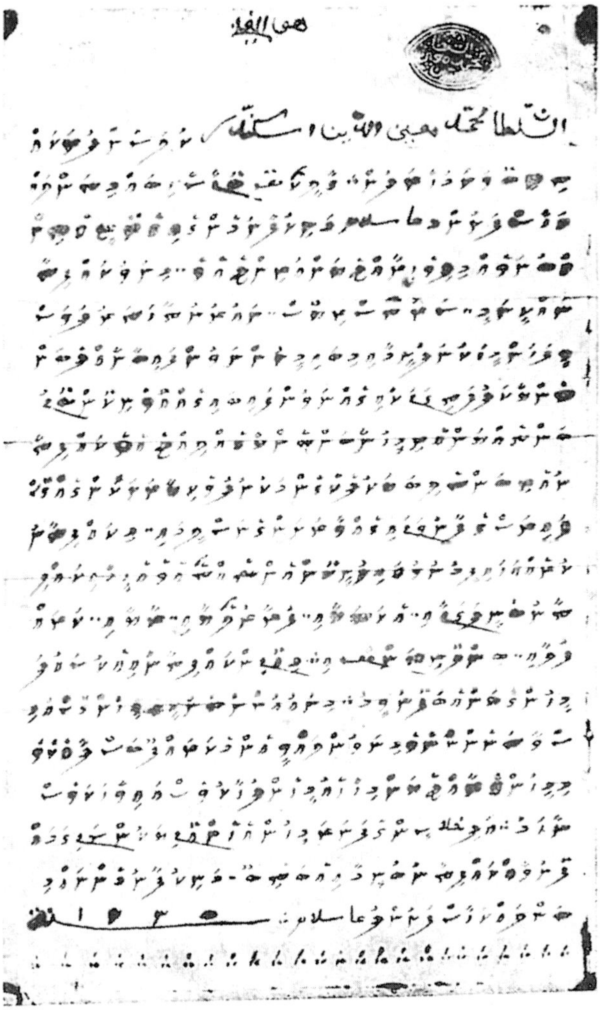

SULTĀN'S MISSIVE: A. H. 1235 (A. C. 1819).

Scale: One-third (approx).

5.	-NA(A)	KÍ	NAMÍ	"SARUTÓSRIYÚS"
		(is)called	(by)the name	Sartorius.
	NA	URUNUTÁ	HATARU	DUVAS
	The ship	grounded	four	days
6.	VÍ	FAHUN	MÍHAKU	NUDUṚÍMÁI
	being	after	by a man	not being seen
	MIBAI	MÍHUN	NAVUN	FAIBÁNÁ(A)
	these	men	from the ship	for landing
	DE	BA(N)-		
	two	boats		
7.	-TE(N)YÁ	KADUFATI GAḌAKÁI GEN		NAVUN
		and a raft taking		from the ship
	FAIBAIGE (A)	OḶENIKOn		BOḌU
	got onto	While remaining (on the sea)		in the big
8	BA(N)TE(A) YAN	ERI		MÍHUNÁ
	boat	(who) embarked		the men
	BA(N)TE(N)YÁ	GE(A)LI(A)JE EVE		KA(A)FITÁ-
	(and) the boat	sunk.		The Captain
9.	-NU	ERI	BA(N)TELI	BAYAKU
		(in which) embarked	the boat	people
	DEL̲EGEN	MAKUNUDU VE	KIYÁ	RAṚAKA(N)
	having seen	Makunudú being	called	to an island
	GENGOS-			
	having taken ;			
10.	-VAI RASGEFÁNU	VAḌAIGE(A)VÁ		RAṚA(N)
	the King	(where) residing		to the Island
	GENASLÍMAI	MI	KA(A)FITÁNU	
	when brought	this	Captain	
11.	KURE(A)	AHAIFÍMU	NUVUGAI	HURÍ KON
	from	We asked	"In the ship	are what
	E(N)CHE(A)-TOEVE		EHÍMÁI	KA(A)FI-
	things"?		When asked	the Captain
12.	-TÁNU	BUNÍ	DAGADÁI	EKATAYÁI FUKÁRU
		said	"Iron,	steel, sheets,
	LÓYÁI	RÁYÁI	KARA(A)	
	copper,	wines,	cloves,	
13.	-FULÁI	BI(N)LÚRI	TA(N)TÁI"	MI ODIN
		glass	dishes.	In this *odi*
	KA(A)FITÁNÁI	EKU	SAUDA	
	the Captain	with	fourteen	

14. MÍHUN GÁYA(N) EBA FONUVÍMU MI NAU
men to Galle We have sent. This ship
URUNU TANA KÍ MI MÍHUN
(where) grounded place called these men (Máldivians)
GOS AI-
gone (and) come

15. -SVÁ TANE(N) NUNEVE MI NAVUN
a place is not. From this ship
LA(A)VÍ E(N)ME KARA(A)FÚ BASDÁ EKEVE
was beached in all cloves bag one.

16. MI MIHUNGE RÁ(A)JEYA(N)
Of these (Máldivian) people to the Kingdom
MÍHA HEU MIHE(N) DUHÁKUVES
such good man at any days
AI VÁHAKA VES
came news

17. NÁHAMU ADI *KALÁSÍNGE* FANARA
We never heard. Further of the sailors fifteen
MÍHUN EHEN OḌIYAKUN SAḌIGAMA(A)
men in another *oḍi* to Chittagong

18. FONUVÁ(A) KA(A)FITÁNU BUNÍMÁI
(whom) to send the Captain having asked
EBA TIBÚ MANIKUFÁNUMENNA(A) MI-
are remaining. To Your Honour these

19. -TA(N) LA(A)KA HÁS FAṚUN
lakhs thousand fold
DUVÁ SALÁM *SANAT* 1235[8]
prayers and) salutations. (Ḥijra) year 1235

Notes

1. The writing (19 lines) on the original Missive covers 12½ inches by 8 inches. Both reduced photographs (**Plates I, II.**) are approximately one-third size.

The Seal is of horizontal *vesica piscis* shape; 1 5 12 inches by 1 inch.

2. *Makunudú* (*Malcolm Atol*):—A large lagoon reef, 15 miles long by 3 miles broad, 10 miles West of Miladummaḍulu Atol, North.

Said to have been unknown to Europeans previous to the Indian Navy Survey of the Máldives in 1834-36. According to native information many ships have been lost with all hands on its barren reef, scarcely a vestige of the wrecks remaining after a few hours, owing to the violence of the surf and the steepness of the reef.

Except Makunudú Island (lat. 6° 25′ N., long. 72° 41′ E.), inhabited, on the N.E., point and a small island N.W., there is nothing but the surf to mark the reef.

3. *Wrecks and Máldivian Humanity*:—Going back to the 17th and 18th Centuries.

In 1631 "the King (S. Muḥammad 'Imád-ud-dín I., A.C. 1629-1658) of the Islands wrote to D. George de Almeyda (Captain of a Portuguese vessel, wrecked in the Group,) condoling his misfortune and sending him a parcel of rice." (*Stephen, Faria-y Sousa, III., 397*).

In August, 1658, the "*Persia Merchant*" was wrecked on Tiladummatí Atol. The fifty survivors (passengers and crew) were well treated by the Islanders, given "toddy to drinke and rice to eate" with "fish and other good things, as hony (jaggery), on which they fed like farmers." Despite some bickering (probably induced by mutual misunderstanding), the shipwrecked Europeans were, after a month's stay, provided with a "a very good boate" (finally "agreed for in 200 pieces of eight"), in which they reached Ceylon at "Caliputeen" (Kalpiṭiya); and (except Mr. William Vassal with twelve others, who were taken to Kandy, and shared the captivity of Robert Knox and his fellows of the "Anne") ultimately found their way to India (*Indian Antiquary, Vol. XXXI., 1902*).

Thirteen years later, Rykloff Van Goens, the Dutch Governor at Colombo, sent a Letter and presents to the Máldive Sulṭán (Iskandar Íbráhím I., A.C. 1658-1698) in courteous acknowledgement of his good treatment of some Hollanders and native sailors, crew of a Jaffna vessel wrecked in his dominions. (*Dutch Records; Resolutions of Council, Colombo, 1671*).

The survivors of the Dutch ship "*Ravestein*," with a valuable cargo of gold, wrecked on the Atols in May, 1726, received every attention. The Sulṭán's tolerant action throughout, under most trying circumstances, justly evoked the gratitude of Governor P. Vuyst; who expressed his "hearty thanks for all the aid afforded and kindness shown," admitting the Sulṭán's "generous and kindly spirit" which had ignored the unruliness of the Captain. *The Máldive Islands*; *Sessional Paper XLIII., 1881, pp. 44-45*).

In 1777 the "Duras," a French vessel, with some ladies on board, was cast away on the Island of Himití (N. Nilandé Atol). All the shipwrecked folk met with the kindest treatment from the Islanders of the Atol where the ship was lost as well as at Málé.

4. *Máldivian Salvage Law*:—"Il se perdit lá (les Maldives) vn nauire appartenant au Roy d' Achen. Le Roy gaigna toute cette marchandise, qui luy appartient selon la coustume." (*Pyrard, Voyage*, 1679, pp. 210-11).

The law at the present day was clearly stated (September 22nd, 1905), by the Prime Minister to H. H. the Sultán in connection with the salved goods from the SS. "Crusader":—"One half of the goods saved by the Máldivians from a vessel wrecked in His Highness' dominions shall be the property of the Máldivian Government and the people who saved them; the other half is the property of the original owners." (*Papers relating to the Máldive Islands, 1904-1910*; p. 9.

5. See *Sessional Paper, XLIII., 1881*, p. 123.

6. *Loc. cit.* p. 130.

7. "*Europa.*":—*Loc. cit.*, pp. 47-8.

8. A.H. 1235 = A.C. October 21st, 1819—October 9th, 1820.

Translation

SEAL.

The Sulṭán Muḥammad Mu'ín-ud-dín.

LETTER.

(We), the Sulṭán Muḥammad Mu'ín-ud-dín Iskandar, a Kshatriya of pure race, Great King of the Universe, send to the Great Lord of Galle Fort countless greetings with our prayers.

A three-masted English vessel of Your Honour's Nationality has been cast away in this Máldive Kingdom. The name of the Captain of the ship is Sartorius.

Four days after the ship grounded, as no one had seen her, the (ship's) people took to the two boats and a raft.

Whilst still on the sea, the men who got into the large boat were lost with the boat itself.

The boat in which the Captain embarked having been seen by some of Our people (Máldivians) they took them (Captain and others) to an Island called Makunudú.

When they were brought to the Island where the King resides (Málé), We asked the Captain:—"What goods are on board the ship?" To this enquiry the Captain replied:—"Iron, steel, copper-sheets, wines, cloves, and glass-ware."

In this *Oḍi* We are sending fourteen men, with the Captain, to Galle.

The place where this vessel was wrecked is a spot which Our people do not frequent.

Only one bag of cloves was washed ashore from the ship.

We have never heard at any time of the arrival in our Kingdom of a man so good as this (Captain).

For the rest, fifteen sailors, who were to be sent to Chitagong in another *oḍi*, are remaining (at Málé), at the request of the Captain.

Lakhs and lakhs of salutations and prayers (We offer) to Your Honour.

(Dated,) A. H. 1235 (A.C. 1819).[8]

EXCERPTA MALDIVIANA.

By H. C. P. BELL, C.C.S. (Retired).

No. 3. "DIVES AKURU" GRAVESTONE EPITAPHS

MÁLE has been the Capital of the Máldive Islands ("*Divehi Rájje*"), and the residence of its Sulṭáns, continuously since the Twelfth Century at least, and in all probability for centuries earlier.

In this Twentieth Century the first, and most persistent, impression left on the European visitor to Mále is not unlikely to be that this much over-populated central Island,[1] which rules the Archipelago, is, in great degree, "a city of the dead."

The appalling redundance of graveyards which meet the eye, almost at every turn, induces reflections inevitably tinged with a sadness that is but half countervailed by that partial heart's ease offered so pathetically by the poet:—

They've a way of whispering to me—fellow-wight who yet abide—
In the muted, measured note
Of a ripple under archways, or a lone cave's stillicide:

"No more need we corn and clothing, feel of old terrestrial stress.
Chill detraction stirs no sigh;
Fear of death has even bygone us: death gave all that we possess"

Into "Sulṭán's Island"—an area, roughly one mile in length, East and West, by half a mile across,—there are crowded at this day no less than twenty-nine Mosques; to the majority of which are attached burial-grounds bristling, all too noticeably, with a veritable forest of stumps,—not live wood but dead stone,—mostly ranged in closest array. No "green graves of sires" these: just stark stiff coral slabs grey, grim and repelling.

It is not unsafe to aver that, during the lapse of the centuries through which Mále's little world has continued to "spin for ever down the ringing grooves of change" since the Island was first occupied, there can scarcely be six feet of Máldive earth (with the exception of the Palace Enclosure and the sites of the more revered Mosques and *Ziyárats*) but have at one period or another held the dead laid "beneath the Churchyard's stone."[2]

No secret is made at Málé now-a-days of the alarming fact that, for some time past, it has been found necessary to make urgently needed room, by clearing away the coral gravestones, (those easily friable monuments of the dead,) and levelling the ground in former, and even some existing, cemetries, in order to receive fresh occupants; or, as frequently, to put "God's acre" so reclaimed to prosaic mundane use in better housing the living and carrying out desirable Civic improvements.[3]

This charge does not apply to the more important graveyards adjoining the chief Mosques and other shrines, *viz*: the *Medu Ziyárat* (traditional burial place of Shaikh Yúsúf Shams-ud-dín of Tabríz, Apostle of Islám to the Máldives); the *Hukuru Miskit*, or "Friday Mosque," (where most Sulṭáns and lesser Royalties are interred, besides specially honoured subjects); *Danna Muḥammad Rasgefánu Miskit: Biharózu Miskit*[4] (the resting place of the great Máldivian hero, Sulṭán Muḥammad Boḍu Takurufánu); and certain others.

But in the case of the majority of Mosques at Mále, imperative demands on available space—dwindling seriously year by year,—whether for further interments or Municipal requirements, have inevitably forced the Government to assert its right to oust even the dead, after due efflux of years, on irresistible grounds of expediency.

Gravestones

At the Máldives gravestones front South, in accordance with strict requirement of Muhammadan sepulture.

In their shape they follow one unvarying design. All alike are elongated slabs, usually from two to four feet in height, with breadth proportionate.[5] According to Muslim custom, those used for females are rounded at the top; in the case of men, the stones taper finally in ogee curve terminating in a point, giving to these slabs the appearance of long shields reversed.

Carved from a close form of madrepore (*M. hirigá*), [6] the better finished head-stones usually exhibit a tall central arched panel, to which the margins of the slabs serve as plain broad framing edged inwardly by neat beading. The panel itself is bordered by a narrow inner frame, slightly ovolo in section, also plain, encircling the inscription, which is often cut between partitions divided horizontally by beaded fasciæ; the whole being so counter-sunk as to leave the letters—if of *Dives Akuru* or *Arabic* character, but not *Tána* which is incised—standing out in mezzo-relievo.

Only head-stones—and but one side of these—bear the engraved record.

The raised outside border, ordinarily left quite bare, is not infrequently covered with beautiful arabesques, which can occupy both flanks of the panel as well as top and bottom of the writing.

The face of the footstone, and the back of both, may be similarly treated.

Coral-stone lends itself admirably to infinite delicacy of involved sculpture; and the Máldivians have brought the delicate art of ornamental lithic chiselling to a very high level, owing to extraordinary skill in manipulation. The chasteness, wondrous variety, and exquisite technique displayed by the stone-masons of these little known Islands have always proved a source of pure delight to lovers of choice artistic work carried, as it is here to a marvellous pitch of perfection when displayed in endless profusion of geometrical and floreated detail of stone carving.

In this respect the chisellers in madrepore are matched only by the unique lacquer workers in their many-sided productions.[7]

Epitaphs

The legend, or epitaph, cut on gravestones at the Máldive Islands is worded either in the Máldivian language (with "*Ḥijra*" and title of the Muslim month always, and name of the deceased most frequently, in Arabic); or entirely in Arabic.

Where Máldivian is employed, the script used is now invariably the comparatively modern "*Tána*" writing (originally formed from a combination of Máldivian and Arabic numerals, with admixture of a few needed Arabic letters), which has wholly supplanted the archaic "*Dives Akuru*" for a long time past.

Even as far back as the commencement of the 18th Century at least only a small proportion of gravestone inscriptions was cut in this rounded character; itself a distinct modification of the oldest known *aksharas*, the "*Evéla Akuru*" of Máldive ***Lómáfánu***, or copper-plate grants by Royalty, which have such close affinities with Siṇhalese lithic inscriptions of the 10th to 12th Centuries.[8]

Probably not more than thirty gravestones and other slab records survive at Mále in *Dives Akuru*.[9]

The use of this medieval script for burial epitaphs, for *Fatkoḷu* (Royal grants on parchment or paper), and for Government Orders has quite died out, almost *pari passu* with the fast disappearing acquaintance with its very alphabet

In the whole of Málé Island at this day the number of persons possessing an intelligent knowledge of the *Dives Akuru* character, and capable of reading it in all its variants and combinations—especially as crowded into these mortuary records—can be counted on the fingers of one hand. This lamentable falling off in epigraphical knowledge has led recently to more than one wholly unexpected—and not greatly relished—discovery, the result of purely fortuitous circumstances.[10]

"Dives Akuru"

All that had been published prior to 1900 regarding that older form of Máldivian script, the *Dives Akuru*, which gradually gave place more and more from the 17th and 18th Centuries to the *Tána* (sometimes called *Gabuli Tána*) alphabet now in universal use at the Máldives, is contained in (i). a short reference, found in the "*Memoir*" compiled by Naval Lieutenants Young and Christopher (*Transactions, Geographical Society, Bombay 1836-8*) to "the most ancient character, called by the natives the *Devehi Hakuru*;" and (ii) the valuable, but incomplete, delineation (18 letters only) of the Alphabet communicated to Dr. Wilson by the latter officer (*Journal R.A.S. 1841, pp.42-76*), and reproduced by Mr. (now Sir) Albert Gray (*Journal R.A.S.* N.S. X, *1878*).

In 1919 the Ceylon Asiatic Society issued in its Journal (*Vol. XXVII, Extra Number, 1919*), with the author's permission, an English Translation by Mrs. C. Willis (revised by Mr. John Harward, President of the Society) of Professor Wilhelm Geiger's scholarly "*Maldivische Studien*, I, II." (1900-1902).

Professor Geiger's "Linguistic Studies" dwell almost exclusively on the Máldivian language; but in his Paper (Plate I) are given two professed lists of the *Dives Akuru* character, side by side with the *Tána* alphabet (*Maldivische Alphabete*), taken from a century-old Vocabulary (*Bibliotheca Leydeniana*) now in the India Library, London.[11]

To Professor Geiger's full and valuable "Studies" (*loc. cit.* pp. 1—102) the present writer, as Honorary Secretary of the Ceylon Asiatic Society, had the fortunate privilege of being able to add four *Appendices*. In the third of these (C) he dealt with "The Old and Modern Máldivian Alphabets."

In illustration of the *Dives Akuru* Alphabet, Mr. Bell supplied a Table (Plates VI, VII) in which are set out "the basal forms—twenty-six (26) in all, inclusive of the *sukun* as nasal and reduplicator—(*a*) of the letters ("vowel consonants") commencing with H and ending at Y and the *sukun*; (*b*) some variants; supplemented by (*c*) the five initial vowels, short and long, and (*d*) their medial signs; with the addition of (*e*) the consonant H, as modified by all its vowel inflections, as well as (*f*) a few compound letters.

The *aksharas* were given both in (i) the purer form ruling in the Southern Atols, and (ii) as now modified at Mále. Short specimens (iii) of the *Dives Akuru* writing, by modern hands, were also offered (Plates VII, IX).

No further light on the *Dives Akuru* script has been afforded since 1919, excepting one gravestone photograph, merely intended to illustrate the peculiar form of the script. (*Bell, Sessional Paper, X, 1921, Plate IX, 14*).

Gravestones A, B, C, D, E

For the present Paper four gravestones with *Dives Akuru* epitaphs, cut in sunk relief, have been selected, as fairly typical, from those photographed at Mále in 1920 and 1922.

These display marked characteristics of the true form of this old alphabet as in vogue from about the middle, or late, Seventeenth Century to the end of the Eighteenth. To their archæological interest as illustrating a type of epigraphy virtually obsolete, they add incidentally material information of historical value confirming the *Táríkh* and lesser Chronicles of the Máldive Islands.

The quartette (B, C, D, E) of *Dives Akuru* records is preceded by one old gravestone (A) in *Arabic*, extreme contrast justifying such insertion.

This Arabic inscription (A), dated A. H. 1103 (A.C. 1692, from the graveyard of Baṇḍára Miskit, is given on Plate I, to left of two in *Dives Akuru*—(B) a single record dated A H. 1141 (A. C. 1729), which immediately adjoins (A) at the same Mosque; and (C) one of four from Dolidán Miskit, dated A.H. 1114 (A.C. 1702).

Plate II (D) and Plate III (E) from Etere-koḷu Miskit contain each a separate epigraph—shown on a larger scale owing to the crowded nature of the writing —also chiselled in *Dives Akuru* characters. Of these (D) is partially dated; but from internal and other evidence their age can be arrived at very approximately.

The *aksharas* of slab (E) are quite unique in the elaboration expended on them by a strange conceit of the stone mason, who skilfully grooved each letter—a *tour de force* that does not make for simplicity in decipherment.

The orthography of these *Dives Akuru* inscriptions is distinctly erratic. The use of variant forms of single letters (e.g., KA, MA, LE) and of compounds (BVA, FRA, SRI, SVA, TRI) side by side with simple vowel-consonants may be noticed; implying that such "vagaries" were countenanced in a script never thoroughly standardised.

Transcripts of the Texts of the five inscriptions reproduced on Plates I, II, III, are followed by Translations, full Glossary, Genealogical Table, and Notes.

Text

A.

BANDÁRA MISKIT

فقد

تو فى

العبد الفقير الي رحمة ربه

العلي الاكبر الخادم

محمد عند السلطان اسكندر

ابن الخازن ابراهيم ابن عمر

من تسع ايام شهر جماد الاخر

سنة ١١٠٣ من هجرة النبي محمد صلي
الله عليه وسلم

وعلي آله واصحابه ذوالعلوم

Transcript

(1) *FAKAD TU''UFFIYA* (2) *AL-'ABDUL FAKÍR ILÁ RAHMAT RABBIHI* (3) *AL-'ALI AL-AKBAR AL-KHÁDIM* (4) *MUḤAMMAD 'INDA SULṬÁN ISKANDAR* (5) *IBN AL-KHÁZIN ÍBRÁHÍM IBN 'UMAR* (6) *MIN TIS'I AYYÁM SHAHAR JAMÁD-AL-ÁKHIR* (7) *SANAT 1103 MIN ḤIJRAT-IN NABÍ MUḤAMMAD SALLALLÁHU 'ALAIHI VA SALLAM* (8) *VA ALÁ ÁLIHI VA AS-SHÁBIHI ZAV IL 'ULUM*

Translation

Verily Muḥammad, son of Íbráhím son of 'Umar, attendant on (*lit.* near) Sulṭán Iskandar (Íbráhím I: A.C. 1648-87), slave of God Most High, Most Great, who sought (*lit.* beggar for) (His) mercy, died on the 9th day of (*lit.* nine days from) Jamád al Ákhir in the year 1103 (A.C. 1692) of the *Hijra* of our (*lit.* the) Prophet.

To him (the Prophet) may God show mercy and blessing, and to his learned relations and friends.

Transcript

B.

BAṆḌÁRA MISKIT
(A.H. 1141)

1\. *ḤIJRAIN*
2 EKU

3\. SÁSTURA
4\. EKU SA-

5\. TÉKA SÁ-
6\. ḶIS (EV)

7\. VANA AHA
8\. RU *SH'ÁBÁN*
7, 8. FANARA

---

9 VI HONIHIRU
10\. DU
11\. TAKANDÚ A-

12\. LI BAḌÉ-
13\. RI TAKU-
13, 14. RUFÁ-
14\. NARA

15\. MÁRANDÚ
16\. ÁMINÁ
17\. KABULÓ-
16\. GE

18\. BADUN
19\. UFAN AISÁ
20\. A BÍFÁ-

21\. NU NIAUVÍ
22\. KAMU HADÁN

C

DOLIDÁN MISKIT
(A.H. 1114)

1\. *ḤIJRAIN*

2\. HÁ HÁI ES-
3\. SATÉKA SAUDA

4\. VI AHARU
5\. *JAMÁD-AL-AWWAL*

6\. BÁVÍS VI
7\. HÓMA DU-
8\. VAHU *AL-VAZÍR*

9\. *ḤÁJÍ ḤUSAIN*
10\. HANDE-
11\. IGIRI KALÉGE

12\. DÍ SANFÁ-
13\. I BÍFÁNU

14\. FURAUTTA VÍ
15\. KAMU HADÁN

Translation

B.

Be it remembered that 'Aishá Bífánu, daughter of (*lit.* born in the womb of) Márandú Áminá Kabuló and (*lit.* to) Takandú 'Ali Baḍéri Takurufánu,[12] expired on Monday the 15th (day) of Sh'ában (month) in the year 1141[13] of the *Ḥijra* era, (A.C. 1729).

C.

Be it remembered that Sanfá Bífánu, daughter of the Vazír Ḥáji Ḥusain Hadégiri,[14] passed away on the 22nd day of (the month) Jamád-al-Awwal in the year 1114 of the *Hijra* era (A.C. 1702).

Transcript

D.

ETERE-KOḶU MISKIT
(Undated)

1. SWAS-
2. TÍ SIRIMA-
3. TA MAHÁ SI-
4. RI KULA SADA IRA

---

5. SIÁKA SÁ-
6. STURA A-
7. UDA KÍRITI KA-
8. TTRI BVANA MAHÁ

---

9. RADUNEVÍ *'UMAR* MA-
10. FAHA
11. KILAGE DIA (FRA)-
12. SÚTÁVE NUFAN *MUḤAMMAD*
13. *AS-SULṬÁN 'IMÁD-*

---

14. *UD-DÍN* RADUNA (Ṛ)
15. BÁRAṚU FAT-
16. TUMA KILAGE KI-
17. HUNUFAN MARIAN
18. KABÁDI KILA-

---

19. GE *'UMAR* FUḶU AṚU TIRÍ-
20. S AHARU VÍ
21. *RAMAZÁN*
22. MAHU SAUDA
23. DU HATARU VA-
24. NA SA'AT FURAU-
25. TTAVÍ
25. HADÁN KAMU

E.

ETERE-KOḶU MISKIT.
(Undated)

1. SWAS-
2. TÍ SIRIMA-
3. TA MAHA

4, SRI KULA BAN MI-
5. BA DA-
6, NÁLA VIRA SI-
7. NGA NAVARANNA KI-

---

8. RTI AUDÁ-
9. NA KATTRI BVA (NA)
10. MAHÁ RADUN

---

11. *AS-SULṬÁN*

---

12 *İBRAHÍM ISKANDAR*
13, KATTRI MAHÁ RA-

---

14. DUNAṚA DI-
15. AFURA-
15, 16. SÚTÁ-
16. VE NUFA-
17. N

---

18. RENDI KABÁ-
19. FÁNU FURAUTTA
20. VÍ KAMU HADÁN

Translation

D.

Be it remembered that Mariyam Kabádi Kilage, daughter (*lit.* born in the womb) of Fátumá Kilage of Báraṛu (island) to the King, Sulṭan Muḥammad 'Imád-ud-dín,[15] a Kshatriya, Mighty Monarch of the Universe, endowed with beauty, of the great glorious race of the Moon and Sun, accomplished in arts and sciences, of unsullied fame, begotten by 'Umar Máfat Kilage, passed away on the 14th day, fourth hour, of the month of Ramazán at the full age of thirty-eight years.

E.

Be it remembered that (Sanfá) Rendi Kabáfánu,[16] born to the Great King, a Kshatriya, Sulṭán Ibráhím Iskandar, endowed with beauty, of the great glorious race (of the Moon and Sun), rich in gold and great elephants, strong as a lion, famed like the nine gems, accomplished (in arts and sciences), a Kshatriya, Mighty Monarch of the Universe, passed away on..............

Glossary

Máldivian	Sinhalese. Etc.	English
Aharu	avrudu	year
Aṭu	aṭa	eight
* Auda, audána	———	———
Baḍun	baḍin	in womb
Bávis	visi deka	twenty-two
Bvana, bovana	bhuvana	world, universe
* Danála	———	———
Dí	dú	daughter
† Diafurasútá-ve	———	———
Du, duvahu	dá, davasa	day
Eku, es, ev	eka, ek	one
Fanara	P. pañchadasa	hrteen
Fánu	vahansé	honorific affix
‡ Fra, fura,-utta,-uttara	———	———
Fuḷu	pirí	full
Ge	gé	genitive case, familv
Há, hái	daha	thousand
§ Hadán	———	———
Hataru	hatara	four
Homa	Sandu(dá)	Monday
Honihiru	Senasurá(dá)	Saturday
Ira	Ira	Sun
Kamu	kama	deed, fact.
* Kattri, Kattiri	———	———
Kihunufan	kusen upan	born in womb
* Kírti, Kíriti	———	———
Kula	kula	race
Mahá	maha	great
Mahu	masa	month

Glossary—*contd.*

Maldivian	Sinhalese, Etc.	English
* Míba	má ibba	great elephants
* Nava-ranna	————	————
‡ Niauví	niyatvi	expired
Nufan	nipan	born
Radun	Raja	King
* Ran	ran	gold
Sada	sanda	Moon
Sa'at	*Arabic*	hour
Sális	sálisa	forty
Sástura	sahasra	thousand
* Sastura	————	————
Satéka	sata	hundred
Sauda	P. chatudasa	fourteen
· Siaka	————	————
Singa	siṇha	lion
Srí, sirí	ṣrí, siri	glorious
* Sirímata	————	————
* Svasti. Suvasti ...	————	————
Tirís	tis	thirty
Ufan	upan	born
'Umar	*Arabic*	age
Vana, ví	vana, vi	being
Víra	víra	strong

* Note 17
† Note 18
‡ Note 19
§ Note 20

Notes

1. MÁLE inhabitants:—Census 1921: males 3,359; females 2,768; total 6,127.

Even in the 12th Century, at the Máldives "*Anberia*" (modern *Hemvéru*, chief "ward" of Mále) "where king and queen reside" was "peopled with a great number of inhabitants" (Edrisi).

2. Not long ago Hoḷudú-nevi-ge Ismá'il Dídí (erstwhile Annual Ambassador to Ceylon on six occasions, and now the invaluable *Míru Baharu* (*Amír al Baḥr*), or Master Attendant, &c., at Mále), given a new residential site, found it productive of numerous long-forgotten graves, yielding human remains evidently once interred in a recognised cemetery.

3. The most recent Municipal action of note in this respect has been the carrying out of extensive improvements at the East side of the Island; when the fine Esplanade and some new roads were formed.

In 1922 Mr. Bell was readily permitted to select for the Colombo Museum any specimens of gravestone ornamentation he desired from a large heap of broken burial-slabs piled ready to be thrown into the sea.

4. See "Plan of Mále" (Sess. Pap. XV, 1921). *Medu Ziyárat, Hukuru Miskit, Danna Muhammad Rasgefánu Miskit*, are on Henvéru Mái Magu; *Biharózu Miskit* on Rad-di-bá Magu

5. The very few gravestones of exceptional size, or unorthodox shape, noticeable anywhere at the Máldives, only prove the rule.

The two largest seen by the writer mark graves of female relatives of Sulṭán Hasan X at Hitadú Island, Aḍḍú Atol; where that nominal ruler, never allowed to reign, died in banishment in A. C. 1758.

A rounded "freak" stone occurs at the *Hukuru Miskit*. Koḷufuṛi Island, Muluku Atol.

6. Máldivians divide the madrepore of their Atols into three main classes: *hiri-gá, veli-gá, rat-gá*, the two latter being coral-sandstone (*hiri* "white;" *veli* "sand," *rat* "red;" *gá* "stone.")

7. "The delightful lacquer-work industry of the Máldive Islands is said to be steadily declining. None is now executed apparently, except for Royalty and the

Nobles. The gradual disappearance of this unique Máldivian art seems inevitable, unless it can be specially fostered by local and foreign encouragement.

"Anxious to see the actual *modus operandi*, Aḥmad Dídí sent the only available worker at Málé to my residence with a half-completed lacquered vase of wood, already lathe-turned and coloured a rich black with bright red borders. Simply standing before me, holding the vase in his left hand, the artificer, with marvellous deftness, ran first one, then the other, of a couple of sharp-edged tools, not unlike short fine chisels, round the face of the black portions, gradually evolving therefrom exquisite foliaged tracery by cutting down to the pale yellow base coating of lacquer which underlies the black. The man worked rapidly, and with no pattern as guide or other adventitious aid, the arabesque design assuming intricate shape with machine-like accuracy." (Bell, Diary February 17th, 1920: Sess. Pap. XV, 1921 p. 61).

8. At this day a few copper-plate grants (*M. lómáfánu*; *S. ṭamba sannas*) in "*Evéla Akuru*" issued by Máldive Rulers are still extant on the Group.

The most interesting is that (like all examined, unfortunately incomplete) granted by Sulṭána Rehendi (Khadíjah), daughter of S.'Umar Víra Jalál-ud-dín, in the 16th year of her reign, A. H. 758 (A. C. 1356). This is being published.

9. All the *Dives Akuru* gravestone epitaphs at Mále, so far as found, were copied by the Archaeological Expedition of 1922; from *Hukuru Miskit* 10, *Etere-koḷu Miskit* 6, *Dolidán Miskit* 4, *Galoḷu Á Miskit* 2, *Baṇḍára Miskit* 1, or twenty-three (23) altogether.

Copies were also made of the only two other inscriptions in *Dives Akuru*; the longest cut on the West wall inside the Portico Entrance to *Hukuru Miskit*, the other on the revetment of *Boḍu Veyo* (bathing tank) adjoining the Hemvéru Maizán-gé.

10. To aid Mr. Bell in epigraphical research the Máldive Government courteously put at his disposal the services of Ḥusain Takurufánu, (Khatíb of Hitadú, Aḍḍú Atol,) then at Mále, whose sound knowledge of *Dives Akuru* script is unquestioned.

Among copies made of gravestone records by this intelligent Khatíb were two which opened—not too pleasureably—the eyes of the authorities responsible for the *laisser faire* manner in which old monuments of the dead are taken for granted, unverified, at Mále.

(i). At Etere-koḷu Miskit, (adjoining the Palace precincts on the N. W.,) close to the Mosque structure stand three slabs, all classed as "gravestones," within their own half-walled enclosure. Until copied by Ḥusain Khatíb, these "graves" had been religiously tended as the presumed resting place of Sulṭán Shujáyi Muḥammad 'Ímád-ud-dín I (A.C. 1620-48), and two of his wives or near female relations.

The first slab (that on the extreme left) proved to be no gravestone at all. It bears merely a variant of three inscriptions, very similarly incised; two on the lintel of the *Hittan Doru*, or Chief Entrance to the Palace, and the third on that of the *Ídu Miskit Doru* gateway through the S. W. wall of the Fort.

These record the capture of Málé in A. C. 1752 by Malabars, the deportation of Sulṭán Muḥammad 'Imád-ud-dín III, the nominal regency of his daughter Áminá Raṇi Kilagefánu, and the administration of the realm by Ḥasan Manikufánu, raised later to the *Masnad* as S. Ḥasan 'Izz-ud-dín (A. C. 1759-67).

The middle slab (Plate II, D.) belongs to Mariyan Kabá, a daughter of S. Muḥammad 'Imád-ud-dín I.

The third (Plate III, E.) is the gravestone of Sanfá Rendi Kabá, one of the five daughters of S. Íbráhím Iskandar II.

(ii). Of the specially reverenced graves, (walled in by themselves on the South-West) within the extensive cemetery attached to *Hukuru Miskit*, there is but one of which the head-stone shows the deceased's epitaph in *Dives Akuru*.

This slab—by some extraordinary laches, difficult to justify—had been, as far as present memory goes back, always deemed to mark Sultán Ḥasan 'Izz-ud-dín's grave; and, as that of the founder of the reigning Dynasty and hero of the mid 18th Century, had been specially honoured to date by his Royal descendants, one or other of whom recited *Fáthiha* there every Friday at the close of *Jum'a*, or midday Muslim service.

Ḥusain Takurufánu's reading of the epitaph on this stone showed it to record in reality the death, not of the Sulṭán but, of his half-brother, ''Ali Raṇṇa Baḍéri Kilagefánu who died, sixteen years later, in A. H. 1196.

The mere occurrence on the slabs at Etere-koḷu Miskit and Hukuru Miskit respectively of the names of Sulṭáns Muḥammad 'Ímád-ud-dín I, Íbráhím Iskandar II, and Ḥasan 'Izz-ud-dín in *Arabic* writing, and the almost universal ignorance of the *Dives Akuru* character prevailing at Mále, had led the authorities blindly to accept current tradition as to the identity of the graves, without deeming it necessary to verify the records.

The Khatíb's discovery was at first disbelieved —even resented—until the present Acting Kází, Ḥusain Dídí Baṇḍára Naib (one of the few remaining *Dives Akuru* scholars at Málé) personally examined the stones and satisfied himself regarding their true contents.

The real grave of Sulṭán Muḥammad 'Imád-ud-dín I is still unknown; that of S. Ḥasan 'Izz-ud-dín was, after much search, traced (by a brass tablet in Arabic clearly recording his death on Ramazán 2nd, A. H. 1180 = A. C. 1767) to the same *Ziyárat*, or roofed tomb, which contains the body of S. Muhammad Muhuy-ud-dín-ul-Ádil (A.C. 1693).

11. Given in Columns I, II of Geiger's Table on his Plate I, and reproduced in C. A. S. Journal (*loc. cit.* 1919, Plate I). The Professor, with no experience of Oriental wile, believed these quaint alphabets (albeit he admits, "widely different from the *Divehi Akuru*") to be "archaic variations of the modern alphabet (*ib.* p. 25)."

This supposition 'Abdul Hamid Dídí Effendí, Máldivian Government Representative, rebutted effectively: "The letters (Plate V) cannot, of course, be called *Dives Akuru.* They were pure inventions of Ḥasan-bin-Ádam of Himití" (*ib.* p. 159); who, in writing the Máldive Vocabulary, no doubt laid himself out deliberately to invent, from the *Tána* of his day, spurious alphabets to foist on to the erudite, but gullible, Dr. John Leyden.

12 *Takandú 'Ali Baḍéri Takurufánu.* The *Táríkh* styles him *Doriméná Takurufánu.*

Sulṭán Ibráhím Muzhir-ud-dín, when Sháh Bandar and Acting Regent, conspired (A. C. 1701) successfully with him, and his own step-father Ḥasan Hakurá Takurufánu of Fasmandú, to oust his cousin. the boy Sulṭán Ḥasan X, son of S. 'Ali VII.

Three years afterwards he himself lost the throne to S. Muḥammad 'Imád-ud-dín Muzaffar II.

13. The letters (line 6) following *sális* = 40 are cut too small for indisputable deciphering; but would seem to be either *ev.* = 1, or *av.* = 8; the former by choice.

14 *Ḥájí Ḥusain Hadégiri.* Quite probably the "Hadégiri Manikufánu," who was a half-brother of S. Íbráhím Muzhir-ud-dín.

15. *S. Muḥammad 'Imád-ud-dín I.* (A. C. 1620-48). Great grandson of 'Ali Khatíb, brother of S. Muḥammad Boḍu Takurufánu (A. C. 1573-85) and Ḥasan Raṇṇa Baḍéri Kilagefánu who recaptured Málé from the Portuguese.

This Sulṭán's father 'Umar Máfat Kilage, was not of noble birth, and lies traditionally under the stigma of having begotten him in the contemptible rôle of "*Medufiri*".

To enable Máldivians thrice divorced to remarry, "vile and abject beings" says Pyrard "are found who, for a money consideration contract a marriage with the women for a few days. By this means the letter of the law is obeyed; and three months after, the former pair are married afresh. The highest ladies in the land are constrained to go through the same business in like case. These middlemen are called *Medu piry*, as who should say 'middle husband;' they are held in great contempt even of the common people, as infamous creatures without honour or conscience. It is a grievous slander even to be called *Medu piry*." (*Hak. Soc. Pyrard*, 1887, I, p. 154).

S. Muḥammad 'Imád-ud-dín doubtless espoused both Fáṭumá Kilage of Báraṛu (Tiladummatí Atol) and 'Aishá Bíbí Kamaná, the widow of his two predecessors on the throne, S. Íbráhim III (A. C. 1585-1608) and S. Husain II (A. C. 1608-20).

By Queen 'Aishá he had the illustrious son who succeeded him as S. Iskandar Íbráhím I (A. C. 1648-87).

16. *Rendi Kabá.* Sanfá Rendi, fifth child of S. Íbráhím Iskandar II (A. C. 1721-50) married her first-cousin-once-removed, Ḍoriméná Manikufánu, son of her great uncle Hóḷi Ḥasan Hakurá Manikufánu brother of her grandmother Mává Kilage.

Their daughter Don Bínage Dídí, married Sulṭán Muḥammad Mu'izz-ud-dín (A. C. 1774-78.)

17. *Máldivian "birudas"*. Word for word meanings:—

D. "Hail! (*Svastí, Suvastí*); endowed with beauty (*sirimata*); of the great glorious race (*mahá sirí kula*) of the Moon and Sun (*Sada Ira*); in arts and sciences (*siáka sást-ura*) accomplished (*auda*); of unsullied fame (*kírtti, kíritti*); a Kshatriya (*Kattiri*); Mighty Monarch of the Universe (*Bvana, Bovana, Mahá Radun*); who is (*ví*)."

E. "Hail! (*Svastí, Suvastí*); endowed with beauty (*sirimata*); of the great glorious race (*mahá sirí kula*) (of the Moon and Sun); rich (*danála*) in gold (*ran*) and great elephants (*míba*); powerful (as a) lion (*víra singa*); famed (like) the nine gems (*navaranna kírtti, kíritti*); accomplished (*audána*) (in arts and sciences); a Kshatriya (*Kattri, Kattiri*); great Monarch of the Universe (*Bvana, Bovana, Mahá Radun*).''

With few exceptions, from the Muḥammadan Conversion in A. H. 548 (A. C. 1153-4) onwards, the *Tárikh* and Lists of Máldive Rulers record the *birudas*, or honorific epithets, attached to each Sultán or Sulṭána.

Variants occur in extant Missives from the Sulṭáns to the Dutch Government during the Eighteenth Century.

Since the British occupation of Ceylon the epithets have been curtailed to half a dozen words, *Kula sundura Kattiri Bovana Mahá Radun* 'Great Ruler of the Universe, a Kshatriya of pure race."

For explanations of *birudas*, mostly similar to the above, appearing in S. Ḥasan Núr-ud-dín's Missive of A. C. 1795 see Bell, Sess. Pap. 1882, pp. 79—80; C. A. S. Journal 1919, Extra Number, pp. 173-9.

18. **Diafurasútá-ve* "begotten." Sometimes used with *nufan* "born." Cf. Siṇhalese *dáva* ("begotten,") *prasútáva* ("delivered,") *nipan* ("born.")

19 As frequently in Latin, English, and other languages, the bald Máldivian word for "died" (*M. maruvejje*) is softened on gravestones by the use of terms approximating to well-known pregnant synonyms so familiar in Europe.

(*a*) *Niau-ví* (Siṇ. *niyat-venava*) "extinguished," "expired;"

(*b*) *Avahára-vi* (so too in Siṇhalese) "(life) abandoned."

(*c*) *Filirá-midi* (Siṇ. *pratirupayen midi*); "released from the image (i. e. body)." Cf. English "shuffle off this mortal coil;" "who pass away, from this our world of flesh set free."

(*d*) · *Furauttara-ví* (Siṇ. *purayen uturanaví*) "coming out of (the city, house, i. e. body)," "crossing," "landing." Cf. English "cross the bar;" "now upon the further shore lands the voyager at last."

---

* For valuable suggestions in regard to the connection with Siṇhalese of the Máldivian mortuary terms, the writer gratefully records his real obligation to that sound, modest scholar Abraham Mendis Gunasékara Mudaliyar, late of the Ceylon Government Educational Department.

20. *Kamu hadán.* "Remember the fact (that)." *Hadán* = Sin. *sandahan* (*veṇḍa*) "remember."

The Sinhalese Inscription (not mortuary) at Kéragala, Ceylon ends in an equivalent periphrasis, "*datuva yahapatayi.*"

By ellipse of "Remember"—the Latin "*Memento*"—the commonest English expression on gravestones has degenerated into the curt cold "Here lies." (*Hic jacet*).

Our forbears showed more reverence for their dead:—

(*a*) "*Mementote Dne Isabelle Le De Spenser comitesse de Warrewic..........obiit Anno Dni. MCCCCXXIX*"

(Memorial to Isabel, Countess of Warwick, 15th Century; Tewkesbury Abbey)

(*b*) "Stay, passenger, why goest thou by so fast,
Read, if thou can't, whom envious death hath plast
Within this monument, Shakespeare, with whom
Quick Nature died..........obiit Ano. Doi. 1616.
Aetatis 53, Die 23 Ap.

(Memorial to William Shakespeare; Stratford-on-Avon.)

21. See Bell, Sessional Paper XV, 1921 pp. 17-22, 74, for summarised account of some Máldive Rulers.

22. *'Aishá Bí Kamaná.* This lady was eighth in direct descent from *'Ali Rasgefánu* (S. 'Ali VI), killed defending his Capital against the Portuguese who captured Mále in A. C. 1558. His daughter Kuḍa Kamaná married Ḥasan Raṇṇa Kilagefánu, younger brother of S. Muḥammad Boḍu Takurufanu with whom he was associated in finally expelling the Portuguese from the Máldives in A. C. 1573.

23. *S. Íbráhím Muzhir-ud-dín.* Connected with the Diyamigilí Dynasty doubly: (i) his Prime Minister, Muḥammad Doriméná Takurufánu (who succeeded him as S. Muḥammad 'Imád-ud-dín Muzaffar II) being his mother's aunt's son (M. *mámage boḍu daitáge dari*), i. e. mother's cousin, or his own first-cousin-once-removed; and (ii) 'Aishá, chief queen of S. Íbráhím Iskandar II, his half-niece.

S. Íbráhím Muzhir-ud-dín's stormy fortunes are touched on in Sess. Pap. *loc cit.* pp. 17-18.

24. *S. Íbráhím Iskandar II.* Died in A. C. 1750, at the age of 42, after a peaceful and prosperous reign of 29 years.

Thereafter ill-luck persistently dogged the Dynasty for many a year.

(i) S. Íbráhím Iskandar's only brother (S. Mukarram Muḥammad 'Imád-ud-dín III was captured by an Expedition sent by Ali Rája of Kannanúr in A. C. 1752, and deported first to India and finally to Maliku (Minicoy), where he died, in 1757.

(ii) S. Íbráhím's only son, seized and carried off with his uncle the Sulṭán and three Ministers, managed to escape; and getting back to Mále in A. C. 1763, succeeded to the throne as S. Muḥammad Ghiyás-ud-dín on the death of S. Ḥasan 'Izz-ud-dín, in 1767.

In 1773 he went the *Ḥajj*; but on his return the following year was not allowed to land, and murdered.

(iii) His son, Íbráhím Kaláfánu, died in 1829 at Fua Mulaku, to which far distant isolated Island he had been banished by the heirs of S. Ḥasan 'Izz-ud-dín.

(iv) Of S. Íbráhím Iskandar's other children by 'Aishá Kabá, five daughters, three died in exile.

(*a*) Áminá, the eldest, married the Vazír 'Ali Sháh Bandar. Owing to trouble arising with Monsieur Le Termellier, Commander of the French *Corps de Garde* stationed at Mále from 1754-9 (Sess. Pap. XLIII, 1881 pp. 33, 45), she was banished but escaped; captured, was again banished; and a third time, after the Sulṭán, her brother, sailed for Arabia.

(*b*) The second daughter, Fáṭumá, had as husband Aḥmad Muhuy-ud-dín Khatíb, who with his brother Muḥammad Shams-ud-dín, the Kází, played traitor to their Sulṭán in 1752; each promptly paying the penalty at the hands of the Malabar invaders.

Íbráhím Siráj-ud-dín, Fáṭumá's son, thrice Kází but banished at intervals, carried on the *Táríkh*, or Chronicle of the Máldive Sulṭans, (begun by his grandfather Kází Ḥasan Táj-ud-din and continued by Kází Muḥammad Muhibb-ud-dín) from A. C. 1761 to 1821.

(*c*) *Mariyam*, the third daughter, was wife of Kází Muḥammad Shams-ud-dín who betrayed S. Muḥammad 'Imád-ud-dín Mukarram III to the Malabars.

Their son, Íbráhím Bahá-ud-dín, was appointed Kází for a while; then banished by S. Muḥammad Ghiyás-ud-dín.

(*d*), (*e*) Sanfá Rendi and 'Aishá Kabá, fourth and fifth daughters, alone seem to have avoided the ill-fortune of their uncle, brother, sisters and nephew: both marrying well, and dying at Mále before the close of the 18th Century.

BANDÁRA MISKIT: DOLIDÁN MISKIT.

A. B. C.

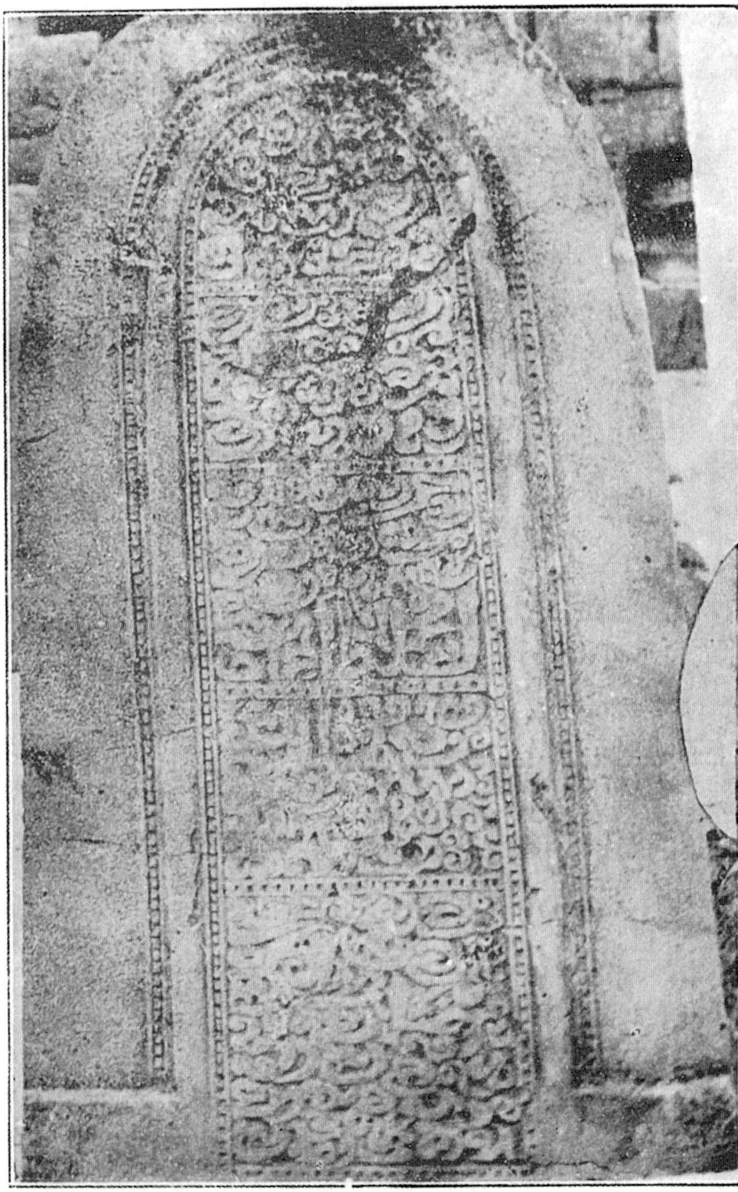

D.

E.

MÁLDIVE SULṬÁNS:

DEVVADÚ, ISDÚ, DIYAMIGILÍ, HURA DYNASTIES.[21]

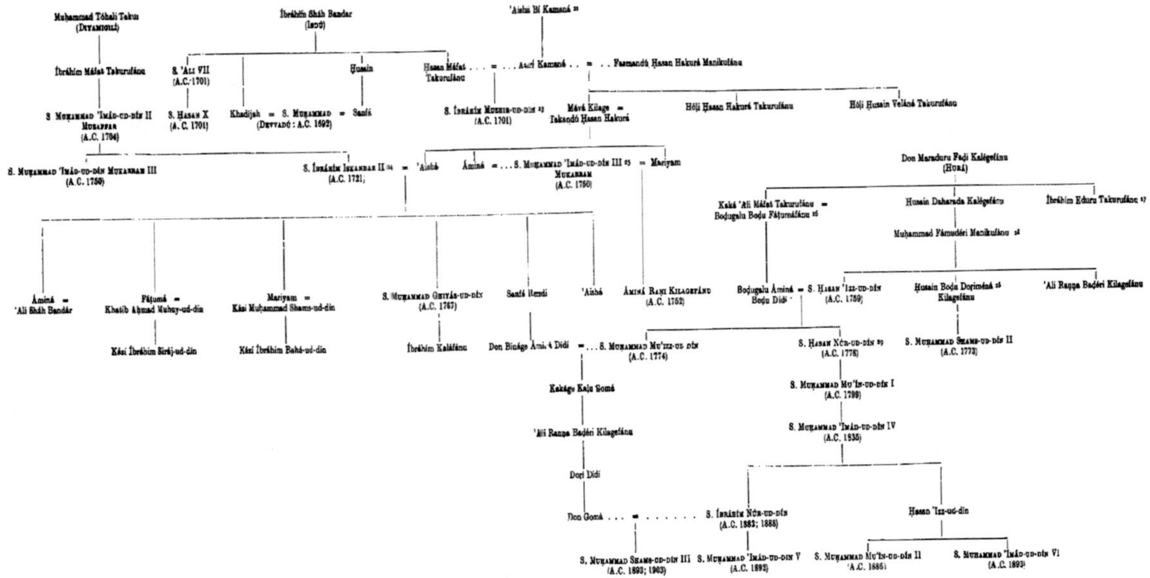

25. *S. Muḥammad 'Imád-ud-dín Mukarram III.* Styled 'Ali Fáṛiná before his accession. Married in turn, Áminá and Mariyam, younger sisters of 'Aishá, his brother's wife.

Mariyam bore him the daughter *Áminá Raṇi Kilagefánu,* whom the Máldivians, after her father's deportation, elected nominal Regent; whilst placing the administration in the hands of a Council of Ministers with Ḥasan Manikufánu (subsequently S. Ḥasan 'Izz-ud-dín) as head.

26. *Boḍugalu Fáṭumáfánu.* In the person of this lady, the Kakáge family of Mále claim descent from Sulṭán Abu Bakr in the eighth degree.

27. *Íbráhím Eduru Takurufánu.* The old Prime Minister at this day, A. Ḥájí Íbráhim Dídí, Boḍu Doṛiméná Kilagefánu,* with his sons (also high officials) Aḥmad Dídí, Kuḍa Doṛiméná Kilagefánu, 'Abdul Majid Dídí, Boḍu Baḍéri Manikufánu, and 'Abdul Hamid Dídí Effendí, Máldivian Government Representative in Ceylon, trace their descent from Íbráhím Eduru Takurufánu, one of the sons of Don Maraduru Faḍi Kalégefánu of Hurá; through Boḍu Murídú Takurufánu, Ḥusain, Aḥmad, and 'Ali Dídís—the three latter, like Íbráhím Dídí himself, Chief Ministers honoured with the highest title, *Doṛiméná Kilagefánu* (Bell, Sess. Pap. XV 1921, p. 67).

28. *Muḥammad Vazír Fámudéri Manikufánu.* Father of S. Ḥasan 'Izz-ud-dín. With his son Ḥusain, taken captive when their Sulṭán was deported to India (A. C. 1752).

The Vazír died there; but Ḥusain returned to the Islands, and became *Boḍu Doṛiméná Kilagefánu.*

S. Muḥammad Shams-ud-dín II was the latter's son.

29. *S. Ḥasan Núr-ud-dín.* Twice went on pilgrimage to Mekka; first in A. C. 1788, and again in 1799.

Unable to get away on the second occasion, owing to persistent harassment by the *Sharif*, the Sulṭán died in Arabia of small-pox.

*Died March 31st 1925, at the age of 80, whilst this Paper was in the press. Ibrahim Didi had for years justly acquired the appellation of "the Grand Old Man of the Máldives" owing to his marked ability and sterling qualities, always devoted to the real interests of his country.

EXCERPTA MALDIVIANA.

By H. C. P. BELL, C.C.S. (Retired).

No. 4. A DESCRIPTION OF THE MALDIVE ISLANDS: CIRCA A.C. 1683.

Foreword.

Thirty years ago that indefatigable Orientalist, the late Mr. D. W. Ferguson, ever keen to snap up all unconsidered trifles of value in his spacious net, as Editor printed in the *Ceylon Monthly Register*, Vol. III, N.S., 1895, pp. 188-9, under the designation of "Olio," copy of an extract ("*A Description of ye Maldiva's*"), which he had himself made from the Original Correspondence of the old East India Company in the India Office.

Mr. Ferguson offered no comments on the Paper; beyond stating that it was "entered in the O.C. Catalogue as written subsequent to 1682"; and that the "timerous old man" of the narrative was "probably Íbráhím Iskandar, who according to Máldivian history reigned from A.C. 1648-9 to 1686-7."

The Paper is of sufficient quaintness and historical interest to warrant its re-publication, with explanatory Notes, in the Journal of the Ceylon Asiatic Society. It is here printed *verbatim et literatim*.

This "Description of the Máldives" may well have been obtained from the Captain of the "Britannia", which reached Calcutta on July 1st 1683 from the Máldive Islands, and reported the exciting experience there of the British vessel "Charles".

The episode is related in "*The Diary of Sir William Hedges*", 1681-87 (Hakluyt Society, No. 74, p.96):—

"July 1.—The Ship Britania, belonging to Mr. Dowglass, &ca., from ye Maldive Islands arrived before ye Factory, bringing advice of ye Charles (a ship belonging to ye Honble Company) arrivall there: and that at their first going ashore, their first salutation from ye Natives was a shower of Stones and Arrows, whereby 6 of their Men were wounded, which made them immediately return on board, and by ye Mouths of their Guns forced them to a complyance, and permission to load what Cowries they would at Markett Price: so that in a few days time they sett sayle from thence for Surrat, with above 60 Tunn of Cowries."

A DESCRIPTION OF YE MALDIVA'S.

The Maldivia Islands are said to contain 72,000 Islands [1] that are above Water, with many Shoals and Banks whereon they take their Cowries having on ym. 2, 3 or 4 foot Water. *The King's Island* or *Residence* is called *Maliva* [2] from wch. all in gen'rall are by us so called, Altho' improperly; Saving that one may term ym.ye Kingdom of *Maliva*.

The King's Island lies in Lattd. No. 4°., 10'.[3] It's Steep too, so yt. we ride at Anchor in 30 fathm. half a Cable's length off Shore in smooth water by 2 *Maquas* [4] ye one provided by ye King & for ye other we comonly pay a *Cady* of Rice (containing 7½ Bengall maunds) they yt. have not Rice pay ye value in othr goods.

The aforesaid *Maquas* are made of wood (being whole trees well trench-nail'd together like a Pyramid) & fill'd full of stones, & swepled round wth large Cables, each of them is carryed off betwixt boats, and sunk where ye Capt. of ye Ship pleases to ride: one of them holds 4 or 5 Tuns of stones and are fit to ride by only Rocky groud.

The East-side of those Islands are bold enough, either one degr. to ye Norwd. or one degree to ye Soard of ye Kings-Island; but to fall to ye Noard is best in ye months of Nov. Xber, Janry. Feby.; and to Soard at other times.—So soon as you can discern ye Islands, you are sure of a boat or *Gunderah* [5] (so called by ye natives) who will take care to anchr. you in clean ground, and ye *Hoveldor* [6] or *Governour* of ye place where you anchr. sends speedily to ye *King* [7] to acquaint him; & in ye mean time will sell you fowles, Fish Coaker-nuts and Plantaines, but dares not deal in any considerable comodity. *The King* so soon as Intelligence is given thereof, Orders his own *Pilotts to* bring you up: for 'tis not safe to do it your selves, Altho' you are never so well acquainted. To fall directly in wth. ye *Island* is not safe but rathr. 8 or 10 Leas Noery or Soby. *The Currents* set many ways amongst ye Islands very strong and ye wind variable. And Wly variation about 10°,,—*The Pilott* yt. carries you in Can't demand above 10 Rupees for ye biggest ship that comes hither [8] and ye greatest caution to take care you come not among them in ye night, thereby to be flung from one to the other, by Tempest's, Storms and Eddys:—

Wood is very scarse upon ye Islands, for they abound with Little more than wth Coaker-nutt & Plantain Trees not fit for fireing. You must not Water upon ye *King's Island* Altho' there be great store of water, for 'tis unhealthy, [9] most of ye Wells being shoal and amongst graves of dead Carkasses of wch this Island is very full. [10] *But* there is good watering upon many other Islands and very safe fetching it: but best when fetch'd by your own people

They have no *Coyne* of their own, save *Larrees* o Silver, being very Course and passe for ye value of a Shilling. 5 is 2 Rups. and sometimes 6, by reason good Silver is very scarse. [11]

The Gold that comes from *Acheen* in uncoyn'd. *Gold Ingott* is better then Coyn'd. *Silver* in *Span: plate* ye *Mexico* is best.

(Merchandize.) Strong water [12] in Cases. A good quantity of broad Cloth, red and green. Knives and Scithers.

Cowries[13] are to be had at any time of ye year, but in Novbr. and Decmr. most, by reason they are brought to ye *King's Island* to Lade ye *Bengall* Shipping. But if you deal wth. ye *King* or his *Noccady*[14] there needs no stay, save ye counting them for they have Thousds. of Tuns buried in ye ground for Store, (and for want of Ware-houses) in this Island wch. is not above 4 English miles in Circuit. Altho' ye 10th part of his Treasure is not here; yet there is sufficient in *Cowries, Amber-grease*[15] and *Sea-Coco.*[16] He is a timerous old man[17] (especially of ye *English* and *Dutchmen*) therefore hides most of his Treasure on some remote Island by *Cowries.*

And to buy ye *Cowrie,* one *Cowrie*[18] qt. 12,000 Cowries; they are worth 2 Rupees ℔ *Cowrie*[18]. they bale them up in bagvs made of *Coire,* or you may throw them into ye Hould loose.

They are admirers of fine silver-wyre-work'd chains wch can't be made of bad and drossy Silver.[19]

They speak a *Language* call'd (*Calko*)[20] but yr. gentry speak *Arrabick*, many speak *Moor's*[21] and are addicted to lying; but have not ye courage to steal, being very effeminate. *We* never sell except ye *Noccady* engages for them. *He* & many of them speak *Portugues,*[22] but few or none *English.*

The Port charges are Large Toll great men, being ye chief of ye Officer's; (Vzt.) *The Treasurer,*[23] *Noccady, Householder,*[24] and other's: To each must be given 150 Bambooes of Rice, wch. are as follows. 14 Parrass in one Cady[25] (or 7½ Hugly maunds) 22 Bambooes in one Parras. *They* weigh ye Goods by ye Maund and Colung,[26] being 7½ galls. to ye maund of Maldivia's qt. 122 galls.[27] More Port charges to each of ye eleven Officer's aforesd. 14 Covett's[28] of Course Callico of a Rupee price To ye *Shabander*[29] a Cady of Rice. To ye *Maabar*[30] a Cady of Rice wch. *he* claims for ye Shipsruddr. To ye *King's Sallareens*[31] (or Life Guards) a Cady of Rice. A Ship of 80, 90 or 100 Tuns pays ye half of these aforemention'd charges.

Notes

1. *The Máldive Islands.* The number of these Islands (Plate I). has been variously stated by old writers:—

Suleimán, Arabian traveller of the Ninth Century, records that "the Islands amount, so it is said, to 1,900". Ibn Baṭúṭa (at the Máldives in A.C. 1343-4) says "about 2,000". "The Moors report that they number 12,000" (Barbosa, A.C. 1518)

According to Pyrard (French captive at Mále, A.C. 1602-7) the Máldive Sulṭán claimed to rule Twelve Thousand islands and Thirteen Atols. (*Ceux du pays me disoient qu'il y en avoit jusques à douze mille. J'estime quant à moy, qu' il n'y a pas apparence d'y en avoir tant. Bien est il vray qu' il y en a une infinité de petites, qui ne sent quasi que des mottes de sable toutes inhabitées. Davantage le Roy des Maldives met ce nombre en ses titres, car il s'appelloit " Sultan Ibrahim dolos assa ral tera atholon", c'est a dire " Ibrahim Sultan Roy de treize provinces et de douze mil isles.*")

The total number of *inhabited* Islands at the present day is 217.

2. *Maliva.* Sc. *Maldiva.*

3. Lat. 4° 10', N. Long. 73° 30', E.; about 415 miles S.W. of Colombo in Ceylon.

4. *Maquas.* Probably corruption of M. *Má-faná* "large coral and wood anchors" The *faná* (coral lump with stick through,) is still so used by Máldive boats in shallow water.

5. *Gunderah.* Arabic, *kundara*, pl. *kanádir* (Ibn Baṭúṭa); Tamil, *kuntará.* Portuguese Historians speak of Máldivian "*gundras*"; and the term "*Gundara-kárayó*" is applied by Siṇhalese in Ceylon to the Islanders and their boats (M. *dóṇifaharu, oḍifaharu*).

6. *Heveldor.* Persian *Ḥaváldár,* " one holding an office of trust." Probably the *Atoḷu-veri,* or Chief Headman of an Atol, is here meant.

7. *King.* M. *Rasgefánu*; but the Arabic title "Sulṭán" is more correctly applied to the Rulers of the Máldive Islands from the Muslim Conversion in A.H. 548 (A.C. 1153-4) onwards.

8. *Pilotage.* Foreign vessels trading to Mále nowadays have to pay Rs. 5 to the *Míru Baharu* (*Amír-al-Baḥr*), or Harbour Master, and a further Rs. 5 to the *Boḍu Baḍéri-ge* (Kachcheri) for Clearance Papers on leaving. All charges formerly paid to other officials

have been abolished; but, as Harbour Dues, from every Foreign vessel is recovered the sum of Rs. 40 per trip for anchorage in the Outer Harbour, which lies between Mále and the islands Fonadú, Dunidú, Fédú and the Galufaḷu reef. Vessels electing to shelter behind Dunidú island during the S.W. monsoon are charged Rs. 25 extra.

9. *Water at Mále.* The well-water at Mále has been more than once strongly condemned. Water, "taken from a well said to be one of the best", when analysed by Staff Surgeon P. H. M. Starr (H.M.S. "Proserpine"), in 1909, was found to be "quite unfit for human consumption, showing contamination, by sewage matter." Of late years a Rain-Water Storage Tank (M. *Fen-tági*), with wide catchment roof, has been built in two of the four Wards, and the erection of a couple more in the others is contemplated.

10. *Graveyards.* "Into 'Sulṭán's Island,'—an area roughly one mile in length, East and West, by half a mile across,—there are crowded at this day no less than twenty-nine Mosques, to the majority of which are attached burial grounds. . . . There can scarcely be six feet of Máldive earth (with the exception of the Palace Enclosure and the sites of the more revered Mosques and *Ziyárats*) but have at one period or another held the dead laid 'beneath the Churchyard's stone.' (C.A.S. Journal Vol. XXIX, No. 77, 1924).

11. *Coinage.* Cowries were the sole Máldive currency until the issue in the Sixteenth Century of the *Digu Lári*, or "long *larin*" (of doubled silver wire stamped with the Sulṭán's name), copied from the Persian *larin*. These elongated coins were certainly struck (*teste* Pyrard) by Sulṭán Íbráhím III (A.C. 1583-1607), if not earlier; as well as by his successors S. Shujá'í Muḥammad 'Imád-ud-dín I (A.C. 1620-1648) and S. Iskandar Íbráhím I (A.C. 1648-1687)

To this last named Sulṭán is assigned the credit of first issuing circular coins. Specimens of his silver *Lári* of A.H. 1075 and 1086 (A.C. 1664-5; 1675-6), 73 grains in average weight, are known. The first known *Kuḍa Lári*, dated A.H. 1105 and weighing 36½ grains, was issued by S. Muḥammad (A.C. 1693-1701) in the year of his accession. (Plate II.).

In A.H. 1146 (A.C. 1733-34), a *Boḍu Lári*, or double *lári*, (146 grs. average weight) was introduced, and ruled with *Lári* struck decennially (A.H. 1153, 1163, 1173) and termed "*Iskandar*" from the original issues; but apparently at the fictitious ratio values of 4 to 1 (*half rix-dollar* to *schelling*).

From A.H. 1184 (A.G. 1770-71), the coinage settled down to *Boḍu Lári* and true *Kuḍa Lári* (weight much as before) at recognised one-fourth ratio. The weights of *Boḍu Lári* and *Kuḍa Lári* have varied since, falling gradually, and are now down to less than half in each case.

12. *"Strong Water"*. The Mâldivians being staunch Muḥammadans, spirits can hardly have found a sale at Mále.

13. *Cowries*. (See *Hak. Soc. Pyrard*, II pp. 429, 452, 444, &c., &c.) Some particulars regarding the trade in Cowries between the Dutch in Ceylon and the Máldives are given under "Trade and Commerce" in "The Máldive Islands" (*Sess. Paper* XLIII, 1881 pp. 98-101).

The Dutch were quick to gauge the advantage of complete control over the trafic in Cowries. Throughout the latter part of the Seventeenth Century, and much of the Eighteenth, they attempted to establish a monopoly, whilst paying less than other nations.

The price to the Dutch in 1669 was 1 1/5 Rds. the *koṭṭe* of 12,000, weighing 24 lbs. In 1697 it rose to 1½ Rds., and up to 1718 fluctuated between that rate and 2 Rds. In 1723 (Sulṭán's Missive in Portuguese) 4½ *koṭṭe* of Cowries were changed with Dutch vessels for a candy (8 Bengal maunds) of rice.

In 1740 the price was fixed at 2½ Rds., the *koṭṭe* of 24 lbs.; but had fallen in 1764 by half a rix-dollar.

For the next twenty years the annual Netherlands' demand for Cowries diminished from 500,000 lbs. (20,000 *koṭṭes*) to as low as 150,000 lbs. or 6,000 *koṭṭes* (now raised to 25 lbs. the *koṭṭe*), needed only if to fill the lower tier of vessels as ballast!

But the Máldive price had risen considerably. Whilst the Dutch Governor in 1777 refused the Sulṭán's request to raise the price to 2 Rds. per *koṭṭe*, English and French vessels paid as much as Rs. 4 at Mále. Owing to other foreigners entering the market, the Dutch in 1795 had perforce to pay Rs. 3 per *koṭṭe*.

In 1836 the price of Cowries at Mále was Rs. 2 per *koṭṭe*; in 1880, nearly half a century later, it had come down to Rs. 1·50; but after forty years further interval, in 1920, stood at Rs. 2·50.

The present quotations are Rs. 5 to Rs. 6 per cwt. at Mále; and Rs. 7 to Rs. 8 per *maund* (84 lbs.) at Calcutta.

Cowries are chiefly gathered in Haddummatí, Huvadú and Ari Atols; the fewest come from Tiladummati (extreme Northern) and Addú (extreme Southern) Atols.

14. *Noccady*. Persian *Ná-khudá*, the Master of a native vessel. At the present time there is but one recognised *Nákudá*, a post of some responsibility, at the Máldives.

15. *Ambergrease*. M. *goma* (raw ambergris); *mávaharu* (prepared ambergris.)

Ambergris is known to be a secretion formed in the stomach or intestines of *Physeter macrocephalus*, or spermaceti whale. It is opaque and soft, and when heated gives out a peculiarly agreeable perfume. Now used only for perfumery, it was formerly freely employed as a medicinal nostrum.

Three grades of ambergris are recognised at the Máldives—*hudu mávaharu* (white), *kaḷu mávaharu* (dark), and *bimbi mávaharu* (speckled). Barbosa (16th Century) specifies these varieties under the terms *ponabar* (white), *puambar* (greyish) and *minabar* (brown).

Large lumps are occasionally washed ashore. The Máldive "*Táríkh*" Chronicle records quaintly how the Islanders bought off their French allies against Ali Rája of Kannanúr, *circa* A.C. 1753, with a huge mass weighing more than 3 cwt. found at Máḷosmaḍulu Atol—ambergris being then valued at Rs. 10 per one rupee weight!

In somewhat recent years a similar exceptional "find" was made; regarding the ultimate disposal of which discreditable rumours still exist.

Ambergris and sea-coconut are Máldive royalties, and highly valued. At least as early as 1706 Rs. 1 to Rs. 2 weight of each of these rarities was included among the Annual Presents to the Colombo Governors and Galle Commanders; and the practice, is believed to be still in force.

16. *Sea-Coconut*. M. *távakkáṛi*, "the hard, (shelled) coconut" (*cf*. Sin. *tavara*, "firm"). This, the double-coconut (*Lodoicea Seychellarum*), from its fruit being carried by currents from the Seychelles and cast ashore frequently on the Máldive Islands, obtained the names *Coco-der-mer* ("sea coconut") and *Cocos-des-Maldives*.

In olden days it was highly valued as an imagined sovereign remedy for all sorts of ailments. (See *Hak. Soc. Pyrard*, I., 229-231; *Hak. Soc.* Barbosa, II, 106 regarding ambergris and sea-coconut.)

17. Mr. Ferguson was right in identifying the "timerous old man" then "King" with Sulṭán Iskandar Íbráhím I (A.C. 1648-87). He was son of S. Shujá'i Muḥammad 'Imád-ud-dín I and Aishá Kabáfanu, widow of that Sulṭán's two immediate predecessors, Sulṭán Íbráhím III, (killed by the Malabar Expedition of A.C. 1607), and Sulṭán Ḥusain II Fámudéri Kilagefánu, who died at Guraidú (S. Mále Atol) in A.C. 1620.

In point of fact Sulṭán Iskandar Íbráhím I, perhaps now in his dotage, had proved himself a masterly Máldive Ruler. His long reign lasted over 39 years, covering, with that of his father, two-thirds of the Seventeenth Century. Skilled in arms and other manly exercises, this versatile Monarch, further, encouraged learning and directed the 'Ulumá to instruct the people; besides appointing salaried teachers.

Many Foreign vessels visited the Máldives during this reign. Trade thrived exceedingly; the more so as Sulṭán Íbráhím put a stop to the exaction of grinding dues and monopolies, formerly levied by grasping officials.

The Sulṭán went the *Ḥajj* twice, in A.H. 1078 (A.C. 1668) and again in A.H. 1093 (A.C. 1682). At Màle his religious zeal showed itself in the improvement of the *Hukuru Miskit* (*Jum'a* Mosque) in A.H. 1085 (A.D. 1674-5), and the erection of its bold cylindrical tower, the *Munnáru*, or Minaret, the most characteristic architectural feature of "Sulṭán's Island" at this day and represented on Máldive stamps. (Plate III).

Sulṭán Íbráhím is said to have been poisoned by a slave girl who bore him a son. This luckless boy succeeded as Sulṭán Kuḍa Muḥammad (A.C. 1687-1691), at the age of six and a half, with his mother as Queen Regent. Both met a tragic death together some four years afterwards.

18. *Cowrie*. The seventh word in the first and second lines, is a misprint in the original MS. for *Cotte* (M. *koṭṭe*).

Cowries are still put up in packages of woven coconut leaves, triangular in shape, tightly stitched with coir at the base or mouth. Each *koṭṭe* contains 12,000 (M. *bára fá*) cowries, and averages 25 lbs. in weight.

19 The handsome gold and silver jewellery of the Máldives is of choice workmanship, and distinctive in design.

20. *Calco*. Manifestly an error. At the Máldives the language of the Islanders is regularly termed "*Divehi bas*"; though at Minicoy (Máldivian in race and speech, but for

centuries held by the Rájas and Bíbís of Kaṇṇanúr, and now grouped by the Indian Government with the Lakkadives) a form of Máldivian is used called "*Máhl*".

21. *Moor's*. Hindustáni; "the Industan language commonly called Moors". The term became obsolete during the first half of the Nineteenth Century.

22. *Portuguese*. This language was greatly in vogue at the Máldives as late as the Eighteenth Century. Three Portuguese Missives of Sultán Íbráhím Iskandar II to the Dutch Governors of Ceylon, dated respectively A.C. 1723, 1734, 1735, are extant.

23. *Treasurer*. M. *Boḍu Baḍéri*. See *Sess. Pap.* XV, 1921 p. 25.

24. *Householder*. Very probably *Má Baḍéri*, the Officer in control of Palace affairs. (*Loc. cit.*)

25. *Cady*. "One *Candiel* is little more or less than 14 bushels" (Linchoten). "Parra" = bushel; "*bamboo*" = seer (Máldive *náli*.) The Máldive *fara* = 12 *náli*.

Taking one seer as weighing 2 lbs., 22 "*bamboos*" × 14 "*parras*" would total 308 seers, or 616 lbs., for the "*candy*" of 7½ "*maunds*", at 82 2/15 lbs., per maund of 41 1/15 seers.

At the Máldives the ruling Dry Measures are :—

Láhi					
4 =	*Náli*				
16 =	4 =	*Kotu.*			
48 =	12 =	3 =	*Fara.*		
192 =	48 =	12 =	4 =	*Muli.*	
1200 =	300 =	75 =	25 =	6¼ =	*Kaḍi.*

Of recent years 50 *náli* have been reckoned broadly, as = 1 *muli*; and 300 *náli*, or 6 *muli*, = 1 *kaḍi*.

26. *Colung*. Perhaps the Máldive *kuladu* (Siṇ. *kalañda*) is meant; but this weight = *bai tola*, half *tola* is used only by Jewellers. The Máldive *manu* (maund) = 84 lbs.

27. Some uncertain writing here. "Maund" dry measure; "gallon" usually liquid measure. The Máldive *adubá* (liquid measure) = 2 quarts, or half a gallon.

28. *Covett*. The more familiar corruption of the Portuguese *covado*, cubit, is *covid*. The term has gone out of use.

29. *Shabander*. This title of *Sháh Bandar* has long lapsed at the Máldives. His duties (cognizance of all matters

Map

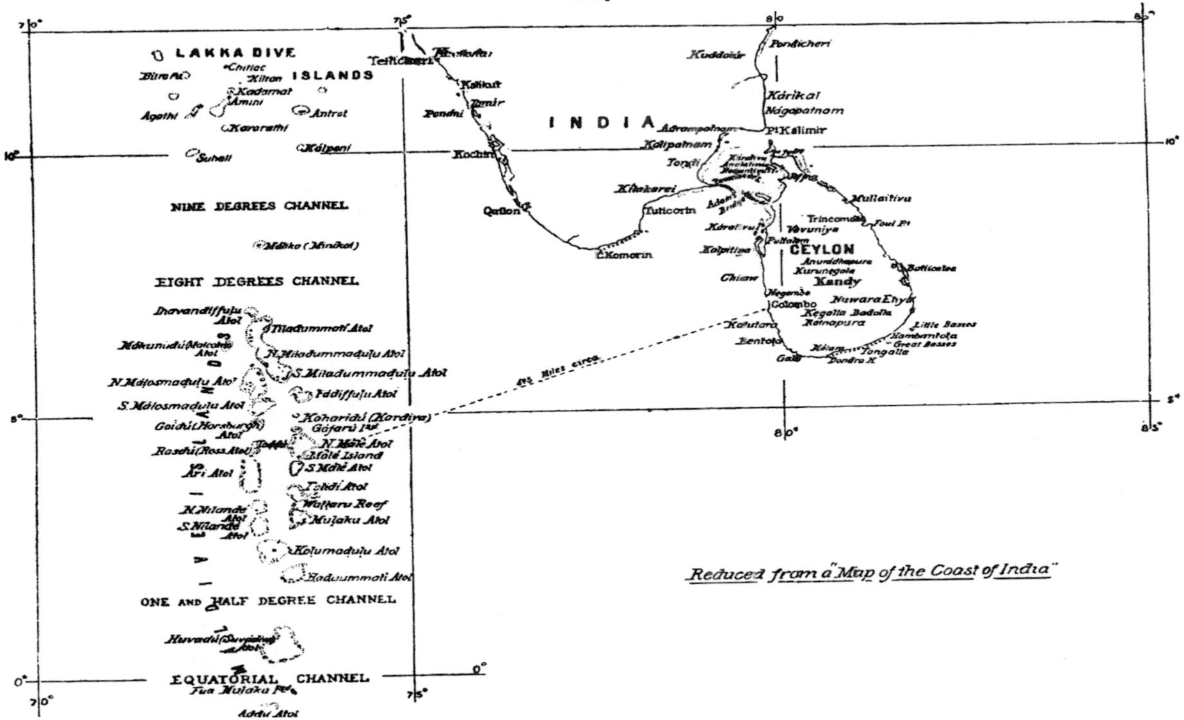

Reduced from a "Map of the Coast of India"

Maldive Currency (Seventeenth Century).

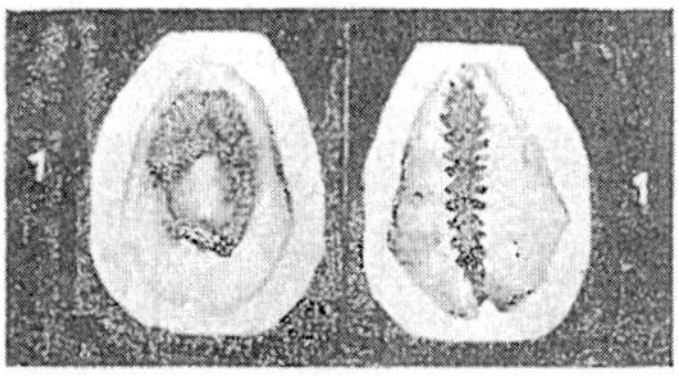

1. COWRIES.

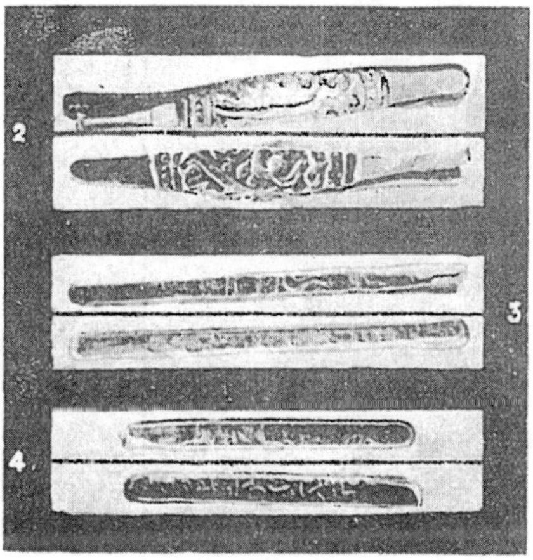

2, 3, 4. DIGU LÁRI.

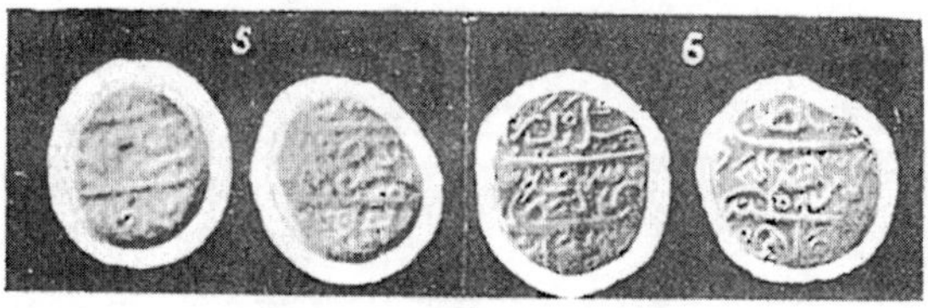

5, 6. LÁRI.

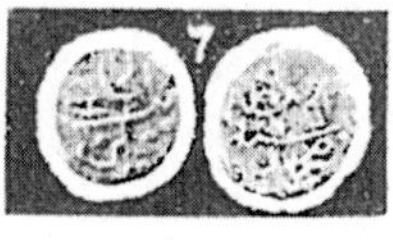

7. KUḌA LÁRI.

PLATE III.

Munnaru, or Minaret, at Ḥukuru Miskit: Male.

View from South-West.

concerning Foreigners and Foreign Trade), devolved at times on the *Velána Vazír*, or the *Bodu Badéri-ge.*

30. *Maabar*. M. *Míru Baharu* (Arabic) *Amír-al-Bahr*. The custom of removing the rudder of native vessels until their departure is still practiced.

31 *Sallareens*. Sc. *Lascarins*. The Máldive term for the Militia at Mále is *Hagu-bé-kalun*. They receive certain allowances in rice, &c., from the Government.

EXCERPTA MALDIVIANA.

By H. C. P. Bell, C.C.S. (Retired).

No. 5. THE MALDIVE ISLANDERS: PHYSICAL TRAITS & GENERAL CHARACTERISTICS

Foreword.

Into his exhaustive and illuminating "*Report on the Census of Ceylon*, 1921," Volume I, Part II, Mr. L. J. B. Turner, M.A., C.C.S., has embodied, by way of profitable illustration, more than a score of excellent vignettes of "Ceylon Type" natives, male and female.

The purpose of the present Paper is to supplement, and round off, the illustrations of the Census Report, with a series of typical group photographs of Máldivians, mainly belonging to the Northern and Southern (as distinct from Central) Atols of the Máldive Archipelago, Ceylon's one Dependency; accompanying the Plates by some description of the physical traits and general characteristics of the Islanders.

No apology seems needed—the writer having been privileged freely to revise for press its Chapter IX (pp.95-108)—for "lifting," from the *Census Report*, (whilst venturing to expand and annotate here and there, *quantum sufficit*) so much of the letter-press anent "The Máldive Islands" as is germane to the subject in hand; in as much as the particulars set out by the Census Commissioner in his Report of 1921 had of necessity to be drawn in great degree from the known authorities—very few in number—who have afforded reliable information in real detail touching the Group.

These are: *Ibn Batúta*, A. C. 1344 (*C. A. S. Journal*, Extra No. 1882); *Pyrard*, 1602-7; *Christopher and Young*, 1835; *Ceylon Sessional Papers*, XLIII, 1881; XV, 1921; *Census Report*, 1911; *C. A. S. Journal*, Vol. XXVII, Extra No. 1919.

Plates.[1]

In regard to the Plates, it appears quite unnecessary to burden this Paper by a superfluity of photographs of Islanders from the Atols which intervene between the three most Northerly (Tiladummatí, Miladummaḍulu and Máḷosmaḍulu), and the two (Huvadú and Aḍḍú, with Fua Mulaku Island midway) lying to the extreme South of the Group.

Physical divergencies shade off so imperceptibly in the natives of these intermediate Atols, that, whilst speech and mannerisms might possibly bewray them, looks and garb would not afford any appreciable differentiation.

Plate I.

Men of Tiladummatí, Miladummaḍulu, and Máḷosmaḍulu, Atols: 1922.

Plate II.

Women, Girls, and Child of Mále Island: 1920; 1922.

Plate III.

Women, Girls, and Children of Mále Island and Mulaku Island (Mulaku Atol): 1920; 1922.

Plate IV

Men, Women, and Boy, of Huvadú (Suwádiva) and Aḍḍú, Atols: 1883.

Plate V.

Men of Huvadú (Suwádiva) and Aḍḍú Atols: 1922.

Plate VI.

Women, Girls, and Children of Fua Mulaku Island and Gan Island (Aḍḍú Atol): 1922.

THE MALDIVE ISLANDS.

The Coral Archipelago known as "The Máldive Islands" extends in the Indian Ocean from lat. 7° 6′ N. to lat. 0° 42′ S., and between long. 72° 33′ and 73° 44′ ; covering 470 miles N. and S. by 70 miles E. and W at widest.

To North, in lat, 8° 20 N., separated by the "Eight Degree Channel," lies the isolated reef-bank of Minicoy (M. *Maliku*), distant 110 miles from the nearest Lakkadive shoal further North, and 70 miles from Ihavandiffuḷu, the most Northerly of the Máldive Atols, to the South.

The Máldives are grouped together in clusters called "Atols" (M *atoḷu* ; Siṇ. *ẹtula*), of which there are nearly twenty in all; but, with an eye to adminis-contrative facilities, the Máldivians themselves have confined the Atols to Thirteen Divisions for some centuries.

Ihavandiffuḷu Atol (included fiscally with Tiladummati Atol) lying since the loss of *Maliku* (Minicoy) to the Rájas of Kaṇṇanúr—at the extreme North end of the Máldive Islands is some 350 miles from the Indian Continent; Mále, where the Sulṭán resides, central, about 400 miles South-West of the nearest port of Ceylon.[2]

1. Inhabitants.

At this day it is not open to doubt that the whole Archipelago—including *Maliku* (Minicoy), now grouped with the Lakkadives and no longer owing allegiance to the Sulṭáns of the Máldive Islands—was occupied, either directly from Ceylon, or, alternatively, about the same time as the B. C. immigration into that Island, by people of Aryan stock and language.[3] This supposition is supported greatly by the close kinship between the Máldive and Siṇhalese languages.

Gradually, from continuous contact and intercourse with natives of the West Coast of India—chiefly Malabar *Mápiḷlas* (vulgarly " Moplahs "),—the influx of Arabs and other aliens, and the occasional importation of African slaves, many characteristics of the original type have been considerably modified. Very markedly is this the case in the Northern Atols, which have been necessarily much more exposed to foreign influence than those lying South.

Muslim predominance, enhanced steadily by regular trade and commerce in the course of three or four centuries at least, culminated in the overthrow of Buddhism, the ruling religion of the Group, and the conversion of the Islanders to Islám in mid-Twelfth Century (A.H.548: A.C. 1153-54).

Since that period the Islands have been governed by a successior of Muḥammadan Sulṭáns (or, very occasionally, Sulṭanas), except during the fifteen years of Portuguese forcible occupation in the Sixteenth Century (A.C. 1558-1573).

2. Population.

The latest Census (1921) gives the full number of inhabited islands as 217: containing 38,174 males and 32,239 females, or a total population of 70,413.

It was to be expected that the Northern Atols should possess most population; to wit, Tiladummati, 10,108; Máḷosmaḍulu (North and South), 7,793; Miladummaḍulu (North and South), 7,021.

The only Southern Atol showing a figure as high as even the last-named is the largest of all the Atols, Huvadú (Suwádiva), with its 7,020 inhabitants.

Mále, the Capital of the Group, though in area approximately but one mile East and West by half a mile across North and South, easily by itself outnumbers, in its over-dense population of 6,127 males and females, that of any of the Atols as a whole, saving the four above specified.

With the exception of 217 foreigners on Mále Island (137 Borahs, 22 Malabars, and 58 Ceylon Moors), the inhabitants of the Máldives were, in 1921, entirely Máldivian, and all Muhammadans

3. Physical Traits.

The Islanders are peopled at this day by a civilized race, originally of Aryan source, which exhibits characteristics both of that and Dravidian type.

In the more Northerly Atols very many present traces of Arab and *Mápilla* (Moplah) physiognomy; this lessens Southwards so gradually as to be hardly traceable step by step.

Most of the types at Mále, and further North, are familiar enough in Ceylon among the Moormen and Southern Indian races. The Southern Islanders approximate much more closely to the Sinhalese.[4]

The Islanders are admittedly a hardy people; due to their predominant occupations, chiefly as sailors and fishermen "elect of the sea."[5] Old persons, both men and women, are quite common throughout the Atols.

In general the natives are of a dark-brown hue; but among the higher classes at Mále are found Nobles (M. *Bodun*) and ladies very much lighter in complexion, owing probably to marriage with light-skinned aliens.

The women are usually somewhat fairer than the men. They have regular features, are shapely in figure, and for the most part goodlooking—some distinctly pretty—when young. For the rest, in stature the majority, like the men, are short, though tall women are to be seen occasionally here and there.[6]

The average height of the men is 5 ft. 2 ins.; but instances are not unknown of individuals, of very fine physique, standing over 6 ft.[7]

Being Muslims, the men, from the Sultán downwards, without exception, keep their heads shaved; as usually their faces also, though free to allow as much hair to grow on the latter as they like—a noteworthy departure from the custom of three centuries back: this permitted the soldiers, officials, and those of gentle birth to wear their hair as long as the women, whilst forbidding all save church dignitaries and *Ḥájis* to grow long beards according to fancy.

4. General Characteristics.[8]

As a race the Máldivians are most inoffensive. Naturally a somewhat timid people, their isolation still induces a certain degree of aloofness and suspicion which in former days was more strongly exhibited.[9]

Crime of a heinous character is scarcely heard of on these Islands; even theft and personal violence are of rare occurrence; murder has been very seldom known.[10]

In their conduct to foreigners the Islanders are thoroughly humane and generous;[11] towards each other noticeably obliging, rendering one another prompt and willing assistance; and to their kindred extremely affectionate.[12]

The Nobility is exceptionally hospitable; and not wanting in a refined sociability, which ever exhales that charming courtesy, the distinguishing badge of the true Muslim gentleman.

Of the natives of the Capital (Mále) it has been remarked recently (1920):

"In regard to the inhabitants of Mále (whose physical characteristics have been frequently described by visitors), it is pleasant to record, with the experience born of close observation, that a delightful spirit of ease and contentment seems to prevail universally. So far as can be judged, the natives appear to be healthy and well-to-do. They go about their respective business cheerfully, and with an air of settled purpose and determination, preserving the while the silent observant demeanour which customarily marks the Muḥammadan. The very bazárs (native and foreign) present none of that noisy bustle and semi-confusion daily experienced in the crowded marts of Southern India and Ceylon.

" Discipline and self-control rule from the highest to the lowest, side by side with the fullest toleration and freedom of action—the latter extending in the case of the ordinary women (albeit under Muslim regime) to the limit of permitting their appearance in the streets unveiled."[13]

5. Dress.

The ordinary dress of the men consists of short drawers (M.*harawálu*); a cloth wrapped round the waist (M.*mundu*), after the Siṇhalese fashion; and a kerchief twisted over the head (M.*ruma*). Sometimes a thin shirt (M.*kuru libás*), generally white, is worn.

The mode of dress in the early Seventeenth Century, as minutely described by Pyrard, must have been both richer and more elaborate. It included the use of turbans and silk scarves.

The women follow the Low-Country Siṇhalese custom of wearing a waistcloth (M.*féli*), which is woven on the Islands themselves, coarse in texture, but striking and tasteful in its colouring—chocolate ground relieved by black and white stripes. The upper part of the body is covered by a long, loose-fitting, coloured blouse (M.*libás*), of cotton or silk, reaching to the knees, short sleeved, and edged at the neck with gold or silver tinsel lace.

Ear-rings, necklace, bracelets and other ornaments may deck the person.

Their luxuriant black hair is bound into a knot—at Mále on the right side of the head, in Atols further South on the top;—upon which a chocolate kerchief of native make (M.*ruma*) is jauntily set.[14]

6. Occupations.

The labouring classes, exclusive of those engaged in pursuits connected with trade, follow various employments as a means of subsistence.

Among the men the occupations much the most favoured are fishing[15] and sea-faring: other industries are husbandry; gathering coconuts; toddy drawing; and a few minor activities.

Less than a score are employed now-a-days in the delicate art of turning out the exquisite and unique lacquer-work produced on these Islands, chiefly for the use of Royalty and the Nobles.

Some choice jewellery is also made in a few islands.

To the women are left, well-nigh entirely, the making of coir; lace-work; mat-weaving; and the collection of cowries.[16]

7. Trade.[17]

Far the largest Export trade of the Islands consists in that well-known comestible of Oriental natives dried "Máldive fish" (M.*kummala-mas*; Siṇ *umbala-cada*). coconuts (M. *káṛi*), and coir (M.*ronu*)—the two latter products being shipped almost exclusively to India. Tortoise-shell (M.*kahabu-fat*) is also regularly exported.

The total Exports from the Máldives to Ceylon rose beyond ten and a half-fold between 1860 (£20,136) and 1919 (£215,906). Over the same period, the Import trade of the Islands grew to more than five times the value of sixty years before: 1860 (£5,101); 1919 (£26,434).

8. Language and Script.

The language (M.*Divehi bas*) spoken by the Islanders is substantially the same throughout the far-flung Group—including *Maliku* (where it is termed "*Máhl*")—though dialectal variations of the Mále standard naturally occur; particularly in the Southern

Atols, which have been less affected by foreign intercourse.

A very large proportion of the Máldivian vocabulary consists (*a*) either of pure Sinhalese words, modified by vowel changes and—owing to Arabic influence—the adoption of the dento-labial consonant "f" for the labial "p," or (*b*) of derivatives from roots common to both languages.

Trade, and other intercourse, with alien races have added a considerable number of words of foreign origin, chiefly Hindustáni.

The oldest form of Máldivian script yet discovered, (i) "*Evéla Akuru*" (lit. "Ancient letters"), is that found on a few copper-plate grants (M.*lómáfánu*) which have survived to this day.

This type, strikingly resembling medieval Sinhalese lithic script, gradually developed into the (ii) "*Dives Akuru*" characters (lit. "Máldive letters"); which, though no longer employed, are known to a limited number of Máldivians on the Group. Both (i) and (ii) are read from left to right.

The third form of character, (iii) "*Tána*" (or "*Gabuli Tána*")—based on Arabic and Persian elements, and, like them, read from right to left—seems to have been in concurrent use with (ii) "*Dives Akuru*" from the Seventeenth Century at least, if not earlier.[18]

NOTES.

1. **Plates**. The men, women, and children of Plates IV (7, 8), and VI (11, 12), and the women and children of Plates II (3), III (5, 6), are dressed in ordinary garb. Most of the men in Plates I (1, 2), V (9, 10), have donned shirts (M.*kuru libás*) for the occasion.

Plate I (1). The Islanders in front belong to Miladummadulu Atol (North); those at back to Tiladummati Atol.*

* Men of Kuḷuduffuṛi and Diddú Islands (Tiladummati Atol) and Má Kaḍudú (Miladummaḍulu Atol, North).

Plate I (2). In the front row the men are from Máḷosmaḍulu Atol (North); those behind from Máḷosmaḍulu Atol (South).*

Plate II. The two female figures of (4) are Málé ladies.

Plate V. The Islanders of (9) came from Huvadú (Suvádiva) Atol; of (10) from Aḍḍú Atol.†

Plate VI. The women and children in (11) belong to Fua Mulaku Island; those in (12) to Gan Island of Aḍḍú Atol.

The mixed Photographs (*Plate IV*, 7, 8) were taken at Colombo in 1883, when Máldive *oḍi-faharu* were visiting Ceylon during the N.E. Monsoon.

Close approximation to Siṇhalese type is well exhibited by some of the Islanders in this Plate.

2. **Map.** For a compact small-scale " Map of the Máldive Islands," See Plate I, *C.A.S. Journal* Vol. XXX, No. 75, 1925.

3. **Date of Occupation.** Such was the tradition among the Maldivians themselves, according to Pyrard, even in the early Seventeenth Century:—

" They hold that the *Maldives* began to be inhabited only four hundred years ago, and that the first who came and peopled them were the *Cingalles* of the island of Ceylon (which is not far distant), and were idolaters, but afterwards changed their religion; it being about one hundred and fifty or two hundred years at most since they received Mahomedanism, through the Moorish and Arabian navigators, who, while trading over all the continent and islands of the East Indies, brought there also their law, which has since remained in most of those parts." (Pyrard, *Voyage*; *Hak. Soc.* I, p.265-6).

Pyrard post-dates the Muslim Conversion of A. C. 1153-4 by at least 250 years, and the original immigration still more egregiously.

4. **Foreign Influx.** " A large number of foreigners from all parts meet there and make it their home; besides many Indians who from time to time are wrecked there . . . . This is why the people living at *Malé* and the neighbouring parts

---

* Men of Inguraidú and Mídú Islands (Máḷosmaḍulu Atol) North and Tuládú (Máḷosmaḍulu Atol, South).

† Men of Gaddú Island (Huvadú) Atol of Huḷudú and Hitadú (Aḍḍú Atol).

towards the North are more polished, genteel, and civilised; while, those toward the South are ruder in language and habits, and also are less well-formed in body, and darker. . . . . The Northern parts, are more frequented by foreigners, who usually marry there. There, too, pass all the ships, which enrich the country and tend to civilise it . . . . Albeit the people of the South are no less well-informed and clever than the rest, perhaps more so in some ways; but as for the nobles, they are all in the North." (Pyrard. *loc. cit.* p.105).

5. **Sea-faring Race.** The Máldive Islanders are expert and intrepid mariners, whose picturesque boats (M.*odi-faharu, ḍóni-faharu* used to be seen in many Indian ports, not infrequently.

Formerly—" sailing upon different stars (by means of their effective, if primitive, nautical instruments) in lieu of points of the compass "—they made long, greatly adventurous, voyages, from the " tempest-haunted " Atols, in their small, light-built, but most sea-worthy vessels, as far as Aden, Calcutta, Penang, Sumátra, &c., braving the storms and formidable currents which sweep round the Indian Ocean and elsewhere. (*C. A. S. Journal,* Vol. XXVII, Extra No. 1919).

6. **Women.** " In truth they seemed to be pretty and engaging enough, as much by reason that they are neatly dressed as that they are well formed, of good figures, and winsome ways; albeit they are of an olive skin, for the most part, although you will find many brunettes, and many quite fair, just as in other parts." (Pyrard, *loc. cit.* p.169).

7. **Stalwarts.** A-Gaḍuvaru Manifuḷu, *ex*-Sulṭan Muḥammad 'Imád-ud-dín V, son of Sulṭán Ibráhim Núr-ud-dín; and Músá *Máfat Kilégefánu*, son of Numara Gaḍuvaru Ḥasan *Fáṛina Kilégefánu*, both now dead, were noticeable in 1920 among such exceptionally tall, well-built Nobles.

8. **General Characteristics.** The Maghrabín traveller in A.C. 1344, Ibn Baṭúṭa, not unnaturally speaks highly of his Muslim co-religionists :—

" The inhabitants of the Máldive Islands are honest and pious people, sincere in good faith and of a strong will: they eat only what is lawful, and their prayers are granted." (*C. A. S. Journal*, Extra No., 1882 p.6).

The "infidel" Portuguese, Barbosa (A.C. 1518), finds few good points:—"The men of the Isles have no weapons whatever; they are feeble folk, yet right cunning, but very clever; and above all things they are mighty magicians" (Duarte Barbosa: *Hac. Soc.* Vol. II, p.104).

Pyrard, the French captive, who spent seven years (1602-7) on the group, is ultra-eulogistic:—

"In short, the people are exceeding adroit, much given to the manufacture of all kinds of things, and excelling therein, even in letters and science, according to their notions; but more especially in astrology, in which they make great business. They are a prudent and circumspect people, very cunning in trade and in social life. And while they are valiant, and courageous, and skilled in arms, they live under a complete system of law and police (Pyrard, *loc cit.* p.106).

For more recent accounts of the Islanders, see the details given by Lieutenants Christopher and Young (*Transactions Bombay Geographical Society*, 1836-8), and *Sessional Papers* XLIII, 1881; XV, 1921.

9. **Misgiving.** Displayed unmistakably less than a century back in connection with the Survey of the Máldive Archipelago by the Indian Navy vessels in 1834:—

"The suspicious nature of Captain Moresby's avowed object co-operated with political circumstances. upon minds whose characteristic trait is fearfulness. They objected to the surveying flags, and were not satisfied until they were permitted to set up their own also." (*Trans. Bombay Geo. Soc., loc. cit.* pp.103-4).

10. **Murder.** For very many years past only two murders are reported to have occurred on the Máldive Islands:—

(*a*) A party of islanders from *Hodaidú* of Tiladummati Atol (who, when seized and tried at Mále, admitted their crime, pleading starvation), landed on *Lubo Kaḍu* an uninhabited island planted with coconuts; and to escape detection, killed the only two watchers.

(*b*) A woman of *Kaḍudú* (Koḷumaḍuḷu Atol) made away with her child, by drowning it.

As punishment at the Máldives in such cases, after trial and sentence by the *Kázi*, the murderers are led round the main streets of Mále with their faces blackened, and a rope round the waist, besides being subjected to other humiliations. They are then taken to the sea-beach and beaten with the official leather thong (M. *durá*) and special rod of four canes tied together (M. *hataru fan etteyo*); chastisement up to 19 strokes being the full tale allowed: thereafter all are banished to various Atols.

The Death penalty has long ceased to be enforced on the Islands.

11. **Humanity,** See *C. A. J. Journal* Vol. XXIX, No. 76, 1925, pp.207-8.

12. **Affection.** When Galoḷu-ge Goma, his aunt, lay slowly dying at Mále in 1922, H. H. the Sulṭán Muḥammad Shams-ud-din III, did not fail to leave the Palace every day to attend on her in person.

13. **Sessional Paper, XV, 1921,** "The Máldive Islands" p.43.

14. **Dress.** In mid-Fourteenth Century, according to Ibn Baṭúṭa, the women would appear to have had no covering either for the head, or for the upper part of the body:—

"The women of these Islands do not cover the head: the Sovereign herself does not so. They comb their hair and tie it up on one side. Most of them wear only a cloth, covering them from the navel to the ground; the rest of the body remains uncovered." (*C. A. S. Jounal,* Extra No. 1872 p.11).

Two centuries and a half had worked great change in both these respects, for Pyrard (*loc. cit.*, pp.166-7; 106-07) writes:—

"As for the women, first of all they have a large coloured cloth of cotton or silk, which covers them from the waist to the ankles, and serves as a petticoat. Above this they wear a robe of taffetas, or of very fine cotton, but very long, reaching to the feet, and with blue and white borders. To give a notion of its shape, I cannot better describe this robe than by comparing it to the chemises which the women here wear. It is a little open round the neck, and fastened with two little gilt buttons, and likewise open at the throat in front, but no further at the breast. . . . Their arms are charged with heavy bracelets of silver, sometimes from the wrist up to the elbow: some of them have them mixed with tin, chiefly the poor, while the rest have them of fine and massive silver."

"The hair, is in general black. . . . They dress it by taking all the hair from the front behind, and drawing it as tight as possible; so that not a hair strays hither or thither; then they tie it up behind and make a large knotted bunch; and in order to enlarge that they use a perruque of man's hair (but as long as a women's), in form like a horse's tail."

15. **Fishing.** Of the male earners nearly 60 per cent., or 14,760, depend upon fishing for their livelihood (*Census Report*, 1921).

16. **Other Occupations.** Coir makers, 9,224; lace-workers, 1,586; husbandry, 1425; mat-weavers, 777; cowry collectors, 348, mostly women. (*Loc. cit.* 1921).

Most coir (of which there are 12 kinds in all) is prepared in Ari Atol.

The cowry trade is rapidly dwindling. In 1911 (*Census Report*), there were 1045 (194 males, 851 females) collectors, or thrice the number of ten years later

Almost all the ornamental "Máldive mats," so highly valued for their choice execution, are made from a rush growing at Huvadú Atol. They exhibit many neat patterns, in which black, brown, yellow and white are blended tastefully.

17. **Trade.** For fuller particulars touching the Trade and Commerce of the Máldive Islands, *Sessional Papers* XLIII, 1881: XV, 1921; and *Census Report*, 1921, may be consulted.

18. **Language and Script.** Regarding the Máldivian Language and Script see *Sessional Paper* XLIII, 1881, *C. A. S. Journal* Vol. XXVII, Extra No. 1919, and Appendices; Vols. XXIX, XXX Nos. 75, 76, 77, 1922-1924.

Máldive Islanders : 1922.

PLATE I.

I. TILADUMMATÍ AND MIỊADUMMADUḶU ATOLS

2. MÁḶOSMADUḶU ATOL.

PLATE II.

Maldive Islanders : 1920, 1922.

3. 4. MÁLE ISLAND

Maldive Islanders: 1920, 1922

5. MÁLE ISLAND.

6. MULAKU ISLAND.

Máldive Islanders: 1883.

7. 8. HUVADÚ AND AḌḌÚ ATOLS.

Maldive Islanders: 1922.

9. HUVADÚ ATOL

10. AḌḌÚ ATOL

Máldive Islanders: 1922.

11. FUA MULAKU ISLAND.

12. GAN ISLAND.

EXCERPTA MÁLDIVIANA.

By H. C. P. BELL, C.C.S. (Retired).

No. 6.—GRAVES OF CAPTAIN OVEREND AND PRIVATE LUCKHAM AT THE MALDIVES.

Prologue.

The countless wrecks [1] that have strewn the "tempest-haunted" reefs of the Máldive Islands during the past four centuries—since European vessels first essayed to pass to and from the Far East through the treacherous lesser "Channels," always more or less dangerous, which separate the Atols—have yielded terribly heavy toll to death; nor less of the drowned than of those who escaped the sea only to find lonely graves, long forgotten, on the shores of many an unknown island.

Whom the breakers grudgingly spared, "Máldive Fever"—that deadly scourge, which has ever clung to the Group—has persistently laid low.[2]

WRECK OF THE "CORBIN."

Ex uno disce omnes. The ship "Corbin" (200 tons), in which was François Pyrard de Laval, sailed for the East, from St. Malo in France, on May 18th 1601, with the "Croissant" (400 tons).

On the night of July 2nd, 1602 owing to gross neglect of ordinary precautions, the "Corbin" drifted on to the reef of Goidú (Horsburgh) Atol of the Máldive Archipelago near the Island of "*Pouladou*" (Fuḷudú).

Pyrard (who returned to France in 1611, to write a full account of his adventures[3]) thus sums up the fate of the "Corbin's" Officers and crew :—

About forty in all survived the wreck (*Hak. Soc. Pyrard*, I, *p.* 60).

The (Second) Mate and two sailors were the first taken to Mále (*p.* 57) ; then the Captain and five or six more (*p.* 59) ; Pyrard himself with two others being tranferred to "*Paindoüe*" (Fehendú) Island.

The King's Officers took more of the crew to Mále ; where the Captain and Second Mate died (*p.* 66).

From "*Pouladou*" the Mate and eleven sailors escaped (*p.* 67) in a Headman's boat, and reached Quilon ; leaving eight, of whom half were sick. The Lieutenant died ; as well as one of the crew who fell from a coco-tree (*p.* 68).

Afterwards Pyrard was taken to Mále, with one of the two sailors at "*Paindoüe* ;" four still remaining at "*Pouladou*" (*p.* 73).

Fifteen or sixteen men had already been brought to Mále ; but Pyrard found only three surviving—two Flemings and one Frenchman. The latter died eight days after Pyrard's arrival (*pp.* 77-78).

The Pilot ("English, speaking no French") and three sailors, had been put to death for an attempted escape (*p.* 79).

Pyrard's companion, left for a time at "*Maconnodou*" (Makunudú, North Màle Atol), was brought to Mále ; making four, two Frenchmen and two Flemings.

Two months later Pyrard arranged for the five others to be brought from "*Pouladou*" and "*Paindoüe* ;" thus making nine at Mále, five Flemings and four French (*ib.*)

Four Flemings got awày, but were drowned (*p.* 86) ; leaving one Fleming and four French. One of the latter, Pyrard's great friend, died (*p.* 87).

This left alive two French—besides Pyrard himself, who was then sick at "*Bandos*" Island (Baḍos, North Màle Atol)—and one Fleming.

Finally, these four were taken to India in February 1607, by the hostile Malabar Expedition which killed the Máldive King (Sultan Íbráhim III: A.C. 1585—1607.)

Whether the Mate, or any of his eleven friends, got back to Europe is not known.

According to this synopsis, almost half of those lucky enough to get to shore from the " Corbin " died of sickness alone, and that in eighteen months or so.

BRITISH DEATHS AT THE MALDIVES.

1. Pilot of the "Corbin": A.C. 1602.

The first English victim to meet his death at Mále was probably the intrepid and ill-fated Pilot of the "Corbin:"[4] who, so long as three centuries and more ago (A.C. 1602). seems to have pioneered an " Escaping Club "—a term made very familiar during the recent Great War

With three companions he lost his life in the first venture, a martyr to that unquenchable spirit of reckless daring characteristic of the British race.

His futile bid for freedom was on this wise :—

" When the news came to the King of the escape of the Mate and the other men from *Pouladou*, he was so enraged that he swore a solemn oath that he would not let one of us go. I was assured by several of the Lords that otherwise he would have provided us with a barque, as we desired.

The Pilot, hearing this resolution, which confined him for life to these Islands, designed to get a barque and escape; like his friends of *Pouladou*. To this end he conspired with three of our sailors, and hid in a wood all that was required. Their design was discovered by the Islanders, who had remarked their goings to and fro the wood by the shore, and played spies over them. They then gave information to the six Elders, called *Mouscoulis* (M. *Muskuḷi-bé-kalun*) who rule the highest affairs of State ; and they in turn informed the King.

Careful observation was made of the carriage of these four, and, on the night on which they were to embark, they were taken in the act by the soldiers, who put their feet in irons.

Two days afterwards the soldiers took them in boats, feigning to take them to some other Island ; and when they were upon the sea they cut off their heads with blows of the *caty* (M.*katu* ; Siṇ. *kętta*,) which is made like a large bill-hook of this country, and of excellent steel, well-polished and highly worked: it comes from the Malabar Coast, and cuts exceedingly well. They felled them by many blows: and one who dealt only one blow was esteemed no good soldier (of the King).

The four corpses were flung into the sea.

After all, it is no wonder that the King was enraged at these attempts to escape on the part of our men; for it is high treason to steal a barque or boat and to depart beyond the realm: that may not be done without passport, and a special and precise permit of the King, even though the boat were one's own. Without that it is death and unpardonable, and no one need hope for the King's mercy if convicted.

This crime is called *odican anpou* (M. *oḍi gengosfu*; lit. "having taken away an *oḍi*").

I heard this sad news, and that of the natural death of our other comrades, as soon as I arrived at *Má.é*.

At the same time one of the King's pilots told me that the twelve of *Pouladou*, who escaped with the Mate of our ship, had arrived at *Coilan* (Quilon) on the Coast, and had been put in irons on a Portuguese galley, where he had seen them; and would be taken to Goa." (*Hak. Soc. Pyrard*, I. *pp.* 78-80)

2. Captain J. C. Overend: A.C. 1797.

Nearly two centuries later another Englishman, a British Officer, to whom the Fates proved somewhat kinder, died at Mále. Also the victim of a wreck (A.C. 1797), Captain Overend was not "done to death," but succumbed to its dread fever (Pyrard, "*Málé ons*"; M. *Mále hun*) within six weeks of reaching "Sulṭán's Island."

Here is the story in brief:—

The "Ketch of Tranquebar," freighted with piece-goods for Colombo by her recent purchasers Captain J. C. Overend and Mr. George Fischer, sailed from "the Island of Veypar near Tuticoryn" on January 6th, 1797, under command of J. H. Thuring, Lieutenant, Marine Survey, Netherlands' East India Company[5].

Owing to stress of weather, and serious leakage, added to want of water and provisions, she was ultimately obliged to steer for the Máldives.

On the 20th they sighted, but could not fetch, "Rája Island" (Mále); and, after beating about for nine days, had "to make (29th) the first Island they could reach," anchoring "in 60 fathoms rocky ground."

"The Chief of the Island," appealed to personally by Captain Overend, "readily promised his aid, but delayed the fulfilment so long that the vessel stranded."

Disaster followed disaster. The Islanders, using violence, "refused to allow the crew to meddle with the cargo," pending a report to their "King"; and proceeded "to remove all the bales as well as the lead."

Sent at first to another Island, the Officers and crew were subsequently brought to "Rája Isle" (Mále). There they were taken before "the Second of the Island," who refused them audience with "the King, but offered "a boat to carry them to Cochin"

Demand for the restitution of the cargo was met by the reply that "very little was saved"; but, upon threat of protest to the Madras Government, the Chief "became more friendly," and promised to "give orders to bring all the cargo that was saved out of the vessel."

Fifteen days elapsed, "but no cargo appeared." The Master (J. H. Thuring), "being attacked with a violent fever, and it increasing daily on shore," was taken off by a chance English ship, and landed at Colombo on April 7th.[6]

Captain Overend had died at Mále on March 16th.

Late in 1800, at the request of the Madras Government, Sir F. North, Governor of Ceylon, forwarded (December 8th,) a translation of the whole correspondence regarding the "Tranquebar" to the reigning Sultan (Muhammad Mu'ín-ud-dín I), with this strong protest:—

"Had Your Highness at that time commenced Your auspicious reign, an act of such outrageous and unwarrantable violence would not have happened

I am confident that Your justice will induce You to make ample reparation for an event so contrary to the hospitality which a friendly nation has a right to find in Your dominions; and so incompatible with those sentiments of friendship and good-will which Your Highness possesses towards the ships and subjects of Great Britain."

The Sulṭán, in reply, sent a "friendly explanation of the case": which seems to have "perfectly satisfied" the Governments of Fort St. George (Madras) and Ceylon.

As the complaint was not pressed for more than three years after the occurrence of the wreck, and in the interval a new Sulṭán had succeeded to the throne, the way was automatically smoothed for plausible excuses.

The only reparation Mr. Fischer obtained was by the sale of a very small portion of the wrecked goods which had found their way to Ceylon.

3. Private V. Luckham: A.C. 1909.

A further century or so had elapsed before a third Englishman was added to the quota of Great Britain's sons who have ended their days at this centre, and Capital, of "The Máldive Islands;" now the sole, isolated, Dependency of Ceylon, and still but little knowm.

On September 9th, 1909, Private Victor Lucknam, R.M.L.I., of H.M.S. "Proserpine," was drowned, whilst bathing off Huḷule Island, about two miles from Málé, on the Eastern reef of North Mále Atol.

Like Captain Overend one hundred and twelve years before (A.C. 1797), Private Luckham was buried on Fonadú, an uninhabited island less than a mile north of Mále.

Full particulars of the accident and burial were furnished by the Commander of H.M.S. "Proserpine," H. J. T. Marshall, in a Report (summarised below) made to H. E. Rear-Admiral Slade, the Commander-in-Chief of the East Indies Station :-

A party of men, under a Petty Officer, had been allowed to go in boats (September 9th) for a picnic to the Island of Huḷulé about two miles distant from Mále. While bathing, Private Victor Luckham R.M.L.I., (who had been swimming about without difficulty between the reef and the beach) was unaccountably overcome, and sank before others could get to his assistance.

The Prime Minister at Mále, (A. Háji Íbráhím Dídí Effendí)[8], at once ordered boats and expert divers to the scene. When the body was recovered, all efforts to restore animation proved vain.

The same Minister, further, sent a party of men at dawn next day to Funidoo (Fonadú) Island to cut the undergrowth, clear the path to the burial ground, and dig the grave.

Private Luckham was buried with full military honours; and mourning flags were hoisted on all the Mosques on shore.

A temporary wooden cross has been set up; and two gravestones will replace it when ready.[9]

No inhabitants are permitted to approach the place, except by order of the Sultan.[10]

Fonadu Island.

To the above Report was appended "*Hydrographic Notes, Etc.,*" by Lieutenant R. Preston, R.N., in which interesting reference is made to Fonadú island and its graves :—

"Funidoo (Fonadú) is a well-wooded islet about 200 yards by 150 N. and S. The undergrowth seems well kept down, and a large well-kept path bisects the island from North to South.

On the South end of the island, at the end of the path, just before coming out on to the beach, is the grave of Captain Overend, H.M.S "Doris," March 16th,[11] 1797; also the grave of Private Luckham, R. M. L. I.

There are numerous graves on each side of the path on the South side: these all had native inscriptions, though (by the size of the head and foot stones and their distance apart) several might be the graves of Europeans;[12] the rest being small and closer together, like the stones in the cemeteries in Malé Island. The native head-stones, some of which were very old, were found among the trees, which had displaced some of the graves.

The trees are apparently kept trimmed; and, I believe, the Sultan sends a party to clear up the island once every year. No one is allowed there at any other time; though some rabbits have been put down to breed.

The island has several varieties of large flowering trees and palms.

The landing place is on the "North side with Dunidoo (Dunidú) island N. 12° W."[13]

Visit to Fonadu: A.C. 1922.

During the Archaeological Expedition's stay at Mále in 1922, opportunity was taken (May 6th) to pay a visit to Fonadú island.

Paired with its similarly verdure-clad, and uninhabited, neighbour, Dunidú, to West, the small island of Fonadú, rising from the bluest of lagoons under the Tropical sun, presents a delightsome picture. Both islands are wooded down to the very beach, in a luxuriant growth of varied jungle-trees and shrubs—notably *Cordia subcordata* (M. *káni*), and the fleshy-leaved *Scaevola Koenigii* (M. *magu*)—for the most part common to the sea-board of Ceylon.

Landing on the Northern side (the usual point of access, and difficult except at high tide) the two particular graves sought—several others lie quite apart—were soon reached along a semi-avenue, partially opened out, which looks across the water Southwards to Mále.

Some "temple-tree" (*Plumeria acutifolia*) saplings were growing on either side of the graves.[14] At head and foot of both stood peaked slabs, of "reverse-shield" shape, carved from madrepore (M. *hiri-gá*), such as mark every adult male interment throughout the many Muslim cemeteries at Mále. All four stones are alike, and measure 2 ft. 10 in. by 1 ft. 1 in., across.

On the head-stone of Private Luckham's grave (which is just North of that said to belong to Captain Overend) has been cut neatly, within 3½-in. framing, in 1-in. capitals an inscription of ten lines. The epitaph runs :—

SACRED | TO THE MEMORY OF | PRIVATE VICTOR LUCKHAM | R.M.L.I. | H.M.S. PROSERPINE | DROWNED WHILE BATHING | AT HULULE NEAR MALE | 9TH AUGUST 1909 | AGED 24 YEARS | PEACE PERFECT PEACE.

MÁLDIVE ISLANDS.

FONADÚ ISLAND.

CAPTAIN OVEREND'S GRAVE · A.C. 1922.

The mason has blundered in one word : AUGUST should be SEPTEMBER.[15]

In regard to Captain Overend's grave (which was photographed: see Plate) what Lieutenant Preston's "*Notes*" had adumbrated proved all too true. Neither head nor footstone bore any incised record ; but across the top of the head-stone. a narrow board, 4 in. only in depth had been affixe

Upon this appear three brief lines of writing, carved in 2-in. letters, blackened :-

CAPTAIN OVEREND R.N. | H.M.S "DORIS." | 1797.

Visit to Fonadu: A.C. 1887.

That the original grave-stone must have disappeared at some time during the period of twenty-two years between April 1887 and September 1909, and the few lines now cut on the strip of plank been substituted, is borne out by the following communication extracted from the Ceylon Press of the eighth decade of the last Century.

On April 14th and 16th, 1887, two very similar letters (combined below) were published in the "Ceylon Times" and the "Ceylon Observer," above the initials "F.C.H.," of an employee in the Basses and Minicoy Lights Office, Colombo at the time :–

"When on shore at Male on the 6th of April I was informed by some of the inhabitants that on the small island of Foonadu (Fonadú) an Englishman, or at least a British subject, was buried. At the same time they showed me a rough copy of the inscription which they had taken from the head-stone of the grave.

Owing to the faulty manner in which it was copied, I was not able to make much sense of the record ; but as the Islanders were very anxious for me to see it, and as Mr. Ibrahim Didi (Prime Minister), with his usual courtesy, placed his boat at my disposal, I very willingly consented to go.

There was no difficulty in finding the grave in question. It was nearly in the centre of the island, and under a large breadfruit tree. The grave was nine (*sic*) feet long, and had a stone at the head and foot. On the former was engraved, in fine bold characters :—

HERE LIETH THE BODY OF CAPTAIN J. C. OVERAND,[16] LATE OF H.M.S. 36TH REGT., WHO DEPARTED THIS LIFE THE 16TH MARCH, 1797.

Can some one of your numerous readers say who this Captain Overand was, and explain by what strange fate he found his last resting place in so lonely and secluded a spot?"

Correspondence of 1800 regarding the loss of the "Tranquebar." having been fortuitously placed in his hands, the Editor, of the "Ceylon Observer," offered this comment (April 18th) :—

"The gallant soldier would seem at the time of his death to have embarked on a private speculation with a Mr. Fischer, having presumably severed his connection with war's hurly-burly and turned his attention to mercantile pursuits.

How, and by whom, the head-stone was carved, and placed to mark the lonely grave, has yet to be explained."

Epilogue.

Every enquiry in 1922 at Mále failed—perhaps not unnaturally—to elicit any information as to when, and by whom, the original grave-stone was set up ; as well as how, and why, the epitaph came to be so drastically altered.

Does Captain Overend's spirit brood still over the weird fate, which, in unwittingly robbing him of his true deserts, has tried to make some amends by posthumous promotion to the Senior Service !

Que diable allait-il faire dans cette galère ? Captain J. C. Overend belonged to the 36th British Regiment of Foot (now the 2nd Battalion, Worcester Regiment), which served for many years in India about this time : he had no connection with the Royal Navy.

Yet mayhap some day this "gallant soldier" shall come into his own again, an it befall that judicious and earnest representation be made, with all due diligence, in the right direction. So mote it be.

NOTES.

1. **Wrecks on the Maldives.**—The Nineteenth Century alone witnessed nearly thirty wrecks, recorded as having occurred on the Máldive Atols. See "List of Wrecks, 1797 to 1800" (*Ceylon Sessional Paper, XLIII.* 1881, *p.* 133. *Appendix*); to which should be added five more of later years.

2. **"Maldive Fever."**—This dire scourge (M. *Mále hun*) has been known and dreaded for centuries past :—

(i) "In the midst of all this a fever seized me, and I was very ill. Everyone who goes to that Island (Mále) must inevitably catch the fever." (*Ibn Batúta*: A.C. 1344).

(ii) "I fell ill at Mále of a severe burning fever, very common there and very dangerous, especially to strangers ; so much so that few get over it—still less the Christians for whom there is no sort of cure. I was ill and in great danger for more than two months, and it was ten months before I was quite well." (*Pyrard*: A.C. 1602). Many of his wrecked shipmates succumbed to the fever.

(iii) Captain Overend died at Mále (March 16th, 1797) within five or six weeks of arrival.

(iv) In 1835, Lieutenants Christopher and Young of the Indian Navy had to leave Mále, fever-stricken, when engaged on the Survey of the Máldive Archipalego, after only three months' stay

(v) Mále is very subject to recurrent waves of this pestilence —apparently a virulent form of what is nowadays termed "Influenza." One such epidemic (300 deaths) struck Mále in the autumn of 1922; aided by its very congested area (6,000 inhabitants to 1½ square miles), bad water, and abominable insanitary conditions.

(vi) All three members of the Archaeological Expedition of 1922 continued to suffer periodically for two or three years after their return to Ceylon.

3. **Pyrard "Voyage aux Indes Orientales"**—Four editions were issued ; 1611, 1615, 1619, all 8vo : 1679, 4to.

4. **Pilot of the "Corbin."**—Pyrard does not record the name of this daring, but luckless, Englishman. He may have already sailed in Eastern seas under Lancaster, who made his First Voyage in A.C. 1591.

5. **Lieutenant J. H. Thuring.**—Leaving the Netherlands' Company Service, he settled in Ceylon. Descendants survive to this day. A grandson, Mr. W. P. Thuring, retired Station Master, C.G.R. (son of the late Dr. J. L. Thuring) died at Colombo on May 11th, 1928, aged 68.

6. **Captain Overend.**—The Captain of this English ship had charge of Captain Overend's watch, sword, trinkets, &c.

7. **Maldive Sultan.**—When the "Tranquebar" was wrecked Sulṭán Ḥasan Núr-úd-dín was on the throne (A.C. 1779-1799). He died at Jeddah in his second *Ḥajj* pilgrimage ; and was succeeded by his son Sulṭán Muhammad Mu'ín-ud-dín I (A.C. 1799-1835).

8. **A Haji Ibrahim Didi. Bodu Dorimena Kilegefanu.**—This greatly esteemed Noble served as Prime Minister to the Sulṭáns of the Máldives, on and off, from 1883 to his death March 31st, 1925 or more than 40 years. *Multis ille flebilis occidit.*

Owing to pre-eminent administrative ability, loyal devotion to the real interests of his country and sterling personal qualities, he justly earned the appellation of "The Grand Old Man of the Máldives."

9. **The Lakkadive Islands.**—Carpenter Primrose of the "Vizier" (wrecked on Cheriyapani in 1853) is the only European (English), so far as is known, to have died on this more Northerly Group.

A roughly carved stone was erected at his grave on Chetlat by the crew of the "General Simpson," wrecked there in 1863.

10. **The Maldive Islands.**—Papers, Part III, p. 49.

11. **Captain Overend's Grave.**—The epitaph as given by Lieutenant Preston includes the month and day (March 16th) of his death.

It is more than probable therefore, that in 1922 a fresh board had replaced that of 1909; for it now gives only the year (1797).

12. **Other European Graves.**—Lieutenant Preston hints at other Europeans having died at Mále and been buried on Fonadú island.

No evidence supporting this presumption was forthcoming, at Mále in 1922, though fullest enquiry was made. It is significant that the graves of Captain Overend and Private Luckham (Christians) are well separated from all others.

13. **The Maldive Islands.**—Papers, Part III, p. 50

14. **Flebile ludibrium.**—One "temple-tree"—*horresco referens*—had been actually planted in the centre of each grave; besides a thriving young-coconut plant on that of Captain Overend!

The Máldive authorities graciously promised to have these "excrescences" removed from the graves. and volunteered, further, that more attention would be paid to their proper upkeep in future.

Horizontal slabs laid between head and foot stones, as suggested on the spot, (1922) would be both economical and effective.

15. **H.M.S. "Proserpine"**—Left Colombo on September 3rd, 1909, "with a Mail for the **Máldive Islands**;" arriving at Mále on September 6th. Private Luckham was drowned three days afterwards.

16. **Mispelt name.**—"F.C.H." spells the Captain's name, as taken from the stone, both OVERAND and OVERAN (the latter doubtless a clerical error) The correspondence of 1800 gives the correct spelling, OVEREND.

EXCERPTA MÁLDIVIANA.

By H. C. P. BELL, C.C.S. (Retired).

No. 7,—"LONU ZIYARAT:" MALE

At the point where Mále, or "Sulṭán's Island," the Capital of the Máldive Group, curls sharply Southwards from East, there juts out from the main Island a small peninsula, known as "*Lonu Ziyárat*," "(Area of) the Sea-(board) Mausoleum[1]."

This tongue of land is, at the present day, again wholly open to access on the Island side, exactly as it had remained up to some three hundred years ago, or prior to the reign of Sulṭan Muḥammad Shujá'i 'Imád-ud-dín I; (A.C. 1620-1648); who, in constant dread of Portuguese attack, erected from coral blocks a stout Fort, which entirely surrounded Málc, and was strengthened by Bastions (M. *Buruzu*), eleven in all, at suitable interspaces[2].

The Bastion,—it has long fallen into complete ruin—guarding the promontory, that projected from the curtain wall where the Fort enceinte runs both North and West, derived its appellation, *Lonu Ziyárat Buruzu*, therefrom.

The term "*Lonu Ziyárat*[3]" in reality covers all graves situated inside the demarcated portion of the peninsula, which stretches 108 yards by 70 yards, but is *par excellence* applicable to the old Shrine Tomb of a famous, if shadowy, Muslim Shaikh.

The actual area contained within bounds is divided clearly into two sections. To left (North) of the bisecting path leading South-East from the Island seaward, the ground seems, now-a-days, to be quite bare of all sepulture; but to right, or South, there are two distinct sets of internment sites, slightly apart, though embraced under the joint appellation "*Lonu Ziyárat.*"

SHAIKH NAJIB ZIYARAT.

Beyond these duplicated grave clusters, at the extreme end of the promontory, stands, entirely isolated, a high-walled structure, commonly styled "*Habshíge-fánu Maqán,*" "Shrine of the African Worthy," to wit, the so-called Shaikh Najíb. But this is only his supposititious burial place; for in point of fact, the Tomb would seem to be merely a cenotaph—the firm tradition being that this Shaikh Najíb actually died at Kurendú Island in Fádiffoḷu Atol when engaged in spreading the Faith.

Nothing more definite appears to be known regarding this highly revered foreign apostle of Islám. That he was a native of Africa (Arabic, *Habshí*), his Ziyárat's nomenclature appears to indicate; and certain it is that he must have lived and died at the Máldives some time between the latter half of the Twelfth Century, when the Máldivians were converted to Muḥammadanism (A.C. 1151) by Shaikh Yúsúf Shams-ud-dín of Tabríz, and the first half of the Fourteenth Century; for the famous Maghrabín traveller of Tangier, Abú 'Abd-Allah Muhammad, usually styled Ibn Baṭuṭa, visited his *Ziyárat* in A.C. 1343, and recorded the fact[4].

The *Najíb Ziyárat* is a roofed building of no size or architectural importance, shut in by tall walls, through which there is but one entrance.

Immediately outside, or North-West of, the enclosed Shrine, a small quadrangular bathing tank (M. *veyo*) has been artificially constructed of dressed madrepore slabs with, a single flight of steps descending to the water (*Plate A*, 1).

"LONU ZIYÁRAT."

Before reaching the Shaikh's *Ziyárat*, about halfway down the path, lie to right, as above mentioned, two sets of customary type graves, connected by the Islanders themselves with Máldivian dead solely.

Of the further coterie, nothing but concreted graves are to be seen, now level with the ground, and mostly without memorial stones—and these few quite bare.

The nearer, or more Western graves, only two in all' stand by themselves, within a bay, low-walled and attached to higher-built precincts, the whole surrounded by rough outer enclosure, accessible, like the Shaikh's cenotaph, from one point only (*Plate A*, 2.).

It is doubtless these very graves that Lieutenants, I. A. Young and W. Christopher, of the Indian Navy saw in 1835:—

> "We visited the graves of the Persians (*sic*) and counted about sixty ; only two of which had inscriptions that were legible, and bearing date 994th year of the Hijra, which would make them 257 year old.
>
> One of these being in appearance less old than the other graves, it seemed probable that it was not the depository of the remains of any of the first settlers, but of those of one of their descendants.
>
> None of these stones are now legible[5]."

With the original manuscript of his P per on the "Vocabulary of the Maldive Islands," Christopher sent Dr. J. Wilson at Bombay "a specimen of the former mode of carving Arabic on stone (at Mâle)": adding that "the stone bears date 994 of the Hegira."

Unfortunately, when editing Christopher's Paper, [6]." Dr. Wilson did not refer in any way to this "specimen"; which was apparently an eye-copy of some portion of the very epigraph now reproduced from photographs made in 1922. (*Plate B* 1. 2).

GRAVE OF SULTAN MUHAMMAD [7]

The oblong headstone, (which is of the familiar peak-topped design denoting graves of males), measures 3 feet 1 inch by 1 foot 1 inch across. The slab, being of coral and uncovered, has naturally weathered greatly from exposure to the elements during a period of four and a half centuries.

It bears nine lines of Arabic script, much abraded in places, cut in bold "sunk-relief" characters, run together in that tantalising monogrammic form so dear to Arabic graphologists, and so heart-breaking to decipher with confidence when worn.

Portions of the record (in particular the names of the deceased Sulṭán, of his father whom he immediately succeeded on the throne, and the date of the former's death) are clear enough ; but in more than one place the reading is very obscure and open to varied conjecture.

Christopher would seem to have misread the first two angular figures in the last line, as "99" instead of "88;" for the actual date on the stone is unmistakable, even at this day, *viz.* "A.H. 884, Rajab 5th" (A.C. 1479, September 22nd).

A poor photograph of the slab itself (*Plate B* 1), and one of a "squeeze" (*Plate B* 2) of the epigraph, taken in A.C. 1922, have been examined by several *'Uluma* at Mále, in Ceylon, and in India.

The Text (*Plate C*) of the record given in lithograph, albeit admittedly not free from doubt here and there, conforms to the version as recorded by M. Ḥusain Dídí, Qázi of the Máldive Islands. It is put forward advisedly as a tentative, though generally reliable. effort by the learned ex-*Baṇḍára Náibu*; who modestly courts amendments by any Arabic Scholar desirous of criticising his reading.

Text, Transcript. and Translation of the Epigraph are offered provisionally :—

Transcript.

1. *HÁZAHI RAHMAT*

2. *ALLAHUMMA IGHFIR HU VA RAHM HU*

3. *TAWAFFÁ ILÁ RAHMAT-ULLÁH TA 'ÁLÁ AL-ÁZAM AL-AKRAM*

4. *AL-MAGHFÚR HÁJÍ 'L-ḤARAMAIN AL-MÁJID ZÚ'D-DAULAT VA'S-SAHÁM VA'S-SUYÚF*

5. *VA'D-DAFATAR MUHAMMAD AL-ḤAFIZ AL-JÁLAB LI-NASR-ILLÁH AS-SULTÁN ṢÁHIB, UL-HAZZI*

6. *'L-ARF'A VA'S-SHARIY'AT ṢÁHIB UL-QALAM VA'L-ḤAJJ LI-BAI-TULLÁH 'L-ḤARÁM*

7. *VA QABR'N-NABÍ 'ALAIHI'S-ṢALÁTU VA'S-SALÁM ÁL AL-KARÍM*

8. *AL-ḤÁJÍ NAṢR-UL-MUKHÁṬIB ḤAZRAT AS-SULTÁN ḤASAN KILAKI LAṬAF-ALLÁH BIHI*

9. *FI YAVMIL ARB'Á 'L-KHÁMIS MIN SHAHRI RAJAB SANAT* 884.

Translation.

This (of Thy) mercy.

O! God pardon and bless him (the deceased).

On the 5th day of the month of Rajab in the (Ḥijra) year 884, entered into the Peace of God, Most Great, Most Bountiful, the pardoned (deceased), the Sultán Muhammad; (who) performed the *Ḥajj* (to Mekka and Medína); (was) glorious, (and) prosperous; (who) excelled with bow and sword; (was) learned in booklore, and a Ḥáfiz; (who) gained the aid of God; lord of fortune; master of Muslim law, (and) pre-eminent writer; (who visited) the Temple (of God) and the Tomb of the Prophet (upon whom be God's mercy and blessing); son of His Gracious Majesty the Sultan Naṣr-ul-Mukháṭib Hasan Kilége the Ḥájí. To him may God be merciful.

HITI DUVAS.

On four days in the year special semi-religious Festivals are scrupulously observed at Mále in remembrance of certain saintly personages, whose memory the Islanders very greatly respect.

These Festivals, termed broadly "*Hiti Duvas,*" comprise two larger (*Boḍu*), and two smaller (*Kuḍa*), functions; one of each category appertaining to *Henvéru Avaṛu* (the Easternmost Ward) and *Máfannu Avaṛu* (the Westernmost Ward) of the quartette into which "Sulṭán's Island" is divided.

All four Festivals occur in the Muslim month of Ramazán; and all are carried out at night: (1) "*Henvéru Boḍu Hiti*" on the 22nd; "*Máfannu Boḍu Hiti*" on the 24th; (3) "*Henvéru Kuḍa Hiti*" on the 26th; and, finally, "*Máfannu Kuḍa Hiti*" on the 28th.

They are held respectively in memory of (*a*) Shaikh as-Sálih Najíb Habshígefánu; (*b*) 'Ali Rasgefánu (Sulṭán 'Ali VI), who fell defending Mále against the Portuguese in A.C. 1558; (*c*) Shaikh Yúsúf Shams-ud-dín of Tabríz, Apostle of Islám to the Máldives, and Sulṭán Sayyid Muḥammad Shams-ud-dín I, (A.C. 1692) jointly; and (*d*) Maulána Al-Fagí Sulaimán of Medína.

The "*Henvéru Boḍu Hiti*" is carried out at the *Lonu Ziyárat* promontory, to South-East; the "*Máfannu Boḍu Hiti*" at a causeway-united site, on the South. These two Festivals are virtually alike; but those of the "*Kuḍa Hiti Duvas*" are chiefly confined to prayer recitals at the respective Shrines.

HENVÉRU BODU HITI.

The following description of the "*Henvéru Bodu Hiti,*" summarised from the writer's Diary of May 20, 1922, may afford a fair idea of the ceremonies, attending that Festival as held on Ramazán 22nd, A.H. 1340:—

Early in the day, the Islanders were made aware, by beat of gong and proclamation, of their bounden duty to attend the Festival at night, subject to dire penalty for default—none the less significant from being unexpressed[9].

In the afternoon we started out, under the sure guidance of the indefatigable H. Ismá'il Dídí, *Míru Baharu* (Harbour Master), to inspect the general preparations for to-night's consummation of the *Boḍu Hiti* Festivities at the *Lonu Ziyárat*

The day was evidently being marked as a semi-holiday. The excellently kept streets seemed alive with many additions to the everyday wayfarers one encounters at Mále; specially noticeable among them being a large number of *Avaṛu-verin* (Ward employees)—the younger blades preening themselves so obviously with evident gusto—, each wearing new *tarbúsh* (fez) and the chocolate-striped *féli* (waist-cloth), Máldive-woven. For the time being, the whole air felt charged with social electricity.

Everything appeared to be well in train; even the streets, beautifully clean at all times, had been given a fresh topping of dazzlingly white coral sand; whilst their cadjan-hidden side fences were lined throughout with a continuous row (in places doubled) of kerosine wind-lanterns ready for lighting at dark.

Immediately North of the *Maizán-Ge*[10], "Council Room", of *Henvéru Avaṛu*, or "Ward," (which was temporarily furnished with coloured glass lamps and a large chandelier, besides neat chairs and small tables,) had been erected a tall ship's mast, from which floated a large flag (M. *boḍu dida*). This flagstaff was enclosed by a low cloth-walled barrier (M. *kóṭṭe, lit.* "fort") termed "*Henvéru Maizán-Ge Doṛu Kóṭṭe,*" joining up the streets *Kebu-alá-Magu* (North and South) and *Bandaru-mati-Magu* (East and West.)

Where the former road unites on the South with ***Bodu Magu,***—the fine broad boulevard which runs due East and West bisecting Mále Island from sea to sea—. stood provisionally a second similar barrier, " *Waḷu Maizán-Ge Doṛu Kötte* "

Just before reaching this point, we diverged, at our cicerone's suggestion, into a cross-street to examine one of the many supplies of eatables provided (all at the expense of the *Bodu Badiri-Ge* or " Government Treasury ") for consumption at the *Lonu Ziyárat* feasting.

Persons are employed for days together, at Government charges, in cooking these toothsome foods for the night s entertainment.

The man who displayed his wares had evidently determined to make a brave show. Outside the entrance to his house, a temporary booth, cloth-covered, had been put up. In the centre was placed on a table a huge brass-tray, about 4 feet in diameter, whereon, as well as round, the purveyor, swelling with honest pride, gradually deposited, for our amused edification, saucer after saucer of victuals galore in seemingly endless variety—-some forty dishes and upwards in all, as actually counted.

As *pièce de résistance*, first brought out, was a large dish of boiled rice, heaped up high : then followed all sorts of novel kickshaws, inviting and otherwise—fish "puffs" and "fingers," and what not, with "cunning cates" innumerable, and varied sweetmeats, some in triangular slices made from edible sea-weed (Tamil, *kaḍal pási*) resembling to sight " Turkish Delight."

The commestibles succeeding one another unceasingly dribbled finally,—*honesta quam splendida,*—to a couple of plantains in one saucer, a single " Cabin" biscuit in another, and a few " Gem " biscuits in a third—perhaps put out as " samples " of a larger supply in reserve.

But why belittle a noble effort? The entire *tour de force*, as piled up on the table "groaning beneath its weight," did, in truth, real and infinite credit to the worthy caterer.

For removal to the *Lonu Ziyárat*, the many dishes are placed in light wicker-work "cages," covered with coloured cloth, and slung on poles by stout ropes[11].

Finally leaving the local "Lyons" in his glory, we went on to the *Lonu Ziyárat* itself, a spit of land running out South-East from the main Island, and picturesquely lapped by the bluest of lagoons.

Where *Báḍi Magu* ("Cannon Street,") and *Lonu Ziyárat-hingá-Magu* unite, a small cadjan hut was put up for the "Sultán's Band" to deposit its instruments, when feasting later in an adjoining large mat-floored shed provisionally set apart for the purpose.

Within the *Lonu Ziyárat* promontory three special structures had been erected for the Night's Ceremony. (*Plate D*).

(i) To right, just beyond the middle *Ziyárat*, or group of graves, rose a commodious room, constructed partly of cadjans partly of zinc sheeting, and divided into sections down its long axis by curtains, with choicest "Máldive mats" many yards in length (M. *boḍu kuná*) laid on the ground.

This spacious "hall" is intended to serve the various officers of Government attending the *Hiti* Festival, when eating the night's banquet seated, *more Arabico*, on the floor[10].

(ii) Nearly opposite, carefully pitched, stood the "*Hiti-Ge*," or Tent, reserved for Royalty.

(iii) Close to it, but nearer the *Najib Ziyárat*, in marked contrast, was a small temporary shed, dubbed "*Kiyveni-Ge*," open at both ends, whose hipped roof nearly touched the ground. Here the *Qurán* is recited in the afternoon of the "*Boḍu Hiti Duvas*."

Outside it were gathered many Muslim dignitaries—notably Sayyid Músá Dídí, Chief *Khaṭíb* of Málé (who also holds the official rank and title of *Fámuladéri Kilégefánu*) and M. Ḥusain Dídí, *ex-Baṇḍára Náibu*, senior of the four Náibs, now acting as Qázi.

The "*Hiti-Ge*" (ii) merits particular description.

A large Canvas Tent, 24 feet square, with but one curtained entrance, made conspicuous exteriorally by broad white and black vertical stripes. Inside, the Tent's sides are lined with rich green felt, as background framing continuous panels, yellow-ochre in colour, which present pseudo-façades (five on each wall) of Muslim Mosques. A valance of pink intervenes, separating walls from horizontal ceiling, which is itself of a rich orange hue. The whole "scheme" displays an Oriental *tout ensemble* truly gorgeous, if inevitably meretricious to Western eyes.

The floor within the Tent was covered by *boḍu kuná* mats, and soft cushions placed thereon at one side, for the use of H. H. the Sulṭán and his nephew when resting to night.

A portion of the *Hiti-Ge* had been curtained off, for dinner to be served to the Royal occupants at the conclusion of all the religious ceremonies.

Night Ceremony.

The weather being propitious, Sulṭán Muḥammad Shams-ud-dín[12], had decided to go on foot to the *Lonu Ziyárat*—one of His Highness' very rare appearances in public—, accompanied by Machchangoli Gaḍuvaru Maniffuḷu, son of his deceased younger half-brother an *ex*-Sulṭán[13].

About 9-30 p.m. the first gun, of a salute of seven[14], was fired from the Palace, announcing the starting of the Sulṭán in procession for the *Lonu Ziyárat*.

From *Henvéru Maizán-Ge*, as far down *Mai Magu* Street as the Eastern Gateway of the Palace Encl sure (M. *Etere-koḷu*), whence Royalty emerged, a vista of fairy lights twinkled ; half way along the street, at the Palace of Prince Ḥasan 'Izz-ud-dín, [15] the Heir Apparent (now in Ceylon), and at the *Medu Ziyárat*[15], shrine sacred to Yúsúf Shams-ud-dín of Tabríz, clustered lamps shone with exceptional brilliance.

The Royal Procession, flanked by torch-bearers, advanced steadily. The Sulṭán, with his nephew immediately behind, was escorted, as on Fridays when attending the *Hukuru Miskit*, or *Jum'a* Mosque' (*Plate F*), in addition to the State Band, (*Plate E*),by *HaguBei-kalun* (Militia) and His Highness' Body Guard.

The latter force, carrying rifles and resplendant in scarlet tunics, gold-striped blue trousers, and red fez, were under the command of young Muḥammad Farid Dídí[16], himself dressed in a neat black uniform overlaid with heavy gold lace.

The regular Royal Insignia—State Umbrella (M. *Hat-koḷu*), Fan (M. *Samara-koḷu*), Sword and Shield (M. *Ogaru Kaḍi-koḷu* ; *Addana-koḷu*), and Palanquins (M. *Dolidán-koḷu*), were borne in the procession by their allotted carriers, headed by the Royal Standard Bearer.

Standing within the *Maizán-Ge*, we were able to get a clear close-up view of the Royal personagea as they passed ; after having paused at certain *Ziyárat* to recite the *Fátiha*, &c.

From the junction of *Kebu-Alá-Magu* with *Boḍu Magu*, the Procession turned sharply Eastward; and, passing the *Dilli Miskit* Mosque (where a third barrier *Kötte* occurred), swerved South-East to reach the *Lonu Ziyárat* area[17].

Arrived there, it marched directly down the promontory as far as the walled-in *Najíb Ziyárat*. The Sulṭán and Prince then entered this greatly reverenced Shrine (tabúed to all laymen), and again recited the *Fátiha*, &c., before emerging.

Escorted back to the privacy of the "*Hiti-Ge,*" the military escort was here temporarily dismissed, except the *Nába* or State Band; for whose performance the Island onlookers, crowding round the "*Hiti-Ge,*" left a suitable space in front of the Tent.

In all, the Band consisted of eleven performers—four beating drums (M. *beru*), four blowing trumpets (M. *tálafili*), and three playing on flagiolets (M. *dummari*).

After changing their robes, &c[18]. for lighter dress and fez, His Highness and the Prince appeared at the door of the "*Hiti-Ge,*" and stood to listen to the *Nába* music. The darkness was well lit up by half a dozen large braziers.

On this occasion. the Band had been voluntarily reinforced both as "Chief Drummer" as well as its "Conductor" by an old Noble (M. *Boduń*); Kakkáge Maniffulu[19], who, though connected with Royalty, deemed it an honour to profer his services for the nonce. Said to be *facile princeps* at Mále as a player on the *beru*, most brilliantly, in sober truth, did he perform his rôle.

As far as the drums were concerned, they were played in perfect rythm—hands working together smoothly throughout at sudden pauses and modulations; but —"tell it not in Gath"!—to one pair of uncultured ears not "educated up to" such sublime heights of musical art, the trumpets and shawns appeared to produce the most appallingly blatant discords.

The whole "concert" only lasted some fifteen to twenty minutes, the tune, or tunes,—due doubtless to lamentable personal ignorance by an European of Oriental music's "idiom"—seemingly changing in no way from first to last.

At the conclusion of the performance their Highnesses retired[20].

G

The subsequent fireworks (rockets), let off as finále to the Festival, provided but a medium show for a rather blasé crowd. Fortunately the rain held up, but heavy clouds obscured the moon.

So was reached "the end of a perfect day" in the life, year in year out, of unsophisticated Islanders, ever temperamentally placid, and, to all appearance, well content with their hum-drum seagirt environment—a seclusion, enlivened, as it is, only by such simple homely rejoicings, and those but at rare intervals.

NOTES.

1. **Plan of Mále Island (Ceylon Sessional Paper, XV., 1921).**

2. **The Portuguese at Mále.** The Portuguese, by invitation of the ousted Sulṭán, Kaḷu Muḥammad, occupied Mále first in A.C. 1518, and built a Fort; but the garrison was soon massacred to a man.

In A.C. 1558, at the instigation of *ex*-Sulṭán Ḥasan IX, Christianised and living at Cochin, after two abortive attempts, the Portuguese captured Mále, killing the Sulṭán ('Ali VI) reigning, and held the Islands under subjection for 15 years, up to A.C. 1573; when their Agent, a half-caste Máldivian, was slain, and Mále recaptured by the Islanders led by Muḥammed Boḍu Takurufánu (immediately afterwards appointed Sulṭán) and his brother Ḥasan.

Mále was not again attacked by the Portuguese until A.C. 1631, That Expedition from Goa was driven off; a fate which similarly befell a second Expedition despatched in A.C. 1649.

This was the last effort of the Portuguese to conquer the Máldives.

3. **Ziyárat.** The Arabic word literally means the "visiting" of Shrines and burial places; hence applied to the sites themselves.

4. **Shaikh Najíb Ziyárat** "On the morrow (of arrival at *Mahal*) I set out with the Captain (of the vessel) and the Qázi; 'Ísá of Yemen, to visit a hermitage (*zavia*), situated at the extremity of the Island, built by the *Shaikh as-Sálih Najíb*" (Ibn Baṭúṭa at the Máldives; C.A.S. Journal, Extra No. 1882, pp. 21, 22).

5. **Transactions Bombay Geographical Society, 1836, (reprint 1844), p. 74.**

6. **Journal, R.A.S., 1838, Vol. VI, N.S. Article III**

7. **Sultan Muhammad.** Son of Sulṭán Ḥájí Ḥasan III, son of Sulṭán Abú Bakr I, son of Sulṭán Ḥasan I (*A.C.* 1388-97) founder of the stormy Hiláli Dynasty, which closed in A.C. 1552 with the renegade Christian King, Ḥasan IX. (A.C. 1550-52)

The *Táríkh* and *Rádavali* Histories give no particulars of this Sulṭán Muḥammad, beyond allotting him respectively 13 years' reign (A.H. 872-85; A.C. 1467-81) and 14 years. The *Lonu Ziyárat* grave record, which highly eulogises him, definitely fixes the date of his death. as having occurred in A.H. 884 Rajab, equivalent to A.C. 1479, September.

Of the Sulṭán his father, the *Táríkh*, confirmed by tradition, speaks with just detestation. He had been Qázi under Sulṭán Danna Muḥammad (A.C. 1420-21); stayed at Mekka over a second *Ḥajj*; brought back 70 slaves to Mále, and employed them in place of his Islander servants. Trouble arose owing to a slave killing a Máldivian.

The Qázi, Ḥasan of Shiráz, insisted on the culprit being punished, invoking on the Sulṭán the punishment of hell in event of refusal. Thereupon, the Sulṭán had the Qázi burnt at a stake—a curious parallel to the *Rájawaliya* story (Englished, p. 26.) of the Ceylon sub-ruler, Kelaṇi Tissa, the Buddhist Elder, and the clandestine letter.

The famous Maulána, Al-Fagi Sulaimán of Medína, then resident at Mále, made futile remonstrance; but ere long God sent His curse upon the inhuman Sulṭán, who died of a terrible and agonising disease.

8. **Hiti Duvas**: The Máldivian word *Ḥiti* (*lit.* "bitter"), as used in connection with *Duvas* ("days"), may possibly derive its association thereanent from the *hiti* curries prepared on the occasion.

9. **Proclamation.** The Crier traverses the main streets of Mále (M. *Koli-hinga-Magu*) proclaiming loudly, to beat of gong (M. *koli*):—*Malin Mudin Khaṭibu rattehi birattehi kuḍi boḍu kamuveri nuveri ule emme aḷutakun aḍu 'Aṣar Namádu faibaigen Lonu Ziyárat doṛa*(ṛ) *Du'averikamu diyaryái uranne mihen ahái dekidene tibi Dua'verikamu nunjaka*(ṛ) *mihaku ahái* - ———.

"All Malins, Mudins, Khaṭíbs and people, small and great, of this Island (*lit.* country) and outside Islands (*lit.* countries) hereby take notice:—To-day, after leaving the '*Aṣar Namádu* (3-30 p.m. Mosque service), (proceed) at once to say *Fátiha* (at the *Lonu Ziyárat*.)

"Should any one hear this (notice), or get word of it, and not attend (as directed) to say *Fátiha*—(woe betide him)!"

10. **Plate XII, 20. (Ceylon Sessional Paper XV: 1921).**

11. **Victuals for Hiti Duvas.** Food is provided for Boḍu Bei-kalun, Muskuli Bei-kalun, Majili-ara-Bei-kalun (Saradáru), the four Koṛi (schools of armed dancers), Kuḍi Bei-kalun, Arihu Bei-kalun, Mudin Bei-kalun, Kiyaveni-verin and Khaṭíbs.

The Boḍu Baḍéri (Government Treasury) is aided in financing expenses (*karadu*) of the Hiti Festivities by outside help. For Henvéru Ward, besides South Mále, Mulaku, Koḷumaḍulu and Haddummatí Atols, some other Departments assist the Treasury; which itself furnishes for one year 2 bags of rice, 3000 *lári*, 125 lbs. sugar, and 3 *aḍubá* of ghee.

Broadly speaking, the varied eatables are classed as *Fudúru-Dolagu*, and beverages as *Bo-Dolagu*; *fudúru* ("food"), *bo* ("drink") *dolagu* ("brass tray"). Distribution of the food (*hiti ken*) is made to groups of consumers, not exceeding twelve persons for each group.

12. **Sultan Muhammad Shams-ud-dín III.** Elder son of Sulṭán Íbráhím Nur-ud-dín, who died in A.C. 1893.

On his First Accession, in that year, as a boy of 12 years, Muḥammad Shams-ud-dín reigned for only three months; but resumed the throne (which he still holds) ten years later, on the deposition of his cousin Sulṭán Muḥammad 'Imád-ud-dín VI in A.C. 1903.

The present Hurá Dynasty, which began with Sulṭán Ḥasan 'Izz-ud-dín (A. C. 1759-67), has ruled 163 years.

13 **Machchangoli Gaduvaru Maniffulu.** Younger son of the deceased ex-Sulṭán Muḥammad 'Imád-ud-dín V styled Á-Gaḍuvaru Maniffuḷu after his supercession. The latter, though but 7 or 8 years of age, was placed on the throne in A.C. 1893 for five months; to be succeeded, then but temporarily, by his elder half-brother himself a lad, Muḥammad Shams-ud-dín the Sulṭán now reigning.

Ex-Sulṭán Muḥammad 'Imád-ud-dín V and his elder son died at Bombay in 1920, when on their way to Mekka. The second son, Machchangoli Gaḍuvaru Maniffuḷu, nephew of the reigning Sulṭán. (whom he accompanied to the *Lonu Ziyárat in* A.C. 1922) died at Mále in A.C. 1928.

14 **Salutes.** In all 30 guns of Mále artillery are fired at various fixed points during the progress of the Royal Procession to and from the *Lonu Ziyárat* : 7 at *Á Kóṭṭe Mati* (outside Palace); 10 (7 + 3) at *Henveru Maizán-Ge Doṛu* (Kóṭṭe); 10 (7 + 3) at *Valu Maizán-Ge Doṛu* (Kóṭṭe); with 3 *Nába Baḍi*.

15. **Plate VII, 9; Plate VIII, 12 (Ceylon Sessional Paper XV: 1921).**

16. **Muhammad Farid Dídi.** Elder son of I. 'Abd-ul Majid Dídí, *Boḍu Baḍéri Manikufánu*, Controller of Revenue and Treasurer, (recently raised to the rank of *Raṇṇa Baḍéri Kilégefánu*) ; himself second son of 'A. Ibráhím Dídí, *Boḍu Doṛiméná Kilégefánu*, Prime Minister to five Sulṭáns, who died in 1925, at the age of 80, greatly mourned.

The *ex*-Prime Minister's eldest son, I. Aḥmad Dídí, *Doṛiméná Kilégefánu*, is Private Secretary to H.H. the Sulṭán, at Mále, as well as Collector of Customs, and Postmaster-General.

The third son, I. 'Abd-ul Hamid Dídí Effendí, has long been the Máldivian Government Representative at Colombo.

17 **Night Route.** The route taken by the Royal Procession from the Sulṭán's Palace to the *Lonu Ziyárat* can be closely followed on the " Plan of Mále " (Ceylon Sessional Paper XV: 1921.)

18. **The Sultan's State Dress.** Turban (*fagudi-koḷu*), white with spike (*turravás-koḷu*)—a form only worn by the Sulṭáns ; shirt (*gamis-koḷu*), trousers (*haruválu-koḷu*) ; stockings, shoes of Delhi pattern (*izzatuge jóḍu*); kamarband (*kamaru-koḷu*), inner robe, (*libás-koḷu*), waist shawl, (*sálu-koḷu*), upper robe (*abá-koḷu*,) handkerchief, held in front (*kuḍa rumà-koḷu*). The Sulṭán's fez (*tarbúsh*) bears as ornament gold-crescent and jewels.

19. **Kakkage Maniffulu.** A great grandson of Sulṭán Muḥammad Mu' ín-ud-dín I (A.C. 1799-1835), through Veoge Maniffuḷu.

20. Interview with H.H. the Sultan. Graciously invited to a short interview with H.H. the Sultán and nephew Prince within the "Hiti-*Ge*," the writer was received by Royalty standing. After the usual formalities (inquiry as to health, &c.,) His Highness touched on the prosecution of the objects of the Archaeological Expedition from Ceylon of 1922: renewing, in kindliest terms, continued promise of the generous and invaluable assistance already afforded the Mission during its visit to the Southern Atols and stay at Málé.

MÁLE ISLAND

1. Shaikh Najíb Ziyárat

MÁLE ISLAND

2. Grave of Sulṭán Muḥammad

MÁLE ISLAND

1.

2.

SULṬÁN MUHAMMAD'S GRAVESTONE

MALE ISLAND

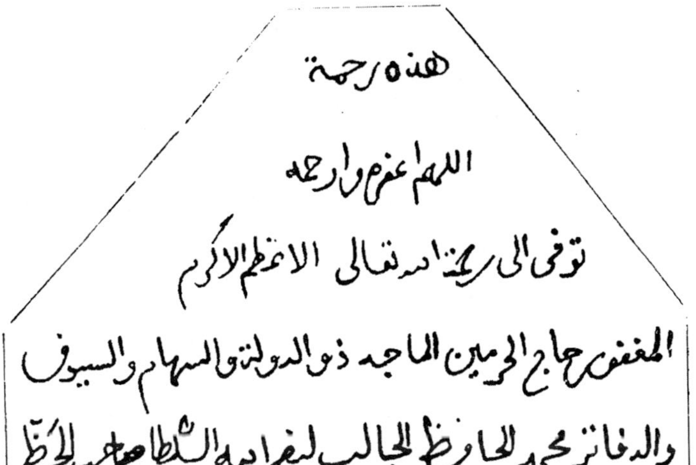

هذه رحمة

اللهم اغفر وارحمه

توفي الى رحمة الله تعالى الاعظم الاكرم

المغفور حاج الحرمين الماجد ذو الدولة والسهام والسيوف

والذخائر محمد الحافظ الجالب لنصر الله السلطان صاحب الحظ

الارفع والشريعة صاحب القلم والحج لبيت الله الحرام

وقبر النبي عليه الصلوة والسلام الكريم

الحاجي نصر المخاطب حضرة السلطان حسن كلوك اطفائنه

في يوم الاربعاء الخامس من شهر رجب ٨٨٤

TEXT OF GRAVESTONE EPIGRAPH

MÁLE ISLAND

"Henvéru Boḍu Hiti" Erections at "Lonu Ziyárat"

MÁLE ISLAND

ROYAL PROCESSION TO "HUKURU MISKIT

Plate E

MÁLE ISLAND

MÁLDIVIAN STATE BAND

EXCERPTA MALDIVIANA.

By H. C P. BELL, C.C.S. (Retired).

No. 8.—MULAKU ATOL : KOLU-FURI ISLAND.

1. MULAKU ATOL.

Mále. Capital of the Máldive Islands. is situated, speaking broadly, about halfway in the long strung-out Archipelago, stretching 470 miles from Ihavandufulu Atol on the extreme North (lat. 7° 6′ N.) to Aḍḍú Atol below the Equator (lat. 0° 42′ S.)

Of the Atols lying directly South of Mále, Mulaku is the third ; separated by *Wádú Kaḍu* Channel (2½ miles, wide), South Mále Atol (20 miles, N. to S.), *Fulidú Kaḍu* (8½ miles), Felidí Atol (22 miles), and *Waṭṭaru Kaḍu* (8 miles), or a little more than 60 miles in total distance.

Mulaku Atol itself has a North and South length of 25 miles. It is separated, on the West, from North and South Nilandé Atols by some twenty miles of open sea, known to Máldivians as "*Hataru Atolu Medu.*" ("Between Four Atols.") Koḷumaḍulu Atol lies S. S. W., across *Má (Kuḍa Huvadú) Kadu*, which is 15 miles in breadth.

Irregular in form. Mulaku Atol bulges on the East from South gradually towards N.E., before curling back ; but runs very straight along its Western reef [1].

Within the Atol's lagoon, (the depth of which varies from 28 to 40 fathoms, sandy bottom), are several coral shoals. Small shallow "passages" occur through the West and North-East reefs.

The Atol contains only 10 of the 217 inhabited Islands of the whole Group. All of these are on the broad, hardly broken, Eastern reef; except Mulaku Island, the largest (lat. 2° 57′ N., long. 75° 35′ E.), which stands nearly one mile inside that reef, athwart *Boḍu Kaḍu* the principal entrance.

From North to South, the occupied Islands are Diggaru, Maḍu-vari, Raiman-dú, Maḍi-fuṛi, Vévaṛ, Mulaku, Muli, Nálá-fuṛi, Váriya-fuṛi and Koḷu-fuṛi; but the two first-named are treated fiscally as appertaining to Felidí Atol, having been peopled by migrants from that Northern neighbour.

Excluding Diggaru and Maḍu-vari, the total population in 1922 numbered 1,744 (males 986, females 758); Nálá-fuṛi containing 388, and Maḍi-fuṛi but 64, persons.

One-fourth of the male population is engaged in fishing operations; whilst coir making occupies a third, or more, of the women [2].

2. KOLU-FURI ISLAND.

Koḷu-fuṛi, the picturesque, among the smaller of Mulaku Atol's inhabited Islands, stands at the extreme Southern end of its Eastern reef.

Approaching from the South, the lagoon is most easily reached through the *Kuraili Kaḍu* passage.

The Archaeological Mission to the Máldives of 1922, sailed through the whole of Mulaku Atol in April of that year; having entered the Atol by the *Boḍu Kaḍu* channel, half-way up the Eastern reef, on April 2nd, visited Koḷu-fuṛi the following day, and emerged on the North, April 6.

Some details of the main features, and incidents, recorded during the few hours spent on Koḷu-fuṛi Island are reproduced from Diary of April 3rd:—

After our inspection of Mulaku Island yesterday, "the *Fatḥ-ul-Majid* (Máldivian Government Schooner), had sailed Southwards down the Atol's lagoon; but was forced to anchor some three miles off Koḷu-fuṛi Island, owing to extensive shallows (M. *faḷu*) intervening between somewhat deeper water.

"A *mas-dôṇi* (fishing-boat) could take us this morning within a mile only of the beach; the rest of the way having to be traversed, for those unable to wade, solely on *kadu-fati* (pronounced *kan̆du-fati*) [3], or native rafts. It being low water at the time, we had to make the last hundred yards over sandy pools.

"The inhabited village on Koḷu-fuṛi is close to the beach as at Mulaku Island; but the houses, and their detached kitchens, are separated by wider streets (*Plate A*). Some dwellings stand within their own cadjan fences.

"Areca and sugar-cane seem to grow rather freely on the Island.

"From the congeries of habitations, a magnificient cleanly kept road, (*Plate B*). flanked on both sides by towering coconut, huge breadfruit, and other fine trees, conducts to the *Hukuru Miskit* ("Friday Mosque") and its well-filled grave-yard.

"Opposite the *Kuḍa Miskit* ("Small Mosque"), reached first along this road, there has been constructed an excellent *Veyó*, or Bathing Tank, (*Plate C*). 30 ft. by 20 ft. with two flights of six matched steps down to the water.

"No tombstones lettered in "*Dives Akuru*" (an older form of Máldivian script) were noticed either at Mulaku or Koḷu-fuṛi; but at the latter Island there is a unique headstone of rounded-fan shape near the *Hukuru Miskit*, besides a typical Máldivian sun-dial (M. *vagutu-gá*).

"At this, the *Khuṭba Mosque*, erected by Sulṭán Ghází Muḥammad Boḍu Takurufánu, in honour of his father Ḥusain

Khaṭíb, are religiously preserved certain " relics," presumably genuine, of the great Sixteenth Century hero of Máldive history, the deliverer of the Islands from the Portuguese yoke. His famous sailing vessel "*Kaḷuwaffumi Oḍi*" is traditionally believed to have been ultimately wrecked off Koḷu-fuṛi, where he lurked oft in safety when warring with the Portuguese [4].

" Obviously the Island *Khaṭíb* was very loath to bring these relics out of the Mosque for inspection, because of their great sanctity in the eyes of Máldivians; but yielded at length to the persuasive H. Ismá'il Dídí, our masterful cicerone. After the recital of sundry prayers by both within the Mosque, the articles were finally produced.

" These antiques consist of an old sword, part of a boat's pennon-staff (*Plate D*), and a choice silk kerchief.

" The sword (which was wrapped in nearly thirty separate cloths) is a very corroded Portuguese weapon ; of which the blade is now much shortened, having broken into two pieces and been roughly clamped together. At present, it is 2 ft. 3 in. long, with 1 in. blade. The Islanders style it *Utímu Baṇḍárange Kaḍi-koḷu* " Sword of the *Baṇḍára* (Sulṭán) of Utímu (Tiladummatí Atol) ".

" As to the flag-staff (M. *féstára*), kept in similar wraps, measuring 3 ft. 6 in., this is little out of the ordinary ;

But the fringed head-kerchief (M. *bolu féli*), 5 ft. 3 in. by 3 ft., is both well-preserved, and exceedingly attractive—its middle and main portion being of brilliant red colour, with chocolate, black and white stripes at each end.

" Of old documents as many as seven *Fat-koḷu*, (Royal Grants,) issued by different Sulṭáns, were produced by the *Khaṭib*. The three oldest belong to the Eighteenth Century and are written in "*Dives Akuru*" characters." [5]

3. MÁLE UNDER PORTUGUESE RULE: A. C. 1558-73

Traditionally, Koḷu-fuṛi Island is so closely connected with Sulṭán Ghází Muḥammad Boḍu Takurufánu, and his long continued warfare with the Portuguese invaders in the latter half of the Sixteenth Century, that excuse need not be offered for interpolating a condensed relation of that internecine struggle.

The "*Táríkh*," or Máldivian State Chronicle, contains a brief narrative,—the more appealing from its simple, semi sophisticated wording,—of the bitter fighting between the Máldivians, (led by the three *Khaṭíb* brothers, Muḥammad, 'Ali and Ḥasan of Tiladummati Atol,) and the Portuguese, during the interregnum at the Máldives; and of the latter's strangle hold on the Islands of more than a decade and a half, after their capture of Málé, following the glorious "martyr's" death of the reigning Sulṭán, 'Ali VI.

This is the stirring story:—

"After reigning for 2 years, 5 months, Sulṭán Ḥasan IX. proclaimed his determination to renounce Muḥammadanism. He left the Máldives in A.H. 959 (A.C. 1551-52) for Cochin, where he embraced the Faith of the Infidels (Portuguese), under the name of Don Manoel[6].

"No less than three Expeditions (the first two disastrous) were despatched to the Máldives by the Portuguese at the instance of the renegade ex-Sulṭán.

"Finally, two and half months after Sulṭán 'Ali began to reign, the third and largest Portuguese Expedition, commanded by 'Captain Adiri Adiri,'[7] attacked Málé vigorously, and effected landing on the West side. Sulṭán 'Ali himself led his soldiers (*Askarun*) against the Invaders. When the Máldivians were driven back near *Ídu Miskit* Mosque, the Sulṭán, his Chief Vazír, and one attendant, alone stood their ground. These three, fighting bravely, were at length shot down.

"Thus the Portuguese took Mále in the month of Ramazán, A.H. 965 (May-June, A.C. 1558).

"Then the Máldivians submitted to Adiri Adiri, who proclaimed himself Sulṭán. He sent Christians to take charge in all parts of the Máldives, and enforced submission.

"The Portuguese ruled with utmost cruelty for several years, committing intolerable enormities: "the sea grew red with Muslim blood; the people were sunk in despair."

"At this juncture God Almighty moved the heart of *Khaṭíb* Muḥammad Takuru, son of *Khaṭíb* Ḥusain, of Utímu Island (Tiladummatí Atol), styled later 'Muḥammad Boḍu Takurufánu Akbar,' to fight with the Infidels, and to end the crying wrongs. Praying to God for wisdom to conquer, he took counsel with his younger brothers, each also a *Khaṭíb*, 'Ali and Ḥasan.

"These three left the Máldives for Maliku Island (Minicoy), which belonged to Áḷi Rája (" Sea King ") of Kannanúr. There they were joined by two other Máldivian brothers, Ḥáji 'Ali and Ḥáji Ḥasan, both skilled in arms. A solemn pact to exterminate the Portuguese was sworn by all; and Muḥammad Takuru elected their leader.

"Thereupon they returned to the Máldives, and commenced an unremitting guerilla warfare; landing on different Islands at night to secure supplies, slaying any Portuguese there, and putting to sea before daybreak.

"In the course of this long struggle for freedom by the three brothers, 'Ali was surprised by the Portuguese and killed; but the other four banded patriots continued hostilities, and in time killed nearly all their enemies on the Máldives, except at Mále itself.

"The conspirators made one abortive attempt to land on Mále; then sought the help of Áḷi Rája, who sent Malabar soldiers to aid them.

"They all reached Mále the night before the day fixed by the Portuguese garrison for the forcible conversion of the inhabitants, on penalty of death for non-compliance. The Islanders ready to die for their Faith, had assembled with arms at the house of the *Qází*, Abu Bakr, prepared to fight to the last.

"The joint force, under Muḥammad Boḍu Takuru, landed secretly when the night was two-thirds spent (i.e. at 3 a.m.). Adiri Adiri was killed by a musket shot fired by Boḍu Muḥammad himself; and the whole Portuguese garrison slaughtered.

"This recapture of Mále took place on Rabi-ul-Awwal 1st, A.H. 981 (July 30th, A.C. 1573)." [8]

4. SULTAN GHAZI MUHAMMAD BODU TAKURUFANU

"Albeit the Portuguese had held the Máldives for 17 (Muslim) years," comments the "*Táríkh*" sententiously, "their rule and power was as transcient as sunbeams."

The Máldivians, "assigning all praise to God for the great victory over the Infidels," at once elected Muḥammad Boḍu Takuru as their Sulṭan.

In organising the State Administration, he associated with himself his brother Ḥasan, under the title *Raṇṇa Baḍéri Kilégefánu*. Ḥájí 'Ali and Ḥájí Ḥasan were appointed respectively *Doṛiméná*, and *Sháh Bandar*, Vazírs.

Sulṭán Ghází Muḥammad "ruled wisely, being just and considerate, protecting the poor, and ever solicitous for the people's interests;" whilst earnestly feeling the pressing call for religious revival.

He was the first Máldive Sovereign to form the *Askarun* into a military body (*Hagu-be-kalun*). Under his brilliant sway the Islands remained wholly peaceful, and free from all injustice, "like unto a festival, or marriage day."

His death occurred on Ramazán 1st, A.H. 993 (A.C. August 17th, 1585) [9].

From this reign dates the steady, if humble, rise of *Divehi Rájje*" (" The Máldive Realm "), Phoenix like, from the ashes of a much chequered past.

5. MALDIVAN FAT-KOḶU.

When " *Fat-koḷu* " (pronounced " *Fai-koḷu* "),—Grants under the Sultán's Seal; written usually on Paper but occasionally on Parchment, *e.g. Kuḍa Huvadú, S. Nilandé Atol* (A.H. 1164), or even Wooden Board *e.g. Gan, Aḍḍú Alol* (A.H. 1063)—first superceded " *Lómáfánu,*" Copper-Plate Grants, at the Máldive Islands is unknown.

But, with much probability, the period may be assigned to the late Sixteenth Century, and the reign of Sulṭán Ghází Muḥammad Boḍu Takurufánu (A.C. 1573-85), that resuscitator of Muslim religious zeal and learning; after the Portuguese had been finally expelled from the Máldives mainly by his action, and the Realm settled down to nearly a quarter-century of peace and order.

For thirty years or more the Máldives had been without *'Ulama*; since the death of Shaikh-al-'Álim-al-Fagí Sulaimán, who came from Medína. All those who studied under this Shaikh had gradually died out, and no *'Álim* remained in the Islands when Sulṭán Boḍu Takurufánu began his reign.

"The Kingdom being, thus, in urgent need of a *Qází* there chanced to return to Mále from Hadramut (Yémen) Shaikh Muḥammad Jamál-ud-dín, a Máldivian, who had acquired his learning in the time of Sulṭán Hasan Shírází VIII. (A.C. 1528-48)."

He was received by Sulṭán Muhammad with greater honours than ever before showered on any learned Máldivian; but, being a recluse, was unwilling to remain at Mále permanently, "caring" (says the "*Táríkh*") "neither for riches, nor to mix with the world. Retiring to Wáḍú Island (Huvadú Atol), he died full of years and honour, leaving many pupils by whom the Faith of Islám was greatly spread."

8. KOḶU-FUṚI FAT-KOḶU.

Among the Royal *Fat-koḷu* Grants belonging to Koḷu-fuṛi, the most valued is that issued under the hand of Sulṭán Muḥammad Boḍu Takurufánu (then styled still Vazir Boḍu Takuru) to the *Hukuru Miskit* of that Island.

This *Fat-koḷu* (*Plates E. F.*), claimed to be quite the oldest extant at the Máldives, is preserved at Mále.

It is written upon ordinary paper in "*Dives Akuru*,"[10] —which continued to be the form of Máldivian characters almost exclusively employed for such special documents during two centuries and upwards; certainly on to the reign of Sulṭán Ḥasan Núr-ud-dín (A.C. 1779-99), when the modern "*Tána*" (right to left writing) seems to have ousted it virtually for every use.

The *Fat-koḷu* runs to twenty-six (26) lines in all, read from left to right: of these lines the three (13, 14, 15), written downwards in the left margin, at right angles to the rest, should come in midway in line 12 of the consecutive Text (*Plate F.*)

This is headed (left top) by what is presumed to be the Sulṭán's manuscript Seal, greatly worn, within rough circular framing. The original legend on the Seal may be tentatively read, *faute de mieux*, as "*Al Gházi Vazír Muḥammad*."

The other Seal has been affixed at a later period; possibly in quite recent years.

In its contents the *Fat-koḷu* deals with the religious donation by the Sulṭán (under the more humble denomination of "Ghází Vazir Muḥammad Boḍu Takuru", which, it is alleged, he adhered to even after being raised to the *Masnad* by the popular voice) to the *Hukuru Miskit*, or *Khuṭba* Mosque, that he had had rebuilt at Koḷu-fuṛi Island.

Produce from the three Islands, Koḷu-fuṛi, Nálá-fuṛi and Medu-fuṛi of Mulakù Atol is specifically assigned as *Waqf* for the upkeep of the Mosque and its services

As customary, the document closes, with an imprecation on the head of any Muslim acting counter to the Grant.

The authenticity of the existing *Fat-koḷu*, *quá* the original document, is accepted unquestionably by Máldivian authorities; and supported by the Seal of *Boḍu Baḍeri Ge*, the Government Treasury, (top right), stamped thereon [11]

It will be as well to leave it at that; *pace* possible misgiving, not unnaturally arising from patent anomalies which differentiate it markedly from quite unimpeachable *Fat-koḷu*, of beautiful execution, granted by Máldive Sulṭáns in later centuries.

That such a *Fat-koḷu* was veritably bestowed on the Koḷu-fuṛi Mosque by Sulṭán Ghází Muhammad need not be doubted for one moment; but the absence in the present document of all dating, an almost illegible Seal, terse diction, crowded script in a running hand, and later insertion of lines slovenly omitted, cannot fail to strike attention.

SEALS

TRANSCRIPT [12]

1. *Al-Ghází Vazír Muḥammad* Boḍu Takru vidáḷín ma· Mulakatoḷa(ṛ) Fra

2. Banḍára fuṛun kan kurevvuma(ṛ) dánai míhunái mi Atoḷu

3. Bó-himanai Váru-bai kán jahadai Ráda Bañḍára uṛun Ras-

4. kamá kemma(ṛ) danmai mi fada emmena(ṛ) vidáḷu fate: mi Atoḷu

5. Koḷu-fuṛi ma heddevi Miskitu machcha(ṛ) mi raṛu Fálabbuái

6. Fálabbaa(ṛ) bima(ṛ) niku(t) nahai rukai: mi raṛu Fáḷabba eḷu-

7. mái mi kan mi Miskita(ṛ) lavvai fechchee : mi Miskitu *Imárat*

8. ko(ṛ) vottelaḷai kunálaḷai fange lai *Imárat* kuḷaima(ṛ) mi Mi-

9. skita(ṛ) hunna huṛi kamái : ihu Miskita(ṛ) hunnahái ruka(ṛ)

10. gahe(ṛ) e fadain-me mi Miskita(ṛ) hunna huṛi kamái: mi raṛun

11. de míhunge boli mi fadain-me ihu Miskita(ṛ) hunna magun

12. nu-uvi hunna huṛi kamái :

13. mi Miskitu kare(n) eḷi

14. nama donu mati mi Miskita(ṛ)

15. hunna huṛi kamái :

16. Naulá-fuṛi Mati Kibaa(ṛ) Don Bíná Nau-

17. lá-fuṛi tibi ru(ṛ) ru(ṛ) fuḷái Medu-fuṛi kiyá ra(ṛ)-gaḍu tibi ru(ṛ)

18. ru(ṛ) fuḷái mi fadain-me mi Miskita(ṛ) *Waqf* ve hunna huṛi

19. kamái : Takru huddain me Miskitu mi fadain *Imárat* ko(ṛ)-

20. bala huṭṭun mi raṛu Hasan Kaló dari-miruminína(ṛ) dáden

21. mi uren mati kamái : mi raṛu Fálabba mi raṛu mi Miskita(ṛ)

22. hunna huddave hunna huṛi kamái : komme míhaku mi Miskitu

23. *Waqfái* ve(ṛ) nu-vá huṛi kamái : mi Miskitu *Waqfái* vevve mi maga(ṛ)

24. lai nu-tibbân bahen bune kame(ṛ) kuḷa komme *Muslimaku Waqf*

25. uvai nahai kuḷa míhuna(ṛ) vá fátuká vá kává huṛi kamái : mita(ṛ) magun

26. Takru kurevvi huddain Músá Náibu Kaló lín.

TRANSLATION [13].

I, Ghází Muḥammad Boḍu Takuru, Vazír, (thus verbally) order:—

To persons going to Mulaku Atol from the Pre-eminent Máldive Government (*Fura Baňḍára*) to get work done, and (those going to take) a Census (*Bó-himanai*), and (to collect) the Poll-Tax (*Váru-bai*) [14] of this Atol and (thôse going) for Royal business (*Ras-kama*) from the Sovereign (*Ráda Baňḍára*)—to all such (persons is directed) this Documentary Order (*Vidálu Fate.*)

Upon the Mosque (*Miskitu*), caused to be built by me at Koḷu-fuṛi (Island)[15] of this Atol, (is bestowed) the *Fálabba* (Government Tree-Tax moiety)[16] of this Island, and the *Fálabba* from coconut trees planted in future on ground (therein).

The work of demarcating *Fálabba* (trees) in this Island (must be done) by (the custodians of) this Mosque [17].

Clause [18]. For providing this Mosque edifice (*Imárat*) with oil lights spreading mats (there in,) thatching with cadjans, and effecting repairs to the Mosque structure (*Imárat*), (the obligation rests) upon this Mosque.

Clause. The coconut and (other) trees possessed by the former Mosque (shall belong), in like manner, to this Mosque.

Clause. (Poll-Tax payments of) Cowries (*boli*) by two persons of this Island to the former Mosque, are to continue in like manner, (to this Mosque.)

Clause. Should a burial occur at (the graveyard of) this Mosque, (provision must be made for) the ***donu-mati*** [19] to this Mosque.

Clause. The coconut trees (*ruṛ ruṛ fuḷái*) on Nálá-fuṛi (Island) which belong to Mati Kibá Don Bíná of Nálá-fuṛi, and the coconut trees in the islet (*raṛ-gaḍu*) known as Medu-fuṛi [20] (are donated), in like manner, to this Mosque, as *Waqf* (religious trust) [21].

Clause. The Takuru has decreed (that) the oversight of this Mosque edifice (shall be entrusted), similarly, to these persons, (to wit), Ḥasan Kaló of this Island, (and his) descendants in perpetuity (*dari-miruminína(ṛ) dáden*).

Clause. This Island's *Fálabba* (income), as allotted (shall pertain) to the Mosque of this Island (undiminished)

Clause. No person shall nullify the *Waqf* (benefaction granted) to this Mosque.

Any Musalman doing aught, by word or by deed, to prevent the *Waqf* remaining as it exists, will incur the punishment of a person who infringes and renders abortive a *Waqf* (religious trust) [22].

Músá Kaló, Náib, wrote (the Decree) made in this wise by the Takuru.

NOTES.

1. **Mulaku Atol.** See Plan accompanying Sessional Paper XVIII, 1881, "The Máldive Islands."

2. **Ceylon Census Report, 1921.** See, for further particulars.

3. **Kadu-fati.** Light (as made at Koḷu-fuṛi Island) rafts of twelve *kadu (Hernandia Peltatia)* logs, lashed three and three together; about 15 ft. by 7 ft. 6 in. in superficial dimensions, but only 5 in. to 6 in. deep, bevelled at each end upwards. Propelled by poles, these primitive rafts do not ride quite clear of the water when mounted. *Kadu-fati* are much used by Mulaku Islanders (who claim to own about 150) when hunting the shell-yielding turtle.

4. **Kaluwaffumi Odi.** The romantic story of the bitter struggle of the *Khaṭib* brothers and their companions—continued harassment of the Portuguese *Vivador* at Báraṛu; descents on different other Islands of the Group from North to South; details of the murder of 'Ali *Khaṭib* at his own house; of the "*Kaḷuwaffumi Oḍi*" of Muḥammad Boḍu Takurufánu; his inaccessible haven of refuge at Koḷu-furi Island when hard pressed—is the subject of much quaint legendary lore and native song at the Máldives.

5. **Kolu-furi Fat-kolu.** Sixteenth Century: A.H. 981-93 (A.C. 1573-85), S. Ghází Muḥammad Boḍu Takuru. Eighteenth Century: A.H. 1153 (A.C. 1740-41), S. Ibráhím Iskandar II; A.H. 1182 (A.C. 1768-69), S. Muḥammad Ghiyás-ud-dín; A.H. 1189 (A.C. 1775-76), S. Muḥammad Mu'izz-ud-dín. Nineteenth Century: A.H. 1218 (A.C. 1803-04), S. Muḥammad Mu'ín-ud-din I; A.H. 1276 (A.C. 1859-60); S. Muhammad 'Imád-ud-dín IV. Twentieth Century: A.H. 1325, (A.C. 1907-08); A.H. 1326 (A.C. 1908-09), S. Muḥammad Shams-ud-dín III.

6. Sultan Hasan IX.—" The Christian King of the Máldives " (A.C. 1550-52) ; fratricide and renegade. " There sprang up, I know not why, between the Máldivians and their Lord, a youth of twenty years, discord of war ; and he, finding himself unable to withstand the force of conspiracy, saved his life, though he could not his Kingdom, by flight to Cochin ; where he trusted to obtain his reinstatement by aid of the Portuguese arms. The Fathers received him into their House, and S. Francis Xavier, who opportunely arrived there (January 14, 1552), solemnly baptised him." (Bartoli, *Asia* III., 201-2).

For the subsequent history of this ex-Sultán and his descendants see *Hak. Soc. Pyrard*, II., pp. 493-508.

7. Captain Adiri-Adiri.—Regarding this scourge of the Islanders, Máldivian tradition preserves certain romantic particulars.

During the reign of S. Kalu Muhammad, (died A.C. 1529) a Portuguese vessel commanded by a Noble of Goa, a relative of the Viceroy, with whom was his young wife, reached Huvadú, or Addú Atol. Kalu Íbráhím Fáriná Takurufánu, of Gáfaru Island, was despatched to seize the ship. He killed the Captain and the crew, but saved the life of the lady, known as " Khánzi Kamaná," then pregnant. Her Portuguese child was brought up as a Muslim, and named Muhammad. After murdering his half-brother, Matukkaláya (son of Kalu Íbráhím Fáriná and Khánzi Kamaná), Muhammad fled to Goa ; whence he returned as " Captain Adiri-Adiri (? Andreas André) with the Portuguese fleet which captured Mále.

8. Portuguese at Male: A.C. 1558-73. Pyrard, writing after his captivity at Mále (A.C. 1602-07), confirms the " *Tárikh* ", and adds some further details :—

" The Portuguese in this way ruled the Islands in peace for the space of ten years, during which time the father of this (reigning) King (Sultán Íbráhim III) and his brother were *Calibes*, each of his own Island ; but, with the pride of their race, would never submit to the Portuguese yoke, nor obey the Governor whom they had left in power. They rebelled and levied a force of men and galleys for war and retired to the Atol *Souadou*, (Huvadú) at the Southern extremity of the Islands, whither the Portuguese dared not follow them ; so that this Atol and the Islands belonging thereto, were never subject to the Portuguese ; nor any of the other Islands and Atols to the South.

" They became in time so strong in men, arms, and ammunition that they, as it were, held Mále and the Portuguese in check, so that they durst not come out without daily experiencing a harassing war." This guerilla warfare lasted for " eight years."

Finally with the aid of four galleys of Malabar corsairs (whom they afterwards plundered), the brothers one night surprised Mále by escalade, and made themselves masters of the place, putting to death upwards of 300 men that were within, and taking prisoner the native Governor sent there by the Portuguese. (*Hak. Soc. Pyrard*, I., pp. 24-48).

9. Sultan Ghazi Muhammad. The *Bihorózu Miskit* at Mále contains his *Ziyárat*. " The Sword of Death " feelingly comments the " *Tárikh* " " severed the thread of life, and his soul was transported to the Great Eternal Throne. His body, enveloped in a shroud and placed in a coffin, was borne by men of eminence to the burial place; where it was interred in special soil. The Earth treats all alike."

10. Dives Akuru. See Ceylon Asiatic Society Journal., Vol. XXVII, Extra Number, 1919. Appendix C. pp. 140-68; Vol. XXIX. No. 77, 1924, pp. 287-303.

11. Bodu Baderi Ge Seal. Within circle:—" *Ad-Daulat min al-Mahal Di biyat* " " The Máldivian Government."

12. Transcript. The Roman transcript, made personally from the *Fat-koḷu* itself, has been most carefully checked with the " *Dives Akuru* " and " *Tána* " copies supplied, on Government direction, by Husain Takurufánu, *Khaṭib* of Hitadú Island, Aḍḍú Atol.

Some points to note in the Text orthography (*Plates E., F.*):—

(i) *Sukun.* This slightly curved diagonal symbol, written above and to right of preceding consonant or vowel, has here five values, viz :—

(*a*) Vowel *u* above consonant, *e.g. Boḍu, hunna*; in contrast to *u* sub-scribed, *e.g. raṛu, huṛi.*

(*b*) " Stop " (equivalent to Siŋhalese *al* sumbol) on consonants; *e.g.* the *s* in *Miskitu.*

(*c*) Mute, when closing certain words ending in a vowel; *e.g. machcha*(*ṛ*), *komme*(*ṛ*), *ru*(*ṛ*).

(*d*) (*e*) Substitute for duplicating medial consonant, *e.g. he*(*d*)*devi, e*(*m*)*mena*(*ṛ*), *hu*(*n*)*na, vo*(*t*)*te, lala. kure*(*v*)*vi*; or for final *n*, *e.g. fadai*(*n*), *Do*(*n*), *furu*(*n*).

(ii) Circular symbol for *r*, combined with preceding consonant and vowel, *e.g. Takru* for *Takuru, Fra* for *Fura.*

(iii) Word coalescence, *e.g.*, *Mulakatoḷu* for *Mulaku Atoḷu.*

13. Translation. Entirely based on oral rendering kindly given to the writer at Mále in 1922 by I. Aḥmad Dídí, *Doṛiméná Kilége-fánu*, son of the late Prime Minister Ḥájí A. Íbráhím Dídí, *Boḍu Doṛi-mená Kilégefánu.*

14. Varu. The term for form and rates of Máldive Poll-Tax per head (M. *Bó-machcha-bahani Váru*) levied from every inhabited Island; now-a-days on the basis of a separate *Váru Fat-koḷu*, or Written Assessment Mandate, for each Island, authorised by the Sulṭán.

The Mandate specifies the number of males in the Island between the ages of 15 and 55 subject to the Tax; with the amount of the different commodities (including money) &c., to be supplied.

The levy is exacted under a fanciful fiction of adult pairs (male and female), termed *Bó-himanai*; males alone being liable to pay the tax (M. *Bai-haru*), but each treated, for the said purpose, as two individuals—one man and one woman.

Theoretically, every Island's assessment is subject to revision once in four years; but usually no change is made during the reign of the Sulṭán issuing the Mandate.

15. Kolu-furi Mosque. The Mosque in the adjoining Island, Váriya-fuṛi, was built by this Sulṭán's elder sister Daita Kamaná.

16. Falabba. Produce Tax (M. *Bin-bai*; *Varuva*), from trees and other cultivations, is levied by the Máldivian Government (M. *Baṇḍára*) in kind, or money, from the occupiers (M. *raiatun*) of inhabited Islands, upon the respective yields of trees and crops, as fluctuating from year to year.

The *Varuva* Tax embraces three sub-divisions.; (*a*) *Fálabba*, (*b*) *Falamadi*, (*c*) *Gován*. These are rated, as under :—

(*a*) *Fálabba*. Half (½) share, equally divided between the Government and the inhabitants, of four special fruit trees—coconut (M. *káṛi*) ; arecanut (M. *fuvak*) ; breadfruit (M. *bambu-keyo*) ; *Pandanus*, or screwpine (M. *kari-keyo*), and the like (M. *talakai* in general).

(*b*) *Falamadi*. One-third (1/3) of all root-crops and garden produce.

(*c*) *Gován*. One-fourth (¼), in inhabited Islands, or one-fifth (1/5) in uninhabited islands, of the three species of fine grain grown at the Máldives, *viz*., *urá* (*Setaria Italica*), Siṇ. *tana-hál* ; *bimbi* (*Elusine coracana*, Siṇ. *kurakkan*) ; *kudibai* (*Panicum miliaceum*, Siṇ. *menéri*).

No rice is grown at the Màldives ; all is imported.

17. Stamping Trees. Trees are stamped (M. *tat-jahán*; *fálabba-kulán*) on the trunk in vertical line, by an iron-shod tool leaving circular mark (M. *tak-kari*), 1¾ in. in diameter. One indentation denotes sole private ownership ; three marks, entire *Baṇḍára* (Government) right ; four marks, half possession in Government, half in the Islanders ; a fifth mark on every twenty-fifth tree (M. *tak-kari ruṛ*, "stamp tree,") signifies Government perquisite.

18. Clause. The recurrence at the end of many sentences of the stereotyped expression "*hunna huṛi kamái*", *lit*. "and (this) was (*hunna*), (and) is (*huṛi*) the fact (*kamái*)," seems to justify its rendering by the legal term "Clause."

19. Donumati. Essential requisites at burials, supplied to the Mosque by the deceased's relatives, *viz*. one coconut plant and one mat.

20. Medu-furi. Uninhabited island lying just South of Nálá-fuṛi ; not to be confused with Maḍi-fuṛi Island between Raiman-dú and Vévaṛ further North.

21. Waqf. *Waqf* (Arabic), *Waguf* (Máldivian) ; bequest for religious or charitable purposes.

22. Imprecation. The curse, as here laid upon any breaker of this *Waqf* benefaction, is far more forcibly worded in *Fat-kolu* Grants issued by later Sulṭáns *e.g*., *Filá-fat*, of Sulṭán Iskandar Ibṛáhím, dated A.H. 1063 (A.C. 1652-53) for *Gan Island*, *Aḍḍú Atol*, :—

"Whoever frustrates, or is minded to harm, and nullify, this (beneficiary) action (*kan*), will go to Hell (*Naraka*), with sinners who destroy the *Ka'aba* shrine (at Mekka), burn the *Qurán*, and worship images (*budu*, *lit*. Buddha)."

Plate A.

MULAKU ATOL : KOḶU-FUṚI ISLAND.

VILLAGE.

Plate B.

MULAKU ATOL : KOḶU-FUṚI ISLAND.

ROAD TO HUKURU MISKIT.

MULAKU ATOL : KOḶU-FUṚI ISLAND.

HUKURU MISKIT.

Plate D.

MULAKU ATOL : KOLU-FURI ISLAND

OLD PORTUGUESE SWORD, &c.

Plate E.

MULAKU ATOL : KOLU-FURI ISLAND.

1.
2.
3.
4.
5.
6.
7.
8.

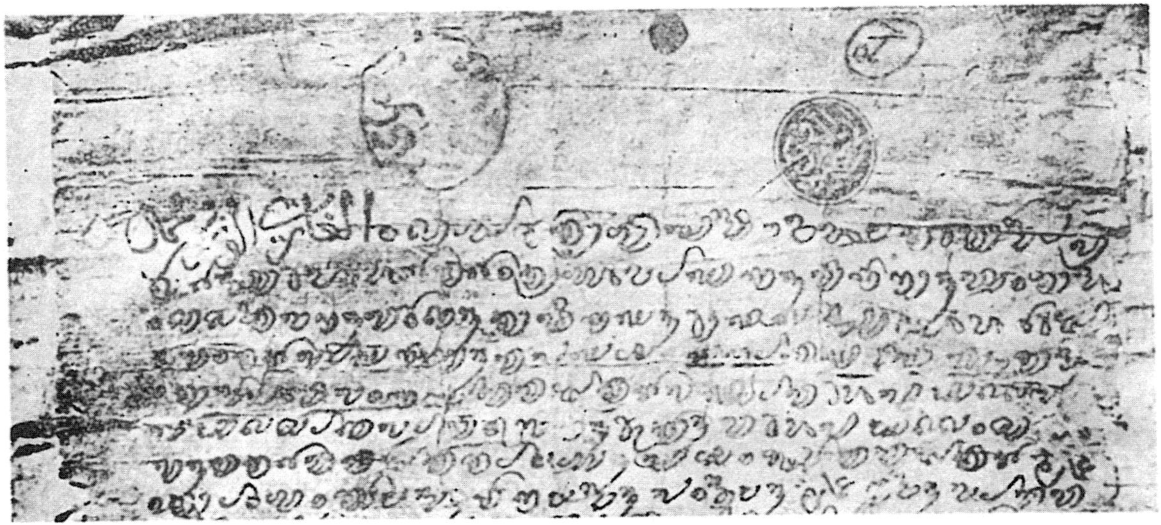

FAT-KOLU.

MULAKU ATOLL: KOḶU-FUṚI ISLAND.

7.
8.
9.
10.
11.
12.-16.
17.
18.
19.
20.
21.
22.
23.
24.
25.
26.

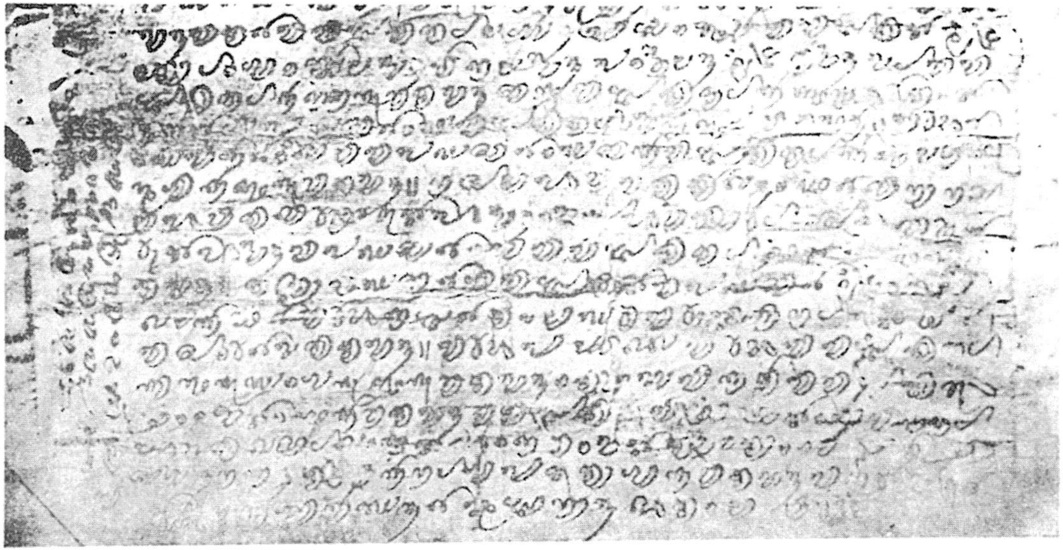

FAT-KOḶU.

* Lines 13, 14, 15 are to left of Text at right angles.

EXCERPTA MALDIVIANA

By H. C. P. Bell, c.c.s. (Retired).

No. 9.—LOMAFANU.[1]

FOREWORD.

Lómáfánu, or *Málófánu*[2], is the Máldivian term equivalent to Sanskrit *Sásanaṃ* and Siṇhalese *Sannasa* ; signifying a Royal Grant inscribed upon one or more Copper, or other metal, Plates.

Prior to 1922 the existence at the Máldives of any such Deeds was unknown to the outside world ; though the fact of their long-established use throughout the Continent of India and Ceylon argued strongly in favour of ultimate discovery of similar *Farman* Plates in the Máldive Islands, so closely connected, since the dim past, with Southern India and this Island.

Patient investigation, during the stay at Mále in 1922 of the Archæological Expedition, elicited ultimately the belated admission that a few Copper-Plate Grants did exist here and there ; but that these, being inscribed in a character for the most part more archaic even than "*Divehi Akuru*," or "*Dives Akuru*" "Island Letters"—its evolutionary derivative, and later form of Máldivian script,—were practically indecipherable by any one on the Group at the present day.

Ultimately, four sets of inscribed Copper-Plates (all incomplete, and one badly injured by fire) were produced, and placed in the hands of the writer for possible decipherment.

Even a cursory examination of the Plates revealed at once the most striking resemblance, ***mutatis mutandis***, of the writing upon them—termed broadly by the Islanders "*Evéla Akuru*" or "Ancient Letters"—with mediæval Siṇhalese letters found on pillar, slab, and rock inscriptions in Ceylon. This similarity proved, generally so marked in its close affinity as to be quite unmistakable to one long familiar with the Epigraphical Records of this Island.

Careful study of the Plates on the spot resulted in much of the Text of those which survive, wholly or partially undamaged, being Transcribed with considerable certainty; and, as regards Translation, in a "prentice-hand" effort (most generously aided by Máldivian scholars to the best of their own knowledge) not, it is hoped, altogether unsuccessful, to convert into English tentatively,—so far as the deficient Plates have permitted,—the Text of at least one, the *Boḍu-galu Miskit Lómáfánu* of Málé,[3] the oldest known Grant extant in "*Dives Akuru*" as distinct from their earlier form conveniently styled "*Evéla Akuru.*"

MÁLDIVIAN LOMAFANU.

The few *Lómáfánu* (single Plates excepted) existing at the Máldive Islands at this day may be listed chronologically, as follows:—

No.	PROVENANCE.	DATE.	SCRIPT.
1	Haddummatí Atol: No. 1	A.M. 582 (A.C. 1195-96)[4]	*Evéla Akuru*
2	Málé: Etere-kolu	A.M. 583 (A.C. 1196-97)[4]	*do*
3	Haddummatí Atol: No. 2	A.H. 636 *cir.* (A.C. 1238-39)[5]	*do*
4	Málé: Bodu-galu Miskit	A.H. 758 (A.C. 1356-57)	*Dives Akuru*

What has survived entire loss, or irreparable injury, in those fuller *Lómáfánu* is being dealt with provisionally elsewhere[3]; albeit of necessity with unavoidable inadequateness, naturally due to the limited knowledge of Máldivian Epigraphy and Linguistics by a comparative tyro.

Similarly, with no little diffidence, the present Paper is offered here; confining itself merely to three "singleton" *Lómáfánu* Plates—stragglers, so to say, from their respective folds, the complete Grants, to which each once belonged.

In an *Appendix* an attempt is made, partially at least, to differentiate and compare the respective types and forms of the "*Dives Akuru*" Alphabet as appearing in the three *Lómáfánu* Nos. 1, 2, 3.

With this semi-apology, for a venture not easy, by a pioneer ploughman of a lonely furrow in a fallow field, too long neglected, this Paper is frankly offered for the kindly criticism of scholars, interested in Oriental languages

(1) LÓMÁFANU: NO. 1.

(*Plate I.*)

This solitary Copper-Plate, measuring 11½ in. by 2¼ in. by 1/32 in., is pierced to left, by a circular hole, for affixing to other like Plates with a metal ring; and is quite bare of any form of border, plain or ornamental.

On each side there are five (5) lines of writing (leaving virtually no margin) in the Máldivian language, with two Arabic interpolated quotations. The Plate shows no numbering.

It is in the possession of Mr. E. 'Abdul Hamíd Dídí, Máldivian Government Representative at Colombo, who kindly loaned it for the present purpose.

As to its true provenance nothing definite seems to be known. Mr. 'Abdul Hamíd Dídí believed that more of the Plates which once formed the whole *Lómáfánu* Copper-Plate Grant were to be found at Mále; but every possible enquiry has failed to bring even a second Plate of the series to light.

This is to be regretted the more as the execution of the single Plate, here reproduced photographically, speaks to exceptional care in its inscribed calligraphy; whilst the verbal style of its contents points to an original document of much scholarly value, when complete.

Towards fixing the period when this isolated *Lómáfánu* was issued, very fortunately important clues are provided by:—

(i) The approximate form of script; (ii) the very noticeable similarity in recurring phraseology; and (iii) valuable historical evidence, presented both in the *Boḍu-galu Miskit* Copper-Plate Grant which has luckily survived in some fullness to this day, and drawn from elsewhere.

(i) Script.

The formation of the engraved characters exhibited by *Lómáfánu* No. 1 much resembles that of the *Lómáfánu* belonging to the *Boḍu-galu Miskit* (Mosque) at Málé.

This Grant,—by an Arabic colophon (in this case prefixed), which bears also the Seal of her father Sulṭán Jalál-ud-dín—is dated *Anno Hijrae* 758 (A.C. 1356–57), or, as given in the body of the Document, the sixteenth regnal year, of the Máldivian Queen, Sulṭána Rehendi Khadíjah; who ruled altogether for twenty-nine years, spread over three periods according to the "*Tárikh*" Chronicle, viz., A.H. 748–64 (first), A.H. 765–75 (second), A.H. 778–81 (third).[6]

(ii) Bodu-galu Miskit Lómáfánu.

In (*a*) the text of *Lómáfánu* No. 1, and (*b*) that of the *Boḍu-galu Miskit Lómáfánu*, are found sentences of absolutely synonymous intent—almost *verbatim* replicas in part—which invoke alternatively blessing, or curse, upon Royalty, Officials, and other persons who uphold, or nullify, the Grant.

A sentence from each *Lómáfánu* may suffice to bear out the close likeness in this respect:—

(*a*) *Lómáfánu: No. 1.*

Text.

(*Obverse: Lines 1-4*).

Mi Hinna Hinna amme tibya meve siṭṭá-kaḷa Muslimán Rahakun Ráda-Ras Kalamidi Raṇi-bihou Faṭamá-Valya Devi

Fradáni Kangati ehen míhaku vyas Muslimunar heu-hiti míhunar vihai nuva-fahi Darmma vaní koru.

Translation.

" (Every) Muslim—(whether) King, Royal Prince, Queen, High-born Noble-man, High-born Noble-lady, Chief Minister, Trusty Personage, or other person—minded to preserve this *Hinna*, as a *Hinna* permanently, will assuredly receive nine-fold blessing (*nuva-fahi Darmma*) that falleth rightly upon persons minded to do good to Muslims."

(*b*) *Bodu-galu Miskit Lomáfanu.*

Text.

(*Plate D, No. 9; Obverse, Lines 1–4*).

Mi Darmya Darmya amme tibya demeve sittá-kala Muslimán kule Musliman Rahakun Rani-bihev Ráda Kumaru Fatamá Devi Mahá Mantri karnna Kangatyakin vata me Rasúlai ekhen Swargga vadunai koru.

Translation.

" (Every one of) Muslim sect—(whether) King, Queen, Royal Prince, High-born Noble, High-born Lady, he who serves as Chief Minister, or (one of) the body of Trusty Personages—minded to preserve this Benefice (*Darmya*), as a Benefice permanently, will verily attain Heaven (as) with the Prophet (Muhammad).

(iii) Historical Evidence.

That the High Post of *Henevi Ras Kinage* (or *Kilage*) —the very patent equivalent of the Sinhalese *Senevi-rada* (*P. Sénápati Rája*, " Commander-in-Chief ")—existed from early days among the State Officials at the Máldives may be taken for granted readily.

(*a*) *Haddummati Lómáfánu : No. 2,*

(*b*) *Ibn Batuta.*

The first references to—or, rather, adumbrations of—the title so far known are furnished by (*a*) the inclusion of

Fehendu-vange Hadi Umari Senevirar ("the General, 'Umar the Ḥáji, of Fehendú Island Family") among the Chiefs who attested *Lómáfánu* Haddummati No. 2, granted by "*Sri Ráarádesvara Mahá Radala*" ("*Tárikh*," No. 7, Sulṭán unnamed ; A. C. 1232-57) in his sixth regnal year, and (*b*) Ibn Baṭúṭa's denomination of the first Máldivian King converted to Islám as *Aḥmad Shanurázaḥ*.

(*c*) *Bodu-galu Miskit Lómáfánu.*

By mid-Fourteenth Century the definite adoption of the title is firmly vouched for by ample testimony.

Besides the distinct mention of "*Kilaki*, Grand Vazír and Lieutenant to the Sulṭána[7]", by the Maghribín Traveller Ibn Baṭúṭa (at the Máldives A.C. 1343–44), in the list he gives of Máldivian State Officials at the time, (*c*) the *Bodu-galu Miskit Lómáfánu* (Plate T, No. 4; Reverse, line 5) specifically alludes to a "*Kakai Mabárak Henevi Ras Kilage*" ("the illustrious Commander-in-Chief, of the Kaká Family"); or, as the Arabic colophon styles him with Oriental bombast, "the erudite Great Vazír, the beneficent, the revered, the illustrious Sharáf-ud-dín Mabárak Shanurázah, who ordered the erection of the blessed Mosque"—the present day *Bodu-galu Miskit* at Mále.

(*d*) *Rádavali.*

Further valuable confirmation is provided by (*d*) the Máldivian "*Rádavali.*" This History calls Queen Khadíjah's second husband,—who (*teste* the "*Tárikh*") usurped the throne for three years, A.H. 775–78—"*'Abd-Allah* (I) *Henevi Ras Kilage*"; and applies the same title to his son.[8]

Upon all the above evidence (i), (ii), (iii) it may be deemed not unreasonable to attribute the Copper-Plate Grant, of which *Lómáfánu* No. 1 formed but one Plate, to Sulṭána Rehendi Khadíjah herself, the bestower of the *Bodu-galu Miskit Lómáfánu*; and to identify her first husband *Muḥammad-ul-Jamíl* (who, the "*Tárikh*" states, ousted her from the *Masnad*, but was murdered after one year's rule, A.H. 764–65, as

Sulṭán Jamál-ud-dín) with the "*Muḥammad Henevi Ras Kiṇage*" of *Lómáfánu* No. 1.

Date of Issue.

If this supposition be correct, the date of the Grant cannot be put later than December, A.C. 1344; for Ibn Baṭúṭa has recorded that "the Vazír Jamál-ud-dín" died in the month of Sh'abán, A.H. 745, and that "the Vazír 'Abd-Allah" then married the Sulṭána.[9]

Contents.

The purport of this *Lómáfánu*—so far as disclosed—is the permanent detachment, on behalf of the ruling Sovereign (unnamed on this solitary Plate), by the Council of State and other personages headed by the Prime Minister, *Muḥammad Henevi Ras Kiṇage*, Commander-in-Chief—of a *Hinna* (delimited area of land) for some set purpose; not definitely ascertainable owing to the absence of other Plates but, in all probability, the endowment by Religious Oblation in *Waqf* of some Mosque.

"In Faith and Hope the world will disagree,
But all mankind's concern is Charity."

Several such Beneficiary Deeds vouchsafed by Máldivian Muslim Rulers, between the Sixteenth and Eighteenth Centuries, are still in existence mostly written on Paper (*Fat-koḷu*): to these should, with little doubt, be added the few (specified above) inscribed on Copper-Plates (*Lómáfánu*) dating back at least to the end of the Twelfth Century.

These Deeds (like similar dedicatory *Sannas* and *Tuḍapat* granted not infrequently by Ceylon Buddhist Kings) concluded, by way of hoped-for potential safeguard, with some form of pious imprecation, more or less stern and bitter, against transgressors; but—in the case of Máldivian Muslim dedications always, and with Buddhist grants occasionally—such malisons were softened down by assurance of countervailing blessing accruing to upholders of the Royal benefactions.

LOMAFANU : NO. 1.

TRANSCRIPT : WORD FOR WORD TRANSLATION.

Obverse.

1. DOSHANÁṚE[10] ANYÁ VAṬṬAINE KRANIMENI
The iniquitous those wrong-doing (who have) committed

LÁNAT LIBENÍ KOṚU *QÁL ALLÁHU TA'ÁLÁ ALÁ*
curse must receive Said God Most High " Know(ye)

LA'ANAT A-
the curse

2. *-LLÁHU 'ALA 'L-ZÁLIMÍN* MI HINNA[11]
of God (is) upon the unjust This Hinna

HINNE-AMME TIBYAMEVE SIṬṬÁKAḶA MUSLIMÁN
as a Hinna (to) continue (who is) minded Muslim

RAHAKUN RÁDA-RAS KALAMIDI[12] RAṆI-
King Royal Prince Queen

3. BIHOU FAṬAMÁ-VALYA DEVI FRADÁNI[13]
High-born man High-born lady Chief Minister

KANGATI[14] EHEN MÍHAKU VYAS
Trusty personages (or) other person if there be

MUSLIMUNAṚ HE-
to Muslims well-

4. U-HITI MÍHUNAṚ VIHAI NUVA-FAHI DARMMA
minded persons due nine-fold blessing

VANÍ-KOṚU *QÁL AN-NABÍ SALLALLÁHU*
(will) assuredly fall Said the Prophet the Blessing of God

'ALAI HI VA SALÁM LÁ'YU MINU
(be) upon him and Peace " Not one of you

AHADUKUM HATTA YU-HIBBU LI
(is) believer (in God) until he loves his

AKHIHI
brother (in Faith)

5. *MÁ YU-HIBBU LI NAFSIHI*
as much as he loves (his) own self"

MI MERUMUN MUHAMMAD HENEVI RAS-
This in conformity with Muḥammad Henevi King

KINAGE-[15]	ÁI	FANSA	FRADÁNI	KANGATI
	and	the Five	Chief Ministers	Trusty personages

FAKÍ	FAḌYÁRU[16]	DETA
the learned	Faḍiyáru	given.

Reverse.

1. FÁTRÁ	DAṚAṚ	LIE	VASSAIDIN	MI
the feet	beneath	written	published	this

MÁ-	FANU[17]	RASGE -	ÁI	RAS-GEVÍ
Great	Deed	the King	and	(has) ended rule

FASDÁKU	BUDAULA-
after	the Government

2. DU	FUṚṚUMÁI	HINNA—	VE	NU-GEVI
	continues	(the) Hinna	existing	without alteration

TIBENI-VE	HINNA	VI	BINEIN	KOMME
(to) remain	(a) Hinna	being	in the conditions	any

EKYAI
one

3. UVAI	NAHAI	BAUHATTAI	KRAMEVE
(by) cancelling	breaking	(and) appropriating	(to) act

SIṬṬÁKAḶA	MUSULIMÁN	RAHAKU	RÁDA-KUMARU	KALA—
minded	Muslim	King	Crown Prince	Prince

MIDI RAṆÍ-
Queen

4. BIHOU	FAṬAMA-VALYA	DEVI	FRADÁNÍ
	High-born man	High-born lady	Chief Minister

KAMUGATI	EHEN	MÍHAKU	VYAS	MUHAMMAD
Trusty personages	(or) other	person	if there be	Muḥammad

KÍ
named

5. FETÁNBRAGE[18]	ṢARÍATU[19]	TIBI	MAGAṚ
of the Prophet	Religious Law	(what) is	according to

NU-ḶI	SUNNÁFATI	AHUVA
without preserving	(by) destroying	perversely

KALAINAṚ	VÁHUṚI	HAIDU
(upon) those who act	(will) ensue	tribulation.[20]

TRANSLATION.

Upon the iniquitous who commit wrong-doing the curse (of God) is bound to fall. The Almighty God has declared :—" Know (ye) the curse of God is upon the unjust."

(Every) Muslim—(whether) King, Royal Prince, Queen, High-born man, High-born lady, Chief Minister, Trusty Personage, or other person—minded to preserve this *Hinna* as a *Hinna* permanently, will assuredly receive nine-fold blessing which falleth rightly upon persons minded to do good to Muslims.

The Prophet (May the Blessing and Peace of God be upon him) said :—" None of you is a True Believer (in God) until he showeth as great love to his fellow (-religionist) as to himself."

In accordance with this (precept of the Prophet), this *Málófánu* (for the *Hinna*), granted by (*lit.* at the feet of) Muḥammad *Henevi Ras Kiṇage*, and (with the concurrence of) the Five Chief Ministers, Trusty Personages, (and) the learned *Faḍiyáru* (Qází), was written and promulgated.

(By its stipulation, even) after the death (*lit.* cessation of Rule) of the King, so long as the Government continues (to last), the *Hinna* is to remain a *Hinna* unalterably.

Should any Muslim— (whether) King, Crown Prince, Prince, Queen, High-born man, High-born lady, Chief Minister, Trusty Personage, or other person—be minded to cancel, break, or appropriate (aught) in (conflict with) any of the conditions (affecting this Deed), he will incur the penalties of those who act perversely by not maintaining, (but) rendering nugatory, the Religious Laws (*Shari'at*) of the Prophet (Muḥammad).

NOTES.

1. **Excerpta Máldiviana No. 9.**—The present Paper could not have seen the light but for the invaluable—and in great degree indispensable—aid most kindly rendered the writer by Máldivian friends.

To E. Ahmad Dídí Effendí, *Doriméná Kilégefánu,* Private Secretary to H.H. the Sultán, to Mr. E. 'Abdul Hamíd Dídí, Máldivian Representative at Colombo, to A. Muhammad Amín Dídí, son of the former, and to the present *Fadiyáru* (Qází) M. Husain Dídí Saláh-ud-dín, just meed of sincerest thanks is frankly due, for consenting, in all generosity, to revise the writer's tentative efforts at translation of the "*Dives Akuru*" Texts as transcribed and furnished to them by him.

For the suggested date periods of the Grants, and other observations offered in the Foreword, the writer must himself accept full personal responsibility; no less than for all matter in the *Appendix* bearing on the form of script displayed by the three *Lómáfánu* Nos. 1, 2, 3 respectively; as well as for the condensed shape into which the running Translations have been finally cast; and finally for the Notes.

2. Lómáfánu.—This term, and its partial metathesis *Málófánu,* as applied to Máldivian Copper-Plate Grants may find derivation in:—*Lómá* = Sanskrit, Páli, *lohamáya,* Sinhalese *lómuwá,* "metal-made," "copper"; *fánu* = Páli *panna,* Sanskrit *pana,* Sinhalese *pan* "leaf."

3. "The Máldive Islands: *Monograph on the History, Archaeology and Epigraphy.*"

4. Lómáfánu : Haddummati, No. 1 : Male.—The dating of these two Grants—a startlingly anomalous and intriguing fact of historical interest and importance, in view of the universal adoption of the *Hijra* era by races who have once adopted the Muslim creed—is thus plainly recorded :—

Text.

Srímat Gadanáditya Má Rasun (eka rádya vina da) tin-vuna (setari-vana) avirodun Sri Muhammadi Fetánbarin (dunie videlai) Swargga vadaigata fás-shatta bay-ási (te-ási) avirodun.

Translation.

"In the third (fourth) year of the glorious Great King Gadanádítiya, (when the kingdom was unified), (being) the 582nd (583rd) year since the illustrious Prophet Muhammad (having illumined the world) attained Heaven."

That the Máldivians should have followed, up to nearly the end of the Twelfth Century at least, the system of *Buddhist Chronology*—by dating their own era, not from the *migration* (*Hijra*) of the Prophet from Mekka to Medina on July 16th, A.C. 622, but from the *death* of Muhammad, which did not occur until ten years later, *viz.*, on June 9th, A.C. 632; as do the Buddhists in reckoning the *Buddha Varsha* from the *Parinirvánaya* of the Buddha in B.C. 544—goes far to show the firm hold that *Buddhism* had secured over the Islanders, and the dilatory change in this respect from the Buddhist cult to Islám, despite Muhammadanism being stringently enforced, as the State Religion, from the date of the Muslim Conversion in A.C. 1153.

The A.H. date 588 is given in the "*Táríkh*" for the accession of *Sultán* (*No. 4*) *Dinei Kalaminjá,* who from his *biruda* is identifiable as "*Srímat Gadanáditya Mahá Rasun*" of the Haddummatí No. 1, and Mále *Lómáfánu.* It is more than likely that this date was equated by the compiler of the State Chronicle, Qází Sheikh Ḥáji Ḥasan Táj-uddín, for the *Anno Hijrae* era with the *Anno Muhammadi* date of that Ruler's accession deducible from the two *Lómáfánu*, viz., A.M. 580, covering the difference of ten years.

5. Lómáfánu: Haddummati, No. 2.—Whether the strange—perhaps unique—"*Anno Muhammadi*" dating for the Muslim era continued to be employed during the Thirteenth Century, the incomplete *Lómáfánu* of Sulṭán Ráarádésvara—the only existing source of information available so far—leave unsettled. The surviving Plates of that Grant nowhere refer to the Muslim year in any form.

Certain it is, however, that a century later the "*Anno Hijrae*" system had taken definite root at the Máldives; for the *Boḍu-galu Miskit Lómáfánu* issued by Sulṭána Rehendi Khadíjah is expressly dated, as recorded in its colophon, in A.H. 758 (A.C. 1356-57).

6. Máldivian Dates. These dates are those of the "*Tárikh*," which the *Boḍu-galu Miskit Lómáfánu* shows to be out by seven or eight years. Queen Khadíjah was on the throne when Ibn Baṭúṭa spent about eighteen months (A.H. 743-44, A.C. 1343-44) at Mále; and this fact fits in well with the sixteenth year of the Sulṭána's reign falling to A.H. 758 (A.C. 1356-57), placing her first accession in A.H. 742, or a year prior to Ibn Baṭúṭa's arrival.

7. Journal C.A.S., Extra No., 1882 : "Ibn Baṭuṭa in the Máldives and Ceylon," page 18.

8. The Máldive Islands : *Sessional Paper* XV, 1921, p. 65.

9. Journal C.A.S., *loc. cit.* p. 36.

10. Doshanáre.—The Mále experts are unable to explain this word, and would connect it with the previous Plate, which is among those missing; but as a very natural derivative from the Siṇhalese *dósha*, "fault", "wrong," the word, as taken to mean "iniquitous" aptly suits the context.

11. Hinna.—A boundary-fixed area, planted or unplanted, belonging either to the Government, to a private individual, or to a family. The Government may bestow the income of a *Hinna* upon a Mosque, &c., or lease it out to any one.

12. Kalamidi.—This title appears in the "*Tárikh*" and "*Rádavali*" Chronicles under the form *Kalaminjá*. It has been explained as signifying "Royal on both sides" (*cf.* Sin. *De-oṭunu meḍa* in Dimbulágala Inscription, Ceylon, *Ceylon Antiquary, III, p. 7*).

13. Fradáni.—*Cf.* Sin. *Pradhána*. The Kandyan Court Ministers, in an *óla* Missive, addressed to the Dutch Council at Colombo in A.C. 1726, style themselves "*Mahá Wásala Pradhánivú Raduḷuvaru*" (*Ceylon Antiquary*, 1915, Vol. I., pp. 118-23); In a *Sannasa* granted six years before they figure as *Siyalu Pañcha Pradháni Amáptavú*. The term *Pañcha Pradháni* occurs in the Hendeniya *Sannasa* (B.V. 2052) of Vikrama Báhu, Kandy, two centuries earlier.

It is not possible to particularise the "Chief Ministers" here grouped as a body of "five" (*Faṇsa Fradáni*). Ibn Baṭúṭa gives the titles of eight, including the *Kilaki*, in office in A.C. 1343-44. The confusion is added to by Pyrard's list (A. C. 1619) of Máldivian dignities, nine in number, at the commencement of the Sixteenth Century; and from the mention (A.C. 1835-36) of six "Vazírs" by Young and Christopher of the Indian Navy—making it certain that the State Offices, and their respective status, have been altered from time to time (See *Hak. Soc. Pyrard*, I, pp. 209-15).

14. Kangati : Kamugati.—"Many other dignities there are of divers degree which the King grants" (*Pyrard, loc. cit.* p. 214).

Influential men, of respectable social standing, might hold lesser minor offices, mostly honorary. Among these "*Kangati nam*" (*Kangati* titles) were in former days several which have seemingly quite died out, *e.g.*, *Dánná, Fenná, Kánná, Kaulanná, Méná, Oliginá, Hirahamádi, Aruvatehi, Wata Baḍéri*, &c. A few still survive, such as *Gaḍahamádi*. *Raṇahamádi*, &c.

15. Kinage.—This term has now been superceded by the form *Kilége* with *fánu* (Siṇ. *vahanse*) honorific attached, *i.e.*, *Kilége-fánu*.

Pyrard supports Ibn Baṭúṭa in attributing special importance to the title:—"The *Quilague*, whom we might call the King's Lieutenant-General; because next to the King, and (in his absence, he is the most powerful in the Government of the State, and without his authority nothing is done. So, if the King wills to do, observe, or execute anything, he is the first to be deputed and receive his commands" (*Pyrard, l. c.* pp. 209-11).

In the course of the Nineteenth Century the title "*Kilégefánu*," once held by the highest Minister only, has been extended gradually to six possible recipients—if all be in office at one time—of whom the *Doriméná Kilégefánu* ranks highest at the present day.

These half dozen *Kilégefánu* Chiefs are :—

1. *Doriméná Kilégefánu*
2. *Raṇṇa Baḍéri Kilégefánu*
3. *Fáriná Kilégefánu*
4. *Fámudéri* (or *Fámuladéri*) *Kilégefánu*
5. *Máfat Kilégefánu*
6. *Dahará* (or *Daharada*) *Kilégefánu*.

Until quite recently they, with the *Qázi*, formed *Is Majilis*, or Chief Council of State (*Raskamuge*) of the Máldive Kingdom.

To the fact that in the Seventeenth and Eighteenth Centuries *Fáriná Kilége* stood first in rank, next below the Sulṭán himself, Máldivian history would appear to point. Thus the following Princes, among others, are specifically styled "*Fáriná*" in the State Chronicle ("*Táríkh*"), and other documents :—Sulṭán 'Ali V (*Dombuláḍ Fariná*); Sulṭán Íbráhím III, son of Sulṭán Muhammad Bodu Takurufánu; Hasan Fáriná, half brother of Sulṭán Íbráhím Iskandar I; 'Ali Fáriná, afterwards Sulṭán Muḥammad Mukarram 'Imád-ud-dín III; and Sultan Muhammad Shams-ud-dín II.

16. Fadiyáru.—The Máldivian term (pronounced *Fanḍiyáru*) for the Arabic *Qázi*.

If *Lómáfánu* No. 1 belongs rightly to Sultána Rehendi Khadíjah, and to the years A.H. 743-44, the particular "learned *Faḍiyáru*" mentioned therein must have been either (*a*) Qází Ísa of Yemen (*Ísá al Yamaní*), or (*b*) Ibn Baṭúṭa himself; who—if he is to be believed—was "constrained" to supplant that Qází (to whom the *Boḍu-galu Miskit Lómáfánu* also alludes), on account of his judicial venality (*Journal C.A.S.*, Extra No., 1872).

17. Má-fánu.—See Note 2 *supra*.

18. Fetánbara.—*Paighámbar* (Persian); which covers both *Rasúl* and *Nabí* (Arabic).

19. Sariatu.—Arabic. *Shari'at*.—"The Laws of Islám."

20. Imprecation.—Two hundred years earlier (A.C. 1133) in an Island Kingdom, separated from the Máldives by thousands of miles, a Christian Sovereign had "granted and confirmed" a "Charter" to "the Church of St. Bartholamew, and to the poor of the Hospital," akin, in its closing adjuration, to that recorded on *Lómáfánu* issued by an Oriental Ruler professing the creed of Islám.

Here are the stirring words of the English document:—"And let all the people of the whole Kingdom know, that I (Henry I, King of the English) will maintain and defend this place even as my Crown; and if any one shall presume in anything to contradict this Our Royal privilege, he, and all and everything that belongs to him, shall come into the King's power. All these things I have granted for ever, for the love of God and the welfare of myself and my heirs, and for the souls of my ancestors.

"Therefore, I adjure all my heirs and successors in the name of the Holy Trinity, that they maintain and defend this Sacred Place by Royal authority and that they grant and confirm the liberties by me granted to it."

But most striking it is to find the Máldivian Muslim objurgation virtually reproduced (save for the more vivid Buddhist penalties in substitution) in a Siṇhalese *Sannasa* (Hendeṇiya) emanating from a Kandyan King in the Sixteenth Century (A. C. 1509-10):—"*Raja Yuva Raja Siṭu Senevirat Ẹpá Mápá Pañcha Pradháni kenekungen wat obakiṅ wat avulak uḍaranayak kala kí kenek ẹt nam, &c.,* . . . ."

(2) LÓMÁFÁNU: NO. 2.

(*Plate II.*)

This single leaf of a Copper-Plate Grant (now as a whole, it is feared, irretrievably lost), is in safe custody at Mále. Weathering has marred a photograph doing full justice.

It was discovered by the writer strung on the same ring as the six surviving Plates (covers excluded) of *Boḍu-galu Miskit Lómáfánu*; and, from its less perfect finish, automatically dubbed itself an interloper.

As with *Lómáfánu* No. 1, no fellow to this Plate is known.

In dimensions it measures 10 1/3 in. by $2\frac{3}{4}$ in.: it is, therefore, slightly shorter than *Lómáfánu* No. 1, but half an inch wider. The ring-hole is on the right side of the Plate: which is exceptional.

The Obverse has six lines, as against but five on the Reverse. The script falls short of the clear cut perfection of characters noticeable on *Lómáfánu* Nos. 1 and 3.

Date of Issue.

Neither its date, nor the name of the Sulṭán by whose order *Lómáfánu* No. 2 was issued, appear on the Plate; which seems to bear, as Máldivian Numbers, *S* (8) and *Ḑ* (9) for its front and back.[1] It may be placed provisionally in chronological order between *Lómáfánu* Nos. 1 and 3.

Contents.

The object of the Document was manifestly the bestowal of a Grant on a Mosque, under *Waqf* conditions, as in the case of *Lómáfánu* No. 1

What is lost, regrettable as it is, in entire absence of knowledge, or even hint, regarding the identity of the particular Ruler on the throne at the date of its execution, or that of any of his Ministers—in contrast to the suggestive information to be gleaned from *Lómáfánu* No. 1—is, however, in no small measure, compensated by two other prominent points in the Text of this unique Plate.

These are centered in :—

(i) The appellation "*Lakká*" (*Lanká*)—still in dispute by Orientalists as far as relates to Ceylon—applied to the Máldives.

(ii) The claim to "*Janman*," or proprietary birth-right, in Landed property on the Islands, asserted almost unequivocally by the Sulṭán reigning at the time of the issue of *Lómáfánu* No. 2, and apparently acquiesced in without demur by his State Officers and subjects;—such vital right, both in regard to Land Produce and Treasury Funds, being now-a-days absolutely denied *de jure* to the Sulṭáns by the *Lex Inscripta* of the Máldive Islands.

(1) "**Lakká,**" (*Laṇká*)

In his closely reasoned Paper (" The Indian Historical Quarterly," Vol. II, No. 2, 1926) Mr. V. H. Vader deals concisely with the situation of " The *Laṇká* of Rávaṇa described in Válmiki's *Rámáyaṇa.*"

Tacitly dismissing the unwisely proposed (*a*) Amarakaṇṭaka mountain, (*b*) Assam, and (*c*) Central India, sites, as all quite unsustainable, he proceeds to tilt vigorously at (*d*) " the almost axiomatic theory that Ceylon was *Laṇká* and *Laṇká* is Ceylon," so persistently urged by many Oriental Scholars.

Upon " more weighty and reliable evidence collected from ancient Sanskṛit literature," Mr. Vader propounds this theory :— " *Laṇká* was the Capital of the big Island known as *Rákshasa Dvípa*, in the midst of the Southern Ocean, and on the Equator or middle part of the Earth."

The question is discussed fully, authorities being quoted to show that "*Siṇhala Dvípa,*" or Ceylon, and "*Laṇká*" were separate kingdoms ; for several reasons clearly set out.

Mr. Vader finally sums up the case for his thesis thus :—

" The present Máldives cover up the same position which once was covered by the *Rákshasa Dvípa*. It extended from 6° North latitude down to 1° South of the Equator lengthwise, while its breadth was from 73½° to 76° West longitude.

" Even the geologists maintain that before the Fourth Millennium B.C. there existed a big Continent in the Indian Ocean. Its extent lay, from the South of Africa, Eastward towards the South of America, to the South of India. In course of time the big Continent became immersed in the waters, and what portions we have now—such as *Malaya Dvípa*, Sychelles, Rodrigues, Chagos, Mauritius, Madagascar, Jáva, Sumátra, Borneo, Ascension, Falkland, Graham, West Antarctica, etc.—are nothing but the mountain tops or plateaus of the old big Continent.

"The *Malaya Dvípa*, or Máldives, is the site of the *Rákshasa Dvipa* of Rávaṇa with its capital *Laṇká Purí*.

Leaving aside the moot point whether Ceylon was, or was not, rightly known as "*Laṇká*" among other names, *e.g.*, *Sinhala Dvípa*, *Támpruparṇa* (*Taprobane*), the existence of an alternative "*Lakká*," or "*Laṇká*," situated to the South-West of Ceylon, is startlingly supported by intrinsic evidence contained in surviving Máldivian *Lómáfánu*

The employment in *Lómáfanu* No. 2 of the term "*Lakká*," as synonymous with "*Divehi Rájje*" of a later period, to denominate "the Maldive Realm." finds valuable collateral support in the *Boḍu-galu Miskit Lómáfánu* (Plate T. No. 3, Obverse, line 3) ; in which distinct reference is made to more than one "*Lakká*"—"*Aahi Lakká Mahi Lakká*, *Laṇká* the "Far" (*lit.* "There") and the "Near" (*lit.* "Here")

These terms may cover the Lakkadive, and Máldive, Island Groups—unless (not impossibly) "*Aahi Lakká*" denoted Ceylon itself.

A further curious point—may be purely accidental, but nathless not to be ignored even if a strange coincidence only—in connection with "*Lanká Purí*" as the presumed Capital of Rávaṇa's "*Rakshasa Dvípa*," is the actual existence of an island at the present day (humble, and uninhabited, but dedicated in *Waqf* to a Mosque), now written and pronounced "*Lankan-fuṛi*," which lies on the Eastern reef of North Mále Atol.

(ii) Sultans' "Janman" Right.

"For many centuries past, and possibly from early days, the form of Government which has ruled at the Máldives has been, to a considerable degree, that of a Constitutional Monarchy.

> 'Broad based upon (the) people's will,
> And compassed by the inviolate sea.'

"The Sultáns of the Máldive Islands (from the date of the Muhammadan Conversion in mid-Twelfth Century,

A.C. 1153) would seem to have held the throne virtually at the will of the Chieftains and people; who have not failed to enforce their power at times by effective Revolution—brought about of late years peaceably, but not infrequently in former days by measures more or less violent and tragic.[2]

"Tenure of land at the Máldives conforms in some points to the Málayáli Fiscal system in vogue for centuries in Malabar, as well as on the Islands off the West coast of India, viz., the Lakkadive Group, including Minicoy (*Maliku*); which latter Island belonged to the Máldive Rulers up to the Sixteenth Century *circa.*

"The *"Janman,"* or proprietary birth-right, claim to *Paṇḍáram* lands and monopoly of all produce, so long maintained over the Lakkadives by the Rájas, and Bíbís. of Kaṇṇanúr, was finally inhibited (with certain concessions to meet all prescriptive allegations) by the British Government of India.

"*Per contra*, for their part, the Sulṭáns of the Máldive Islands have never, *as of right*, established exclusive *"Janman"* claims of possession to land, or produce, of any Islands in their Dominion as distinct from, and independent of, the *Baṇḍára* or Government right.

"The soil of *Divehi Rájje*, ('The Island Kingdom,') is vested in the Government (M. *Baṇḍára*) inalienably. Land can neither be seized *de jure* by the Sulṭáns, under pretence of *"Janman"* right; nor conveyed by them *suâ sponte*, either to Máldivian subjects (Mále Island furnishing the sole partial exception) or to Foreigners.

"The Máldive Sulṭáns, in short, were never absolute personal owners of either the soil, or the produce, whether in (*a*) the whole, or (*b*) certain Islands, or (*c*) parts of Islands, of the Máldive Archipelago.

"Despite, however, the well-established Máldivian Unwritten Law, viz., that the Sulṭáns are not unconditioned proprietors of the land, Máldivian history discloses, beyond question, that taking advantage of the weakness of their Governments, or of the flexible disposition of their subjects, Sulṭáns have, on occasions, acting with high-handed and unjustifiable assertion of "*Janman*" right, alienated Islands for their own interests or that of favourities, besides reserving Islands in their names for *Waqf* benefit of Mosques.

"Islands thus irregularly transferred by one Sulṭán were generally allowed to remain uninterruptedly *in statu quo* by his successors, on grounds of expediency, or as convenient precedent for justifying plausible similar action at will to their personal advantage." [3]

LÓMÁFÁNU : NO. 2

TRANSCRIPT : WORD FOR WORD TRANSLATION.

Obverse.

1. BÁRA	RAṚ	NAGAI	DEMAVE	MI
Twelve	Islands	selected	given	this

BAHÁI	MI	EMME	VERI-TAKUN	HITAṚA	DURO-
saying	these	all	Officials	to the mind	rich

2. AKAI	HAMA	BÁRA	RAṚ	BÁRA
	sufficient	twelve	Islands	from twelve

ATOḶUN	NU-FENI	MUḶI	LAKKÁIN	BÁRA
Atols	not finding	from the whole of	Lakka	twelve

RAṚ	DE-
Islands	

3. MÁVE	BUṆEGEN	:	UTTARAIN	NEKURANDU-AI	:
given	saying		from the North	Nekurendú and	

KALAIDU-AI	:	LANDUV-A
Kalaidú and		Landú

4. I	:	IGURAIDU-AI	:	KÁṚIDU-AI	:	HUḶULE-AI	:	ELA-AI	:
and		Iguraidú and		Káṛidú and		Huḷule and		Ela and	

KAṆI-
Kaṇi-

5. (MÍ)DU-AI	:	FOṆADU	DE	TUḌI-AI	:	MADIṚI
Mídú and		of Foṇadú	two	portions and		Madiṛi

VILIGILLI-(A)I	:	NELENDU-AI
Viligili and		Nelendú and

6.	MÁI	RASGE	TUḌI	AVAHÁRA
.	ma and	Royal	portion	private

TUḌI	MI	DE	TUDIAR	VANAHAI	HI-
portion	to these	two	portions	what exists	Hi-

Reverse.

1. TADU	MÁMENDU	GAḌAI	MI	BÁRA	NAGARU
tadu	Mámendú	reservation	these	twelve	(Island) villages

DA(NÁ)RU	MACHCHAṚ	VANNA	EMME	TA-
Mosque	upon	being	all	things

2. KETAI	:	MI	RADUNGE	AMILLA	UKAS	MATÍN
		this	King's	own	property	out of

SIRI	SÁSTRA	FAṆA	MI	HAṆE	FÁ-
glorious	sciences	plate	this	narrow	notification

3. ḶA	KOṚU	MI	BÁRA	NAGARU	HINNA
	having made	these	twelve	(Island) villages	Hinna

KURAVVAI-GENFI	KAMÁI	:	MI	BÁRA	RAṚA
caused to make	the fact		These	twelve	Islands

RAS	BO-
Royal	Cowries

4. LI	RAHURÁ	:	GOI-MAS	:	*QALAM*	GOVI-BAI	:
	Toddy Tax		Fish Tax		*Qalam*	Cultivators Tax	

FÁLABBA	MI	VERÍ-NAṚ	ME	TIBIMAṚ	MI
Tree Tax	to these	people	this	belonging	These

5. NAGARUKU	SAMUDDURE	FUṚI	HIKUNAS	MI
(Island) villages	in the sea	islet	dried up	this

RAṚ	MACHCHAṚ	ME	TIBENA	HUṚI	KAMÁI
Island	upon	this	belongs	is	the fact

TRANSLATION.

. . . . . . should be selected and given.

Upon this statement, as the twelve Islands from the (above specified) Atols did not appear to be sufficiently productive in the opinion of all these (State) Officials, (they) declared that twelve Islands should be given from the whole Máldive Kingdom (*Muḷi Lakká*).

(Accordingly) the following Islands were selected from Northwards,[4] (viz.):—Nekurendú (Tiladummatí Atol), Kalaidú (South Miladummaḍulu Atol), Landú (South Miladummaḍulu Atol), Iguraidú (North Máḷosmaḍulu Atol), Káṛidú, Huḷule (North Mále Atol), Ela (Koḷumaḍulu Atol), Kaṇi Mídu (Nilande Atol), two portions of Fonadú (North Mále Atol), Mádiri Viligili[5] (North Mále Atol), Nelandú (North Nilande Atol),......(including) the Royal portion, and private portion, with what (produce) exists (therein), as well as, (in Haddummati Atol), a reserved portion of Hitadú and Mamendú Islands—everything in these (above) twelve Islands (*lit.* villages) being (bestowed in *Waqf*) upon the Mosque.

(His Majesty), having caused these twelve Islands, (drawn) from the King's own property, to be constituted a *Hinna*, proclaimed the fact by this glorious, scholarly *Málófánu* (*lit.* narrow Plate).[6]

From these twelve Islands (the taxes)[7] *Ras-boli*, *Rahurà*, *Goi-mas*, *Qalam*, *Govi-bai*, *Fálabba*, were allotted to these persons (as custodians for the upkeep of the Mosque).

(Further), it is decreed (*lit.* is the fact) that an eyot (*fuṛi*) which has emerged (*lit.* dried up) from the sea[8] at any one of these Islands (*lit.* at this village)—this (too) belongs to this Island.

NOTES.

1. **Máldivian Numeration.** In old Documents this ran thus:—*M* (1), *F* (2), *D* (3), *T* (4), *L* (5), *G* (6), *Ṇ* (7), *S* (8), *Ḍ* (9).

2. **The Máldive Islands:** *Sessional Paper XV, 1921.*

3. **The Máldive Islands:** *Monograph on the History, Archaeology and Epigraphy.*

4. **Islands.** The sequence of the Islands starts from the Northernmost Atol (Tiladummatí), but at once becomes irregular.

5. **Madiri Viligilli.** "Rowed across from Mále to Viligili Island. It is occupied by *Rá-veri* (Toddy Drawers), under their own Headman. The houses are poor and few, surrounded by coconut and breadfruit

trees. Most of the Island is under dense sea-board jungle, interspersed with sporadic coconuts......

"The Mosque, about a quarter of a mile from the dwellings, is a building of no merit, covered by galvanized sheeting, half walled, half wooden-barred, having but one doorway. There are stepping-stones from the square ablution-tank (*hauz*) to the Mosque entrance, to save feet pollution.

"With men and boys, the women here came out to be photographed, near their houses. In Mále, the latter 'run like hares,' if approached camera in hand.

"This Island lives well up to its name *Madiri Viligili.*" Mosquitoes (M. *madiri*) abominably aggressive: by contrast, Mále is very free of these pests." (*Diary, May 2, 1922*).

6. Sultáns' "Janman" Right. By Mále authorities the sentence from *Má Radunge amilla* (Reverse: line 2) to *fáḷa koṛu* (line 3) in the Text, is considered "very complicated, and its meaning not at all clear." They, however, frankly admit that "either the Sulṭán of the day must have proclaimed that he reserved these Islands for the Mosque as of indefeasible right; or that he asserted forcibly and wrongfully such personal claim, and autocratically proclaimed the fact."

7. Taxes: *Ṛasboli.* Royal Cowries, *i.e.*, Cowries paid as Poll-Tax (*Váru*); *Rahurá*. Toddy (unfermented) Tax; *Goi-Mas*: Fish Tax; *Qalam*: Tax Collector's Fee (*lit.* "pen-fee"); *Govi-Bai*: Cultivation Tax; *Fálabba*: Tree Tax. For *Fálabba* see *Journal C.A.S.*, XXXI, 82, 1929, pp. 414-15.

8. Island Erosion. "They (the natives) observe the Atols to be washing away: in some, coconut trees are standing in the sea; elsewhere, the black soil of the Island is discernible thirty feet from the beach at low-water. The South-East side of an Island in Fádiffuḷu Atol is entirely gone, and marked only by a tree in the water. Some Islands are said to have disappeared entirely, *e.g.*, Wádú in Miladummaḍulu Atol, now a rocky shoal but once an Island.

"It is, however, acknowledged that reefs have risen from the water, and gradually formed Islands. The inhabitants of Mále remember the outer edge of a circular reef in their harbour which had two fathoms in the shoalest part, but is now dry at low water" (*Moresby, "Report on the Maldives,"* 1835, *circa*).

LÓMÁFÁNU: NO. 3.

(*Plates III, IV.*)

The left half of a broken Copper-Plate, which must once have formed portion of an important *Lómáfánu*, was presented to the writer in 1922 by Hoḷudú-nevige Ḥáji Ismá'il Didi,[1] for many years past, the *Míru Baharu* (Arabic, *Amír-al-Bahr*), or Harbour Master at Mále. It has no claimant, and is said to have been found *perdu* somewhere at Mále among other "unconsidered trifles."

The fragmentary Plate measures roughly about 7 in. horizontally by 3 in. in regular breadth.

As most customary, the Plate is pierced near the left side, and bears the first portion of five lines on Obverse and Reverse face alike.

Its script is beautifully engraved, the characters being boldly incised, and clear beyond possibility of confusion.

Contents.

By extraordinary good luck, though but half of the Plate is available—the Máldivian numbering, *Ṇ* (7) and *S* (8) on Obverse and Reverse respectively, fixing this as the fourth in order of the original set—so much of the Text as is forthcoming contains definite historical particulars, (besides veiled suggestions, partly divulged, partly shadowed). which enable the period of the *Lómáfánu's* execution, and the identity of the Royal Grantor, to be deduced with virtual certainty.

Succinctly stated these clues (i), (ii), (iii) are as follows :—

(i) Al-Gházi Íbráhim Fáriṇá.

"The Great King Íbráhím Fáriṇá, the Ghází," (at the present day spoken of at Mále by tradition, and in song, as "*Íbráhím Kaláfánu*)," is styled precisely, as on this half Plate, "*Al-Ghází Íbráhím Fáriṇá*" in an old *Fat-koḷu* (Paper Grant) in which Haññа Mídú Island of Ari Atol figures conspicuously.

This *Fat-koḷu* opens with a reference to the circumstances attending the tragic death, by spear thrust, of Al-Gházi Sulṭán Íbráhím (III) son of Al-Gházi Muḥammad Boḍu Takura martyred (*shahid vejje*) on Wednesday, the 28th of Shawwàl, A. H. 1017, when fighting against the evil-minded Malabars (*Hóḷín*) who had descended upon Mále in fourteen vessels (*Gurábu*) ; the Muslim burial, and the erection of a stone-built tomb (*Ziyárat*) to the slain Sulṭán at Haññа Mídu; and the appointment of its caretakers; together with mention of the names of the two wives, 'Aishá Bíbi Kamaná and Nazarat Kamaná, who had accompanied the Sulṭán on his flight.[2]

(ii) Length of Reign.

The "*Táríkh*" and "*Rádavali*" Chronicles agree with the *Lómáfánu* in allotting a period of twenty-four (24) years and two (2) months to the reign of Sulṭán Íbráhím (III, A.C. 1585–1609), son of Sulṭán Muḥammad Bodu Takurufánu (A.C. 1573–85).

(iii) Succession to the Throne.

From the same Histories is gained the further information that, after one intervening reign—that of Sulṭán Ḥusain (II) Fámudéri Kilégefánu (A.C. 1609–20)—the throne passed to Sulṭán Muḥammad 'Imád-ud-dín (I), A.C. 1620–48, whose parentage is given.[3]

This Ruler, the nearest living relative to the deceased Sulṭán Íbráhim (III), was his great-nephew, in as much as Sulṭán Muḥammad 'Imád-ud-dín's great-grandfather 'Ali Khaṭíb—"*Al-Gházi* Ali Katíbu Takura" of *Lómáfánu* No. 3—and Sulṭán M. Boḍu Takurufánu were half-brothers.

Enough is left on the broken Plate (albeit but the last syllable "*ná*") to identify "Áminá Mává Kilage" as the mother of the "male child" (*furaddinúda*) "Muḥammad Kalaminjá"[3] of the "*Rádavali*" history; besides affording the strongest presumption that her own mother's name Mariyam Kabádi Kilage, (as occurring in the "*Táríkh*"), filled the missing part of line 4 (Obverse); and that the latter lady was a daughter (*dí*) of "Ali Katíbu Takura" mentioned in the first part of the same line.

Date of Issue.

The issue of *Lómáfánu* No. 3 (to which the partial Plate belonged) may, therefore, fairly be assigned to Sulṭán Muḥammad Shuj'ai 'Imád-ud-dín (I), commonly known as "*Boḍu Rasgefánu*," who reigned from A.C. 1620–1648.

By collation with existing *Fat-koḷu* of Sultān Iskandar Íbráhím I (A.C. 1648–87), son of Sulṭán Muḥammad 'Imad-ud-dín I, gaps in the text have been partially filled with confidence ; in addition to other *lacunae* closed up by the supplementary information drawn from the Chronicles.

(3) LÓMÁFÁNU : NO. 3

TRANSCRIPT : WORD FOR WORD TRANSLATION.

Obverse.

1. MAHÁ RADUNE VANA *AL-GHÁZÍ* ÍBRÁHÍMU
Great King being the Gházi Íbráhím

FÁṚINÁI [. . . . . . SA]
Fáṛiná

2. -UVÍS AVERUDU DVI MÁSÁIN REDALI
twenty-four years two months reigned
[. . . . .]

KURAV [VAI . . . . SHAHID VEJJE SATÁRA AVERUDU]
having martyr become seventeen years

3. DAHA MÁSÁIN MI LÓKA MEDUN
ten months this world from midst

BAIBAA[. . . . .]
departed

4. EB-BAFAI *AL-GHÁZÍ* ALI KATÍBU TAKURAGE
one-father the Gházi 'Ali Khaṭíb Takura's

DÍ : [MARIAN KABÁDI KILAGE DÍ
daughter Mariyam Kabádi Kilége's daughter

KABÁ ÁMI-]
Kabá

5. NÁ MÁVÁ KILAGE KIHUNU : FURADINNÁDA
Áminá Mává Kilége born to male child

[. . . . . SVA]

Reverse.

1. -STI SRÍMATA MAHÁ SRÍ
Hail! Endowed with beauty great glorious

KULA	SUNDURA	SÁIKA	SÁSTURA	[AUDÁNA . . . .
race	pure	all	sciences	[accomplished . . . . .]

. . . .]

2. FURA	UTTARA	KATTIRI	BUVANA	MAHÁ
pre-eminent	noble	Kahatriya	Universe	Great

RADUN[4]	EKU	RÁJJE	FURAGAḶA	[UDDAḶA KOṚU
King	(as) one	Kingdom	all the Islands	embellishing

KELA	AḌḌÚ	MI	DE-]
Kéla (Island)	Addú (Atol)	these	two

3. MEDU[5]	EKAṆU ONNAMI	KOṚU	ANEKANEṚ
between	one together	having made	(to) any other

NETÍ KOṚU[.	MI	DEHAIN	BAA]
denying	this	country	fear

4. NIRUBÁ	KOṚU :	BARI	KUSHA	MI
without fear	having made	weight	wisdom	this

AMATTAVI	KOṚU :	FURA	MÁ[6] [LE . . . . . .
exclusive	having made	Ancient	Male

. . . .]

5. MI	DARUṆI	MATÍ	SARUMÁṆA	BINÁ
this	fertile area	upon	cleared	ground

KURAVVAIGEN	SAVÁLA	[. . . . .]
getting worked	famed	

TRANSLATION.

When the Great King Íbráhím Fáṛiná, the Ghází,...... had reigned for four and twenty years and two months, [and after seventeen years and] ten months [had elapsed since, as a martyr, he had] departed from this world, (there succeeded to the throne) a male child [begotten by 'Umar Máfat Kilége, and born to Kabá Ámi]ná Mává Kilége [daughter of Mariyam Kabádi Kilége, who was a] daughter of 'Ali Khaṭíb Takura, the Ghází, half-brother [of the Sulṭán Muhammad Boḍu Takurufánu, the Ghází].

Hail ! the Great Ruler of the Universe—a pre-eminent noble Kshatriya........(learned in) all sciences, (descended from) the great glorious pure race, endowed with beauty—

having embellished as one Kingdom all the Islands [between Kéla and Aḍḍú Atol] making it his own domain, and that of no other (Ruler), banished fear from this country, freeing it from alarm.

Having (thus), with weighty wisdom, established exclusive (Sovereignty), (His Majesty) caused ground, cleared in a fertile area, to be cultivated at Ancient Málé,........the famed...........

NOTES.

1. **H. Ismá'il Didí.** The erstwhile sprightly young Ambassador to Ceylon in the Eighties of last Century. He has gone on the *Hajj* Pilgrimage, thrice since; and is one of the State Officials most trusted at this day.

His all-round efficiency, and knowledge of Siṇhalese, coupled with a happy temperament, rendered his services invaluable as cicerone to the Archaeological Commission of 1922.

2. **Haññá Mídu Fat-kolu.** The full passage in the Text runs:—

Hijrain eku sástura satára vana averudu *Shawwál* mahu Buda arávis duvahu *Al-Ghází Muḥammad Boḍu Takuraṛ* fut *Al-Ghází Ibráhím* Fáriná Kilage faivánái *hasad* verikamu Hólinge dolos-de Gurábu ais mi Kinage faivánái mi uren hagurámа koru mi uren elli lónsiakun mi Kinage gaikolu gehi *shahid* vejje hidu mi Kinage Ziyárat aigen Haññа Míduvaṛ gos Ziyárat mi raru Miskit doṛun Binkoṛ kiavvai mi Kinage Ziyáratu gau-gassavai mi kankama kemi míhen kuravvaifá tibe mi Kinage faiván daṛu de Abi-Kabalun kamu tibi *'Aishá* Bibí Kamanái *Nasarat* Kamanái.

Pyrard (who was held prisoner at Málé at the time) has left interesting details of the tragic, but justly deserved, death of Sulṭán Ibráhim of evil memory, and its sequel. The following is an extract :-

"The eight Galleys that were bidden to go after the King came up with him and to close quarters; whereupon the King, attempting to defend himself, was slain by a pike-thrust, followed by sword-cuts; his wives were taken prisoners, and his nephew was drowned.

"No harm, however, was done to the wives, save that they lost all their trinkets, which were seized by the soldiers and mariners, these being the most dangerous fellows at pillage: these mariners are called *Maucois* (Mukkavar).

"The cause of the taking and death of the King was that there was no wind, but the greatest calm possible; and that the enemy's Galleys were better for rowing than those of the King, which were only good for sailing, and of no use for oars. Had there been but a little wind they could not have caught him; but his ill-fortune cast him into this fate, which he fully merited for the great cruelties he had used. His hour was come, and for my part I hold that it was by the mercy of God he was thus slain." (*Hak. Soc. Pyrard*, Vol. I, page 314).

3. **"Rádavali."** The account in the "*Rádavali*," short as it is, of the reigns of the four successive Sulṭáns, Muḥammad Boḍu Takuru-

fánu (A. C. 1573-85), Ibráhím (III) (A. C. 1585-1609), Ḥusain (II) Fámudéri Kilégefánu (A. C. 1609-20), and Muḥammad 'Imád-ud-dín (I) (A. C. 1620-48), makes matters clearer :—

8. *Muḥammad Boḍu Takurufánu.*

Text.

Mi Radunge (*'Ali* Kalaminjá) Kafirunái toḷi *shahid* vejje fahu MG aharu MM mas foiṛ Utímu *Ḥusain Khaṭíb* Kalogeṛ diafurasútáve *Áminá* Dio kihunufan *Al-Ghází Muḥammad* Boḍu Takuraṛ : Suvastì Sirí Kavunsarádítta Buvana Mahá Radunevep. Mi Kalá raskan kuḷa aharu MM mas G.

Translation.

"When MG (16) years and MM (11) months had elapsed since this King (S. 'Ali VI) was slain by the Infidels, and became a martyr, Muḥammad Boḍu Takura, the Ghází, begotten by Ḥusain Khaṭíb of Utímu (Island) and born to Áminá Devi, (was elected Ruler).

"(His title, as proclaimed, was) :—Suvastí Sirí Kavunsarádítta Buvana Mahá Radun.

This King (lit. Personage) reigned MM (11) years G (6) months.

8. *Ibráhim (III).*

Text.

Mi Radunaṛ me (*Al-Ghází Muḥammad Boḍu Takura*) diafurasútáve Bauraṛu *Fáṭumá* Dio kihunufan *Al-Ghází Ibráhim* Kalaminjáṛ : Sirí Sandu Suvaru-gai Loka Mahá Radunevep. Mi Radunge raskan kula aharu FT mas F. Mi Radunge *shahid* vi *Hijrain* 1017 vana aharu.

Translation.

"(Then succeeded) Ibráhím Kalaminjá, the Ghází, begotten by this last King (Muḥammad Boḍu Takura), and born to Fáṭumá Devi of Bára Island (Tiladummati Atol).

"(His title, as proclaimed, was :—Sirí Sandu Suvaru-gai Lóka Mahá Radun.

"This King reigned FT (24) years F (2) months, and became a martyr in A.H. 1017 (A.C. 1609)."

8. *Ḥusain (II) Fámudéri Kllégefánu.*

Text.

Mi fahu Fámudéri Kilagefánu niyauvi *Hijurain* 1029 vana aharu.

Translation.

"After this, Ḥusain Fámudéri Kilégefánu (reigned, and) died in the *Hijra* year 1029 (A.C. 1620).

8. *Muḥammad 'Imád-ud-dín (I).*

Text.

Mi Radunge (*Al-Ghází Ibráhim*) *shahid* vejje MṆ aharu MO diha mas vejje imaṛ fahu furaddináda *'Umar* Máfahaṛ Kinagoṛ diafurasútáve nufan *Kabá Áminą* Mává Kinage kihunufan Muhammad Kalamiṇjár: Suvastí Sirí Kula Sundura Audána Kíriti Kattiri Buvana Mahá Radunever. Mi Kalá raskan kuḷa aharu FD mas F.

Mi Bodu Rasgef ..nu avahára ví aharu *Hijrain* 1058.

Translation.

"When MN (17) years and MO (10) months had expired since this King (Íbráhím III) was slain by the Malabars, and became a martyr, Muhammad Kalaminjá, male child, begotten by 'Umar Máfat Kilége, and born to Kabá Áminá Mává Kilége (came to the Throne).

"(He was proclaimed as):—Suvastí Sirí Kula Sundura Audána Kíriti Kattiri Buvana Mahá Radun. This King reigned FD (23) years F (2) months.

This (King styled) Bodu Rasgefánu expired in A.H. 1058 (A.C. 1648)."

4. S. Muhammad 'Imád-ud-dín (I). His epithets are limited by the "*Tárikh*" to :—Sirí Kula Sundura Kattiri Buvana Mahá Radun.

To distinguish them, Sultans M. 'Imád-ud-din I, M. 'Imád-ud-dín II, and M. 'Imád-ud-dín III are conveniently styled by the respective epithets Shuj'ai, Muzaffar and Mukarram.

Sultans' *birudas* are given full rein in *Lómáfánu, Fat-koḷu,* and State Missives to Dutch Governors of Ceylon.

5. Kela : Addu. In *Fat-koḷu* granted in A.H. 1063 (Gan Island, Addú Atol) and A. H. 1074 by Sultán Iskandar Íbráhím (A.C. 1648-87), son of Sultán Muhammad 'Imád-ud-dín I, the Máldivian Ruler asserts right to exclusive sway from Kela Island in Tiladummati Atol, the Northernmost of the Máldive Group. to Addú Atol, at the extreme South

But in another *Fat-koḷu* of Hitadú Island (Haddummatí Atol) dated A.H. 1074 (A.C. 1665-66) the claim boldly and bombastically runs from Maliku (Minicoy) Island—raided by the Máldivians in this reign, but not held long—to Addú Atol (*Eku Rájje furagala uddala koṛu Malik-Aḍḍu mi de medu ekuṇu onnavi koṛu anekaku nan neti koṛu*).

Minicoy (originally Máldivian) had long been added to their Lakkadive Islands acquisition by the Rájas of Kaṇṇanúr.

6. Mále. Several important structural improvements at Mále are attributed by the "*Tárikh*" to Sultán Muhammad 'Imád-ud-dín I.

He constructed the Fort (still standing, and repaired in great part) with bastions (*Buruzu*), joined up by curtain-walls, and many embrasures and convenient gateways; besides mounting extra guns obtained from Achin.

Further, he built a Breakwater to shelter Máldivian craft : this Inner Harbour is in existence and kept dredged at the present day.

Previously, the same Sultán had rebuilt the Palace Enclosure, (*Etere-koḷu*) and surrounded it with a Moat; which was not completely filled in until the close of the Nineteenth Century.

APPENDIX.

Origin of the "Dives Akuru."

The obvious affinity of the "*Divehi Akuru*" or "*Dives Akuru*" writing—a kinship disclosed *a fortiori* in its older form, dubbed for the nonce "*Evéla Akuru*" "Ancient Letters"—to the mediaeval Sinhalese of Ceylon, combined with a like element of Tuḷu, or, possibly, of an older Grantha type, *Arya Eḷuttu* (Tuḷu-Malayálam) prevalent in the Malabar Districts of Southern India, indicate convincingly its almost certain origin; and strongly suggests the former inclusion in the Alphabet of a fuller list of characters covering aspirates.

So far as it survives at the present day, the "*Dives Akuru*" alphabet has been manifestly made to fall into line, as far as practicable with the simpler modern Syllabary based on Persi-Arabic characters, known as the *Tána* Alphabet.

Evidence is still not, and perhaps may never be, forthcoming as to the full original extent of the "*Evéla-Dives Akuru*" as compared with Sanskṛit and other Indian alphabets; but the existence, to this day, at the Máldives of Grants on Copper-Plates, styled "*Lómáfánu*," of a date as early as the Twelfth-Thirteenth Centuries, has at least proved that the complement of letters still retained then, in addition to its aspirate form DH, the dental D side, together with the regular use of the palatal sibilant Ṣ,—both almost abandoned by the Fourteenth Century.

Syllabary.

A duplicate syllabary, in two parallel lines, of the "*Dives Akuru*" Alphabet, as formerly current at (1) Mále (Central Atol) and (2) Aḍḍu (Southernmost Atol) of the Máldive Islands, was supplied by the writer to Journal, Ceylon Asiatic Society: Vol. XXVII, Extra No. 1919.

On two Plates (VI, VII) are there set out, as Type 1 (Mále) and Type 2 (Aḍḍu):—

(*a*) Basic form of *aksharas* (consonants with inherent vowel A)—twenty-five (25) in all—, besides the *sukun* symbol ; (*b*) some variants ; (*c*) a few compound letters : (*d*) the five (5) vowels, short and long ; and (*e*) the respective vowel-signs.

To the above was added tentatively, summarised explanation of the Alphabet's general usage.

The opportunity afforded in 1922 of studying at Mále itself lithic Inscriptions, and *Fat-koḷu* (Royal Grants on Paper) issued by Máldive Sulṭáns in " *Dives Akuru* " characters, has necessitated certain desirable amendments (doubtless still capable of further improvement) to that preliminary sketch.

These appear in the statement given below :—

Alphabet.

The Consonants and Vowels which constituted the full " *Dives Akuru* " Alphabet, (now in usage but rarely) may be, grouped, broadly, according to phonotic values, as follows :—

	CONSONANTS							VOWELS	
Divisions	Surd		Sonant					Sonant	
	Tenues (Hard)	Sibilant	Mediae (Soft)	Nasals.	Liquids.	Sibilant.	Aspirate.	Short	Long
1. Gutturals ..	K	—	G		—	—	H	A	Á
2. Palatals ..	C	Ṣ	J	Ñ	Y	—	—	I	Í
3. Cerebrals ..	Ṭ	SH	Ḍ	Ṇ	ṚḶ	—	—	—	—
4 Dentals ..	T	S	D	N	RL	Z	—	—	—
5. Labials ..	P	—	B	M	—	—	—	U	Ú
6. Gutturo-Palatals ..	—	—	—	—	—	—	—	E	É
7. Gutturo-Labials ..	—	—	—	—	—	—	—	O	Ó
8. Dento-Labials ..	F	—	V	—	—	—	—	—	—

Consonants.

"*Dives Akuru*" consonants, like those of Sanskrit, Sinhalese, and other Indian cognate alphabets, are in reality "vowel-consonants," *i.e.*, each basal *akshara* includes the short vowel A, unless superceded by insertion of other vowel-signs, or the vowel-eliminating *sukun*.

As with Sinhalese, etc., the addition of these symbols in no way affects the shape of Máldivian *aksharas*, beyond the modification due to such inflexions.

Vowels.

In "Type 1" (Mále), distinct forms are used, both as Initials and Medials, for the vowels A, I, U, E, O, in accordance with the Sanskrit-Sinhalese canon; whilst those of "Type 2" (Southern Atols) are merely derivatives, sign-modified, of the Máldive consonant transcribed as A.

Dipthongs AI, AU, EU, OU, are made up from the vowel-consonant with the respective additional vowel attached.

In "*Evéla Akuru*" (older form of "*Dives Akuru*") the doubled *Kombuva* symbol—as in Sinhalese—stood for AI.

Vowel-Signs.

A. Á.

Short A, as stated, is inherent in every *akshara*, or "vowel-consonant"; unless the latter be bereft of its vowel by the *sukun* eliminator.

For long Á, the Máldive sign exactly resembles the Sinhalese *Elapilla* symbol; written detached to right of the consonant.

I. Í.

Short I has three symbolic forms:—

(i) Placed above consonants, like Sinhalese *Ispilla*.

(ii) Modified *Ispilla*; differing only from Sinhalese *Elapilla* (long Á symbol) in being united to the consonant on its right.

In form (i) long Í is differentiated by a knot; in form (ii) by curl, or kink.

(iii) I, Í, signs are, in the third form carried almost round the consonant from right to left, in combination with R symbol—conforming exactly to the Sinhalese complex known as *Uttara rakáránṣaya*.

U. Ú.

Four symbols are utilised for U :—

In the first two forms short U follows the Sinhalese *Pápilla* usage, *i.e.*, Form (i), long narrow loop to left; Form (ii), curl to right; both written below the consonant;

Form (iii) shows a small loop united to the consonant's right arm inside;

Form (iv) closely resembles the *sukun* symbol.

Long Ú, in form (ii) adopts a small stroke cutting the curling *Pápilla*.

E. É.

E is represented :—

(i) Earlier, by a small helix, like the Sinhalese *Kombuwa* symbol, preceding its appropriate consonant.

(ii) Later, by tiny circle, or oval, bisected horizontally in lieu of the helix—a slovenly devolution.

O. Ó.

For O the above derivative E symbols of the Sinhalese *Kombuwa* serve, when followed by consonants inflected with the *Ẹlapilla* sign.

Sukun.

The *Sukun*—an undulating stroke drawn diagonally upwards to right above the *akshara*—has three uses :—

(i) Medial : Reduplicator of succeeding cosonant.

(ii) Final : Equivalent of certain silent *aksharas*.

(iii) Final : Vowel-eliminator, or "stop," to consonants —possibly an attempted combination of the two kinds of Sinhalese *al* mark.

LÓMÁFÁNU NOS. 1, 2, 3: EPIGRAPHY.

It remains to offer some comments on an epigraphical analysis of the three *Lómáfánu* under review.

Consonants.

A.

The Siṇhalese medieval type of A is noticeable in "*Evéla Akuru*" *Lómáfánu* (Mále; Haddummatí) as existing side by side with the later Máldivian "*Dives Akuru*" form found in *Lómáfánu* Nos. 1, 2, 3.

A solitary spreading variant of this older type occurs (See C.A.S. Journal, Extra No., 1919, Plate VI) in *Lómáfánu* No. 1 (Obverse, line 1, *anyá*); in this respect assimilating to the *Boḍu-galu Miskit Lómáfánu*, which furnishes four or five examples.

D.

The Siṇhalese DH, or aspirated form of dental D, had virtually ousted the unaspirated letter by mid-Fourteenth Century.

Once only is the unaspirated D found in this trio of Plates, and that in *Lómăfánu* No. 1 (Obverse, line 5, *Fradáni*): in its congener, the *Boḍu-galu Miskit Lómáfánu*, the simple D is equally scarce, occurring but thrice on the six surviving Plates.

In Copper-Plate Grants engraved in the "*Evéla Akuru*" of the Twelfth-Thirteenth Centuries, both the aspirated and unaspirated forms of dental D are employed at will (*e.g.*, *Dabudu*, *Dabudhu*, *Dhabudu*), for the modernised *Da*($\bar{m}$)*bidú* Island, Haddummatí Atol; proving the steady "passing" of ordinary D.

K.

Though not figuring either in the "*Evéla Akuru*" Plates, or in "*Dives Akuru*" *Lómáfánu* even up to the first half of the Seventeenth Century, it may not be inapposite to note the sudden introduction of a freak form of the letter K resembling a bold figure "3" (See C.A.S. Journal *l.c.*, Plate VI) into an Inscription and *Fat-koḷu* of the latter part of the same Century.

M.

Two types of M are to be seen in *Lómáfánu* Nos. 2, 3 :—

(i) Large : (*hama*, L. 2 ; *máhá*, L. 3); descendant of the medieval Siṇhalese M.

(ii) Small : (*mi*, L. 2 ; *Ibráhímu*, L. 3) ; more frequently used than the large (i) type.

Lómáfánu No. 1, and *Boḍu-gálu* Mi*skit Lómáfánu* use a medium size of type (i).

N.

Regarding Nasals four points stand out :—

(i) Dental N is occasionally given duplicated value, in monogrammatic form,—as, indeed, are T (*vaṭṭai*, L. 1); T (*bau-hattai*, L. 1 ; *uttura*, L. 3) ;—by a small curl at its bottom (*vanna*, L. 2 ; *onnumi*, L. 3).

Full dental N, appears as terminal, with the *sukun*.

(ii) The form of "stop," rising from single looped back of the letter, is employed in *Lómáfánu* No. 1 alone (*merumun, ehen*).

(iii) This florid modification of the vertical Siṇhalese *al* symbol will be noticed to have degenerated further in the later *Lómáfánu* Nos. 2, 3, by the entire letter N being transmogrified into two loops attached to the *sukun* (*verí-takun*, L. 2 ; *kihun*, L. 3).

(iv) A diminutive vermiform symbol, somewhat like tiny F of the modern Máldivian *Tána* Alphabet,—a tailed evolution seemingly of the Siṇhalese *anusváraya*, or *binduva*, attached to the head of the consonent—is freely used ; as :—

(*a*) Half, or full, nasal medial (*Kangati*, L. 1 ; *passim*, L. 2).

(*b*) Final full N (*uttarain*, L. 2 ; *másain*, L. 3).

The same symbol may also be employed to duplicate consonants, with no nasal influence, (*Lakká*, *samuddre*, L. 2 ; *Rájje*, L. 3).

T. Ṛ.

Cerebrals Ṭ and Ṛ are both manifest derivatives of the Sinhalese lingual surd Ṭ.

This Ṛ is met with frequently single, (*koṛu*, L. 1, 2 ; *raṛa*, L. 2 ; *Fáṛinai*, L. 3) ; and once double (*fuṛṛurai*, L. 1).

Ṭ. appears in a few words. both singly (*Faṭamá*, L. 1) and doubled (*vaṭṭai*, *siṭṭákala*, L. 1).

R.

The ordinary R is at times replaced by two symbols, each clearly of Sinhalese birth, and largely utilised in that script.

(i) *Réphaya* : (*Darmma*, L.1)

(ii) *Uttara rakáránṣaya* : (*passim*, L. 1, 2, 3).

Ṣ.

By the Sixteenth Century palatal Ṣ, found twice (Obverse, line 5, *fanṣa* ; Reverse, line 5, *ṣariatu*) in *Lómáfánu* No. 1, had seemingly quite dropped out of employment.

In "*Evéla Akuru*" *Lómáfánu* it already appears linked up at choice with dental S (*e.g.*, *fassima*, *fasṣima*).

Y.

The Sinhalese *Yanṣaya* symbol, as adopted, is resorted to in *Lómáfánu* 1 (*tibya* ; *Valya*).

Conjunct Consonants.

(i) *Entire Letters.*

BV, *b(u)vana*, L. 3.
CHCH, *machcha*, L. 2.
DV. *dvi*, L. 3.
KL, *k(u)ḷa*, L. 3.
KSH, *k(u)sha*, L. 3.
MM, *komme*, L. 1.
NB, *Fetánbrage*, L. 1.
ṚṚ, *fuṛṛurai*, L. 1.
SD, *fasdáku*, L. 1.
SG, *Rasge*, L. 1.
SK, *Ras Kinage*, L. 1.
SL, *Muslimán*, L. 1.
SS, *vassaidin*, L. 3.
ST, *Svasti*, L. 3.

NN, *hinna*, L. 1.
NR, *Rahakun Ráda*, L. 1.

STR, *sástra*, L. 3.
SV, *Svasti*, L. 3.
TT, *uttarain*, L. 2 ; *amattavı* L. 3.

(2) *Entire Letter and Symbol.*

BB, *fálabba*, L. 2.
BR, *Fetánbrage*, L. 1 ; *Ibráhimu*, L. 3.
DD, *samudd(u)re*, L. 2.
FR, *f(u)ragala*, L. 2 ; *f(u)radinnáda*, L. 3.
JJ, *Rájje*, L. 3.
KR, *Tak(u)rage*, L. 3.
LL, *Viligilli*, L. 2.
MM, Muhammad, L. 1.
MM, amme, L. 1.
NB, medun baibai, L. 3.
NDR, sund(u)ra, L. 3.

NE, *Radun eku*, L.
NF, *genfi*, L. 2.
NG, *Kangati*, L. 1 ; *Radunge*, L. 2.
NM, *másainmi*, L. 3.
NN. *hinna*, L. 1 *vanna*, L. 2.
NR, Muslimán *Rahaku*, L.1; *masain Redali*, L 3.
ṄṢ, *fanṣa*, L. 1.
NS, *matin siri*, L. 2 ; *kuravvaigen savála*, L. 3.
ṬṬ, vaṭṭai, L. 1.
TT, bauhattai, L. 1 ; uttura, L. 3.
TTR. Kat(ti)ri

Vowels.

A.

Types 1, 2.—(i) Initial : *anyá* (spreading variant), *ahuva*, L. 1 ; *akai*, L. 2 ; *averudu*, L. 3 ; (ii) Medial : *Kiṇage-ai*, L. 1 ; *nagai*, L. 2 ; *Fáṛinai*, L. 3.

Á.

Types 1, 2.—Initial : Medial. *Nil*

I.

Type 1.—(i) Initial : *nil* ; (ii) Medial : *vaṭṭai*, L. 1.
Type 2.—(i) Initial : *Iguraidu*, L. 2 ; *Iburáhimu*, L. 3 ; (ii) Medial : *nagai*, L. 2 ; *Fáṛinai*, L. 3.

Í.

Types 1, 2.—Initial : Medial. *Nil.*

U.

Type 1.—(i) Initial : *uvai*, L. 1 ; (ii) Medial : *nil.*

Type 2.—(i) Initial : *uttara*, L. 3 ; (ii) Medial : *budauludu* L. 1 ; *sauvís*, L. 3.

Ú.

Types 1, 2.—Initial : Medial. *Nil.*

E.

Type 1.—(i) Initial : *ehen*, L. 1 ; Medial : *lie*, L. 1.

Type 2.—(i) Initial : *emme*, L. 1, 2 ; *ela*, L. 2; *eb-bafai*, L. 3 ; (ii) Medial : *passim.*

É.

Types 1, 2.—Initial : Medial. *Nil.*

O.

Type 1.—(i) Initial : Medial. *Nil.*

Type 2.—(i) Initial : *onnami*, L. 3 ; Medial : *nil.*

Ó.

Types 1, 2.—Initial : Medial. *Nil*

Vowel-Signs.

A.

Inherent in every basic consonant, forming one syllable.

Á.

Like Siṇhalese *Ẹlapilla* symbol; following *akshara* to right detached (*passim*).

I. Í.

Form 1.—Like Siṇhalese *Ịspilla* symbol ; above letter :—(*a*) Short : *passim* (L. 1) ; *nil* (L. 2, 3) ; (*b*) Long : *Rasgeví*, (L. 1).

Form 2.—Like Siṇhalese *Ẹlapilla* symbol ; but attached to side of letter :—(*a*) Short : *vihai* (L. 1) ; *mi* (L. 2) ; *Iburáhímu*, (L. 3) ; (*b*) Long : *Iburáhímu* (L. 3).

U.

Form 1.—Like Siṇhalese *Pápilla* ; loop to left at bottom of letter : (*koṛu*, L. 1).

Form 2.—Like Siṇhalese *Pápilla* ; right curl at bottom of letter : (*Ráhaku*, L. 1) ; *nufeni*, L. 2).

Form 3.—Small loop inside right limb of letter : (*buṇegen*, L. 2 ; *Iburáhimu*, L. 3).

Form 4.—*Sukun*-shaped up-stroke to right above letter : *míhaku* (L. 1) ; *verí-takun* (L. 2) ; *Radunai* (L. 3).

U.

Forms 1, 2, 3, 4.—*Nil.*

E.

Form 1.—Like Siṇhalese *Kombuwa* symbol, but diminutive : precedes *akshara* (*passim*, L. 1).

Form 2.—Small round, or oval, symbol, bisected horizontally ; similarly placed (*passim*, L. 2, 3).

É.

Forms 1, 2.—*Nil.*

O.

Forms 1, 2.—*Kombuwa*-shaped like E, but with the addition of *Ẹlapilla* symbol attached to the following *akshara*.

Ó.

Forms 1, 2.—*Nil.*

Sukun.

The *sukun* possesses triple power :—

(i) Medial : Reduplicator doubling succeeding consonant (*amme*, L. 1).

(ii) Final : Equivalent of silent *akshara* Ṛ (*míhunar*, *daṛaṛ*, *magaṛ*, L 1).

(iii) Final : Vowel-eliminator to consonant (*lánat*, *Ras*, *merumun*, L. 1).

Calligraphy.

A final word regarding the execution of these *Lómáfánu*.

Lómáfánu No. 1.—It would not be easy for an engraver to improve generally on the finish of this Plate—its horizontal regularity of line, and the perfect delieation of the neatly incised writing, whether *Arabic* or " *Dives Akuru.*"

Save for the omission, and subsequent insertion, of three letters, the graphology of this Plate is up to the standard of the best examples of Sinhalese Copper *Sannas*.

Lómáfánu No. 3.—This half-plate *Lómáfánu* displays equal precision in the work of the engraver's tool, and the sharpness of the bold script. It is quite free of any carver's errors.

Lómáfánu No. 2.—Obviously *Lómáfánu* No. 2 falls somewhat behind the skilled execution, so strikingly displayed in *Lómáfánu* Nos. 1, 3.

The crowding of a sixth line on to the Obverse, the omission of an *akshara* in *Mídu* and *Danáru*, the hardly parallel lineal spacing, added to more shallowly engraved writing, stamp it as the handiwork of a less efficient worker.

The two short vertical lines (reminiscent of Sanskrit and other Indian inscriptions), found in *Lómáfánu* Nos. 2, 3, and represented by *colons* in the transcript, would seem intended to serve the same purpose as the horizontal Siṇhalese *Kuṅḍali*, or pause symbol.

MÁLDIVE ISLANDS

A

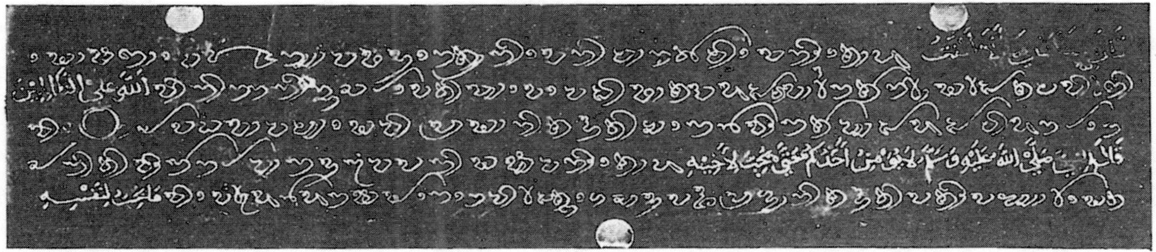

B

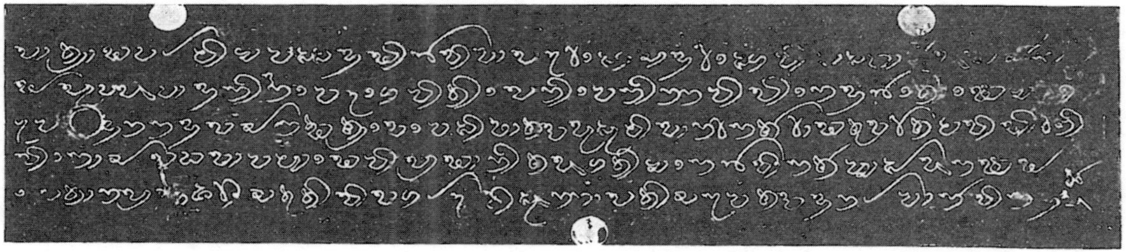

Lȯmáfánu No: 1.
Scale : Half size, *circa*

MÁLDIVE ISLANDS

Plate II

A

B

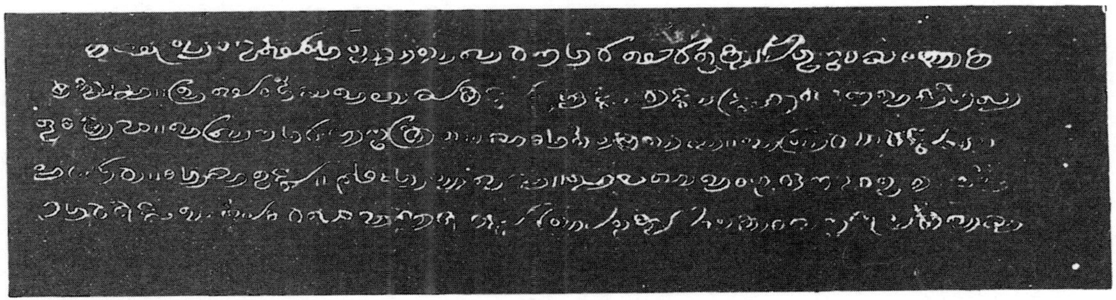

Lómáfánu No: 2.

A

Lómáfánu No: 3.
Scale : Five-sixths

B

Lómáfánu No: 3
Scale : Five-sixths.

EXCERPTA MALDIVIANA.

By H. C. P. BELL, C.C.S. (Retired).

No. 10.—THE PORTUGUESE AT THE MALDIVES.

FOREWORD.

"Lead, O God, the Máldive Race
Along Thy Prophet's way,
Ever staunch to Muslim Faith,
Until the Judgment Day."*

The purpose of the present Paper is to bring into one concentrated focus all known references of any moment, or their gist, on the above subject occurring in European and Máldivian records, Such references have been made available—and that often but partially—, up to the present, only in scattered writings more or less difficult of access.

The main authorities, from the European point of view, are to be found in (*a*) the Portuguese Archives † and Histories relating to the East, (*b*) in Pyrard's *Voyage to the East Indies*, together with notices summarised in (*c*) *Ceylon Sessional Paper XLIII*, 1881, and in (*d*), the *Hakluyt Society Pyrard*, 1888, Vol. II., *Appendices* A, B; whilst on the Oriental side the sole source of information is furnished by the "*Tárikh*," or State Chronicle of the Máldive Sultáns, which still remains unpublished.[1]

By way of comparison and contrast in the narratives, it will be most convenient to group accounts by Portuguese, French, and other Western writers, separately from the particulars derivable from the Máldive Chronicle.

* See *infra*, p. 96 for the prayer of Muḥammad Boḍu Takurufánu, the Máldivian national hero of the Sixteenth Century. This, old "slogan" (so to say) of the Máldive Islanders, remains undiminished in its intense fervour.

† *Archivo Portuguez Oriental* (*Goa*); *Livro das Monções* (*Lisbon*).

CONTENTS.

These fall suitably into three broad Periods.

1. FIRST PERIOD: A.C. 1500-1550.

(1) *PORTUGUESE REFERENCES.*

A.C. 1498.

East Indian Trade.

The Portuguese first showed their flag in the East at the very close of the Fifteenth Century.

When Vasco da Gama, rounding the Cape in A.C. 1498, reached Calicut (*Kaḷḷikkóḍḍai*), he found Oriental trade and commerce well mapped out and established.

Vessels from Further India and China bound for Aden and the Red Sea touched at Ceylon, the Máldives, or Malabar ports (Calicut in particular) before striking across the Indian Ocean, and up the Red Sea to Jeddah, or on to Suez for delivery to merchants at Cairo.

As a second route the ships made, by way of Calicut and other ports on the West Coast of India, for Cambay, and thence to Ormuz; from which great emporium, their cargoes were transported by caravan routes to Baghdad, Damascus, and ultimately to Europe.

Everywhere free trade prevailed, united with commercial security and at least rough justice.[2]

It was upon such inexhaustibly rich prey that the Portuguese "swooped" greedily.

A.C. 1500.

Upon the arrival of the second Portuguese Expedition to the East Indies, under P. Alvares Cabral, off Malabar in A.C. 1500, owing to "the bitter rivalry" existing between the Zamorin of Calicut and the Rája of Cochin, the latter, eager for Portuguese support, allowed them to establish a Factory.*

From Cochin, that "coign of vantage," the Portuguese first commenced—and long continued—to harry the seas of Western India, until, "by conduct not to be distinguished from common piracy, they broke up link by link, the commercial chain which had hitherto extended from Genoa and Venice to Malacca and Pekin."

The Muḥammadans—the "*Moros*" (Moors) of Portuguese writers—held most of the carrying trade at the time; and to every one of them, when seized, confiscation of goods, slavery, and even death, were meted out inexorably, albeit engaged on "lawful occasions" of immemorial Eastern commerce.

A.C. 1503.

Portuguese encounter Máldivians.

In A. C. 1503 the Máldive Islanders learnt their initial cruel lesson from Christian hands.

Four Máldive *gundras* † were sighted by Vicente Sodre, ‡ off Calicut, laden with dried fish (*peixes seccos bonitos*),

---

* With an eye to the main chance, the Portuguese (who had already in A.C. 1502, exploited Cannanore), ready ever to play rival Rulers against one another, made very advantageous terms ere long with the Zamorin, obtaining in A.C. 1513 permission to construct a Fort at Calicut.

Goa, after its capture in A.C. 1510, supplanted Cochin (lost to the Dutch in A.C. 1663), as the Portuguese headquarters in India; though not officially recognised as such until A.C. 1530. (Logan; *Malabar Gazetteer*, 1915, 50).

† Arabic *kundura* (pl. *kanádir*). The Siṇhalese still call a Máldive boat (M. *dóṇi*, *oḍi*) by the term *gundura*, and the Islanders *Gundura-kárayó*.

‡ Gaspar Correa, *Lendas da India* (Ed., 1864), I, 341-2.

coir (*cairo*), and cowry shells (*caury*),—the last then in great request in Bengal as currency. In addition, these vessels contained "great store of silks, coloured and white, and many brilliant tissues of gold, made by the Islanders themselves, from thread obtained from Moor ships which visited the Islands by bartering for salt, earthenware, rice and silver."

The Máldivians of the *gundras* lost all their goods, which were sent to the Factory at Cannanore (*Kaṉṉanúr*)—whose Ruler, *Áḷi Rája* ("Sea-King"), the Portuguese, under Vasco da Gama in A.C. 1502, had got to agree to a fixed scale of prices, whilst ensuring by the issue of passes a safe passage to all Cannanore merchants *—and were warned imperatively against further such trading ; as for the Calicut Moors one-hundred (*cem*) were fettered and burnt in one of the vessels incontinently.

A.C. 1510.

"Mamalle, Lord of the Máldive Islands."

Seven years later, in 1510, the great Alfonso d Albuquerque, second Viceroy at Goa, peremptorily dealt with "*Mamálle*" (*Mammáli Marakkár*), a predominant Mápiḷḷa merchant who lived at Cannanore and was styled "Lord of the Máldive Islands" (*O Senhor das Illas de Maldiua*).

The monopoly of trade with the Máldives was held by this man—the "*Saracenus quidam Mamelles nomine*" of Osorius, —under an agreement with their King,—whereby Máldive goods (dry fish, coir, cowries and fine silks) were obtained at definite prices in exchange for rice and earthenware—to such a degree that "*Mamalle*" virtually supplied all the coir for the use of India.†

To counteract the influence of this Moor, the Máldive Ruler sought the alliance of the Portuguese, undertaking

* Logan, *Malabar Gazetteer*, 41.
† Correa, *loc. cit.* II, 129.

to render them tribute on condition that they would compel "*Mamalle*" to renounce his pretensions.*

Albuquerque ordered "*Mamalle*" forthwith to remove his Factors, and to cease trading with the Islands, "as these belonged to the King of Portugal, who would hinder no one from trading there"; naively insisting, further, that "*Mamalle*" should in no way hamper the Portuguese if they visited the Máldives for trade purposes.

Against appeal by the Moor for retention of his monopoly, the Viceroy was obdurate, fixing the tale of annual delivery to the Portuguese, free of expenses, at one thousand (1,000) *báres* of fine, and one thousand (1,000), of coarse, coir, each *bár* to weigh four *quintales* and a half.†

"The foregoing agreement," adds Correa, "was duly observed during the government of Alfonso d' Albuquerque; but his successors, understanding how to profit themselves by the trade, gave it over to their servants and friends, and violated the contract. The ships and armadas sent by the Factor of the King of Portugal reduced his profit to nothing, and did much robbery and mischief at the Islands."‡

After the departure of Albuquerque the Máldives became "the happy hunting ground" of Portuguese first-hand pirates; and equally so for those sent to capture the filabusters. §

A.C. 1517.

Portuguese obtain Factory at Mále.

Ultimately on the information given by the ex-Viceroy to the Court of Portugal regarding the Máldive Islands, and the advantages to be derived from them, Lopo Soares, Albuquerque's successor in the Government of India, on orders from home, despatched Don Juan de Silveira in A.C. 1517 to come to terms with the King of the Máldives and to form a solid establishment in his Kingdom.

---

* Lafitau, *Découvertes, etc., des Portugais*, I, 552.
† Correa, *loc. cit.* II, 130.
‡ *Loc. cit.* II, 130.
§ *Loc. cit.* II, 508.

"He had been instructed to promise all that was desired, and obtained what was wished." *

A.C. 1519.

Portuguese Garrison at Mále annihilated.

In further pursuance of this project a Flotilla was despatched to the Islands in A.C. 1519 by the Viceroy, Diogo Lopes da Sequeira, under João Gomes Cheiradinheiro. It consisted of four vessels, a *carevella* (three-masted galley-rigged barque), a *catur* (smaller vessel) and two *fustas*, (pinnaces), furnished with artillery and all necessaries, and carrying one hundred and twenty men. †

After roving to harry and rob the Islanders and others according to fancy, João Gomes landed at the principal Island *Mafacalou* (Mále) [3] where the King of the Islands dwelt. Settling himself on part of the Island, he fortified it well by strong palisades, with shelter inside for men and guns. The place was very strong, and adjoined deep harbourage for the Portuguese vessels, whence they used to emerge to rob what they could : on shore, much Máldive produce—coir, cloth and dry fish—was taken from the inhabitants, but paid for at the pleasure of the Portuguese.

The actions of the foreign garrison became so intolerable that the Máldivians sought urgent intervention from "*Baleacem*," a great Moor merchant and noted corsair of Calicut ; and, in his absence, successfully invoked the aid of "*Patemarcar*" (*Pata Marakkár*), another powerful Moor and Chief merchant at Cochin, who, after Portuguese seizure of some of his ships, had turned to buccaneering.

Twelve Malabar *paraos*, well manned, sailed for Mále and fell suddenly, with fire-bombs, upon the Portuguese ships lying unaware in harbour. Six *paraos* attacked

---

* Lafitau *loc. cit.*

† Correa, *loc. cit.* II, 568-70 ; Faria y Sousa, *Asia* (Stevens, 1695, I, 219).

the *fustas* and *catur*, the other six the *carevella*, speedily killing all those on board. They then assaulted the Fort, which was undefended on the seaside, and killed and wounded many: the remainder, who fled through the thickets, were slain by the Islanders in revenge for the many misdeeds committed by the Portuguese.

In this assault João Gomes and all his men were killed, the *carevella* burnt, and the other vessels seized, with all the artillery and rich booty accumulated by the Portuguese.

The King of the Islands eagerly participated in the spoil, including two large cannon (*dous tiros grossos*) which the Moors could not carry off in their *paraos*.

Thus the Máldivians regained their freedom from partial thraldom to the Portuguese; but retained it for but three decades.

During the ensuing thirty years no further assault was made by the Portuguese on Mále itself; but notices occur in their Histories of the continuance of quasi-legalised piratical raids by them among the Islands.*

A.C. 1525.

"Mamalle" captured and killed.

"*Mamalle*, the most honoured Moor in India, a titular King of the Máldives"—was chased in A.C. 1525 by Vicente Sodre with four vessels, captured, and put to death.

The fame of this noted Muslim corsair of the Sixteenth Century was such that, on Maps of even two centuries later,† it gave his name, in "the Channel of *Mamalle*" (*Canal de Mamale*), to the present day "Nine Degrees Channel" between the Lakkadives and Minicoy Island.

A.C. 1540.

In A.C. 1540 Gonzale Vaz, going to the Máldive Islands on his own account, seized a "Moor" (Máldivian) who had robbed and killed some Portuguese a few days previously.

* Correa, *loc. cit.* III, 70, 288.
† Stavorinus, *Voyages*, III, 280 (English Translation, 1798).

Gonzale Vaz took prompt revenge upon the particular Island where the Portuguese had met their death. Its Headman, was seized, put in chains, tortured and heavily mulcted before being released. *

A.C. 1545.

" Cojezemecadim " Corsair

An offer made in A.C. 1545 by the Viceroy, through Belchior da Sousa, of the title and advantages of "Lord of the Máldive Islands" to "*Pocoralle,*" *regedor* and general factotum at Cannanore, and brother of "*Mamalle,*" on condition of his effective aid in capturing the notorious and elusive Moor "*Cojezemecadim*" (*Kóya Shams-ud-din*)—the special *béte noir* of the Portuguese at the time,—came to nothing, owing to native mistrust and tergiversation. †

(2) *MÁLDIVIAN REFERENCES.*

The limelight bearing on Portuguese connection with the Islands can now be switched on appropriately to Máldivian recorded history—albeit lamentably meagre, as told in its "*Tárikh*"—covering approximately the first half of the Sixteenth Century.

"TARIKH" CHRONICLE.

50. S. Kalu Muhammad.

(A.H. 807 : A.C. 1491-2)

He (S. Íbráhím II, 49) was succeeded by Sulṭán Muḥammad, son of Sulṭán 'Umar (II, 45) Mahá Radun, son of Sultán Yúsuf (II, 38), son of Sultán Hiláli Hasan (I, 29).

51. S. Yúsuf III.

(A.H. 807-8: A.C. 1491-3)

When he (S. Kaḷu Muḥammad) had occupied the throne for nine months, Yúsuf, the brother of Sulṭán

* *Loc. cit.* IV, 152.

† *Loc. cit.* IV, 421-2.

Muhammad (50), son of 'Umar (II, 45), seized the throne by force. He called himself Sultán 'Umar.

After reigning for two and a half months, he died in the year 808 of the *Hijra* era.

52. S. 'Ali IV.

(A.H. 898-900 : A.C. 1492-5)

Then 'Ali, son of Kai-Ulanná Kilége, son of Máfat Kilége, son of S. Husain (I, 31) ascended the throne.

53. S. Kalu Muhammad.

(A.H. 900-915 : A.C. 1494-1510)

After he (S. 'Ali IV, 52) had held the throne for two years and four months, Sultán Hiláli Muhammad (50), who had previously ruled for only nine months, seized the Sultánate in the *Hijra* year 900, with the assistance of *Áli Rája* of Kannanúr.[4]

54. S. Hasan VII.

(A.H. 915-16 : A.C. 1509-11)

When he (S. Kalu Muhammad) had reigned for fifteen years, Sultán Hasan (VII), son of Sultán Yúsuf (51), took possession of the throne.

He died in *Hijra* 915, after ruling for two years.

55. S. Shariff Ahmad.

(A.H. 916-18 : A.C. 1510-13)

Then the throne was filled by As-Sharif Ahmad of Mekka.

He died in *Hijra* 918, after reigning for two years and nine months.

56. S. 'Ali V.

(A.H. 918 : A.C. 1512-13)

Thereupon 'Ali, son of Hirratu (*Mává Kilége*) of Nelláidú (Island, Tiladummati Atol), ascended the throne.

When he had been reigning for nine months, the twice deposed Sultán Hiláli Muhammad (50, 53) went to Kannanúr on the Malabar Coast, and signed a Treaty with *Áli Rája*, in which he agreed to pay him yearly a substantial sum for his aid.

He (S. Muḥammad) was given a large force of soldiers, with whom he sailed for the Máldives.

But, on leaving Kaṇṇanúr Harbour, they were met by several Portuguese vessels, which prevented them from continuing their voyage, and held them as prisoners until (annual) payment of a large sum of money was agreed to.

On this being guaranteed, they were released by the Portuguese; who then accompanied them to the Islands. Both fleets anchored in Mále Harbour; and (forcibly) secured the throne for this said Sulṭán Muḥammad.[5]

The combat was fought in *Hijra* 919.

57. S. Kalu Muhammad.

(A.H. 919-35 : A.C. 1513-14).

Annual Tribute to Áli Rája.

After he recovered the throne the Sulṭán, in accordance with his compact, began to pay yearly the amount agreed upon.

This Tribute was continued by the Sulṭáns who succeeded him, until the reign of Sulṭán Íbráhím Iskandar (I, A.C. 1648-87), son of Sulṭán Muḥammad 'Imad-ud-dín (I, A.C. 1620).

The Sulṭán (Íbráhím Iskandar I), deeming that such payment to two foreign nations was made through ignorance, and was humiliating to Máldivians, enjoined on his son and his successors—and, indeed, all future Rulers (of the Máldive Islands—not to continue this Tribute, which was forbidden by their Religion and would bring a curse on their country.*

Sulṭán (Kaḷu) Muḥammad was a selfish, heartless, and deceitful tyrant, who had no love for his subjects, caring for them not at all, but ruling with an iron hand.

When he had resumed the throne, this Sulṭán imagined that he would have a long and peaceful reign. He gave no thought to the hidden future, or deemed that, when on his death-bed, there would be no one to help him.

Verily not long was it before the Messenger of Death appeared before him, and summoned him from the pomp and glory of his throne. His useless, emaciated body was consigned to the earth to rot. Persons avoided even the mention of his name. "For God, it is not difficult to do whatsoever seemeth good unto Him."

---

* See *infra*, p. 109.

This Sulṭán's (full) reign lasted thirty years and nine months, covering the three periods of his occupation of the throne.

His death occurred in *Hijra* 935.

58. 8. Hasan Shírází VIII.

(A.H. 935-55 : A.C. 1528-1549)

He was succeeded by his son, Ḥasan (VIII), born to a woman whom his father had brought as a concubine from Shiráz in Persia. For this reason, Ḥasan assumed the title of "As-Sulṭán Ḥasan As-Shírází."

He died in *Hijra* 955, after reigning for 21 years.

59. 8. Muhammad

(A.H. 955-57 : A.C. 1548-51)

Then Muḥammad, son of the half-brother of the Sulṭán last mentioned (Ḥasan VIII, 58), ascended the throne. His father was 'Umar Máfat Kilége, son of Sulṭán Kaḷu Muḥammad (50, 53, 57), son of Sulṭán 'Umar (45), son of Sulṭan Yúsuf (38), son of Sulṭán Hiláli Ḥasan (29).

2. SECOND PERIOD: A.C. 1550-1700

(3) *PORTUGUESE, &c., REFERENCES.*

The opening of the second half of the Sixteenth Century was to usher in at the Máldives perhaps the greatest revolution that has marred their fitful history—a *débâcle* culminating in the flight from the Islands of the last Sulṭán, caitiff, fracticide and apostate alike, of the Hiláli Dynasty which had occupied the throne, with little intermission, for more than a century and a half.

Let François Pyrard de Laval (one of the survivors of the ill-fated French ship "Corbin" wrecked on the Group in A.C. 1602, and captive at Málé for five years) tell, in his own intriguing fashion, the story—as he learnt it on the spot less than fifty years afterwards—of the abandonment of his Kingdom by Sulṭán Ḥasan (IX)—that brother-slayer and renegade, "inspired of God"—to find refuge at Cochin, and baptisement there as a Christian; followed by some account of the *bouleversement* which shortly ensued, and continued during the Portuguese occupation of the Islands for fifteen years and upwards from A.C. 1558*:—

FRANCOIS PYRARD DE LAVAL.

S. Hasan IX.

Titular Christian King.

About fifty years before this time the King of these Islands (S. Ḥasan IX), who was of noble and ancient lineage, seeing that he was but ill-obeyed, and was unable to withstand a formidable rival who wished to depose him, was inspired of God with a resolve to quit all.

He departed secretly with his wife and some of his family, without saying a word of his destination to anyone, and went straight to Cochin; where he became a Christian, along with his wife and some of his followers; sending back such as would not be baptized.

For this cause his rival, who was his near relative, was at once accepted as King. The name of the latter was *Haly* ('Ali) of the other *Assan* (Ḥasan). †

This former King, then, when he became a Christian at Cochin wrote word to all his subjects that they should become Christians and pay him their wonted tribute; otherwise he would come and see to it with a large army of Portuguese, who had promised him their aid.

The new King and the Máldive people made answer that they would no longer acknowledge him; that if aught was due to him he might come and get it; and that if he preferred to be a Christian he should remain where he was—as for them, they would sooner die than change their faith.‡

Hearing this, he asked the aid of the Viceroy of the Indies at Goa: who promised it; but on terms that he should not go in person, as it was feared that he would not agree with his people, or might bring the Portuguese into difficulties.

---

* Pyrard, *Voyage* (Hak. Soc., 1887, I, 244-51).

† S. 'Ali VI married 'Aishá Kabáfánu, daughter, by Buraki Rani, of S. Kalu Muhammad; S. Ḥasan IX was the latter's grandson through S. Ḥasan Shirázi VIII.

‡ The strict Muslim penalties for apostacy, originally enforceable—death to the man; for the woman incarceration—no longer rule generally.

The Portuguese armed force set out, but was not able to effect anything, losing a galley with three ships, and a goodly number of men ; and so were constrained to retire.

8. 'Ali VI.

Portuguese Capture Mále.

The following year they returned with a stronger force and better pilots, and the new King went out bravely to meet them, though he knew himself lost ; he might perhaps have escaped but he preferred to die in battle rather than to retreat with shame.*

He was vanquished and put to death, and the Portuguese made themselves masters of Mále ; where they built a Fortress, and thence sallied forth to compel the submission of the other Islands, and put many of the inhabitants to the sword.

Interregnum.

Then they assembled all the Chiefs of the Islands and told them they desired to leave them at peace, and not to constrain them in any way, nor to change their religion, if only they would pay the (titular) King his dues.

These terms being accepted, they left one of the Island Chiefs to govern, and to remain always at Mále with the Portuguese Commandant ; on terms that he should take no political measure but after consulting the Portuguese and the Island Chiefs, and that all the trade should be in the hands of the Portuguese alone.

The Governor appointed by the Portuguese to rule under them as Viceroy was a Lord, a native of the Islands and of their religion ; but he did everything in the name of the Christian King who lived in Portuguese territory.†

In this way the Portuguese ruled the Islands in peace for the space of ten years ; during which time the father of this King (presently reigning, Sulṭán Íbráhím III) and his (the former's) brother were *Catibes* (Khaṭíb), each of his own Island, but, with the pride of their race, would never submit to the Portuguese yoke, nor obey the Governor whom they had left in power.

* Fleeing in battle before the face of Infidels is classed among the seventeen *Kabira* or "great sins" of Islám. As the reward of those who fall fighting against Idolaters, Paradise is promised (*Qurán, Sura*, xlvii, 4-7).

† Regarding the birth, upbringing, and base character of this Portuguese Muslim, see *Monograph on the Máldives*, p. 27. § and Journal C.A.S., 1929, xxxi. 82. p. 413.

On the contrary, they rebelled and levied a force of men and galleys for war, and retired to the *Atollon* (Atol) *Ouadou* (Huvadú) otherwise *Souadou*, at the Southern extremity of the Islands, where the Portuguese dared not follow them, nor cross the *Candou* (M. *Kadu*) or Channel, of the said *Atollon*; so that neither this *Atollon* and the Islands belonging thereto, nor any to the South of that Channel were ever subject to the Portuguese.

These two brothers then built a strong Fort;* and being distant about eighty leagues from Mále, where the Portuguese were, they became in time so strong in men, arms, and ammunition, that they, as it were, held Mále and the Portuguese in check, so that they durst not come out without daily experiencing a harassing war.

This lasted for eight years, at the end of which arrived four galleys of Malabar corsairs for the purpose of war and pillage, as was their wont. The two brothers accosted them, and agreed with them to make war upon the Portuguese on terms of half the booty

Máldivians retake Mále.

So one day, getting word that the Captain of the Fortress and Island of Mále was gone to Cochin with a goodly number of Portuguese soldiers, they could not miss the opportunity, and resolved to attack the Fortress: which project they carried out so well, that one night they surprised it by escalade, and made themselves masters of the place, putting to death upwards of three hundred men that were within, and taking prisoner the Native Governor who was set there by the Portuguese.†

The place being taken and sacked, the Malabars, having got their agreed share of the spoil, were going home, leaving the two brothers masters of the town; but they, jealous to see so much of the riches of the Islands being carried off, resolved to attack the Malabars. This they did, and, after a long engagement, at length were left victorious, and got both the booty and the galleys, sending the men back to the Malabar coast; and thus repaid with treachery the good service they had of them.

---

* No known remains of any Fort exist in Huvadú (Suvádiva) penultimate Atol to the South. Probably Pyrard meant the old Fort on Hitadú Island of Addu, the Southernmost Atol, ruins of which are still to be seen. See *Monograph on the Máldives*, pp. 118, 121, 140.

† The "*Tárikh*" says he was killed. See *infra*, p. 120.

In this manner the two brothers became Kings of the Islands, and equally shared the throne without any quarrel between them.* They were both men of great valour, and were acknowledged as such by the people.

As for the Portuguese, they were indignant at the rebuff they had received at the Máldives, and were resolved to avenge it; so the next year they sent an army to the Islands, and carried on the war for a long time; but the two Kings defeated all their forces. This war lasted three years.

These Kings were very powerful, and possessed two Fortresses, that of Mále, and the other at the Atoll of *Souadou*, or *Ouadou*, in an Island called *Game*. †

At length both parties considered that it would be for the good of the country and of trade to come to some sort of understanding, rather than to continue this war to a doubtful issue.

Treaty between Portuguese and Máldivians.

Accordingly, they made a Treaty, with these conditions, viz., that the Máldive Kings and their people should be left in peace to possess the Islands in like manner as their predecessors, save that they should give a certain pension to their Christian King, his successors and heirs, to be rendered at Cochin, but without acknowledging him in any other way: on the other hand, the Mahometan Kings at the Islands should not be allowed to take the title and name of King ‡ though they were to be absolute in all things, but only that of Prince, Duke, or the like; also, that those two (brothers) only should be entitled to this name, in their language *Quilague* (*M. Kilége*), and that they should be responsible for the payment of the pension of the Christian King; who, on his part, was allowed to have a Factor there.

Furthermore, all natives of the Máldives desiring to traffic with other countries, were bound to take a passport from the Portuguese; as were all the other Indians that were at peace with them.

---

* Pyrard would seem to be wrong in speaking of an actual Duumvirate. The "*Tárikh*" merely states that, after his election as Sulṭán, Muḥammad Boḍu Takurufánu allotted "very responsible duties" to his brother and gave him the high title "*Raṇṇa Baḍéri Kilégefánu*.

† See *supra*, p. 89.

‡ *Brutum fulmen*. Every Máldive Ruler continued to style himself "*Sulṭán*" (Arabic) and "*Mahá Radun*" (Máldivian).

Such were the terms of this Peace, which has endured to the present day (A.C. 1619).

(4) *MÁLDIVIAN REFERENCES.*

The important events recorded by Pyrard, on the strength of oral tradition, appear set down by the compiler of the "*Táríkh*" with an unsophisticated charm, not free of that quaint romance and fervent religious tone so marked throughout this valuable, if strangely uneven, Muslim Chronicle.

"TÁRÍKH" CHRONICLE.

60. S. Hasan IX.

(A.H. 957 : A.C. 1550)

When he (S. Muḥammad, 59) had reigned for two years and four months, his brother Ḥasan seized the throne, after murdering him.

Having ruled for two years and five months, he determined to change his religion, and proclaimed his intention publicly in the 959 year of the *Hijra*.

Titular Christian King.

He then departed for Cochin, where he embraced the Infidels' Faith, and even adopted their mode of dress.

After residing there for two years, he went to Goa; where, some time afterwards, he married a Christian lady of good birth, by whom he had several children.

61. S. Abu Bakr II.

(A.H. 962 : A.C. 1554-55)

At the Máldives Abu Bakr (II), son of Íbráhím Fáṛiná Kilégefánu,* ascended the throne after a while. The name of his mother was Sanfá Diyo.

He reigned for four months, and died a martyr's death in *Hijra* 962.

62. S. 'Ali VI.

(A.H. 965 : A.C. 1557-58)

He was succeeded by 'Ali (VI), son of 'Abd-ur-Rahmán, Prime Minister. His mother's name was Sitti Kabádi Kilége of Feridú (Island, Ari Atol).

---

* More than probably the Chief of that name who aided "Buraki Rani" to secure the throne for "Kaḷu Muḥammad," by the murder of her brother, Sulṭán 'Ali V. See *infra*, p. 119, Note 5.

Ten months later he was killed in battle with the Christians.

Know the origin of this war.

The Sulṭán Ḥasan, who had become a Christian, desiring to convert the Maldivian Ministers and Chiefs, sent a Portuguese vessel to bring them to Cochin.

On arrival at Mále, the Captain of the vessel informed the Ministers, etc., that he had come there to remove them to Cochin at the request of their Sultan. The inhabitants held a meeting, and decided not to go, or obey the orders of their infidel Ruler. Then they fought the invaders, killing all of them, and seized their goods.

Those who took part in the fighting against these invaders were the aforesaid Sulṭáns Abu Bakr (II) and 'Ali (VI) with their supporters. All this took place before they came to the throne.

Again those (the Portuguese) at Cochin sent a fresh force, which also was defeated, and all slain by the Máldivians, who seized the ship with its entire cargo and arms.

For the third time, a force, fully armed, was conveyed in a great fleet to Mále, under the command of Captain Andiri Andiri.* Sultan 'Ali had then been on the throne for two months and fifteen days.

Portuguese Capture Mále : A.C. 1558.

The enemy landed one night on the West beach of Male with their cannon. Thereupon Sulṭán 'Ali accompanied by his soldiers, armed with swords, lances, bows and arrows, sallied forth to oppose the invaders. The Sulṭán, bearing sword and shield, marched at the head of his soldiers. He had gone as far as the *Íḍ* Mosque † when he found that the soldiers had all deserted him, with the exception of the Prime Minister and his personal attendant—the only two that remained with him. Then these three warriors, facing the enemy, charged them with the courage of lions. The foe astounded at their bravery ceased advancing, and, terror-stricken, began to fire on them from a distance, until they had killed all three.[6]

Then, without much resistance, they (the Portuguese) seized the Kingdom.

---

* See *supra*, p. 88.

† The *Ídu Miskit* at Mále is situated at the Western extremity of *Máfannu Avaru* (Ward): The Sulṭán visits it for worship, in full State, on *'Íd-ul-Fitr*, the annual Muslim "Lesser Festival."

Sulṭán 'Ali died in *Hijra* 965, at the end of the month Sh'abán. and Andiri Andiri ascended the throne.*

God knoweth better than we (men) what happened at that time.

Interregnum.

(A.H. 965-81 : A.C. 1558-73)

After seizing the Kingdom, Andiri Andiri declared himself Sulṭán of the Máldives.* He sent Christians to the different Atols to act as Headmen.

Thereafter, the invaders, strengthening their position, ruled for several years. They were a treacherous, cruel and iniquitous people. The sea ran red with Muslim blood. Property was seized publicly, and the people harshly treated. (The Muslim) Religion was persecuted during their rule, causing the Máldive people great sorrow. Pious persons were put to death ; looting and destruction became of common occurrence.

Then God took compassion on His people and decreed that they should be freed from the yoke of these foreigners. One of His servants, named Muḥammad Khaṭíb, son of Ḥusain Khaṭíb Takurufánu of Utímu (Island, Tiladummati Atol), was inspired by God to fight against them. He was a brave and powerful man, styled Muḥammad Boḍu Takurufánu, a name now famous—

> " O God, grant us strength to preserve this Shrine,
> " making it always redolent of scent and fragrance of
> " sweet-smelling flowers.
> " We pray God that He will keep our swords ever ready.

God inspired him (Muḥammad Khaṭíb) to fight with these Infidels in order that the Máldives might be freed from tyrants, and the enemies of Islám destroyed ; that peace might be spread amongst the inhabitants, the " fire of injustice extinguished," and the power of the Infidels be crushed.

This keen-sighted and wise personage Muḥammad Takurufánu, thus firmly resolved, earnestly prayed God to grant him the strength and will to accomplish what he planned. He took counsel with his brothers 'Ali Khaṭíb Takurufánu, and Ḥasan Khaṭíb Takurufánu, who agreed to join him.

* This assertion of the Chronicler is not borne out by Pyrard.

Getting together swords, guns, lances, bows and arrows, and accompanied by only a few friends, but trusting in God, they (the three brothers) ventured out on this great emprise. For the purpose they built a very fast-sailing vessel* which they loaded with arms, food and clothing, and set sail for Maliku (Minicoy Island); where they placed their families for safety.

Maliku belonged to *Áḷi Raja* of Kaṇṇanur.

When these men landed at Maliku they met two sage Máldivians named Ḥájí 'Ali and Ḥájí Ḥasan, brothers, who had been on pilgrimage to Mekka and Medína. These two men were masters of fence and javelin usage. They had gone the *Ḥajj* before the Christians invaded the Máldives.

Muḥammad Khaṭíb acquainted them of the conquest of the Máldives by the Christians, of the cruel treatment of Máldivians, and of the plan to wage war against the Christians; whereupon they consented to unite with him. Unanimously they elected Muḥammad Khaṭíb as leader, and swore by God that these Idolators and enemies of Islám, should be once for all exterminated, and their heads severed from their bodies; that they (the conspirators) would not desist until they had achieved their object; and that they would abide by the orders of Muḥammad Khaṭíb Takurufánu, and never desert him.

Then they offered prayers to God, inspired with courage by two verses of the *Qurán* :—

> "How often, by God's will, hath a small number
> "vanquished a numerous host. God is with the
> "patient."
>
> "Then We gave punishment to those who were guilty:
> "To help Believers (Muslims) is ever incumbent on Us."

Guerilla Warfare.

Thereafter they started warfare, and began to kill the Christians wherever they found them. They would land at an Island at night, and after killing the Christians, load their vessels with provisions and water, and depart early in the morning by sea. During daytime they concealed their vessels from the enemy; when night fell, they acted as before. 7

* For the tradition connected with this famous Máldivian vessel, "*Kaḷu Offumi*" *Oḍi*, see C. A. S. Journal, XXXI, 82, pp. 403, 412.

Albeit 'Ali Khaṭíb died the death of a martyr, the remaining (banded) four, in no wise disheartened, carried on the struggle successfully with renewed courage, under God's constant aid, until but few of their enemies were left alive.

When the Christians found their numbers dwindling, the remnant went to Mále, where they began to keep watch on the movements of this warrior band; which would approach Mále, sailing round it without finding a site to land, because the Island was so well guarded, sentinels being posted round the whole fortifications. They (the conspirators), therefore, left Mále for a while.

The Christians at Mále, thinking that they would never return, relaxed their watchfulness.

Meanwhile the band of Máldivians went to Kaṇṇanúr, and obtained from *Áḻi Rája* a sufficient force of soldiers; with which they returned to Mále on the very day, on which the Infidels had decided to command all the Islanders to become Christians and worship their idols, under threat of death on refusal.

That very night the (Mále) Islanders held a meeting at which they agreed to die in their Faith. They assembled in the house of the *Qázi* Abu Bakr, son of Don Kurali Faḍiyáru Takurufánu, son of Sharaf-ud-ḍín Ismá'il Fámudéri Faḍiyáru Takurufánu; and vowed not to obey Andiri Andiri's command to embrace his religion, but to fight to the death against those sent to compel them. They then collected knives, swords, lances, bows and arrows, and even clubs, and prepared to meet their enemies.

Then Muḥammad Khaṭíb made a vow that, if they succeeded in retaking Mále from the Christians, he would recite the *Maulud** to the Prophet every year near the Shrine of Shaikh Yúsuf of Tabríz.

Máldivians retake Mále: A. C. 1573.

The same night, after offering prayers to the Omniscient God, when two-thirds of the night had passed, Muḥammad Khaṭíb Takurufánu anchored off Mále, and landed when the Christians were making merry with song and carousal.[8]

---

* *Mawlud.* The ceremonies and service on the anniversary of the Prophet's birth.

The real, or suppositions, *Ziyárat* Shrine (*Medu Miskit*) of Shaikh Yúsuf of Tabríz, the Apostle of Islám to the Máldives in mid-Twelfth Century, stands on the South side of Henvéru Mái Magu street opposite to *Hukuru Miskit*, Mále's Chief Mosque.

Andiri Andiri's supporters then emerged and began to fire on the Muslims, who returned the fire. The fusilade of the Christians was unavailing but the Muslim's fire began to take effect. The fighting continued until God weakened the Christians, and they offered to surrender. Many had already died, and the survivors were mortally wounded.

The calamity, fear and sorrow, which they (the Portuguese) suffered, were sympathised in neither by Heaven nor Earth, which wept not for them. Their rule and power proved as transcient as sunbeams. Their name was detested by the people, and their might had departed for ever.

They had been masters of the Máldives for seventeen years.

This famous combat was fought, and won, in *Hijra* 981 on the 1st day of the month Rabi-ul-Awwál by Muḥammad Khaṭíb Takurufánu, the Great (who uttered this prayer):—

> "May God the All-knowing keep them (Máldivians) ever in the True Religion of His gracious Prophet." *

63. S. Gházi Muhammad Bodu Takurufánu

(A.H. 981-93 : A.C. 1573-85)

There was rejoicing then in all parts of the Máldive Islands; and, by the Grace of God, the Sulṭánate fell to Muhammad Khaṭíb Takurufánu, the Great.

> " God giveth power to whomsoever He pleaseth.
> " Of His creatures some He raiseth to high place;
> " others doth He beggar.
> " Heaven and Earth are subject unto God's rule, for
> " God is Almighty."

The long-suffering Muslims, their faces radiating happiness, assembled before the Great Takurufánu, who came to meet them, his broad brow bright with light sufficient to fill the four corners of the world. They kissed his hands and offered prayers that his rule might long continue. He, in turn, offered prayers for the prosperity and health of his subjects.

They (the Islanders) then took the oath of allegiance to him as Sulṭán.

---

* The Arabic (transcript) runs:—*Va da'u il-Allah-is-sami 'l. 'Alim an yasbita hum fi Din-il-Qavim* va millat in-*Nabi-il Karim*.. For rough adapted "slogan" in English, see *supra*, p. 76.

After he acquired the throne, he built a Palace, made regulations for the Government of the country, and reduced all into order.

Upon his younger brother Ḥasan Khaṭíb was bestowed the title of *Raṇṇa Baḍéri Kilégefánu* with very responsible duties.

(5) *PORTUGUESE, &c., REFERENCES.*

Of the Revolution at the Máldives in A.C. 1550, and its immediate aftermath, Bartoli, a Jesuit Historian, has written :—

S. Hasan IX.

"There sprang up, I know not why, between the Máldivians and their Lord, a youth of twenty years (S. Ḥasan IX), discord and war; and he, finding himself unable to stand the force of the conspiracy, saved his life, though he could not his Kingdom, by flight to Cochin, where he trusted to obtain his reinstatement by aid of the Portuguese arms.

"The Fathers received him into their House; and S. Francis Xavier (who opportunely arrived there), instructed him as far as needful, and solemnly baptised him."*

Regarding the subsequent fate of the exiled Sulṭán Ḥasan IX, and the titular Máldivian Royalties of his family during the century succeeding the Mále Revolution, Portuguese archives at Lisbon and Goa, supplemented by other authorities, afford casual glimpses—mostly of the abject mercenary side—of these *rois en peintre*.

Abandoning, after three years' abortive effort, all attempts to force a Christian King upon the Islanders, since their recapture of Mále in A.C. 1573, the Portuguese resorted to utilising Treaty claims of the banished family as justification for extracting needful supplies of produce (chiefly coir) for their own needs.

On their part, the individual Princes eked out petty lives, wholly inglorious and at times sinking to lowest depths of moral turpitude, as half-caste pensioners in an alien land.

---

* *Asia* III, 201-2. The Sulṭán's conversion is attributed by other writers to Padre Antonia Heredia (or Eredia.)

The sorry account, condensed and co-ordinated below, of "*Dom Manoel*," ex-Máldive Sulṭán Ḥasan IX, and his ill-starred projeny living in India until extinguished finally in A.C. 1655, appears for the most part in *Hakluyt Society Pyrard, II, Appendix B.*

TITULAR MÁLDIVIAN CHRISTIAN KINGS.

Máldivian lady = **Dom Manoel** = Portuguese lady
(ex-Sulṭán Ḥasan IX)

Dom Francisco | **Dom João** = Dona Francisca Vasconellos | **Dom Pedro** | Daughters

Dom Philippe | Dona Inez = a *Fidalgo*

Dom Luis | (?) **Dom Malavis**

Dom Manoel.

Dom Manoel's Máldivian wife became a professing Christian at Cochin; but he also married a young Portuguese lady of much virtue and noble blood.

His family comprised three sons, (who adopted the Portuguese names Dom Francisco, Dom João, and Dom Pedro), besides one daughter at least.

In regard to his virtual tribute to Portugal, Don Manoel was treated not unfairly.

"As for the Christian King, "says Pyrard," he gave a third part of his revenue to the King of Portugal. This revenue consists of cowries and coir, which is rope made of the coco-tree.

"They (the Máldive Kings) send every year at their own expense four ships, of a hundred and fifty tons burthen each, laden with it; that is at the risk of the Máldivians until the ships get beyond the Banks at the (Northern) end of the Islands—beyond that point, the risk is with the Christian King."*

* Pyrard, *loc. cit.* I, 250-51.

Dom Manoel was, however, permitted to exercise occasionally "sovereign rights," in addition to the extent of granting, at Cochin, "Letters Patent" to Portuguese exploiters of "voyages" (privilege of trade in the East to a private vessel) on their own account, subject to confirmation by the Viceroy at Goa.*

But repeated appeals made by him to the King of Portugal for reinstatement on the Máldive throne were studiously ignored. "Ever hoping to regain his own, Dom Manoel lived and grew old in privacy at Cochin; and finally died in great affliction about A.C. 1583, when fifty years old and upwards."

His widowed Queen was granted proper provision for herself and her daughter.

Dom Francisco.

Of the sons, Dom Francisco, the eldest, who had sailed for Europe with a returning Portuguese fleet, met a violent death in a brawl, A.C. 1581 at Lisbon; where he had gone to make representations at Court concerning the petitions of his father.

Dom João.

The titular sovereignty thus passed to Dom João. This Prince proved a thorn in the side of the Portuguese, as testified by the Royal Despatches :—

"I am informed by you that the King of the Islands," wrote the King of Spain (Philip II)† to the Viceroy (Despatch, February 6th, 1589), "that the King of the Islands has married a sister of Antonio Teixeira de Macedo, against your opinion.

"Owing to his excesses and misconduct in the married state, I think it well done on your part not to have delivered my Letter to him; and that you ought to

* *Arch. Port. Or.* Fasc. V, No. 350.

† Philip II. of Spain annexed Portugal in A.C. 1581. Seven years later (A.C. 1588) he made the disastrous attempt to conquer England with the Great Armada.

endeavour to train this King, who, as you know, is very young, in all the affairs of my service ; and also in those which will be serviceable to himself in order that he may know how to govern well."

Request made by Dom João for assurance of 200 *cruzados* increase to his wife's pension, out of the Máldivian revenue accruing to him, was met by semi-refusal.

"I deem it undesirable to yield to his request," runs the Despatch of March 8th, 1589, "without information from you as to his present conduct."

Dom Joao and his younger brother Dom Pedro seem to have paid no heed to Royal admonitions. For, two years later, a stern Despatch of January 12th, 1591, whilst waiving deserved death penalty closes with the definite order for their solitary incarcaration:—

"I approve that execution be suspended on the King and his brother, although their misdeeds merit natural death ; but I ordain that they be kept in prison separately, and securely, until my further pleasure be known."

But the pension of the King's wife was increased from 500 to 700 *pardaos* a year.

The two Princes were held in pseudo-honorary confinement for ten years at Goa, where they had been transferred. They constantly clamoured for freedom and permission to return to Cochin ; but all appeals availed nothing, and they remained, by orders from Spain, under the immediate surveillance of the Viceroy—"the misdeeds committed by the brothers when at Cochin having been so outrageous, and so scandalised the whole of India, that it were better not to speak of them."

There is an unfortunate hiatus in the Royal Despatches between A.C. 1598-1606.

Dom Philippe.

The death of Dom João occurred during the Vice-Royaltyship of Ayres de Saldaña, A. C. 1601-04.

Pyrard was at Mále when Dom Adrian de Gouveia went there, about A.C. 1605-06, as Portuguese Ambassador of the exiled King Dom Philippe,* a boy of thirteen, son and successor of Dom João.

In A.C. 1606 Dom Philippe complained to the King of Spain that the revenues from the Islands had dwindled to 5,000 from 18,000 *xeraphins* in the time of his grandfather Dom Manoel and his father Dom João, owing to the negligence of the Viceroys.

He begged that he be granted :—(*a*) A salaried honorary office in order to maintain his position; (*b*) a suitable pension, with other assets for his staff,; and (*c*), as virtual dowry to his sister Dona Inez, that her projected husband be made "Captain" for three years of one of the Portuguese Fortresses; concluding, characteristically, with the modest requests that (*d*) orders be given that no Captain, *Vedor da Fazenda*, or other official, of Cochin or elsewhere in Malabar (under pain of chastisement and suspension from office) be permitted to enquire into the merchandise brought from the Islands by his vessels; and (*e*) that the Viceroy should equip an armada to bring the Islands into greater obedience, that so he (Don Filippe) might acquire a greater revenue—otherwise that he be excused from further payment of tribute under the Treaty.

To this "nothing venture, nothing have" petition the King (Philip III) yielded concessions; but not till three years later (Despatch, November 4th, 1609) :—

(*a*), (*b*) To Dom Philippe was granted one habit of Christ, and therewith a pension of 150 *pardaos* payable from Ceylon sources; (*c*) his sister Dona Inez might be married to a *Fidalgo* of standing and appointable to the "Captaincy" of a Canara Fortress; (*d*) in regard to revenue, the *Vedor da Fazenda* at Cochin would be directed to take, from

* See *infra*, p. 106.

the Máldive consignments brought over, only so much coir as was needed for the public service; (*e*) *Áḷi Rája* (*Adarrajao*) of Kaṇṇanúr was to be warned not to meddle with the Máldive Islands and Dom Philippe's property, and (*f*) finally, the pension of the Queen-Mother, Dona Francisca, might be raised from 700 *pardaos* to 1,000 a year, but without the grant of a "voyage."

The not illiberal, if dilatory, terms accorded by the European Monarch did not satisfy the young Prince and his mother; who persisted in pressing for further concessions.

Again the King, some two years later (Despatch, March 28th, 1612), exercised a certain generosity :—

(*a*) Dom Philippe's allowance was increased to 200 *milreis*; (*b*) the Fortress of Daman, instead of Canara, was granted for three years to the husband of Dona Inez; (*c*) the pension of Dona Francisca might be paid in silk; (*d*) further pressure would be put upon the Rája of Kaṇṇanúr not to interfere; also (*e*) a reliable Agent would be sent to the *de facto* Máldive Ruler threatening him with invasion, in failure of better fulfilment of the Treaty; and (*f*), lastly, the officials of Malabar would be debarred from issuing trade passports to the Máldives on their own account.

Interesting side-lights are cast on Dom Philippe by a few Europeans then in India.

(1) FRANÇOIS PYRARD DE LAVAL.

Pyrard, who became acquainted with him and his mother whilst at Goa (A.C. 1608-10), after the Frenchman's deliverance from captivity at the Máldives, records :—

"I have seen at Goa the grandson of that Christian King Dom Manoel, aged fifteen years, with his Portuguese mother. He is named Dom Philippe. The Portuguese gave him the title of Majesty calling him 'King of the

Máldives,' and honour and respect him greatly. The King of Spain gives a pension both to him and to his mother.

"They were lodged near the Jesuits' College, in a very handsome house.

"The little King has a suit against his uncle Dom Paulo (Pedro) who resides at Cochin, and is married there; for that he also calls himself 'King of the Máldives.'

"This uncle is married to a *Metice* (half-caste) lady, nobly born and vastly rich, who maintains him in comfort; for without her he has only his pension from the King, which is small, and very often—indeed usually—but badly paid."*

(II) PIETRO DELLE VALLE.

The next notice of Dom Philippe, as far as known, is found in the discursive Letters of the Roman Traveller, Pietro della Valle.

In describing the Feast of St. John the Baptist, which he witnessed at Goa in A.C. 1623, he writes :—

"I went to see the sight in the Street of St. Paul, at the house of one whom they call the 'King of the *Máldiva* or *Máladiva* Islands.'

"Of these Islands an ancestor of this man was actually King; but being driven from his country by his own people, he betook him to the Portuguese, and became a Christian, in the hope of getting back to his own country and regaining it with their aid. But the Portuguese taking no steps in his behalf, he and his descendants remained thenceforth deprived of their Kingdom and with the empty title alone, which, the Portuguese, having formed connections with them, still preserve to them; and, since a number of merchant vessels come from these Islands to the Portuguese ports, they compel them to pay a little tribute, as it were, to their legitimate Lord, who thus (albeit the Harbour Officials, through whom the transaction is necessarily conducted, appropriate more than one-half) draws at the present day about 3,000 *crowns*, and therewith supports himself."†

* Pyrard, *loc. cit.* II, 293-4.

† *Viaggi*, Pt. 3, Letter iii. (English ed., II, 606).

Portuguese Attack on Mále: A.C. 1631 (or 1632).

So pressingly did Dom Philippe continue to pester the Government of Spain for active support towards securing full, and more punctual, payment of his Máldive revenues, that in A.C. 1631 or 1632 the Viceroy was ordered by the Spanish King (Philip III) to send an Expedition to the Islands.

Fifteen ships, under the command of Domingos Ferreyra Belliago, Chief Captain of Canara, sailed direct for Mále.

"But the King of the Máldives was advised of the coming of the Armada, and when it arrived he was well fortified; The only entrance to the Island (Mále) was blocked with ships; and it was more impossible to enter by any other way, because the whole Island is encircled by rocks and reefs, as may be seen by the (accompanying) Plan, with the mode of the Fortification.

"For some days the said Armada fired upon it (Mále) with cannon, and then seeing it was impossible to force an entrance, and that the time spent was all wasted, returned to Goa." *

(III) PHILIPPUS A SANCTÂ TRINITATE.

The only other mention of Dom Philippe so far forthcoming is made by Philippus a Sanctâ Trinitate, Carmelite monk, who was at Goa, A.C. 1631-1639, and often interviewed him :—

"He was of a middling colour, that is somewhat dark and tanned, after the black skin of his father, with some of the whiteness of his mother.

"It was arranged that he should come to Europe with me, for he believed that by his presence he could obtain of the King of Spain what he failed to get by letters, seeing, as he saw, that either the commands were not efficacious or that he was mocked in India.

"As only some of the Islands persevered in acknowledging his sovereignty he had not much revenue.

---

* *Ressende*, Sloane MS 197, fol. 377, See *infra*, p. 107.

"He died while yet young and unmarried, leaving as his successor (to the titular sovereignty of the Islands) a nephew on his sister's side; though his father's brother (Don Pedro), in reliance upon the laws and customs of the Máldive Kingdom and the acceptance by the people * claimed the throne as rightfully his in a lawsuit still pending. †

(IV) FRANCISCO DE SOUSA.

The pitiable end of this ill-fated family of exiled Máldive Kings is given by Franciso de Sousa :—

"The last King of the Máldives was Dom Luis de Sousa,‡ who on the 22nd October, 1653, attempted with other *Fidalgos*, (gentry) to depose the Viceroy, Dom Vasco Mascarenhas, Conde de Obidos. For this cause he was imprisoned at Mormugao until the 10th November, A.C. 1655, in the Viceroyalty of Dom Rodrigo Lobo da Silveyra, Conde de Sarzedas; and for the same cause was sent a prisoner to Portugal in the ship "Nossa S. de Grava," in the year A.C. 1656.

"The ship, dismasted in a storm off the Cape of Good Hope, put back to Mozambique, but, before reaching port, the King was dead.

"He left no legitimate successor; and named the King of Portugal as his heir to the Eleven Thousand Islands." §

(6) *MÁLDIVIAN REFERENCES.*

The only notices of contact with the Portuguese during this period occurring in Máldivian Chronicles relate to the two hostile Expeditions against the Máldives, despatched respectively, in (i) A.C. 1631 (or 1632), during the course of the reign of Sulṭán Muḥammad 'Imád-ud-dín I (A.C. 1620-48), and that (ii)—the last effort of the Portuguese, already losing their hold in the East, to conquer the Islands—which his son Sulṭán

* "The *Laws and Customs* of the Máldive Islands," together with the definite "*Acceptance by the People*," still stand as the absolute recognised *Lex Scripta* and *Inscripta* governing the *Right of Succession, &c., to the Máldive Throne*. See Papers connected with the First, and Second, Accession of the present Sulṭán, Muḥammad Shams-ud-din III, in 1893 and 1903 (*Máldive Islands*, Part I).

† Latin Ed., 1649, 98; French Ed., 1652, 226.

‡ Probably son of Dona Inez, sister of Don Philippe, see *infra*

§ Franciso de Sousa, *Oriente Conquistado*, C.D., 67.

Ibráhím Iskandar I (A.C. 1648-87) had to meet in A.C. 1650, very shortly after mounting the throne.

Although not mentioned in the "*Tárikh,*" Pyrard's account, as that of a personal witness at Mále itself, *circa* A.C. 1606 of the Embassy sent to Sulṭán Ibráhím III by the titular boy King of the Máldives, may not unfitly find insertion here. A semi-Máldivian record, of historic interest, it throws additional light on the contemptible character of the Máldive Ruler of the day, who ere long met a deservedly tragic death at the hands of Malabar Mápiḷḷas. *

FRANÇOIS PYRARD DE LAVAL.

S. Ibráhím III : A.C. 1585-1609.

Portuguese Embassy to Mále : A.C. 1606 circa.

" About a year before we left the Máldives, there came to the King (Sulṭán Ibrahím III) an Ambassador from the Christian King of these Islands, who lived at Goa; of whom I have already spoken. This Ambassador was a Portuguese, and told me he had been at Rochelle in France. He was about fifty years of age, and was named Dom Adrien de Gouia. He came in considerable state, accompanied by some other Portuguese and Christian Indians.

" The subject of his visit was a certain dispute which existed between that young Christian King and his uncle, Dom Paulo (Dom Pedro), who resided at Cochin, the latter wanting to take part of the tribute coming to the said King.

" A suit was pending about it in the Parliament at Goa for a long time, during which this Dom Paulo enjoyed the receipt of it—for, under the Treaty of Peace, the Máldivians were not obliged to pay the tribute elsewhere than at Cochin, where the uncle was.

" At length, the Parliament of Goa having ordained that the Christian King, Dom Philippe, should have of the Máldive King and all the Chiefs of the country a certificate to the effect that they recognized him as the King, he therefore sent this Embassy with a quantity of presents.

" But the Máldive King took but little notice of it, and the Ambassador waited there for two months without getting an audience; such was the pride and haughtiness of this

* See Journal C.A.S., 1930 : XXXI, 83, pp. 561, 565.

King in a matter wherein he perceived no gain for himself; and when he was got to do business with them, his demeanour was exceeding proud. In fine, it was four months ere the Ambassador got his despatch; which was granted, when he asked it, with offerings of the rarest gifts. as well from his master as from himself."*

Of the assaults on Mále made during the first half of the Seventeenth Century, the "*Táríkh*" alludes to (i) the first and more formidable, with not unjustifiable pride, accompanied, *more Máldivico*, by pious Muslim comments; whilst (ii) the second attack is dismissed in contemptuously incisive words, spiced with some diverting braggardism.

"TÁRÍKH" CHRONICLE.

8. Muhammad 'Imád-ud-dín I: A.C. 1620-48.

Portuguese Attack on Mále: A.C. 1631, circa.

In the fifth year of his reign, A.H. 1034, a Portuguese named "*Balayágu*" came to the Máldives with a large fleet, fully manned and armed, to attack Sulṭán Muhammad 'Imád-ud-dín (I, A.H. 1029-58).

Then the Sulṭán, summoning his Vazirs and soldiers, obtained from them an oath to fight against the Portuguese fearlessly without fleeing; thus inspiring them with courage. His *Qází*, Muḥammad Fadiyáru Takurufánu, son of Ḥasan Naibu Takurufánu of Mídú (Island, Addù Atol), also encouraged them.

At the time there were neither Fort walls nor Bastions; nor many cannon. They (the Islanders) had only five guns, † yet did not they display any signs of cowardice during the fight.

The Portuguese commenced to fire the cannon mounted on their vessels; but God protected the inhabitants against the bombardment. The cannon shots fired from the Mále Forts hit both vessels and men of the enemy

God filled the hearts of the foe with fear, so that they fled from Mále terror-stricken. The people of Mále ceased not firing until the enemy fled

* Pyrard, *loc. cit.* I, 293-4.

† *Ressende*, with exaggeration not unexpected, shows thirteen canon, seven unmounted, and six simultaneously firing on the ships, from rough ramps and a central Bastion, where three flags fly (Plate III).

In the course of their flight the Portuguese burned the Mosque in Viligili Island. They returned to Goa wholly disheartened.

Sulṭán Muḥammad 'Imád-ud-dín and his subjects obtained the victory over their enemy; albeit they had fewer cannon and soldiers than the foe.

God gave them the victory: to God that is no hard matter; for hath He not said in the *Qurán* :—" He, the Mighty and the Merciful, helpeth whom He pleaseth."

This battle took place in *Hijra* 1034.

Thereafter, to supplement the Palace fortifications, he (the Sulṭán) built a Bastion provided with embrasures and called " *Boḍu Kóṭṭe*." He also built other Bastions in different parts of Mále, and, between every two (curtain), walls entrances and crenelles so as to prevent a foreign foe from invading the Island.*

Then he constructed a (partially) encircling Breakwater, leaving only gaps sufficient to allow passage to *dóṇis* and *oḍis*. This breakwater is to be seen at this day.

Thus did he make of Mále a Fortress very strongly defended.

Further, he equipped a large vessel and sent it to Achin to procure some big cannon: it brought to Mále fourteen bronze guns.

Subsequently, by the grace of God, this Sulṭán recovered from ships wrecked in different parts of his dominions a large number of cannon. For as soon as vessels are wrecked, they are deserted by those on board; who make for the Malabar Coast of India in small boats, taking only money and light articles and abandoning their cannon and other goods. It was in this way that Sulṭán Muḥammad 'Imád-ud-dín acquired a large quantity of cannon and other property.

8. Ibráhím Iskandar I: A.C. 1648-87.

Portuguese Attack on Mále: A.C. 1650.

In the second year† of his reign Dom Laviz and Dom Malaviz came in ships to attack the Máldives. They were brothers and reported to be the two sons of the daughter of

* Twelve Bastions in all at this day; two completely demolished; others virtually abandoned. The *Bodu Kóṭṭé* (main Bastion), and *Ñána Buruzu*, alone mount guns—but of very limited, if any, effectiveness.

† The *Tárikh* gives "9th year, A.H. 1059," wrongly.

Sultán Hiláli Hasan (IX), who became an Infidel and went to Goa.*

Information being brought to Sultán Iskandar of the advent of these brothers, with several vessels fully armed, the Sultán bethought him of fighting them; and summoned to the Palace his three half-brothers † and the Ministers. After consulting them he decided to oppose the invaders.

When the Muslims (Máldivians) began to fire on these Infidels, God granted them the victory over their enemy. Don Malaviz was killed in the attack, his brother Don Laviz wounded, and several of those who accompanied them were also killed. The few survivors withdrew their Fleet without accomplishing their object, and sailed away.

This great and famous battle was fought in the *Hijra* era year 1059.

These people (the Portuguese) had not the courage to come again to (attack) the Máldives.

After this episode the (Tribute) payment was stopped that had been made since the reign of Sultan Hiláli (Kaḷu) Muhammad grandfather of the Sultán who became an Infidel and went to Goa.

Sultán Iskandar having gained this victory no longer paid the stipulated sums of money, either to the Portuguese or *Áḷi Rája* of Kaṇṇanúr.‡

This Sultán (Iskandar Íbráhím I) made the Máldives independent, and himself became a great ruler.

3. THIRD PERIOD: A.C. 1700-1930.

From the first, the three objects of the Portuguese in the East were "Conquest, Commerce and Conversion"; and for all three their central position on the Malabar Coast served them well.

Between A.C. 1500 and 1600 they enjoyed the monopoly of Oriental Trade; but towards the close of the Sixteenth Century decadence was setting in and they could

* Sons of Dona Inez, grand-daughter of ex-Sultán Ḥasan IX.

† Muhammad *Doriméná*, Ḥasan *Fáriná*, and a third unnamed; sons of Queen 'Aishá Kabáfánu by S. Ḥusain II, *Fámudéri Kilégefánu*. She subsequently married S. Muhammad 'Imád-ud-dín I, to whom she bore S. Iskandar Íbráhím I. Her first husband had been the despicable Sultán Íbráhím III, well-known to Pyrard.

‡ See *supra*, p. 85.

scarcely hold their own against native enemies. The State itself derived little gain from trade profits, while it had to bear continuously great strain in men and money for needs of the East

Portugal had been incorporated with Spain in A.C. 1581 by Philip II after the battle of Alcantara; and the conditions during the "Sixty Years Captivity" (A.C. 1581-1640) under three Spanish Sovereigns, Philip II, III, IV, were not wholly ended until the coronation of João IV of Braganza as King of Portugal in A.C. 1640, followed forty years later, by the Spanish renouncement of claim in A.C. 1683; finally breaking an unhappy coalescence which had ever inured to the disadvantage of the Portuguese.

At many parts of the world the English, French and, in particular, the Dutch had begun to harass Portuguese trade, and seize their possessions.

Before the end of the Seventeenth Century the Dutch (who had gradually established Factories on the Continent of India, in Ceylon, Sumatra, and the Moluccas (as well as on the Persian Gulf and Red Sea), ruled without rival, and gradually expelled the Portuguese from almost all their territorial possessions.

The further history of the Portuguese in India is a distressing chronicle of pride, poverty and misfortune. Pressed by native Rulers upon the land, on the sea they gave way to more vigorous European enterprise.*

Little wonder, therefore, that the humble and isolated Máldive Islands escaped further hostile attention from the Portuguese after A.C. 1650, falling, as they were, steadily from supreme power in the Orient.

With delightful naiveté the Máldivian Chronicler, writing not many years later, says that after the last Portuguese

* Encyclopaedia Britannica; Imperial Gazetteer of India, II, 451.

ineffectual bombardment of Mále in A.C. 1650 "these people dared not to come again to attack the Máldīves."

But that sullen hatred and dread of this persistent Infidel enemy still continued to exercise the minds of the Islanders, is borne out forcibly by an Arabic Inscription carved in A.H. 1087—nearly forty years after the later attack—on a Bastion in Mále Fort, which frankly sets out that the express purpose of its erection was to serve as "a bulwark to repel the accursed *Farángi*." *

Time is a mighty soother: before the lapse of a further century from A.C. 1650, all open rancour at least had melted between these once bitterest of foes, so long bent on internecine struggle at every encounter.

(7.) *MÁLDIVIAN REFERENCE.*

8. Íbráhim Iskandar II: A.C. 1721-50.

Portuguese Missives from the Sultán.

How friendly—superficially at least—had become mutual relations, a side-light, as intereesting as unexpected, was furnished by the discovery among the Colombo Archives in the Eighties of last century of three Missives from the reigning Máldive Sulṭán (Íbráhím Iskandar II, A.C. 1723-1750), sent under his Royal Seal and Signature, to the Dutch Governors at Colombo (A. Moll with Council, and Dedrick Van Domburgh, respectively) in A.C. 1723 and 1734, 1735.

These Letters, strange as it may seem, were indicted—of all foreigners—by Portuguese scribes—, in all probability, Captains, &c., of vessels trading to Mále.

The unique Missives relate mainly to the reciprocal trade (rice and spices *versus* cowries) between the Dutch in Ceylon and the Máldive Islands.

Indirectly they bring out the proverbial mercenary spirit of the Hollanders, and the disgusted acquiescence of

* See *infra*, p. 124. A century earlier the Portuguese poet Camoens, (*Luciads* I, 99), had, for his part, paid all Muslimáns as hearty a compliment—"the malignant crew who follow the base Mahomet" (*malina gente que seque o torpe Mafamede*).

the Máldive Sultán, forced to accept, with very obvious reluctance, the unconscionable bargains made by a fresh European race too powerful to resist—grinding terms which may possibly have driven the Máldivian Ruler to fraternise with the Portuguese, quondam deadly foe of the Islanders.*

With this sole minor piece of evidence so far bronght to light in proof of amicable intercourse, nominal at any rate if not more, between Máldivians and Portuguese, the curtain falls on all further known relations for still another century—to be lifted again but once more, and that under unwonted—and in one sense happy—circumstances, viz., on the occasion of the Portuguese Merchantman "Prazer e Allegria" being wrecked on the Máldive Islands in A.C. 1844.

(8.) *PORTUGUESE, &c., REFERENCES.*

8. Muhammad 'Imád-ud-din IV: A.C. 1835-1882.

Wreck of "Prazer e Allegria" on the Máldives: A.C. 1844.

The account of the disaster, and its satisfactory sequel, puts *finis* to the long chapter of checquered history, opening with ruthless emphasis in A.C. 1503, and closing four centuries and upwards later with "the Star of Peace" risen brightly upon two alien races, each worshipping one and the same God under differing lights, for whom finally

"Grim-visaged War has smooth'd his wrinkled front."

The wreck of the "Prazer e Allegria" in A.C. 1844, has been the last occasion on which Portuguese and Máldivians have come into touch at the Islands.

The following details, somewhat curtailed, of the disaster are taken from a translation of the statement made to the English Commandant at Galle by Major Manuel Guides de

* A cyclone, which struck the Northern Máldive Atols in October, 1733, overwhelmed many Islands, with great loss of inhabitants and boats. The heavy calamity was bowed to by the Máldive Ruler with Muslim resignation (*Mas em tudu consolo com vertrade de Deus*).

Quinhones,* who sailed from Portugal in charge of a large body of Convicts and "Relief" of Officers and others:—

"I have to communicate events connected with the wreck of the Merchant Ship 'Prazer e Allegria.'

"Freighted in Lisbon, on account of the Portuguese Government, to convey to Goa eighty-four (84) Convicts, and five (5) Lieutenants (one, A. J. de Soyza Alvia, belonging to the Army in Portugal, with his wife), two First Sergeants, a Writer (A. J. de Silva Milheirio) of the Custom House of Mozambique, and myself, as Major and Governor of Bahiá de Lorenzo Marques, with my wife and three children.

"We left Lisbon on November 8th, 1843, and reached the Cape of Good Hope without other mishap than the death from scurvy of twenty-nine (29) Convicts.

"On March 16th, 1844, between 8 and 9 in the morning we discovered, to leeward, seven Islands, all in a line, and one Island ahead. The Captain told us that they were the Máldives. He continued on the same course, the current then running three miles an hour towards land. At half past one o'clock in the afternoon, the boatswain inquired of the Captain whether he wished to tack; but was directed to continue on the same course.

"At about 4 o'clock in the evening the ship was so near land that we could see the people distinctly; and it was then that a little boat manned by blacks, and with an English Jack fixed at the poop, came off from one of the Islands. Approaching the ship one of the Moors pointed towards a channel which lies between three or four Islands. The Captain hailed the Moors, and told them to come on board; but seeing the Convicts they immediately departed through fear, lowering the Jack.

"Thus we were committed to the current, which every moment drove us much nearer land, and upon a reef of coral which lies opposite the second Island. The night was dark, and there was lightning; the breakers dashed incessantly on the sides of the ship, forcing her more and more on to the reef; at length the rudder broke, and the ship rested; but a large leak was sprung. All of us worked the pumps, but it was impossible to reduce the water.

* The original Statement in Portuguese of Major de Quihones and the Sultán's Missive to the Ceylon Government on the subject, are not forthcoming.

"At about 11 o'clock the cock-boat was let down; in which work we had laboured a good deal, as she had been much obstructed by the rigging. The Captain ordered the sailors to take soundings all round: they found the depth was seven (7) fathoms, and cast a small anchor. Upon this we all hauled on the cable, with a view to save the ship: in this manner were we engaged until daybreak, expecting every moment to become victims.

"The morning of the 18th saw us surrounded by reef shelves. The Captain having had the cock-boat manned despatched it towards the channel above mentioned. It finally landed on the third Island, which was some two leagues distant.

"The cock-boat having returned to the ship all the passengers and crew were saved.

"This Island is called *Muḷi** and is ruled by a Moor named Íbráhím, who is under subjection to the Sulṭán. The place near which we were wrecked is called *Muḷi Faḷu*.

"On the following day, the Captain despatched the cock-boat, the long boat, and a hired *katamaran* in order to procure more provisions, if possible; but all the three boats were sunk by the billows. The Convicts (who had been rowing), and a sailor, were drowned; the rest, with much difficulty saved their lives by swimming.

"Having remained five days on the Island of *Muḷi* the ship-wrecked survivors one hundred and four (104) in number went on to 'King's Island,' where the Sulṭán resides. We were kindly received, and provided with a house and such food as could be had in the country.†

"The Sulṭán‡ promised to have us conveyed, in his own vessels, to Goa, after one month, it being impossible for him to do so earlier.

---

* It is difficult to fix this Island's position in the absence of any clue to Latitude or Longitude, or the name of the particular Atol to which it belongs. There is a *Muḷi* Island in *Mulaku Atol*, but it lies on the Eastern reef, whilst the Portuguese Transport should ordinarily have encountered the Máldives from the West, voyaging round the Cape of Good Hope.

† For amplest confirmation regarding the never-failing humanity, and kindly treatment, displayed by the Màldive Islanders for centuries past towards all those ship-wrecked on their danger-haunted Atols, see *The Màldive Islands* (Sessional Paper, XLIII, 1881, pp. 127-131); Journal C. A. S., 1923, XXIX, 76, pp. 206-214.

‡ S. Muḥammad 'Imád-ud-dín IV, grandfather of Muḥammad Shams-ud-dín III, the Sulṭán now on the throne.

"But having been informed by the Foreign Traders staying in the Island that in the beginning of May the sickness called 'Intermittent Fever'* prevails there, the Captain hired two *Katamarans* for 1,700 English Company's Rupees, to be paid at Goa. He conveyed thither ninety-three (93) persons in all, namely four (4) Lieutenants, a detachment of the Naval Battalion (consisting of one (1) Second Sergeant, two (2) Corporals and twenty-two (22) soldiers), the Ships Company, and the Convicts.

"It was impossible for me to proceed in the *Katamarans* as my eldest son was very sick of the fever. I, therefore, determined to stay at the Máldives, and remained there up to April 11th ; when, with my family, I left in the Merchant Brig 'Faṭh-ul-Rahmán'; and on the morning of the 15th arrived at Point de Galle.

"We took seven days to get from the Island of *Muli* to the 'King's Island,' sailing only by day, and staying the night at seven small Islands.

'The King's Island, (Mále), which is superior to all, is (according to the information of the inhabitants), a little more or less than two miles in length and one in breadth.

"It is furnished with artillery, but badly fortified.

"In the Harbour were riding at anchor nineteen (19) Merchant Brigs, four (4) from Chittagong and the others of Moors."

All those who reached Ceylon, among whom were two ladies and three children, after proceeding to Colombo from Galle, were duly provided with food and lodging and liberal advances (amounting to some Rs. 7,000) by the Ceylon Administration ; and ultimately given free passage to Bombay in the Mail Boat 'Seaforth.'

In thanking Sir C. Campbell, then Governor of Ceylon, for the ready British hospitality extended to the Portuguese castaways, the Governor of Goa, Jose Ferreira Pestana, wrote on June 10th, 1844 :—

"I have informed Her Majesty, my August Mistress (Queen Dona Maria II), of the great kindliness shown by

* The dread "Máldive Fever" (M. *Mále huma*), which inevitably seizes all Europeans who sojourn at Mále for any length of time. See *Ceylon Sessional Paper*, XLIII, 1881, p. 8: *Monograph on the Máldive Islands*, p. 7, †.

Your Excellency to Portuguese subjects; and, on Her Majesty's behalf, I desire to thank Your Excellency for the ready hospitality given to them. They will never forget the extreme kindness they met from Your Excellency, as well as from the inhabitants of Colombo and Galle.

"I profit by this occasion to present to Your Excellency my sincere protestation of friendship and high consideration."

NOTES.

1. Tárikh.—The original manuscript of the "*Tárikh,*" or "Chronicle of the Sulṭáns of the Máldive Islands," up to that date, is said to have perished in the conflagration of the Royal Palace, when Mále was sacked and Mukarram Muḥammad 'Imád-ud-dín III, the Sulṭán then reigning, deported by the Expedition despatched by *Áli Rája* of Kaṇṇanúr in A.H. 1166 (A.D. 1752).

Entered in a "ledger-form" volume, the existing copy—examined by the writer in A.C. 1920 and 1922—contains 132 leaves (water-marked for the year 1820), all but 15 of which bear writing covering space 13½ in. by 7½ in.

Its language and character are Arabic. Written in excellent script, the headings, important names, etc., are emphasised by being recorded in red ink.

The "*Tárikh*" consists of three separate Parts *:—

Part I: A homalectic treatise of hortatory advice (drawn from the *Qurán*, etc.) to Rulers of the World;

Part II: Starting with the Biblical Adam, passes, in rapid sweep, on to the Prophet Muḥammad, his four successors, and subsequent Khalífas, down to Abu 'Abd Allah Muḥammad al-Muqtafí who died in A.H. 555 (A.C. 1160);

Part III: The "*Tárikh*" proper. It embraces wholly, or in part the reigns of seventy-six (76) Rulers belonging to at least six Dynasties

This History extends from the twelfth regnal year (A.H. 548: A.C. 1153-4) of Sulṭán Muḥammad ul-Ádil to the twenty-third year (A.H. 1237: A.C. 1821-22) of Sulṭán Muḥammad Mu'ín-ud-dín I, great-grandfather of the present Sulṭán, Muhammad Shams-ud-dín III, —a period of nearly 670 years in all.

The composition of the "*Tárikh*" was undertaken successively by three erudite members of one family—father, nephew and grandson—each, in due course, *Qázi* of the Máldive Islands.

Shaikh Ḥáji Ḥasan Táj-ud-dín, Qází, the first Chronicler, brought the "*Tárikh*" manuscript up to A.H. 1137 (A.D. 1724-25).

It was carried on to A.H. 1174 (A.D. 1760-61) by Ḥáji Muḥammad Muhibb-ud-dín, Shaikh-ul-Islám, Qázi, son of Ḥasan Táj-ud-dín's brother, Ḥusain Afíf-ud-dín, *Baṇḍára Naibu*.

---

* An English Translation is contemplated by competent Arabic scholars at Mále, in collaboration with the present learned Qazi of the Máldive Islands, M. Husain Dídí Saraf-ud-dín.

From this date until the year A.H. 1237 (A.D. 1821-22)—or by Muslim lunar reckoning exactly a century from the conclusion of Ḥasan Táj-ud-dín's instalment—the "*Táríkh*" was continued by Ibráhím Siráj-ud-dín, Qází, son and nephew respectively of the dastardly betrayers of their Sovereign in A.H. 1166 (A.C. 1752), viz., Muḥammad Shams-ud-dín, Qází, and his brother Aḥmad Muhí-ud-dín, Chief Khaṭíb of Mále, whose father was Ḥasan Táj-ud-dín Qází.

2. East Indian Trade: Fifteenth and Sixteenth Centuries.

Calicut.

"*Calicut* is a perfectly secure harbour," writes the traveller 'Abd-ur-Razak (*circa* A.C. 1442), "which, like that of *Ormuz*, brings together merchants from every city and from every country. In it are found abundance of precious articles, especially from Abyssinia, Zirbad, or Zanguebar.

"It contains a considerable number of Mussulmáns, who are constant residents.

"Security and justice are so firmly established in this city, that the most wealthy merchants unload there (considerable cargoes), and unhesitatingly send (them) into the markets and bazárs, without thinking of any necessity of checking the amount, or of keeping watch over the goods.

"At Calicut every ship, whatever place it may come from, or wherever it may be bound, when it puts into this port is treated like other vessels, and has no trouble of any kind to put up with." (*India in the Fifteenth Century*).

Ormuz.

Of *Ormuz* 'Abd-ur-Razak (*loc. cit.*) says :—"It has not its equal on the surface of the globe. Merchants of Egypt, Syria, Turkistan, China, Java, Pegu, Bengal, the Máldives, Malabar, Cambay, and Zanguebar, from all countries resort hither ; and, in exchange for the commodities they bring, they can, without trouble or difficulty, obtain all that they desire. Bargains are made either by money or by exchange

"Persons of all religions, and even idolators, are found here ; and no injustice is permitted towards any person whatever."

Máldive Islands.

Writing in A.C. 1619 Pyrard (*Loc. cit.* I, 236—42) particularises the special items of trade at the Máldive Islands :—

"There is a great trade at the *Máldives*, and they are much frequented for their commodities. You see merchants from all quarters, as Malabar men from Barcelor, Onor, Bacalor, Cananor, Calecut, Tananor, Cochin, Coilam, Cael ; Guzeratis from Cambaye, Surat, and Chaul ; Arabs, Persians, men of Bengal, St Thomas, and Masulipatam, Ceylon, and Sumatra, who bring goods in demand there, and take away what the Máldives produce in abundance.

"First, of the *Coco* tree, which grows naturally at the Islands without any cultivation, they make many sorts of goods in demand with the foreigners ; for instance, cordage, with which all the vessels of the Indies are equipped ; the coco fruit, which is carried [illegible] quantity to the coasts of Arabic and Malabar and throughout India, that more than a hundred ships are laden with it every year, as well as with the oil and honey of the same tree; and the leaves which serve for sails: but the greatest trade is in cordage.

"There is another kind of wealth at the Máldives, viz., certain little shells (*Couries*), containing a little animal, large as the tip of the little finger, and quite white, polished, and bright .... They call them *Boly*, and export to all parts an infinite quantity, in such wise that in one year I have seen thirty or forty whole ships loaded with them without other cargo.

"All go to Bengal, for there only is there a demand for a large quantity at high prices. The people of Bengal use them for ordinary money..........All the merchants from other places in India take a large quantity to carry to Bengal, where they are always in demand; for they are produced nowhere but at the Máldives..........

"The Máldives have also an infinite abundance of *Fish* of all kinds ....; they also sell a large quantity, both cooked and dried, to foreigners.

"This commodity is in great demand in all parts of India, notably in Sumatra, whither whole shiploads are carried.

"*Tortoise-shell*, called *Cambe* (*M. kahambu*) is much valued in the Indies. It is found at the Máldives, and is largely traded in......

"The people of the Máldives likewise make a good traffic in *Rush Mats* (M. *kuna*) of perfect smoothness, which they make very prettily of divers colours, adorning them with patterns and figures so neatly that nothing can be nicer. The Portuguese and Indians alike prize them, so that there is much trade in them.

"Thus also with *Cloth of Cotton and Silk*, which is brought to them raw, and by them worked up.........

"So the Máldives are frequented from all quarters for their commodities, inasmuch as they possess so many things that foreigners prize and require.......

"I have heard it said by the Islanders that the trade and prosperity of the Islands were never so great as when the Portuguese governed there."

3. **Mafacalou.**—The modern *Mále*, or "Sulṭán's Island"; from the complex *Mahal* "Palace" + *Diva* "Island," Mále has given its appellation to the entire Máldive Archipelago.

Thus Ibn Baṭúṭa (Fourteenth Century) has:—"*Dhibat-al-Mahal*," with "the principal Island *Mahal*, the province after which all the Islands are called."

Barbosa (Sixteenth Century) writes:—"The King, a Moor, resides at *Mahaldiu*.

Pyrard (early Seventeenth Century) explains more fully:—"L' isle principale, comme j'ay dit, s'appelle *Male*, qui donne le nom a tout le reste des autres : car le mot de *Dives* signifie un nombre de petites isles amassees;" and elsewhere: "Ce Royayme en leur langage, s'appelle *Malerague*, Royaume de *Male*, et des autres peuples de l' Inde il s'appelle *Male-divar*, et les peuples *Dives*."

Mafacalou may stand, as part for the whole, not improbably for the modern *Máfannu* (*Avaṛu*), or Western Ward of Mále, + "*koḷu*" (honorific suffix); for Al-Ídrísí's (Twelfth Century) gives similarly *Amberia* (modern *Hemveru Avaṛu*, the Eastern Ward), "where the King and Queen resided."

4. Áli Raja.—In consequence of his interference in A.C. 1549-50 on behalf of the Lakkadive Islanders oppressed by the Portuguese, the Kolastiri, or Chirakkal, Rája was enabled to establish his authority over all those Islands.

Subsequently he transferred them, in *jaghir* with the honorary title of *Rája*, upon "*Áḷi Rája*," or "*Áḍi Rája*," ("Sea-King") the Head of the Máppiḷḷa community of Cannanore (*Kaṇṇanúr*), in return for stipulated *peshkash* of 6,000 *fanam* a year.

This status persisted until the invasion of Malabar by Haidar 'Ali of Mysore in the Eighteenth Century; when the Cannanore family, taking advantage of the gradual dismemberment of the Chirakkal territories, asserted its own independence, and became the seat of a Muḥammadan State (Logan, Malabar, 1915; Ellis, *Short Account of the Laccadive Islands and Minicoy*, 1924).

Regarding the *Áḷi Rája* of his day, Pyrard (*loc. cit.* II, 324) writes :—"This King of *Cannanore* is very wealthy, and very powerful; for his subjects are numerous. He is called "*Ali Ragea*," and is a Muḥammadan. Owning many vessels he is strong on the sea, and for the purpose of trade in India has many Agents and Factories.

"The Lakkadive Islands ("*Les Isles de Díuandurou*") as well as some thirty of the Máldives belong to him.

"The Portuguese are at peace with him, and are allowed to occupy a small Fort in Cannanore. The other Kings of India, however, do not style the Ruler of Cannanore "King," asserting that his title has accrued by force alone."

Cannanore was stormed by the British in A.C. 1791, and the Lakkadive Islands (including Minicoy subject to that State) sequestered by the Indian Government. Ultimately, during the Nineteenth Century liberal concessions were granted; and an equitable division of those Islands between the Cannanore Ruler and the British Crown now obtains.

The "*Táríkh*" testifies that the Máldive Islands (ever coveted by the Cannanore *Áḷi Rájas* and Bíbís) have been not infrequently attacked by these Malabar Máppiḷḷas. On two occasions (A.C. 1607 and A.C. 1752), Mále itself was captured temporarily, and the respective ruling Sulṭáns killed or deported to India.

5. S. 'Ali V.—The legend of the intrigues of "*Buraki Raṇi*," the infamous elder sister of Sulṭán 'Ali V (56), ending with the deliberate murder of her brother, is of tragic interest, and doubtless rests on a substratum of truth.

Buraki Raṇi claimed the throne, but her younger brother "*Dombulá Fáriná Kilége*" was appointed Sulṭán (as 'Ali V). Their aunt, younger sister of S. Abu Bakr (39), was mother of "Raddebá Magu Kaḷu Muḥammad Manikufánu" (afterwards S. Kaḷu Muḥammad, 50, 53, 57). Kaḷu Muḥammad wished to marry Buraki Raṇi, but his mother opposed; and he was banished by S. 'Ali to Wádú Island in Huvadú Atol.

The Sulṭán permitted his sister Buraki Raṇi to follow, accompanied by Kaḷu Ibráhím of Gáfaru Island, who had served the family since childhood. Instead of making for Huvadú Atol, they sailed to Achin; and thence back to Goa.

The Portuguese being promised share in the Máldive revenues, Buraki Raṇi was escorted by a Portuguese armed vessel to Gáfaru

Island. From there Kaḷu Ibráhím was sent to Málé to bring about, (with the connivance of his step-father Huḷudeli Don Yúsuf, the Sultán's sword-bearer), the murder of her brother, Sulṭán 'Ali, was inveigled into leaving the Palace, attacked, ham-strung, and left to die.

Buraki Raṇi then seized the throne by the aid of her Portuguese allies, recalled Kaḷu Muḥammad from exile, and married him. He thus resumed the Sulṭánate for the third time.

Later he banished Buraki Raṇi to Tiladummati Atol, and married Shírází Fáṭuma Kamaná, by whom he had the son Ḥasan VIII, (58), who succeeded him on the throne.

6. Death of S. 'Ali VI.—"Some of the inhabitants who saw their Ruler and the two others lying dead on the battle-field, buried them where found, and enclosed the spot with a rubble wall. Some time afterwards, the water of the lagoon surrounded the site.

"Since their death, all the Sulṭáns, from that date up to this day, have visited their graves, and prayed for their souls" (*Táríkh*).

A small causeway now connects the *Ziyárat* islet with Málé Island. The Religious Ceremony held at the site annually on Ramazán 24th, which is attended by Máldivians from the Sulṭán downwards, is styled "*Máfannu (Avaṛu) Boḍu Hiti*" (See *C. A. S. Journal*, 1928, XXXI, 81).

7. Death of 'Ali Khaṭíb.—"In this way they had carried on for some time, when one night 'Ali Khaṭíb Takurufánu remained in his own house till daybreak. The others having departed before dawn without noticing his absence, 'Ali Khaṭíb and his wife hid in a house in one of the Islands; but the Christians (Portuguese) had wind of it, dragged him forth, and decapitated him.

"Thereafter they sent his head to Andiri Andiri (at Málé) and cast his body away. It was buried by some of the Muslims of that Island; while the head was recovered from Andiri Andiri, after much entreaty by the inhabitants of Málé, and buried in an Island hard by, called Fonadú" (*Táríkh*).

8. Death of Andiri Andiri.—"He (Muḥammad Takurufánu) approached the house which Captain Andiri Andiri occupied, and found him seated facing the door, with his attendants standing round. All were in the light thrown by a lamp suspended from the roof. Then Muḥammad Khaṭíb Takurufánu took careful aim, fired at, and wounded Andiri Andiri; who, after returning the fire in the direction from which he was shot, fell to the ground. After firing Muḥammad Khaṭíb had taken cover behind a coconut tree; thus escaping." (*Táríkh*).

PLATES.

Plate I.

Málé ("Sultán's Island.")—Reduced from larger photograph (See *Monograph on the Máldive Islands*). View taken in A.C. 1922 from H.M.S. "Comus" Cruiser, anchored off Málé in North Málé Atol Lagoon.

Bodu Kótté Buruzu, the largest Bastion of the fortifications, stands out, with other buildings, white against dark background of trees. Directly behind this Bastion, within the Fort Wall, lies the grassy Northern Esplanade in front of the "Palace Enclosure" (M. *Etere-kolu*).

Plate II.

Mále.—Reduced photograph of Survey Plan, (as lithographed 80 feet to an inch), of Mále Island, made by Islanders under orders of the Máldivian Government in A.C. 1922. (See *Loc cit*).

The Plan, admirably executed, is in considerable detail, showing the sites of the Palace, the Fort Bastions, Esplanades, Streets, Mosques, Tanks and Chief Residences.

Plate III.

Portuguese Attack on Mále : A.C. 1631 circa.—Photographic reduction of Ressende's Sketch Plan. (See *Hak. Soc. Pyrard*, II, 996-07).

Seemingly the only defences then existing, from East to West, or left to right, were three make-shift ramps—converted later into the Bastions (*Buruzu*), *Oikoḷu*, *Ñáne*, *Ranjehi*, with the *Boḍu Kótte Buruzu* and its annexe on the West, and a further ramp where *Á Buruzu* Bastion now stands. From these bulwarks six cannon are shown returning the fire of the Portuguese Fleet, and seven more guns lie together unlimbered.

The fifteen vessels engaged in the bombardment are depicted as drawn up in three lines—six, five and four from front to back.

The sole entrance into the Inner Harbour through the Breakwater, marked, is the modern central passage (M. *kadimma*). At this day there are five other lesser entrances (M. *neru*).

A "horse-shoe" moat would appear to surround the Palace precincts; which are triangularly shaped with base facing North. The modern "Palace Enclosure" (M. *Etere-koḷu*) is quadrangular.

The five outermost islands at the top of the Sketch Plan and its photograph, represent some of those (*e.g.* *Farukolu-fuṛi*, *Furanna-fuṛi*, *Lankan-fuṛi*, *Himma-fuṛi*, *Hurá*) lying along the Eastern reef of North Mále Atol; the three at bottom (*Guli-fuṛi*, *Girávaru*, and possibly *Wabbin-faṛu*) stand on the Western reef; the four islands to right (South) of Mále Island are doubtless intended for *Finoḷu*, *Embadú*, *Wádú* and *Velessara*, of South Mále Atol; the four to left (North) nearest to Mále in the lagoon probably denote the Islands *Huḷule*, *Fonadú*, *Dunidú* and *Madiri Viligili*; the remaining two, with others—mere outlines—further back, should signify some of the central islands, *e.g.*, *Baḍos* (*Boḍu* and *Kuda*), *Fédú*, *Baros*. *Ihura*, *Ára*, *Tulágiri*).

Plate IV.

Portuguese Cannon.—This gun, lying unmounted at the *Boḍu Buruzu* Western annexe, very closely resembles that dredged from the bed of the Colombo Harbour in 1888, which is now in the Colombo Museum.*

It measures, over all, 8 ft. 3 in. in length, with circumference at muzzle 2 ft. 3½ in.; the bore is 7 in.

Besides astragal bands and other mouldings at the mouth and other points, there are emblazoned on the top of the cannon, in relief, the Portuguese Royal Arms—Crown, surmounting Shield with quincunx "inescutcheons," each bearing "bezants five"†—footed by "Armillary Sphere" or lined Orb, besides additional designs and ornamentation. Rings for hoisting are affixed.

---

* Not improbably one of the cannon of the unfortunate Portuguese ship, commanded by Francisco Pereira, which foundered in a storm within Colombo Harbour, A.C. 1613 *circa*. The two other Portuguese vessels of three returning from Negapatam, were also both lost. but elsewhere. (*Bocarro*).

† See Plate (*Archaeological Survey, Ceylon Sessional Paper*, XIX, 1892, pp. 30, 31) figuring the slab discovered at Menikkaḍawara.

Camoens (*Luciads*, III, 53, 54) describes the Portuguese Royal Arms heraldically in verse. "On every cinque a cinque is shown"; and that "the thirty silvers wherewith God was sold . . . . be fully told, counteth for two the one that central lies." (Burton).

Possibly this cannon may be even one of the pair abandoned to the Máldivians four centuries ago by their Malabar allies, after the recapture of Mále from the Portuguese in A.C. 1519. (See *supra*, p. 82).

Plate V

"Á Buruzu" Bastion.—View of the exterior from the Breakwater (M. *tori*), which divides the Inner Harbour from the Lagoon on the North.

This semi-circular Bastion, the first to South-West from *Boḍu Kóṭṭé Buruzu*, tapes at base 65 ft. 8 ins., with radial axis 81 ft. 6 ins. There are remains of eleven embrasures, more or less perfect; but no guns.

Ressende's Sketch Plan, and the Arabic record (Plate VI) may well imply that this Bastion was not built until after the later Portuguese attack on Mále of A.C. 1650.

Plate VI.

Arabic Inscription.—The photograph shows an Arabic record, in Kufic character,—taken as being dated A.H. 1087 (A.C. 1688-87)—carved on madrepore slabs forming the inner face of *Á Buruzu* Bastion where it projects furthest forward.

There are two lines of high-relief characters, stretching 10 ft. 4 in. by 2 ft. 2 ins., in a counter-sunk panel, within oblong framing of guilloche embellishment.

The record relates to the construction, or rebuilding, of this Bastion by order of Sulṭán Íbráhím Iskandar I (A.C. 1648-87), son of Sulṭán Muḥammad 'Imád-ud-dín I. But the *Hijra* date is rather obscure. If A.H. 1087 be the correct calculation (as worked out by Muslim experts) the inscription was cut between A.C. 1686, March, and A.C. 1687, February, the latter the last year of Sulṭán Íbráhím Iskandar's reign.

MÁLE

Plate I.

Mále Island : View from Lagoon, North : A.C. 1922.

MÁLE

Plate II.

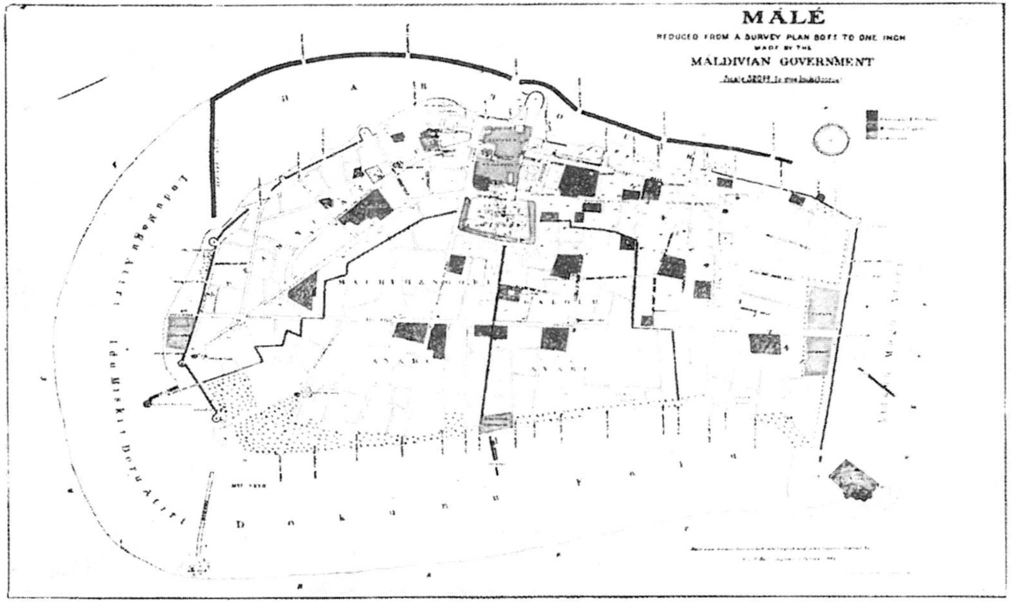

Mále Island : Plan : A.C. 1922.

MÁLE

Plate III.

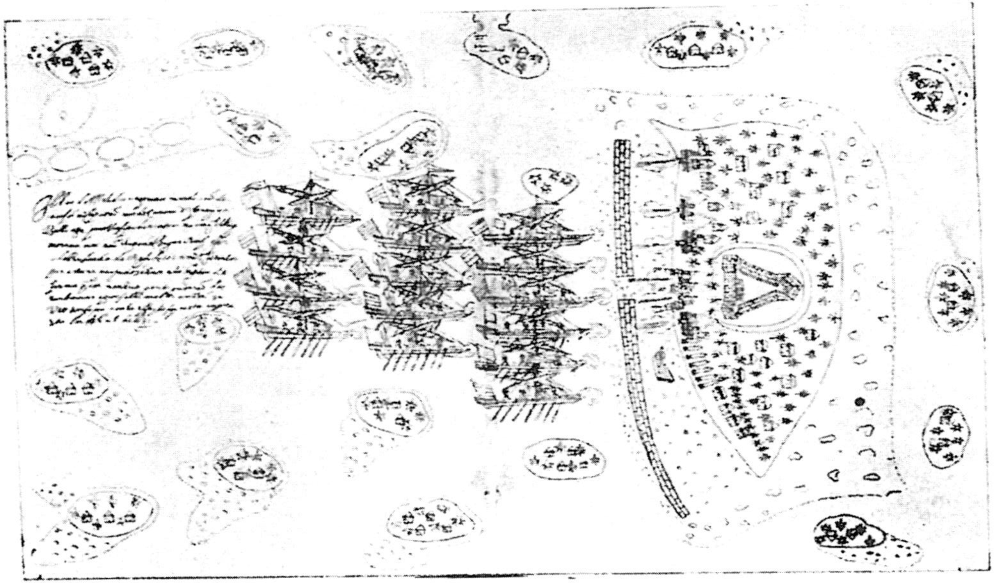

Portuguese Attack on Mále: A.C. 1631 *circa*.

Portuguese Cannon at Mále.

MÁLE

Plate V.

"Á Buruzu" Bastion: from Breakwater, North: A.C. 1922.

Plate VI.

Arabic Inscription at "Á Buruzu" Bastion.

Text.

المبارکـة المنصورة المرکلم لدفع فرانع الملاعين
امر بالاتخاذ هذا الخما ل المطار *
السلطا ن ابن السلطان محمد الصور مرا سع
سنة من هجرة سيد المواسمطاالغازي ابراهيم اسكندر

Transcript.

1. *Al-mubárakat ul-mansúrat al-Markám lidafa'i Farángi al-mala'ín amara biti kházi hazal khimal al-matár.*

2. *As-Sulṭán ibn as-Sulṭán Muḥammad as-Súr Marási'a sanat min Hijrat saydat al-ma-vá-si-m-ṭá al-Ghází Íbráhím Iskandar.*

Translation.

"The Ghází Íbráhím Iskandar, the Sulṭán, son of the Sulṭán Muḥammad as-Súr Marási'a, ordered this blessed victorious bulwark, (called) "*Markám*," to be built as a defence to repel the accursed *Farángi* (Portuguese), in the *Hijra* year 1087 (*al-ma-vá-si-m-ṭá*.) *

---

* Calculated apparently thus : l = 30 ; m = 40 ; v = 6 ; $á$ = 1 ; s = 60 ; m = 40 ; $ṭ$ = 9 ; $á$ = 1; total = strictly 187, but taken as = 1,000 (one thousand) + 87 (eighty-seven), or 1087 in all.

EXCERPTA MÁLDIVIANA.

By

H. C. P. BELL, C.C.S. (Retired).

No. 11.—DUTCH INTERCOURSE WITH THE MÁLDIVES : SEVENTEENTH CENTURY.[1]

FOREWORD.

This Paper is limited to information, (much too scanty, but all so far known to the writer), put together from mere fugitive extracts met with in the Dutch Archives stored at Colombo.[2]

These extracts contain sporadic hints, rather than real notices—Pyrard de Laval's *Voyage* and *Memoirs* of Dutch Governors of Ceylon excepted—, regarding the trade and political intercourse between the Máldive Islanders and the Hollanders in Ceylon (who gradually acquired possession of its ports and sea-board hinterland) in the course of the Seventeenth Century.

What appears below must, therefore, necessarily be taken as an incomplete outline sketch. Future research, whether in Ceylon, at Batavia, or at the Hague, will doubtless disclose many further particulars supplementing the present scraps.

Earliest Dutch Exploration of the East.

Spain and Portugal held the monopoly of Trade with the East until A.C. 1594 ; when Philip II's ill-advised and "despotic effort to humiliate the commerce of Holland acted as an immediate stimulus to its expansion by that country."

---

1. The writer most gratefully records his great obligation to the Very Reverend Father L. Vossen, S.J., of the Papal Seminary, Kandy, for valuable aid, unselfishly spared, from heavy calls on his time towards the due translation of the Dutch extracts quoted below.

2. See *Ceylon Antiquary*, 1915-16, I, 118.

Within a year, the Spanish Ruler's "tyrannous veto" was countered by the Dutch organisation of "*La Companie des Pais Lontains*"; and definitely clinched in 1602 by the inauguration of the "*Nederlandsche Oost-Indische Compagnie,*" ushering in an era of splendid trade growth in India and the Far East, during two centuries.

Cornelis Houtman—the pioneer Dutch Voyager to the East—rounded the Cape in 1595; followed three years later (1598) by Jakob van Nek, and by other Expeditions in rapid succession.

At Ceylon, landfall was made by the Dutch for the first time, when Joris van Spilbergen on May 30th, 1602, anchored off Batticaloa; and provisional negotiations were entered into with the Sinhalese King (Vimala Dharmma Súryayá I.) at Kandy.

Sebald de Weert's visit, later in the same year, ended tragically.

Trade at the Máldive Islands.

A high Dutch authority writes[1]:—

"Mainly created for purposes of commerce, the Company remained true to her origin: commercial profit was ever the object of her endeavours. For that purpose she entered into Agreements with Native Princes and peoples; whereby she obtained the articles of trade mostly in demand, and, as far as possible, to the exclusion of all others.

"But without, and sometimes against, her will, she also thereby got possession of an ever-increasing extent of territory, and found herself, after that of merchant, playing the rôle of sovereign."

The Seventeenth Century.

The Seventeenth Century was, so to speak, the heyday of Máldive trade.

Pyrard de Laval (captive at Mále, A.C. 1602-07) saw it fast rising to its height; and more than a hundred years later, during the reign of the prudent Sulṭán Ibráhím Iskandar II. (A.C. 1721-50), it showed but faint signs of decay.[2]

From Pyrard is drawn this succinct record[3]:—

"Commerce at the Máldives is extensive, and they are much frequented for purposes of trade. From all quarters—merchants from Malabar, Barcelor, Onor, Bacalor, Cananor, Tananor, Cochin,

---

1 M. A. van Rhede van der Kloot, Gouverneur General, &c., van Nederlandsch-Indie.

2. Harris, Voyages, 1744, I, 715.

3. Hak. Soc. Pyrard, I. 236-41 (condensed).

Coilam, Cael, Guzerat, Cambaye, Surat and Chaul; Arabs, Persians, natives of Bengal, St. Thome, Musulipatam, Ceylon and Sumatra, bring commodities in demand there, and take away products in which the Islands are so rich; to wit, the cordage with which all the vessels of the Indies are rigged; coconuts, exported in such quantity to Arabia, the Malabar coast, and all parts of India, that every year more than 100 vessels are loaded therewith, as well as, from the tree, oil and honey (jaggery) and platted leaves (cadjans) of which they make sails. But the greatest traffic is in (coir) rope.

"Also they vend little shells (cowries), very smooth and glittering: these go only to Bengal. I have seen 30 or 40 ships laden without any other commodity: these shells pass there as money. For a fardel (*koṭṭé*) of shells,—each fardel containing 12,000,—20 measures of rice are given. Máldive fish is in great demand throughout India.

"Besides these they have a sort of tortoiseshell called *cambe* (M. *kahabu*). It goes off best in Cambaye.

"They also make fine reed-mats, and cloths of cotton and silk.

"In exchange merchants export all the necessaries of life; yet everything is cheap, because of the number and frequency of ships."

Máldive Cowries.

Until the demand for Cowries, induced by the Dutch, rendered the export of these shells to Ceylon profitable, Máldive boats visiting the Island loaded up mainly with Máldive Fish (*commala-mas*, M. *kaḷubili-mas*, dried bonito) and Coconuts.[1]

Other products of the Máldives were held beneath notice, and no restrictions placed on their free sale; but the Dutch were not slow to gauge the advantage of a complete control over the traffic in *Cowries*. This monopoly they attempted, with much success, to establish throughout the latter part of the Seventeenth and Eighteenth Centuries.

Dutch Exploitation of the Máldives: A. C. 1602—1640.

It goes without the saying that some at least of the earliest Dutch ships, on their voyages to and from the Further East, must have touched at the Máldives, which lie athwart the regular course.

That this actually was the case is confirmed by a Dutch Minute on record of 1602; adumbrating even then the trade advantages potentially derivable from the Islands:—

"The Factors of the Company at Middleburg report (April 20th, 1602) that they had spent five days at the Máldives, and that business could be done there."[2]

---

1. Abbe Raynal, II, 83.
2. Dutch Records, Batavia.

But nearly forty years were to elapse before the Dutch, engaged in their grim struggle to oust the Portuguese from Ceylon (a consummation not fully realized until A.C. 1658) —whilst obstructed persistently, and at times openly opposed, by the machinations and treachery of the Kandyan Ruler, Rája Siṇha II. (A.C. 1635-87), their nominal ally under the Boschouwer Agreement, 1612, and Westerwold Treaty, 1638—, found themselves, owing to constant calls on their blockading fleets, in no position to spare a ship to "try out" the capabilities of Máldive commerce by special exploitation through a direct visit to the Group.

But in 1640, the Dutch "despatched a vessel, laden with rice, to ascertain the nature and prospects of trade at the Máldive Islands." [1]

What success attended this venture is not known.

A. C. 1640—1663.

A ten-year Truce between the Portuguese and Dutch expired in 1650; and strenuously renewed hostilities did not again cease until terminated by the Dutch capture of Colombo in 1656 and Jaffnapatam two years afterwards.

Save for a single reference in 1645 to a Missive from the Máldive Sulṭán, the period between 1645 and 1663 would appear to be virtually blank in regard to allusions in the Ceylon Archives to further trade between the Dutch and Máldivians.

In 1649[2] the Islanders had themselves to meet, and successfully beat off, the final attempt by a Portuguese Expedition from Goa to reconquer the Máldives; having less than twenty years earlier (1631 or 1632), repulsed a similar attack on Mále. [3]

Máldive Boats Yearly Visits to Ceylon.

In spite of the marked silence during the above period in the Resolutions and State Registers regarding the Islanders' annual arrivals at Galle, and later at Colombo as well, it may be taken for granted that these hardy mariners, "elect of the sea," rarely failed—as up to this very day—to visit Ceylon yearly in their small, but exceptionally seaworthy, craft, in order to dispose of the humble products of the Atols.

---

1. Resolutions : Dutch Council, Galle ; November 20, 1640.
2. C.A.S. Journal, 1931, XXXII, 32, 33.
3. *Loc. cit.* 33, 34.

A couple of casual entries, touching such visits, may be quoted for their bald unpretenciousness :—

A. C. 1647.

(i) ***Resolution : May 31st, Friday, 1647.***—" On the 27th instant anchored a *gundura* (native vessel) wherein are fifteen Máldivians, with only some drinking water as provisions.

" Laden with coconuts, their boat was driven past the Fort, and reached shore in the River ; being unable to continue the voyage at the present time.

" Upon the proposition of N. J. Overshie, Commandeur, to the Council (of seven Members), it was decided, whilst deeming it not advisable to grant them too long a stay, to allow the above-said Máldivians to remain on here until the month of September next ; in order to obtain similar friendly action in case of like mishap on our side. A measure of rice will be granted daily to each man for his sustenance.

" Resolved thus in the Fort of *Negumbo*." 1

A. C. 1663.

(ii) *Resolution : October 25th, 1663.*—" Entered (Colombo) Harbour two Máldivian vessels ; one rather large. The owners (who came in them) assert that they contain, respectively, 25,000 coconuts with 16,000 *commela-mas* (dried fish), and 40,000 coconuts with 60,000 *commela-mas*.

" On being interrogated for some information, they (the Máldivians) declared that they knew nothing, and that the Island from which they came was called *Cardiva* (Káṛidú, North Mále Atol)."

" After the audience, they were permitted to sell their goods free (of duty)." 2

Dutch Quest of Cowries : A.C. 1649.

The annual supply of Cowries brought to this Island by the native vessels being at times inadequate to meet the growing behests of the Batavian Government, the Dutch Governors of Ceylon re-initiated occasional visits to the Máldives by Hollanders, in their own ships, " to negotiate for larger importation."

Thus in 1669 the " Cockatoo " was despatched and returned with 27,578 lbs. weight of these shells. The price then ruling was Rds. $1\frac{1}{8}$ the *koṭṭé* :—

Resolution : February 4th-18th, 1669.—" Resolved to send the yacht of Vryburger Gerrit van Oldenburgh, called the " Cockatoo," to the Máldives to purchase cowries and ambergris."3

The " Instructions " issued to Marten Gillisse, Chief Mate, and David Sontyn, Purser, would seem to be wanting.

1. Resolutions : Dutch Council, Negombo.
2. Resolutions : Dutch Council, Colombo.
3. Resolutions : Dutch Council, Colombo.

Resolution: June 11th, 1669.—" The yacht 'Cockatoo,' having brought 1,149 *cottys* of cowries at 12,000 shells per parcel (*koṭṭé*), it is decided to store them at Galle for transport by ships returning Home (Europe)." [1]

" Memoirs " of Dutch Governors.

The Máldives receive but meagre attention in the " Memoirs " (hitherto published) of the Dutch Governors of Ceylon, left for the information and guidance of their successors, during the Seventeenth Century.

The only three special allusions with which the writer is acquainted, appear in "Memoirs," separately printed, viz., those of the Governors (A) Ryckloff van Goens, Senior (1657-63; 1665-75), (B) Laurensz Pyl (1680-92), and (C) Thomas van Rhee (1693-97).

(A). Memoir of Governor Ryckloff van Goens, Senior: A. C. 1663.

In his " Memoir " (dated December 16th, 1663) Ryckloff van Goens, father of an equally distinguished son and later Governor, found nothing further to note down than the following briefest of paragraphs touching the Máldives :—

" The trade with the Máldive Islands for Cowries (*cauris*) and sometimes for a great quantity of Ambergris (*Amber de Grys*), could also yield profitable advantage.

" What has been written to Batavia upon this subject, and the reply sent by Their Honours for attention, will be seen by Your Honour in the File of Letters (*Brief-Boek*): and will enlighten Your Honour, more particularly according to experience in the course of time." [2]

(B). Memoir of Governor Laurensz Pyl: A. C. 1688.

A quarter of a century later the price of Cowries was 3¼ *larins* per *koṭṭé*, [3] and the Dutch were anxious to establish an exclusive contract with the Sulṭán.

Governor Laurensz Pyl wrote briefly on 1688 :—

" The Company is very glad that the Sulṭán has always entertained friendly feelings towards them.

" As regards the commercial relation, however, between the Company and the Sultán there is room for an Agreement to be entered into." [4]

---

1. *Idem.*

2. Valentyn, Ceylon, 161.

3. Regarding prices, etc., paid for Cowries by the Dutch, and other European traders, in the East during the Eighteenth Century, see Ceylon Sess. Pap. XLIII, 1881, 98-101.

4. See *infra* p. 239.

4

Upon each successive Governor was constantly impressed from Batavia the duty of inciting the Máldivians to furnish larger supplies of cowries (*den Maldivers in den aanbreng van cauris meer en meer ta animeeren*) ; whilst the purchase price was studionsly fixed below the fair market value.

(C). Memoir of Governor Thomas van Rhee : A. C. 1697.

At the very close of the Seventeenth Century the state of the trade with the Islands is thus described by Governor Thomas van Rhee (February 25th, 1697) :—[1]

"For several years consecutively various vessels have arrived, both here (Colombo) and at Galle, from the Máldive Islands with *commbela-mas* (dried fish), and with cowries. The latter we have bought, for transport to the Netherlands, at Rds. 1½ the *cotty* (*koṭṭé*) of 12.000 weighing 24 lbs.

"In exchange, they obtain from the Company arecanuts and spices ; which, however, do not amount to much. For Colombo and Galle arecanuts they pay Rds. 6½ per *ammunam* of 24,000 ; for those of Calpetty (Kalpitiya), Rds. 5.

"We have assisted them, now and again, by selling some necessaries for their vessels ; with the view of including them to bring here more of their cowries : this would be of advantage, as these shells are much cheeper than those obtained in Bengal.

"Their Excellencies at Batavia have also earnestly recommended us to foster the Máldive sea-farers in every way (*ons ook seer ernstig recommandeeren de Maldives vaerdaers in alles te caresseeren*)."

"Màssives" from, and to, Máldive Sultáns.

In what year the Sulṭáns of the Máldives first commenced the despatch of State Missives to the Dutch in Ceylon is unknown. Further, prcof of regular continuity of such practice from the start is more than doubtful : no more than three instances have come to light as yet in the Ceylon Dutch Records.

From at least A.C. 1711 onwards, however, the custom would seem to have become recognised by the Máldivians as an definite yearly obligation.

Not a single original Missive received from any Sulṭán during the Seventeenth Century has been yielded by the

1. Dutch Records, Colombo.

Archives [1]; but, of Ceylon Governor's Replies, three are extant.

Of these, two are embodied in Dutch Resolutions—the first (No. 1, 1645) rather strangely jumbled; the second (No. 2, 1671) covering the substance of the Sulṭán's communication as well as the Dutch Governor's response; the third (No. 3, 1688), and latest, the draft of the original Arabic Reply of the Governor of which a Dutch Translation exists.

Taking this triplet *seriatim* :—

No. 1. Governor Jan Maatsuycker's Reply to the Sultán's Missive: A.C. 1645.

The reference occur in a Resolution of the Galle Council. Summarised it runs :—

(*a*) December 21st, Friday, 1645.—"Resolved to present to the King of the Máldives two (2) metal pieces (Ordnance), and five (5) rolls of Satin; that thereby we may enjoy his friendship (*ten eynde zyne vrundshap daar door mogen genieten*)," [2] whilst making a return for the presents received from him.

(*b*) "Resolved, unanimously, to send back the Máldivians with a polite Reply to their King, and a present of merchandise, instead of despatching the two metal pieces (Ordnance) and appurtenances."

(*c*) "The Captains of the vessels which arrived from the Máldive Islands on November 26th last, brought a Letter from the King, together with (the under-specified) presents :—

"Five (5) *bhárs*, fine Coir; twelve (12) *bhárs*, coarse Coir; sixty-three (63) *parras*, Cowries; one hundred and sixty (160) pieces of *Commela-mas* (dry fish).

"(These are) valued here at :—20 Rds. the *bhár* of fine Coir; 40 Rds. the *bhár* of coarse Coir; 63 Rds. the 63 *parras* of Cowries; 320 Rds. the 160 *parras* of *commel-mas* at 2 Rds. per *parra*.

"Pursuant to the Sulṭán's Order given to, and the Letter brought by, him, the Ambàssador desired that, in return for the above presents, the request of the King be granted, viz., that two metal pieces (Ordnance) and appur-

1. The first original Missive of a Máldive Sulṭán extant in Ceylon is that of 1713 in *Tána*. See C.A.S. Journal, 1923, XXIX, 196-206.

2. For reciprocal presents, which always accompanied the Missives of the Sulṭáns and Dutch Governors in Ceylon, see Sess. Pap. 1881, XLIII, 49-52.

tenances, should be sent together with some grenades, and a Dutch *Couttapel* (Gunner), to remain during one monsoon.

Resolved by the Council of State, after mature deliberation, lest the men (Máldivians) should be too long detained, to give them leave to depart, taking a friendly Reply to their King;—wherein it be stated, apologetically, that our strength of *Couttapels* is limited (besides giving other reasons as detailed in our Reply); and that, in lieu thereof, the following articles be sent (as return presents):—

	Rds.
"Three (3) pieces of Satin at 25 Rds. each ..	75
One (1) piece double Red Damask ..	40
One (1) Japan lacquered Counter ..	34
Six (6) Muskets, with accompaniment (ammunition, &c.)	18
Six (6) Fine lacquered Pikes	12
Six (6) Grenades	6
Three (3) Grasshopper guns (*Springhanen*) ..	15
One (1) Match-lock gun inlaid with silver ..	25
Six (6) Ceylon *Matties*	6
Total. Rds.	231

"Thus Resolved, unanimously, in the Town *S. Crux de Gale.*"

(Signed) JAN MAATSUYCKER.

December 21st, 1645.

Sultán Muhammad 'Imád-ud-dín Shuja'i I: A.C. 1620-48.

The Ruler on the Máldive throne in 1645 was Sulṭán Muḥammad Shuja'i 'Imád-ud-dín I.

Great great nephew of the Máldivian hero, Sulṭán Boḍu Takurufánu (who in A.C. 1573 delivered the Islands from the intollerable Portuguese Rule of 15 years), he was forced in 1631 or 1632 to repulse a formidable assault by the inveterate alien Goa foe; and later to crush the serious rebellion of his Queen's brother (Sámiya Kilêge), who was captured and died in banishment at Fua Malaku Island.

To this Sulṭán Mále owes its Fort and Breakwater.[1]

1. Monograph (Máldive Islands) p. 30.

The appeal to the Dutch for arms in 1645 gave ominous signs of that lowering Portuguese storm, which broke on the Islands within four years (1649), at the outset of a new reign.

Survey of Lakkadive and Máldive Islands: A. C. 1671.

From 1668 the Dutch in Ceylon had been greatly exercised by anxiety as to the safest course for vessels to select in voyages from, and to, Persia.

A definite decision was come to in 1671, and "Instructions" issued for a complete Survey both of the *Baxos de Padua* (Lakkadives) and the Máldive Islands. [1]

During the prosecution of the Survey the Dutch Captain was enjoined to deliver a Letter from Governor Rycklof van Goens, Senior, to the reigning Sultán of the Máldives.

The lengthy Resolution on the subject, dated Colombo, January 16th, 1671, is given below, somewhat abridged :—

Dutch Council Resolution, Colombo.

"The Noble Company at Batavia having been informed last year that we would despatch one of our best-rigged brigs to examine the *Baxos de Padua* (Lakkadives), and, concurrently, to map the Máldive Islands, accurately, in order that the valuable ships of the Company might utilise them when voyaging from, and to, Persia, or from Home ; and as at present we are well provided with brigs—it is Resolved to send thither (the two Island Groups) the brig "Snipe" under charge of Arent Conink, Chief Mate (returned from Persia in Acting Command of the "Amerongen") who has already gained much experience of that route, and is besides, as sober and careful as one would wish.

"As he will visit the Máldives, it is further Resolved to carry over there a reasonable cargo to be exchanged, if feasible, against its value in Cowries—whereby commerce will be promoted in future ; supplementing it with a very civil Letter to the King of the Máldives about His Highness' treatment of certain Dutchmen and Moors, who were driven there in a vessel from Jaffna ; and adding suitable directions for the provisional Captain regarding a sufficient crew for the return voyage.

Instructions.

"For Captain Arent Coninck, who goes from here with brig "Snipe" to visit the Northern Máldive Islands; and, if

1. The British surveyed the Máldives, 1834-5.

possible, also the Southern Máldives, in order to map them; and moreover to try to traffic in Cowries at the Chief Island of the Máldive King."

"Set your course along the South Indian Coast nearly to Bacheloor, without touching at any of the Company's Settlements, either on the Malabar or Canarese coast, unless compelled by necessity; lest time, already very short, be wanting to complete everything satisfactorily.

From the latitude of Bacheloor, strike Westward to make to North of *Baxos de Padua*. (Lakkadives). These Banks Your Honour will duly visit, noting all contours.

South of these Banks at the 11th Degree North latitude occur various Islands; of which the closest to the Mainland, or most Easterly, called *Lumenia* ("Amini")—is not on the Charts. We ourselves touched at in the year (16)57 · there is good provisioning and water. To the West of this Island bottoms vary; sometimes 20 fathoms, then 6, then 30 and more: depths should be sounded.

Your Honour particularly should take as accurate observations as possible by both Sun and Stars: this is of the highest importance; as the voyage is undertaken chiefly in order that, from the experience acquired by Their Honours' ships coming from Home, from Persia, and from other quarte s, may in future pass through free from fear. Your Honour must spare neither pains nor labour between the 9° and 11° North latitude—especially from 8°·30 and 10°·15′, the customary passage. Islands lying between these points should be mapped with great care.

Beyond 8° latitude Your Honour will pursue, your course Southwards, either to East or to West of the Máldive Islands; traversing them occasionally, given sufficient sea-room.

Having reached the "King's Island," you will hand over Our Letter to the King, together with the presents, and use all means to barter the small cargo taken by you for Cowries; making careful entry thereof in your Journal.

Take care that no unpleasantness arises with the Islanders, guiding yourself entirely according to the "Instructions [1]" (enclosed herewith) given to Captain Maerten in February, 1669.

---

1. See *supra* p. 230.

When the business here is completed we desire you, if time and weather permit, to push on to the 4° South parallel where the Southern Islands occur; keeping good look out, star-board, from 1° North to 2° South, for the *Diego Royes* Islands.[1]

Having reached the limit of the Southern Máldives, the wet season (Monsoon) will probably have set in. Your Honour should, then, steer a course along the East side of the Máldives, as close as seamanship allows, until again attaining 8° North latitude.

From there, making for Cape Comorin, and so to Tuticorin, you will return to Colombo.

May God Almighty have your voyage in His good keeping.

(Signed) RYCKLOFF VAN GOENS.

Colombo, 16th January, 1671.

No. 2. Governor Rycklof van Goens' Letter to the Sultán: A. C. 1671.

" Rycklof van Goens to the Mighty Lord, *Mahamedy Umbrayime* (Íbráhím, son of Muḥammad), Ruler of the Máldive Islands.

"Herewith is being forwarded to Your Highness copy of Our Letter, sent thirteen months ago by the hand of one of Your Highness' subjects, the contents of which bear on the mariners (since returned safely), who drifted (to the Máldives) from Jaffnapatam and were, by Your Highness' Orders, well received, and despatched to Tuticorin.

"For the above friendly actions, We thank Your Highness very greatly; and, to gain further assurance Ourselves, and to assure Your Highness, of firm friendship, We send this ship to Your Highness with the Letter; adding thereto :—.

"Ten (10) lbs. Cinnamon; six (6) lbs. Cloves; six (6) lbs. Mace; six (6) lbs. Nutmegs.

"These articles will be presented to Your Highness by the *Commandeur* of this little vessel.

"May Your Highness be pleased to extend to him a helping hand, in furtherance of his trading; and to favour Us with an answer, so as to confirm Our friendship the more.

1. Concerning the mythical *Diego de Roys* Islands, see Hak. Soc. Pyrard I, 49. They are entered on Old Maps variously, as lying to South West of the Máldives, or on the Equator in long. 70' E. The *Chagos*, though further South, were doubtless meant.

"With renewed salutations, We commend Your Highness to God's protection,

Your Highness' good friend,

(Signed) RYCKLOFF VAN GOENS.

Colombo, 16th January, 1671.

Sultán Ibráhím Iskandar I : A.C. 1648-1687.

"The Mighty Lord, *Mahamady Ubraime*, Ruler of the Máldives" Governor Ryckloff van Goens addressed in his Letter of 1671, was Sulṭán Ibráhím Iskandar I, son of S. Muḥammad 'Imád-ud-dín Shuja'i I and Aishá Kabáfánu, "thrice crowned Queen."[1]

He succeeded to the *Masnad* in 1648, when eighteen, and reigned until 1687.

One of the Islands' most puissant Monarchs, he has left his mark on Máldivian History. The Portuguese were finally routed in 1649, when Mále was attacked by a powerful fleet—the last effort to retain drastic grip on the Group; and the Kaṇṇanúr (Áḷi Rája) Rulers' long-standing enforcement of Annual Tribute terminated.

At home, he carried out extensive religious improvements; and performed the *Ḥajj* pilgrimage twice (1667; 1682).

Circular coinage was first struck in this reign.[2]

No. 3. Governor Laurensz Pyl's Letter to the Sultán: A. C. 1688.

Of this Letter to the boy Sulṭán, Kuḍa Muḥammad, son of S. Ibráhím Iskandar I, two copies exist, one in Arabic, the other in Dutch, differing little in wording.[3]

The accompanying Plate shows a photographic reproduction of the Letter, to exact size. The English Translation given below has been made from both versions.

---

1. Chief Queen of Sulṭán Ibráhím III (Kaláfánu : A.C. 1585—1609); Sulṭán Ḥasan II (Fámudíri Kilégefánu : A. C. 1609—20); Sulṭán Muḥammad 'Imád-ud-dín Shuja'i I : A. C. 1620-48).

2. Monograph (Máldive Islands) p. 31.

3. The Arabic Text contains the following additions to the version as given by the Dutch Translation :—

(i) Heading : *Bismihi subhánahu va ta'ala*, "In the Name of (Him), the Glorified, the Most High.

(ii) *Muḥarram 2nd* (October 17th); date of the Missive's despatch.

(iii) To "Silver cloth, with filigree ornamentation," is added "called *Zarbáf* (scarf) for neckwear."

" Laurensz Pyl, Counsel in Ordinary of India, Governor and Director of the Island Ceylon, the Madura Coast, tenders to his powerful Majesty, the Sulṭán, Lord of the Máldive Islands, his wishes for a prosperous reign, long life, and perfect health.

" Your Highness' Missive has been handed to Us, to Our exceeding happiness, on November 2nd last, by Your Highness' *Nákuda Ḥáji* 'Ali ; who has, further, brought from Your Highness (the following presents) ; for which We desire to thank Your Highness :—

" Silver Cloth, 2 lbs. in weight, ornamented with gold and silver filigree work ; two (2) Máldive Turbans ; four (4) Máldive Mats ; one thousand (1,000) pieces of *Commela-mas* (dry fish).

" According to Your Highness' request, We have been helpful to Your Highness' people in everything ; and have taken over, both here and at Galle, the Cowries brought by them, at 6¼ *larins* the *cotty* (*koṭṭé*) of 12,000 shells ; closing accounts with them.

" In response to the desire of Your Highness to live in friendship with the Honourable and Illustrious (Netherlands) Company, We are similarly disposed ; and, for the fostering of good commerce, desire to enter into a Contract of greater amity and trust with Your Highness.

"To treat regarding this, with the greatest benefit, profit, and advantage, may it please Your Highness to send here some Persons of Importance, with credentials ; whom We undertake to meet with full reasonableness.

" We have had verbal communication (regarding this matter) with Your Highness' *Nákuda Ḥáji* 'Ali ; and he, on his part, has consented to inform Your Highness.

" As acknowledgement of Your Highness' benevolence towards Us, to this Reply We have added (the under-mentioned gifts) :—Ten (10) lbs. Cloves ; ten (10) lbs. Mace ; ten (10) lbs. Nutmegs ; fifty (50) lbs. Cinnamon ; ten (10) ells of Red cloth ; one hundred (100) ells of the same. For these We ask Your Highness' kind acceptance.

" May God keep Your Highness, and all Your subjects, in lasting health and prosperity."

(Signed) LAURENSZ PYL.

December 4th, 1668.

Governor Laurensz Pyl's Reply to the Sultán's Missive.
December 4. A.C. 1688.

باسمه سبحانه وتعالى

لورنس فيل ارد فنيشيا كوفرندور اندركتول بجزيرة سيلان في ارض مادري ارسل الى سلطان
محمد ابن سلطان ابراهيم بجزيرة ديو محل طول الله تعالى عمره وسلمه في الدنيا والآخرة
وبعد فان مكتوبكم في صحبة نخودا حاج على مع جماعاته كلهم قد وصل الينا ثاني يوم
شهر المحرم الحرام وعرفنا جميع ما فيه من الكلام وفرحنا لمجيئه الينا من جانبكم الشريف
ومع ما تضمن من الهدايا وهي الثوب المذهب المسمى بازرباف اثنان وعمامة ديو محل
طاقتان واربع من الحصير الكبار والف سمك مبلس وان الله تعالى يتقبل احسانكم وخيراتكم
واما ما طلب السلطان محمد حفظه الله تعالى من عندنا انه نعين بعض جماعاته فنحن ان شاء الله
نعينهم مثل نعين جماعاتنا فنعرفكم ان لوري الذي الينا قد ساعدنا ببيعه في كل واحد
من كتي بعنا لكم بستة لاري وستة مكاس والسبب في ذلك لما كان السلطان محمد يريد الصحبة
مع كمفني دايما الى نهاية افرح كمفني بذلك وايضا يمكن ان يكون بينكم وبين كمفني بافعال
البيع والشرى مصالحة ثم اذا ارسلتم الينا في السنة الآتية ارسلوا برجل معتبر من اهل
العقول حتى يتأكد صحبتنا معكم بذلك الرجل صحبة الحاج على وقد قلنا للحاج على ذلك بذلك
المقال وقد صار بيننا وبينه وعلى انه سيقول لكم هذا الكلام ثم بعد ذلك لما كان السلطان محمد
يفرح بارسال المكتوب الينا مع ما تضمن فيه من الهدايا فان الله يتقبل ذلك منكم فنحن نرسل
لكم بعشرة كيني قرنفل وعشرة كيني زهر جوز الطيب وعشرة كيني جوز الطيب واربعة باع جوخ
احمر ومائة كتة سكر بنكالي وخمسين كيني قرفة ونسال منكم يا سلطان محمد حفظه الله تعالى
ان تقبلوا هذه الهدايا منا فالحاصل ان جميع امور [illegible] وعينكم تسلموهم الى الارادة الله تعالى

Sultán Kuḍa Muḥammad: A.C. 1687—91.

Sulṭán Íbráhím Iskandar I died from poison administered by his son's mother, a concubine named Mariyam.

The young Prince, only six years of age, was faithfully guarded by the Vazírs; but the Queen Mother, Mariyam Kabáfánu, by basest influence gained absolute power. Many leading Vazírs were banished, or replaced by her relatives and favourites.

Thereafter, Mariyam threw all decency to the winds—openly playing the role of a later day Catherine II of Russia. Nominally married to a commoner, on whom High Rank was conferred, she encouraged unrestricted vice in every form.

In 1691 piratical vessels from the Malabar Coast descended on Tiladummati (the most Northerly) Atol: committing much depredation, before Máldivian boats could be equipped to encounter them.

The Máldivians drove the enemy off. Mariyam, with her son, then sailed to meet the victorious boats returning to Mále. During the firing of a salute on the Royal *Oḍi* sparks fell into the Powder Magazine, and the vessel blew up.

Of the Queen the body was not found: that of her son, though recovered, was so badly burnt that he succumbed to his injuries almost at once.[1]

With the death of Kuḍa Muḥammad, the youthful nominal .lṭán, the direct Utímu Dynasty of Máldive Sulṭáns came to end.

Political Status of the Màldive Sultáns.

No show of force was needed on the part of the Dutch unlike their Portuguese fore-runners to secure a recognition of their Suzerainty—inherited, so to say,—over the Máldive Islands.

With a wise discretion the Sulṭáns have voluntarily placed themselves, for three centuries and more, under the virtual protection of the dominant European Power in Ceylon, and courted its alliance; having finally thrown off the intolerable yoke of Portuguese thraldom, which lasted little short of a hundred years (A.C. 1558-1649).

---

1. Monograph (Máldive Islands), pp 32-33. *Enda Miskit.* "The burnt (Queen's) Mosque" still stands at Mále to recall the episode.

British-Máldivian Treaty : A.C. 1887.

Under the State Agreement, concluded on December 16th, 1887, between the British Crown, as represented by His Excellency the Governor of Ceylon, the Hon. Sir A. H. Gordon, G.C.M.G. (later Lord Stanmore) and His Highness the Sulṭán of the Máldives, Muḥammad Mu'in-ud-dín II,[1] the Máldive Islands definitely became the sole *Political Dependency of Ceylon* ; but with full unrestricted freedom, *caeteris paribus*, in all matters relating to Internal Administration.

" By this Compact the Sulṭán, on his side :—

(*a*) Recognized conclusively, on behalf of His Highness and his Successors, the Suzerainty of the Sovereign of Great Britain over the Máldive Islands.

(*b*) Disclaimed all right, or intention, to enter into Negotiation, or Treaty, with any Foreign State, except through the Ruler of Ceylon.

" With equal explicitness the British Government engaged, *per contra* :—

(*c*) To protect the Máldive Islands always against all Foreign Enemies.

(*d*) To abstain, to the furthest extent justifiable, from all interference in the Local Administration of the Group, or intervention in its Internal troubles.

---

1. Sulṭán Muḥammad Mu'ín-ud-dín II. Eldest son of Prince Ḥasan 'Izz-ud-dín, the blind incapacitated elder brother of Sulṭán Íbráhím Núr-ud-dín. The latter immediately succeeded his father (Sulṭán Muḥammad 'Imád-ud-dín IV, A.C. 1835-1882); and died in 1892.

For two years, 1886-88, he peaceably abdicated (willingly or on pressure) in favour of his oldest nephew; who ruled as Sulṭán Muḥammad Mu'ín-ud-dín II, dying in 1888.

In 1893 abortive efforts were made by rival Ministers to place on the throne, in turn, (i) the eldest—only 8 years old—of three boy-sons of Sulṭán Íbráhím Núr-ud-dín by different beds, under the name of Sulṭán Muḥammad 'Imád-ud-dín V ; and (ii) the only son of the same Sulṭán's senior wife—a lad 13 to 14 years of age.

Further scheming culminated finally in the appointment (first as *Regent* and later as *Sulṭán*) of the eldest son of Prince Ḥasan 'Izz-ud-dín by his second bed; who assumed the title Sultán Muḥammad 'Imád-ud-dín VI (A.C. 1893-1903).

Ten years later he was deposed by the Ceylon Government: and the Sulṭánate definitely restored, to (ii) his eldest cousin, the rightful heir, reigning at this day as Sulṭán Muḥammad Shams-ud-dín III.

"The future status of the Máldive Sulṭáṇs, and the degree of their Dependence on the Paramount Power, the Crown of England, became thus unequivocably defined, once for all, in 1887." [1]

1. Monograph (Máldive Islands) p. 49.

EXCERPTA MALDIVIANA.

BY

H. C. P. BELL, C.C.S. (Retired)

No. 12.—MÁLDIVIAN PROVERBS.[1]

FOREWORD.

"A Nation's Proverbs," rightly has it been said, "are as precious as its ballads, as useful, and perhaps more instructive."

"Despise not the discourse of the Wise, but acquaint thyself with their Proverbs: for of them thou shalt learn instruction." Thus wrote Jesus the son of Shirack, in his "*Wisdom*," or "*Ecclesiasticus*" (VIII. 8) some twenty centuries ago.

"Wisdom manifests herself in divers forms, but seldom perhaps in any more acceptably, or impressively, than when she clothes herself in proverbial guise."

Yet for the definition of a *Proverb*, with complete accuracy, there standeth forth—Who ? Echo answers—"Who ?"

"Much matter decocted into few words" (Fuller); "Shortness, sense and salt" (Howell); "Wisdom of many, wit of one" (Lord Russell);—these and other attempted solutions (including Erasmus' well-known, but inadequate, "*Celebre dictum scita quâpiam novitate insigne*") all fall short more or less of solving fully the "complex," so quaintly assayed by a Latin poetaster—

Omne Epigramma sit instar apis, sit aculeus illi,
Sint sua mella, sit et corporis exigui.

"Proverbs and bees should—an they do not fail—
Have honey, body slight, and sting in tail."

1. For the never failing generosity, and courteous readiness to aid students in Máldivian literary research, the writer is almost entirely indebted to his kind friends at Málé, the State Ministers A. Ahmad Dídí, *Doriméná Kilégefánu*, his son A. Muhammad Amín Dídí, and M. Ibráhím Dídí, a cousin, who supplied the Proverbs printed in this Paper, as well as others.

But etymologically, at all events, the verbal interpretation of the Latin *proverbium* (*pro* + *verbum*, "publicity saying") and its Greek correlative *paraemia* (*para* + *oimos*, "wayside expression") tends to show unmistakably that "triteness, common usage, and popular acceptance" are essential features of the Proverb, or Adage (? *ad agendum aptum*), its near parallel.

The languages, whether of Europe and America, of Asia and Africa, or the Seven Seas of the World, have, each and all, their special stores of wit and wisdom in the shape of Proverbs; albeit, so much appears akin to the rest, that careful study would seem to point "either to some same origin, or to the hypothesis of an universal wisdom manifesting itself vicariously in the pithy savings of all nations, barbarous and civilized."

Oriental Proverbs are still but little known in Europe outside a small circle of Orientalists, and even they have to a great extent overlooked them. On Proverbs of the four main languages (Dravidian) of Southern India. (*Tamil, Telugu, Kannarese*, and *Malayáḷam*), like *Siṇhalese*[1] (Áryan) in Ceylon, "Collections" have been issued, from time to time; but all are capable of much extension.

MALDIVIAN PROVERBS.

The fortunate opportunity of a few months' sojourn during 1922 in the little known Máldive Islands—Ceylon's Muslim Dependency—afforded the writer the welcome chance of acquiring a casual, though but partial, "batch" of Proverbs current on the Group.

From this windfall a random selection is offered in the present Paper; limited, of set purpose, to half-a-hundred—lest peradventure Don Quixote's heavy curse do light upon him from readers justifiably resenting the gratuitous annoyance of "damnable iteration."[2]

In regard to the broad nature of Máldivian Proverbs, it is not surprising to find the "tang of the sea" largely pervading many a *tritum vetustate proverbium* of these hardy sea-faring Islanders of "*Mehi Laka*" ("*Cis-mare* Lanká,"

1. Several 'Collections":—*Specimens of Siṇhalese Proverbs* (L. de Zoysa Mudaliyar) Journal C.A.S., 1870-1872: 1881; *Athitha Wākya Dipaniya* (Mendis), *Siṇhala Upamā* (N. Mendis, 1890), &c.

2. "Heaven confound thee: sixty thousand devils take thee and thy Proverbs!"

Máldives), whose boats have long frequented far-flung Eastern harbours: in this respect at least differentiating them noticeably from their more land-bound progenitors with wider interests, dwelling in "*Aḥi Laka*" ("*Trans-mare Lanká*," Ceylon).[1]

But, as with Siṇhalese Proverbs, "the saving grace of spicy humour" displays itself not infrequently in their Máldivian congeners—at times with a refreshing unsophisticated frankness startling to ultra-refined ears.

For the rest, it should be remembered that "the vagueness of their epigrammatic brevity allowing great variety of meanings, the play upon words, and alliterations, may cause the true point to be missed in the translation of many."

SINHALESE, AND OTHER PARALLEL, PROVERBS.

The marked affinity of the Siṇhalese language with the Máldivian form (in particular the purer dialect of the Southern, and more distant, Atols, which retains fuller elements of its original source, owing to less intercourse both with Western India, and Muslim influence during centuries of Arabic and Persian trade) is, as was to be expected, very patently exhibited to no small degree in the mutual similarity of the proverbial lore of both races.

Interesting proofs of distinct Muslim contact with the Archipelago, and Islamic infiltration—mainly in the Northern and Central Atols—crop up; but these only go to emphasize further the greatly preponderating general resemblance—so manifestly derived from the erst-time Siṇhalese parental stock, after the Aryan migration into Ceylon from the Indian Continent.

To bring out this close kinship between Siṇhalese (S. *Upamá*) and Máldivian (M. *Musáḷu*) Proverbs the more effectually, all examples of the former quoted have been placed immediately below the equivalent, or semi-co-efficient, paraemiology of the Islands.

---

1. "*Mehi Laka*" (*lit.* "Here Laṇká"); — "*Ahi Laka*" (*lit.* "There Lanká"). Terms used in the old Máldivian *Boḍugaḷu Lómáfánu* (Royal Copper Grant). Plate T, observe, line 3.

Finally, to illustrate, *pro tanto*, the cosmopolitan currency of similar " wise-sayed saws " throughout the world, sporadic instances of kindred quips are interpolated from occasional other Eastern sources, as well as European languages mainly Latin.[1] These can doubtless be greatly supplemented by other students, attracted to the subject.

MALDIVIAN PROVERBS

(I.) GENERAL

1.

Funet fáya(ṛ) fen furun.

" (Like) pouring water into a broken pot."

Similes.

(*a*) *Kẹdichcha kaléṭa watura wakkaranná wágẹyi* (S).

" Like pouring water into a broken pot."

(*b*) *In pertusum ingerimus dicta dolium* (L).

2.

Furifá huri baḍiyale(ṛ) guḍu guḍe(ṛ) nagáṛe.

" The water-pot that is full will not shake (*lit.*) make *guḍu guḍu* sound)."

Simile.

(*a*) *Piriṇu kalé diya no-selveyi* (S.)

" In a full pot the water will not shake."

3.

Saṭṭi nubai bat-koḷu heyo.

" The cooking-pot may be bad, (but) the rice (boiled therein) good."

Similes.

Kavuru gini molevvé mokada apé bata pẹhichchi nam (S).

(*a*) " What boots it who kindles the fire, if our rice be boiled."

(*b*) *Mẹṭiyen wat mokada balalá míyá ẹllí nam* (S).

" What matters it if the cat, though made even of clay, catch the rat."

4.

Vaḷe(ṛ) nuteḷeneye dánñe teḷeni.

" The well will not break, should the *dánné* [2] (snap) "

Simile.

(*a*) *Édaṇḍa giyáṭa toṭupalat yayi-da* (S).

" Though the *édaṇḍa* (single log bridge) be washed away (*lit.* go), will the ferry go too ?

---

1. (A), Arabic ; (E), English ; (F), French ; (Gr), Greek ; (H) Hebrew ; (I) Italian ; (L) Latin ; (S), Siṇhalese ; (Sc.), Scotch ; (Skt.), Sanskrit ; (W.A.), West African.

2. *Dánné* :—Long-handled scoop with coconut-shell head.

5

5.

Nuro dariyaka(ṛ) kiren nulibeneye.
"The babe that cries not will get no (breast) milk."

Simile.

(a) *Ëñdú-koṭalu kiri erenne* (S).
"When the infant cries the (breast) milk will rise."

6.

Rihe fái maṛcha(ṛ) foi veṛṭunu ḥen.
"Like the (grain) pounder falling on (one's) sore foot."

Similes.

(a) *Gahen veṭunu minihâṭa goná ẹnná wágeyi* (S).
"Like the ox goring the man fallen from the tree."

(b) *Koré piṭaṭa maré* (S).
"The pangs of death added to lameness."

(c) "Heaping Pelion on Ossa." (Gr.)

(d) *In flammam flammas, in mare fundis aquas* (L).

7.

Veṛṭen dátá gá ko(ṛ) fállye.
"Pushed down when falling."

Simile.

(a) *Vẹṭenṭa yaddí tallu kaḷá wágeyi* (S)
"Like pushing down (one already) falling."

8.

Baḷuge nagu kita(ṛ)me varaka(ṛ) henien kamaku tede(ṛ) nuváneye.
"Drag at a dog's tail as long as you choose,
Effort to straighten will be of no use."

Similes.

(a) *Balu walgé ẹda arinṭa bẹruwá wágeyi* (S).
"Like failing to straighten a dog's tail."

(b) *Bihiráṭa gítiká moṭada* (S).
"Why sing to the (stone) deaf ?"

9.

Gini dun mihá rat mala(ṛ) biru ḡannáneye.
"He who has known the hurt of fire's power,
"Feareth the sight of nature's red flower."

Similes.

(a) *Gini penellen beta ká aya kaná mediriyá duṭuwám duwanná wágeyi* (S).

"Like the person (once) beaten with a fire-brand running away on seeing a fire-fly."

(*b*) "He whom a snake has bitten dreads a glow-worm." (W.A.).

10.

Tiya ketaṛṭak gui runleyṛ.

"Like stooling into (one's) feeding plate."

Simile

(*a*) *Kápu paté runnák men* (S)

"Like stooling into (one's) feeding plate."

(*b*) *Magna movet stomachum fastidia si puer unctis Tractavit calicem manibus* (L).

(*c*) "Throw no stones into the well whence you have drunk" (Heb.).

(*d*) "It's an ill bird which fouls its own nest" (E).

11.

Vehen oṛwwá fen negun.

"Collect water whilst it rains."

Similes.

(*a*) *Galáyana waturen dótak gattat lába lu* (S).

"Even two handfuls got from running water are gain, 't is said."

(*b*) "Make hay while the sun shines" (E).

12.

At ot echche(ṛ) du nukuraṛe ane(ṛ) eṛche(ṛ) libene kama(ṛ).

"Part not with what is held, counting on something better."

Similes.

(*a*) *Miṭé un kurullá ẹralá gahe un kurullá ẹllímaṭa giyák men* (S).

"Like releasing the bird in (one's) fist when going to catch the bird on the tree."

(*b*) *Até neti muttu ẹtté múdin etarayi* (S).

"Things unpossessed (*lit.* not in hand) are (as though) overseas."

(*c*) *Certa amittemus dum incerta petimus* (L).

(*d*) "A thousand cranes in the air are not worth one sparrow in the fist" (A).

(*e*) "A bird in the hand is worth two in the bush" (E)

13.

Vaḷi riti tilatuniṛyáye.

"The knife is beautiful, if the blade be sharp."

Similes.

(*a*) *Le coûte en ôte le goût* (F).

(*b*) " The worth of anything is just as much as it will bring "(E).

14.

Kuriot gerige fide fennani.

" The back of the ox in front (moving ahead in single line) can alone be seen."

Similes.

(*a*) *Anungé ẹhé kuna mólgahak vágeyi penenava lu,*
Tamunge ẹhé kuna abamal rénuwak vágeyi penanavá lu(S).

" Dirt, 't is said, in others' eyes appears like a rice pounder ; dirt in one's own eye like a mustard seed."

(*b*) *Crimine qua cernunt aliorum, non sua cernunt*
Hi sapiunt aliis, desipiuntque sibi (L).

(*c*) " Why beholdeth thou the mote in thy brother's eye, but considereth not the beam that is in thine own eye ? " E).

15.

Boḍu nagulaṛe duniyege kanta(ṛ) dani.

"In the world things (may take) shape like a lizard's tail."

Similes.

(*a*) " Fine by degrees and beautifully less " (E)

(*b*) " Much cry, little wool" (S).

16.

Kanun eṛlá gá gaḍa(ṛ).

" (Like) the stone thrown by the blind man."

Similes.

(*a*) *Gal kípayak gehuwot ekakwat wadí* (S).

" If several stones be thrown, one at least will hit.

(*b*) " Drawing a bow at a venture " (E)

17.

Numoṛe gurábára(ṛ) dai gannáneye.

" Parrots, (even if) speechless, (can) bite hard."

Similes.

(*a*) *Nidiyena díyan kubuddaṇṭa epá* (S).

" Rouse not sleeping leopards."

(*b*) " Let sleeping dogs lie."

(*c*) " Still waters run deep " (E).

18.

Hiyanfia(ṛ) muḍi negun.
To jump at one's shadow

Similes.

(*a*) *Nurussana minihage sevanẹllat ẹda lu* (S).
"Even the shadow, 't is said, of a hated man is distorted."
(*b*) "Shadows to night,
Have struck more terror to the soul of Richard
Than can the substance of ten thousand soldiers"(E)

19.

A kukuḷaka(ṛ) gá biheke tiya eḷuni.
"Like the pullet that laid (its first) egg."

Similes.

(*a*) "Salt will not itself say 'I have a pleasant taste'."(W.A.)
(*b*) "Blowing one's own trumpet" (E).

20.

Kukuḷa(ṛ) vure bis doṛivun.
"The egg becomes older than the hen."

Similes.

(*a*) *Kimbul pẹṭavuṇṭa pínáṇṭa uganuwanne kavuḍa* (S)
"Who teaches young crocodiles to swim?"
(*b*) "Teach an eagle to fly"; "a dolphin to swim"(Gr).
(*c*) *Sus Minervam docet* (L).
(*d*) "Teaching your grandmother (to suck eggs)" (E).

21.

De midá fehi·buḷala(ṛ) vi varevántiya
"(Like) the cat chasing two ṛats (simultaneously)."

Similes.

(*a*) *Flare simul et sorbere hand facile est* (L).
(*b*) "One eye looks not simultaneously on a *Kra* monkey and an *Asibe* baboon" (W.A).
(*c*) "He who would grasp too much, will hold nothing" (It.).
(*d*) "Vaulting ambition which o'er leaps itself" (E).

22.

Giteyo eḷi guḷiyakun vahe(ṛ) nufiláneye.
"A vessel which held (*lit.* into which has been poured) ghee will not lose its smell."

Simile.

(*a*) " You may break, you may shatter, the vase as you will,
The scent of the roses is over it still " (E).

23.

Ala gahakun keyo nirḙ(ṛ) nufaḷáneye.
" From a yam's root, springs no plantain shoot."

Similes.

(*a*) *Non generant aquilae columbas* (L).
(*b*) " The crab's daughter beareth not a bird " (W.A.).
(*c*) " Do men gather grapes of thorns, or figs of thistles ? " (*E*).

24.

Danna mis ará gala(ṛ) arannñá danna mis váneye.
" He who stands on the (same) rock as the learned will be deemed to be learned."

Similes.

(*a*) *Uttamayinge guṇa uttamayó danit* (S).
" Good men's merits are known to the good."
(*b*) *Noscitur a sociis* (L).
(*c*) " Even foolish men to eminence may rise,
By following closely actions of the wise.' '(Skt.)
(*d*) " Keep gude company and ye'll be counted ane of them " (Sc.).

25.

Bo foti gaye tiya huri.
" Like wearing ostentatious (*lit.* thick) clothing."

Similes.

(*a*) *Simia simia est, etiam si aurea gestat insignia* (L)
(*b*) " Trumpeter *unus erat qui* coatum scarlet *habebat,*
Et magnum periwig, tied up with the tail of a dead pig."
(*c*) " Let ne'er your gear o'ergang ye " (Sc.).
(*d*) " Like hedgehogs dressed in lace " (E)

26.

Tan ottá goḍi jehun.
" (Like) arranging the seats while there is space."

Similes.

(*a*) *Omnem crede diem tibi diluxisse supremum* (L).
(*b*) "The Bird of Time has but a little way to flutter,
—And the Bird is on the wing " (E).

27.

Beru fuḷali jehimá gifili fen waḷun gele(ṛ) weṛtun.

" (Like) a brick falling from the back rooms's well when the garden gate is opened."

Similes.

(*a*) *Dolendi modus, non est timendi* (L).

(*b*) " The leaf crackled, and your slave fled " (W.A.).

(*c*) " Conscience does make cowards of us all " (E).

28.

El Banḍára de geriye taḷáne waraka(ṛ) teḷiya ḍeṛe.

" (They are but) two Government cattle : let them fight as much as they like."

Similes

(*a*) *Ácháriyáṭa mayináhama epánam magé balláṭat epá* (S).

" If the blacksmith needs not the bellows, my dog even will not want it."

(*b*) " Hippoclides don't care " (Gr.).

(*c*) *Nil est ad nos* (L).

(*d*) " Fight dog, fight bear ; wha wins deil care!" (Sc.).

29.

De kaḍiye(ṛ) ek urayaku nonnáneye.

" Two swords cannot be kept in one scabbard."

Similes.

(*a*) *Eka Pansalé inná Mahanun Unnansélát kuḍamiṭa harawágannawá lu* (S).

" Even Buddhist Monks, 't is said, living in one *Pansala* come to loggerheads."

(*b*) " Two crocodiles do not live in one hole " (W.A.).

(*c*) " Two of a trade seldom agree " (E).

30.

Iburáhimaku maṛcha(ṛ) kibihinnek erima ehinna(ṛ) duniye ran vihene viṛye.

" The world becomes golden to the ant which climbs on to an *Ìbráhim* (gold coin)."

Similes.

(*a*) *Ratran ṭika kẹraḷu kaṭussá vage* (S).

" Like the piece of gold tied round the neck of the chameleon." [1]

(*b*) *Asperius nihil est humili cum surgit in altum* (L).

(*c*) " Set a beggar on horse back, etc." (E).

---

1. See the story in Louis de Zoysa's Proverbs, No. 222 (C.A.S. Journal, 1872).

(*d*) " Gold ! Gold ! Gold ! Gold !
Bright and yellow, hard and cold
How widely its agencies vary—
Now stamped with the image of Good Queen Bess,
And now of a Bloody Mary " !

31.

Kamaku terene kama(ṛ) libeni.
" Do something; gain something."

Similes.

(*a*) *Ata nohollá kaṭa hollaṇṭa bẹhẹ* (S).
" Without exertion (*lit.* moving the hand) one cannot eat (*lit.* move the mouth)."
(*b*) *Nil sine magno Vita labore dedit mortalibus* (L)
(*c*) *Il n'ya pas d' omelette sans casser des oeufs* (F).
(*d*) " No pains, no gains " (E)

32.

Kukuḷu govi kamaku aṛye(ṛ) nuvileṛeye.
" If hens crow it is not dawn."

Similes.

(*a*) *Kaṭa baha ẹti gẹ́ni ẹtikaraṇa kikilit añḍalanavá lu*(S)
" The hen too, 't is said, will crow that is reared by a gabbling woman."
(*b*) " Whistling woman, crowing hen,
Pleaseth neither gods nor men " (E).

33.

Tiya fenuni hudu kaḷake.
" Like a white crow "

Similes.

(*a*) *Rara avis in terris, nigroque simillima cygno* (L).
(*b*) " Very like a whale." (E).

34.

Midalu hattin wafen bovuma(ṛ).
" The rat gnaws into the young coconut : the bat drinks the water."

Similes.

(*a*) *Nẹṭum gẹhum Kapurálaṭa lu,*
Bat ṭika Ṭikirálaṭa lu (S).
" The dancing (labour) falls to the *Kapurála,* the boiled rice to *Ṭikirála,* 't is said."
(*b*) " Some have laboured, others profited " (Gr.).
(*c*) *Sic vos non vobis.* (L.)
(*d*) *Les foux font des festins, et les sages les mangeṇt* (F)
(*e*) " One soweth, another reapeth " (E).

(2.) SEA-FARING

35.

Ganfá dáni boḍu mahe.
" Huge was the fish that escaped "

Simile.

Giya Lúlá maha eká lu (S).
" The *Lúlá* that got away was the immense one, 't is said."

36.

Fetunu Oḍi ṛiyá daṛu viyas kanaku at daṛu nuváṛe.
" Even if you sink under a (capsized) *Oḍi's* [1] mast, get not caught in a blind man's grip."

Simile.

(*a*) *Kanáṭa ahuvuna bẹlimẹkká wágeyi* (S).
" Like the flea caught by the blind man."

37.

Ek donu gá de buḷiye tiya jehi.
" Like baiting two hooks on one line."

Similes

(*a*) *Duos parietes de eadem fidelia dealbare* (L).
(*b*) "Killing two birds with one stone." (E).

38.

Bas nuvike Oḍiyeṛge dirubala(ṛ) náráṛe.
" Station not yourself at the *Oḍi's* bow unless you (can take) command, (*lit.* sell not your words).

Similes.

(*a*) " Command will show the man " (Gr.)
(*b*) *Rex est qui metuit nihil,*
Rex est quique cupit nihil (L)
(*c*) " A subjectless King is no King " (W.A.).

39.

Mále dán Kelaya(ṛ).
" Going to Kelaya (in Tiladummati Atol, Northernmost) in order to reach Mále " (Central Atol).

---

1. *Oḍi* :—Máldivian sailing vessel Cf. *Dóṇi*, No. 48 *infra*.

Similes.

(*a*) *Parangiyá Kóṭṭé giyá wágeyi* (S).[1]
"Like the Portuguese going to Kóṭṭé."

(*b*) *Prendre le chemin des écoliers* (F).

40.

Ronu eduru.
"Master of Rope—(making)."

Similes.

(*a*) *Aliquis in omnibus, nullus in singulis* (L).

(*b*) "Was everything by starts, and nothing long."

(*c*) "Jack of all trades, master of none" (E).

41.

Amá kiti fara(ṛ) diyun.
"Going to pick shells, only because (his) mother bade him."

Similes.

(*a*) *Stultitia est venatum ducere invitos canes* (L).

(*b*) "Where the mind inclines, the feet lead" (A).

(*c*) "He ne'er did a gude darg (day's work) that ga'ed grumbling about it" (Sc.).

(3.) MUSLIM

42.

Burudá gai mu kurun.
"To make sure of *Burudá*."[2]

---

1. *Portuguese going to Kóṭṭé*:—See De Quieroz (Book 2, Chapter 1) and De Zoysa's *Sinhalese Proverbs*, No. 17, Journal C.A.S., 1870.

On the first arrival of a Portuguese Fleet at Colombo (November, 1505), the Admiral, Don Lourgenço de Almeyda, sent two successive Ambassadors, Fernao Cutrim and Payo de Souza, to the Sinhalese King then reigning at Kóṭṭé.

Though Kóṭṭé is situated but some six miles from Colombo, "through the industry (*sic*) of the Cingalas," each Ambassador "spent three days on the journey, going uphill and down dale and crossing the same river (Kélani Gaṇga) several times." Remonstrance with those who guided them was met by open laughter. the intention of the Sinhalese being "to secure themselves from any danger."

As counter to this Proverb, runs :—"The longest way round is the shortest way home."

2. *Burudá* :—Arabic *Burdah*. An Arabic poem, said to have been composed about A.H. 810, eulogising the Prophet Muhammad, and inculcating moral precepts. This poem is now-a-days at times recited at social gatherings, where the guests are hospitably entertained.

Similes

(*a*) *Eamus quo ducit gula* (L).
(*b*) " When the stomach calls, wisdom falls " (A).
(*c*) ' Ilka man as he likes—I'm for the cook " (Sc.).

43.

Danbera(ṛ) vure Tagudi diguwun. [1]
Tagudi (playing) becomes longer than *Dan-beru*.

Similes.

(*a*) *Omne nimium nocet; ne quid nimis* (L.)
(*b*) *Injussi numquam desistant*
" Though unasked, they'll play and play,
Till patience self is worn away."
(*c*) " Nothing is there to come, and nothing past,
But an eternal now does always last " (E).

44.

Miskit hulu jehi mihá hedeniye.

" (Like) the man who set fire to the Mosque (at dead of night, loudly denouncing ' Somebody ' as he emerged)."

Similes.

(*a*) *Wañdința giya Déválé ìeé kaḍá veṭuná vágeyi* (S).
" Like the *Déválé* falling on one's head when entering for worship.
(*b*) " There's many a slip 'twixt cup and lip " (Gr.)
(*c*) *Acta exteriora indicant interiora secreta* (L).
(*d*) " He who gets between the onion and its peel will not emerge free from the stench " (A).

45.

Ar-Rahumánu Surat faṛaifi viyyá Fabiya(ṛ)yi gá nujehi nudáneye.

" He who begins (reading) ' *Ar-Rahmán Súrat* ' [2] will not fail to meet (the words) ' *Fa-bi-yayi* ' "

---

1. *Damberu.*; *Tagudi* :— Tunes played on two Máldivian " tom-toms, so named."

2. *Ar-Rahmán Surat.*—Surat 55 of the *Qurān* entitled "The Merciful." The sentence " *Fa-bi-ayyi-alai-Rabbi-kuma-tukazzi-bán*" (" Which, therefore, of your Lord's benefits will ye ungratefully deny ? " : *Sale*, 1734 ; " Which, then, of the bountees of your Lord will ye reject ? " : *Maulāvi Muhammad 'Ali*, 1917) is intercalated, or repeated by way of burden, throughout the Chapter of stanzas no less than 31 times, in imitation of Psalm 136 of the Biblical King David.

Similes.

(a) "You sing the same (old) song" (Gr.).
(b) *Citharaedus Ridetur chorda qui semper oberrat eadem* (L).
(c) *Occidit miseros crambe repetita magistros* (L).
(d) "To harp on the same string" (E).

46.

Ibilihu kaivanña(ṛ).
"(Like) the wedding of Ibilis (Satan)."

Similes.

(a) *Cras te victurum, cras dices, Postume, semper,*
Dic mihi cras istud, Postume quando venit (L).
(b) "Defer not till to-morrow to be wise,
To-morrow's sun to thee may never rise."
(c) "Procrastination is the thief of time" (E).

47.

Mekunu fumune kamaku Gahaka(ṛ) nufume veneye.
"Though the *Mekunu* (springing fish) leap, the *Gahaka* (limpet) cannot leap."

Similes.

(a) *É kelen mé keṭe'a pennuma muwage tit mękéda* (S).
"Will the deer change its spots, albeit it leap from that jungle to this jungle?"
(b) "Can the Ethiopian change his skin or the Leopard change his spots?" (E).

48.

Mohana(ṛ) Doṇi din hen.
"Like the *Dóṇi* (sailing vessel) given to Mohan."

Similes.

(a) *Upadinṭa issara pekinivęla kapatekeyi* (S).
"Like trying to cut the umbilical cord before the child is born."
(b) "The she-goat has not yeaned, but the kid plays before the house" (Gr).
(c) *Ante victoriam canere triumphum* (L).
(d) "To swallow gudgeons ere they're catch'd,
And count their chickens ere they're hatch'd (E)."

49.

Nálafuṛi fagira(ṛ) geri din hen.

"Like the cow given to the beggar of Nálafuri (island).

Similes.

(*a*) "None gets the cow but the Qàzi" (A).

(*b*) "He who eats the hen of the Sultan will return her to him a cow" (A.)

(*c*) *Apres donner il faut prendre* (F).

50.

Kuḍa Tu(ṛ)tu Didige moho(r).

"Like the (house) nails of Kuḍa Tuttu Dídí." [1]

Similes.

(*a*) *Diruit, aedificat, mutat quadrata rotundis* (L).

(*b*) *A l'aeuvre on connait l'artisan* (F).

(*c*) "A crooked stick (betrays) the carpenter" (W.A.)

---

1. This man, when building his house at Mále, was perplexed by the surfeit of nails he seemed to hold, and finally drove all remaining over into one post !

EXCERPTA MÁLDIVIANA.

No. 13.—SOME POLYGLOT MISSIVES OF SULTAN IBRAHIM ISKANDAR II.

BY

H. C. P. BELL, C.C.S. (Retired)

FOREWORD

The present Paper is a partial tentative endeavour, however limited, possibly to induce other students working on "off-set branches" of Ceylon History, to pay same meed of justice, far too long overdue, to that still but little known Coral Archipelago, the Máldive Islands, Ceylon's single Dependency.

From old times styled by its own inhabitants "*Divehi Rájje,*" or "The Island Kingdom," the Group, lying in the Indian Ocean four hundred odd miles South-West of Ceylon, was in the Sixteenth Century more fully defined by Portuguese Historians as "*Dolos Assa Ral Tera Atholon*" ("The Twelve Thousand Isles and Thirteen Atols").

Strange—parlous strange—that nearly a century and a half of well-recognized, if spasmodic, connection since A.C. 1799 with the British Crown, (though not clinched definitely until the tardy British Máldivian Treaty of A.C. 1887) should have passed, leaving the outside world's acquaintance of the Máldive Islands so slightly advanced, beyond the admirable. albeit greatly wanting, records penned by virtually no more than four visitors—(i) Ibn Baṭúṭa (Abu 'Abdullah Muḥammad), Maghribín Traveller, who was at the Máldives, A.C. 1343-44 ; 1346, (ii) François Pyrard de Laval, the Frenchman, five years (A.C. 1602-07) captive at Málé, (iii) with Lieutenants W. Christopher and I. A. Young, Indian Navy Surveyors of the Group (A.C. 1835 *circa*)—save for the scanty. haphazard particulars furnished by a few sporadic writers in quite recent days.

The Máldivian field, remaining fallow for fuller exploitation, is wide ; but, with the exercise of steady patience and tact, will not fail to be made more and more open to judiciously conducted investigations by the courteous Muslim Ruler of the Islands, the Málḍive Sulṭán of the time being, and his peaceful law-abiding subjects ; *pace* a marked racial timidity—now gradually diminishing—that seeks nothing better than to be " left severely alone " to work out for themselves, their own humble future, wholly unfettered and unharassed by doubtfully welcome alien exploiters—*Timeo Danaos et dona ferentes*—after bitterest experience in the Sixteenth to Eighteenth Centuries, not yet forgotten.

This instalment of the " *Excerpta Máldiviana* " series, as its predecessors, is offered to the Ceylon Asiatic Society in the hope of aiding *pro tanto* in the direction urged above.

The Paper could not have been made available to the public but for the ever ready courtesy, and unbounded generousness of the Very Reverend Father L. Vossen, S.J., Principal of the eminent Papal Seminary at Kandy, who has personally favoured the writer with translations of (*a*) very numerous *Dutch* versions of Missives and Replies, from and to, the Máldive Sulṭáns, and (*b*) of *Portuguese* Missives of the Sulṭán Íbráhím Iskandar II, made through the agency of obliging Goanese Students of the College.

In like manner, for the rendering into English of (c) the *Arabic* and (d) the *Máldivian* Missives, unstinted gratitude is due to E. 'Abdul Hamid Dídí Effendi, for many years Máldivian Government Representative at Colombo, able son of that incomparable Prime Minister to five Sulṭáns, A. Ebráhim Dídí, *Boḍu Doṛiméná Kilégefánu*, who ended forty and more years of faithful and invaluable service to his country in 1925.

EXCERPTA MALDIVIANA : No. 13.

1. ANNUAL MÁLDIVIAN EMBASSY TO CEYLON.

Now-a-days it is common knowledge in Ceylon that an Embassy arrives at Colombo year by year—usually during the course of the last three months—bearing from the Sulṭán on the throne of the Máldive Islands to the Ceylon Government a State Missive, accompanied by customary trifling Presents of indigenous products.*

It remains in doubt at what period exactly, since the Sixteenth Century and Portuguese provisional hold of the group, these Annual Missives assumed the general character of Tributary Homage—virtually implied, though for diplomatic reasons camouflaged under semi-disguised phraseology—which grew into regular recognized practice, steadily pursued and tacitly established. But certain it is that not until the Treaty of A.C. 1887 with the British Crown was the relative Status of the Máldive Sulṭáns placed on a definite footing.

The date of the supercession of earlier relationship on terms of—at least conveniently assumed—equality, as drawn

* Journal, C.A.S., XXIX, 76, 1923, p. 194.

from the spasmodic inter-exchange of Missives from Máldive Sulṭáns and Replies thereto by the Dutch Governors at Colombo, would seem to fall about the commencement of the Eighteenth Century.

2. STATUS OF MÁLDIVE SULṬÁNS : SIXTEENTH CENTURY.

By the repulse of the last two attacks on Mále, in A.C. 1631 *circa*, and A.C. 1650, respectively, the Máldive Sulṭáns had thrown off, once for all, the galling Portuguese yoke of a hundred years—during the fifteen years, A.C. 1558-1573, a ruthless domination, suffered grievously on the Group itself ; if in the subsequent spell exercised vicariously from Cochin and Goa with less drastic force.

During this latter period of hateful Tributary submission to "the accursed *Farangi*," the compulsory recognition of *de facto* vassalage needed no annual epistolary confirmation; in as much as the tender of a Yearly Exaction had been embodied in a crushing *soi disant* "Treaty."*

3. STATUS OF THE SULṬÁNS: SEVENTEENTH CENTURY.

Examination, in the Eighties of last Century, of the Dutch Archives of Colombo and Galle has yielded so far but three references—and those at irregular intervals—to any mutual communication between the Hollanders in Ceylon and Máldivian Sovereigns, viz., in the years A.C. 1645, 1669, and 1688.†

The relations between the Dutch Rulers of Ceylon's sea-borde and the reigning Máldive Sulṭáns, certainly to A.C. 1688, clearly indicate a Political Status of presumed reciprocal equality and friendly intercourse, free from all taint of

---

* *Loc. cit.* XXXII. 84, 1931, pp. 13-15.
† *Loc. cit.* XXXII, 85, 1932, pp. 233. 237, 239.

subservience by the latter to the Netherlands East India Company.

"In response to the desire of Your Highness," wrote Governor Laurensz Pyl in A.C. 1688 "to live in friendship with the Honourable and Illustrious (Netherland's) Company. We are similarly disposed; and for the fostering of good commerce, desire to enter into a Contract of greater amity and trust with Your Highness."*

Little doubt that the prestige of that enlightened Máldive Sovereign Sultán Íbráhím Iskandar I, during the forty (40) years (A.C. 1648-1687) of his masterly reign, still made itself felt with the Hollanders, despite the Sulṭánate having passed at the Islands to a boy but twelve years old, his ill-starred son, Sulṭán Kuḍa Muḥammad, cursed with an unspeakably depraved slave-born mother, whose deserved tragic end he was soon (A.C. 1691) to share.†

4. STATUS OF THE SULTÁNS: EIGHTEENTH CENTURY.

In chronological order, the next Royal Missive (Dutch Translation only) at present known, is dated A.C. 1711—an hiatus of close on a quarter of a century; filled at the Máldives with a plethora of stirring events—(*a*) the closing years of the historically prominent "Utímu Dynasty" (A.C. 1573-1692), (*b*) the Rule of a learned Arab *Shaikh* (A.C. 1692), followed, (*c*) by a Máldivian *Qázi* of Huvadú Atol (A.C. 1692), (*d*) the succession of the short-lived "Isdú Dynasty" (A.C. 1701-1704), doomed to romantic collapse with the Sulṭán Íbráhím Muzhir-ud-din's, bold but abortive attempts to regain the throne, after (*e*) the selection during his absence of the *Doṛiméná*, or Chief Vazir, to fill the *Masnad* (A.C. 1704), under the title of Sulṭán Muḥammad 'Imád-ud-dín II Muzaffar.‡

* *Loc. cit.* p. 239.
† *Loc. cit.* p. 240.
‡ Monograph (Máldive Islands), pp. 32-37.

5. SULTÁN MUHAMMAD 'IMÁD-UD-DÍN II.

He held the throne to A.C. 1721, as the first of four Sulṭáns of the "Diyamigili Dynasty," so dastardly extinguished after seventy years by the murder of his grandson, Sulṭán Muḥammad Ghiyás-ud-din in A.C. 1774.

At the door of an "Act of God,"—the wholly unsuspected escape from shipwreck of Sulṭán Muzhir-ud-dín and his young nephew, ex-Sulṭán Ḥasan X, when returning from the *Hájj*, and their repeated desperate efforts to recapture Málé,—may not unreasonably be attributed the all-important change in the Political Attitude towards the Dutch Power in Ceylon of successive Sulṭáns during the Eighteenth Century, and the British Rule which superceded it—a real desire, if never definitely shown, which ran, barely varied, continuously for not far short of two hundred years; to be cemented finally by the Express Stipulations of the British Máldivian Treaty of December 16th, 1887.

6. SULTÁN'S MISSIVES: A.C. 1711, 1713.

This supposition is strengthened by hardly mistakable inferences, deducible from Royal Missives as early even as October 20th, 1711 (Dutch Translation) and October 16th, 1713 (*Tána* Original).*

The former Letter, received by the Dutch from Sulṭán Muḥammad 'Imad-ud-dín II, contains this pregnant passage :—

"As We am but little, whilst Your Excellency is a Great Lord, We are in need of Your Lordship's help, and at all times.

"We pray that should any person from among Our people come to seek from Your Excellency aid and support against Us, Your Excellency will not lend ear to them.

* Journal, C.A.S. XXIX, 76, 1931, pp. 202-203.

"In the year 1711 from the birth of *Ísá Nabi* (Jesus Christ), on the 28th of the month of Rabi-ul-Awwal (May 5th), Our enemy (the ex-Sulṭán) had gathered together a great number of soldiers from several peoples to make war with them against Us. But he has been forced, without having done Us any harm, to disband his armed body, and to withdraw, on the 29th of the month of Rabi-ul-Ákhir (June 14th.)

"We were prevented, by the importance of affairs, from writing to give Your Excellency information of it (hitherto).

"God has now driven away the said enemy from here."*

Two years later (October 16, A.C. 1713), His Highness records :—

"We have experienced at all times the goodwill of the Rulers at Colombo, and assistance from them. Be graciously pleased not to (*lit.* do not) break the friendship which exists between Us. (Your Excellency is) the Lord (*Sahib*) who, like the shadow of a tree, doth protect Us. Everything that befalls Us, and the difficulties which beset Us, are known to Your Excellency, by reason of Our (*lit.* being the persons) ever keeping (Your Excellency) informed regarding all Our affairs.

"Do not, (We entreat), deprive Us of Your Excellency's sheltering care, under which We abide.

"Should any persons inimical towards Us either have gone, or been driven out of their course, to any place belonging to Your Excellency, kindly have them sent (*lit.* send them) back to Us."

As the Eighteenth Century advanced, the *quasi*-suppliant wording of the Sulṭáns' Missives, however diplomatically worded in this regard, never ceased to harp on a presumed (if ever tactfully disguised) inferential dependence on the European masters of coastal Ceylon.

7. BRITISH-MÁLDIVIAN TREATY : A.C. 1887.

Finally, under the State Agreement concluded on December 16th, 1887, between the British Suzerainty as represented

* Dutch Records, Colombo.

by His Excellency the Governor of Ceylon, the Hon. Sir A. H. Gordon, G.C.M.G. (later Lord Stanmore) and His Highness the Sulṭan of the Máldives, Muḥammad Mu'in-ud-dín II, the Máldive Islands became *once for all a Political Dependency of Ceylon*, under definite British protection; but with the proviso of full unrestricted freedom, *caeteris paribus*, in all matters relating to the Internal Administration of the Group.*

8. EXTANT SULTÁNS' MISSIVES AND GOVERNORS' REPLIES.

Omitting Arabic Missives and English Replies from A.C. 1822 to the present day, a sum-total of the unique Máldivian Missives, seventy (70), or so in number, have come to light.

These Documents comprise (*a*) Actual original existing Missives despatched by Máldivian Rulers, (*b*) Official Dutch and English Translations of (*a*), (*c*) Translations of other Missives whose Texts are not forthcoming, together with (*d*) Replies of Dutch and British Governors' extending from the seventh regnal year (A.C. 1711) of Sulṭan Muḥammad 'Imád-ud-dín II Muzaffar to the twenty-third (A.C. 1822) year of Sulṭán Muḥammad Mu'ín-ud-dín I—when (or may be a few years later) *Arabic* script began wholly to oust Máldivian *Tána* for Missives from Sulṭáns of the Máldives.

In the annexed "*Tabulated Statement*" are listed the (i) number and (ii) written character of the Missives despatched between A.C. 1711 and 1822 by the several Sulṭáns of the Máldives, so far found in the Colombo Archives† or elsewhere.

9. FORM AND SCRIPT OF MISSIVES.

No Máldive Missive as yet traced is inscribed in the archaic "*Evéla*", or slightly later "*Dives Akuru*", Alphabet.‡

* Journal, C.A.S. XXXII, 85, 1932, pp. 240-41.
† See Appendix A.
‡ *Evéla Akuru*; *Dives Akuru*. See Journal, C.A.S. XXIX, 77, 1924, pp. 283-303; and references given.

Much the majority is in a comparatively modern *Arabic-based* Script known as "*Tána*": for not more than four (4) was *Arabic* itself utilised, despite seven-hundred years lapse (A.C. 1153-1822) since the Muslim Conversion; whilst a few *Portuguese*, and even *French*, interlopers have occasionally crept in.

From the death of Sulṭán Muḥammad Mu'ín-ud-dín I in A.C. 1835—a period of a hundred years which has witnessed the reigns, sometimes broken, of seven (7) Sulṭáns—all Missives would appear, as stated, to have been studiously confined to pure *Arabic* script.

Every Máldive Sulṭáns' Missive known is a single-page document. Some are of considerable size, and many beautiful specimens of calligraphy, in which Red and Black Characters are freely commingled; and one at least further embellished by a broad border bearing foliated arabesque ornamentation in gold leaf.*

10. DATING OF MISSIVES.

Of the original Missives, that of A.C. 1713, the earliest discovered, when the Record Office was searched some fifty years ago, bears—as do several others—the *Christian Era* dating; but far the most, inclusive of the latest *Tána* Missive (*Anno Ḥijrae* 1238 or A.C. 1822); are dated from the *Hijra* Era counted by Muhammadans from the Prophet's migration in A.C.622; though sometimes *Anno Hijrae* and *Anno Christi* appear together side by side.

11. SEALS OF MÁLDIVE SULTÁNS.

The Royal Sign Manual on Máldive Rulers' Missives invariably consists of the *Seal* of the Sulṭán, either actually

* Missive from Sulṭán Ḥasan Núr-ud-dín, dated A.H. 1208 (A.C. 1793-94). This coincides nearly with the issue of the only *Gold* coins ever struck at the Máldives, viz., "*Bai Mohori*" in A.H. 1202 (A.C. 1787-88), and "*Mohori*" in A.H. 1207 (A.C. 1792-93), respectively. Both of these were fashioned of the gold recovered from a French vessel wrecked on the Atols.

on the throne, or assumed to be still reigning though absent from the Realm.

They bear its legend inscribed within horizontally ruled lines and a frame; affixed above the Text, or high up on the margin of the Document.

In size and outline the Seals have tended to vary more and more, as Dynasty succeeded Dynasty. Thus, the four (4) Diyamigili Rulers confined themselves exclusively to Large Seals of Octagonal shape, slightly cusped, and measuring nearly two (2) inches across.

This design was initiated by the first Sulṭán of the ilk, Muḥammad 'Imád-ud-dín II Muzaffar (A.C. 1704-21); but, on the extinction of his line seventy years later, continued by Sulṭán Muḥammad Mu'iz-ud-dín, (A.C.1774-79) elder son of Sulṭán Ḥasan 'Izz-ud-dín I (A.C. 1759-67) first Sovereign of the Muli Dynasty.

Sulṭán Ḥasan 'Izz-ud-dín had himself used a Smaller Seal, Round or Oval.

His youngest son, Sulṭán Ḥasan Núr-ud-dín, (A.C. 1779-99) wavered in the selection of his Seal from Octagonal and Large Oval to an Horizontal *Vesica Piscis* form of Small Size.

Sulṭán Muḥammad Mu'in-ud-dín I, son and successor (A.C. 1799-1835), usually preferred a Bold Circular Seal.

The Pinnated Oval, (varying slightly in measurement but usually not large), has seemingly been repeated annually from A.H. 1251 (A.C. 1835)—possibly earlier—onwards.

12. CONTENTS OF SULTÁNS' MISSIVES.

During both Dutch and British times later, after the usual formal enquiries regarding, and prayer for, the Governor's health, the Sulṭáns' Missives contained, ordinarily speaking, the following chief heads :—

(i) Solicitation for continuance of the friendship and favour of the Dutch (or British) Government in Ceylon.

(ii) Appeal for protection against enemies.

(iii) Request for arrest of any Máldivian rebels, and their deportation to Málé.

(iv) Desire for aid to Máldivian subjects chancing to be wrecked on Ceylon, or other Dutch held, shores.

(v) Typical Oriental apology for possible shortcomings on the part of the yearly Ambassadors; with request that their return to Málé be expedited.

(vi) Occasionally there is embodied reference to further subjects of more or less importance—some of special urgency.

(vii) In addition, unfailingly, a list was affixed of the usual complimentary Presents customarily tendered—with perchance the ultra-submissive stereotyped request (so common to the East) for the favour of their gracious acceptance despite regretted unworthiness.*

In brief, these Annual Missives, cling so closely to a cut-and-dried formality as to differ, on the whole, but little—save on exceptionl occasions—during their long-standing existence.

13. REPLIES OF EUROPEAN GOVERNORS IN CEYLON.

The monotonous verbiage repeated *ad nauseam*—but ever most courteously—of the Sulṭáns' Missives applies, not unnaturally, in considerable degree to the Replies of

---

* *Presents.* For details regarding these yearly mutual Presents, see Sessional Paper XLIII, 1881, pp. 49-52.

Very occasionally the Dutch sent (as to the Siṇhalese Kings of Kandy), in addition to the ordinary articles—mostly spices—presented specimens of fauna not found at the Máldives, *e.g.* two buffaloes and two monkeys in 1727, and "a couple of deer, very pretty," in 1728.

Dutch and British Administrators at Ceylon; including (until modern days) those of Commandants at Galle no less than Colombo Governors.

European Governors—Dutch and British alike—for their part readily have :—

(*a*) Promised to do everything in their power to promote the good understanding always subsisting with the Sulṭáns,

(*b*) Undertaken to succour any stranded Máldivians ; stipulating for the same friendly reciprocal office on the part of the Sulṭáns towards Foreign Subjects, European and other, castaway on the Máldive Atols,

(*c*) Expressed approval of the conduct of the Envoys ;

(*d*) Notified, in conclusion, the due receipt and despatch of the mutual Presents.

As a matter of course, very exceptional items now and then find place in the Replies—British no less than the Dutch ; but such, "interpolations" have rarely proved of more than ephemeral moment.

In one most noteworthy respect alone do the Missives and Replies on record from the period of the British occupation of Ceylon, differ *toto caelo* from those of the Dutch period.

Without exception they are free from all vestige of that wholly discreditable mercenary spirit—not to put too fine a point on it—exhibited in unconscionable Trade harrasment (nothing short of peremptory demand at times) by the Hollanders for the supply of *Cowries*, year in year out, from the Máldive Rulers and their subjects—insatiable greed of "the daughter of the horse leach crying 'Give 'Give' "—basest, insistent pressure for augmenting delivery of "Cowries, more Cowries, and still more Cowries" to serve as Currency *passim* wherever backward races clamoured for them.

The long correspondence between the Dutch Governors in Ceylon and Sultán Ibráhím Iskandar II in this connection, reveals to the full the lowest depths of Europeans'Commercial Morality ruling in the East during the Eighteenth Century ; but not confined.—let it be recorded in all fairness—to the Hollanders alone—for French and English ships, to their lasting disgrace, played an equally degrading role to the best of their more limited opportunities.*

14. POLYGLOT. MISSIVES OF MALDIVE SULTÁNS.

As stated, all but a very small proportion of Máldive Sultáns' Original Missives forthcoming, in the long series extending from A.C. 1713 to A.C. 1822, were written in the present-day Máldivian character styled "*Tána*," which directly superceded the comparatively old-time "*Dives Akuru*" Alphabet on the Islands.

The exceptions in alien tongue and script, from a total of fifteen (15) Original Missives, belonging to the thirty (30) years' reign of Sultán Ibráhím Iskandar II. are :—*Portuguese* three (3), *French* one (1), and (greatly curious) but two (2) in *Arabic*,† albeit the Máldives had been converted to Islám since A.C. 1153 as recorded above.

---

* That quaint American cynic J. R. Lovell should have lived a century or so earlier, to lash with his scathing verses ("*The Biglow Papers*") these miserable mercenary European exploiters of Oriental Trade in the Eighteenth Century :—

"It ain't by princerples, nor men,
My preudunt course is steadied,—
I scent wich pays the best, an' then
Go into it baldheaded.

"This doth my cup with marcies fill,
This lays all thought o' sin to rest,—
I *don't* believe in princerple,
But, O, I *du* in interest.

"This heth my faithful shepherd ben,
In pasturs sweet heth led me ;
An' this 'il keep the people green
To feed ez they hev fed me."

† The two Original Arabic Missives forthcoming are dated in A.H. 1134 and 1135 respectively (A.C. 1722 and 1723) ; but the Dutch Translation of a Missive (script unspecified) of the former year, may possibly refer to a third Missive in Arabic.

These "polyglots" bear dates as follow : *Arabic*, A.H. 1134, Rabi-ul Ákhír 14th (A.C 1722, January 21st), 1135 Rajab 24th (A.C. 1723, April 19th); *Portuguese*, May 1st. 1723, May 9th, 1734, May 19th. 1735 ; *French*, June, 1726.

From these six (6) Letters, one of each foreign language, is being used to illustrate the present Paper, together with a single specimen of the nine (9) *Tána* Missives.

15. SULTÁN 'IBRÁHÍM ISKANDAR II.

Of the reigns of the ten (10) Sulṭáns who ruled the Máldive Islands during the Eighteenth Century, that of the second Sovereign of the Diyamigili Dynasty, Sulṭán Íbráhím Iskandar II (A.C. 1721-1750) stands out probably as the most prosperous. He succeeded his father, Sulṭán Muḥammad 'Imád-ud-dín II Muzaffar in A.C. 1721 at the age af 13, and reigned for 29 years in peace and honour till A.C. 1750.

If, *teste* Pyrard de Laval, the Seventeenth Century witnessed Máldive Trade at its heydey, it assuredly had suffered little or no dimunition—in one notable direction actually acquired vast expansion—during the first half of the Eighteenth, under the wise, and tactful administration of Sulṭán Ibráhím the Second.

16. MÁLDIVE COWRY TRADE.

The Trade in Cowries, in particular, overshadowed every other branch of commercial intercourse between the Máldivians and European exploiters—themselves open rivals, battling for the greatest share of Sea-borne Trade with the Islands, chiefly in the exclusive monopoly of dealing for wholesale shipments of the tiny *Cypraa Moneta* molusc, then, and for many years to come, accepted .broadcast throughout Asia and Africa as indispensable substitute for, or supplement to, metal coinage.

By the Hollanders, requirements were pushed persistently, as almost tentamount to peremptory orders, up to well-nigh intolerable limits. Even in A.C. 1722 the annual demand amounted to no less than " 20,000 tons *pro patria*." These shells were customarily shipped from Mále, as convenient ballast, in Dutch vessels specially chartered by their East Indian Company, and despatched from Colombo to Europe, and elsewhere.*

Correspondence between the Máldive Sulṭáns and the Dutch Governors in Ceylon throws a flood of lurid light upon the one time derisive proverbial policy (alluded to above) in " Matters of Commerce," of the Hollanders—followed, if to a lesser degree, by other would-be cultured nations of Europe—as exemplified in their dealings with these semi-unsophisticated Eastern Islanders, and like races.

17. SEAL OF SULTÁN ÍBRÁHÍM ISKANDAR II

Text.

الواثق بالملک ال اکبر
السلطان ابراهیم اسکندر ابن
السلطان محمد عماد الدین محب الا

Transcript.

AL-VÁZIQ BIL MALIK-UL-AKBAR
AS-SULṬÁN ÍBRÁHÍM ISKANDAR IBN
AS-SULṬÁN MUHAMMAD 'IMÁD-UD-DIN MUHIBB ULÁHI.

---

* *Cowries.* For partial summarised notice of the Dutch-Máldivian Cowry Trade from A.C. 1663 to 1795, Sessional Paper XLIII, 1881, pp. 98-101 may be profitably consulted. See too Appendix B.

" The Dutch, with everything originally in their favour, from the illiberality of their Commercial Policy, saw a trade that, judiciously fostered, would have continued to yield them ample profits, gradually slip through their hands to the enrichment of other nations."

Translation.

The Puisant King, the Great,
The Sulṭán Íbráhím Iskandar, son of
The Sultán Muḥommad 'Imád-ud-dín, beloved of God

18. POLYGLOT MISSIVES: A.C. 1723, 1723, 1726, 1732.

The Quartette of Polyglot Missives is dealt with below in Chronological Order.

No. 1. ARABIC: A.H. 1135 (A.C. 1723).

Contains eighteen (18) lines of horizontal script, (6 in. by 6¾ in.), with eight (8) more (3 in. by 5½ in.) written upside down and diagonally from the bottom of the right margin.

The writing is neatly executed in a firm hand, as would befit an erudite *Qázi*, *Naib* or other competent Arabic scholar.

Already, thus quite early in Sulṭán Íbráhím's reign, the contents point unmistakably to "a cloud" of obvious dissatisfaction, "the size of a man's hand,"—which steadily grew as year succeeded year until it may well have threatened to culminate economically in distressful "abundance of rain," far from anticipated at the outset. by a disgruntled Sulṭán and his subjects.

In absolute justice, be it said, full perusal of the long and unedifying commercial correspondence between the Dutch Governors in Ceylon and the Máldive Ruler at Mále clearly exculpate the latter with the Islanders from all cause for dissatisfaction, and redounding greatly to the credit of a quiet God-fearing race abominably coerced by callous Western exploiters.

Text.

(*Plate I.*)

Translation.

" 'To the One (and Only) Almighty God, the All Generous Creator, We offer (Our) prayers, desiring from Him the bestowal (on Your Excellency) of greatness, lasting rule, and power to defend Your Excellency's Government, raised high in nobility mid the fortunate, (and) elevated, to lofty status over (Your Honour's) people.

" 'Grant (O ! God) to the Dutch Governor (*lit.* Him) boldness and wisdom, and make His enemies subservient to His will : grant Him strength to perform good actions, with the courage and trustiness of a bird in full flight ; and keep Him in possession of the Fort of Colombo, so that, by the Grace of God Almighty, He do not depart therefrom.

" 'Look upon Him with loving kindness, unalloyed, (in such wise that) He be guarded against all evils and base influences.' "

" After offering these (the above) prayers, with all due respect, and never-failing supplication, as ever (hitherto) offered, We notify (*lit.* write these words to) Your Excellency, famed for generosity, contentment, clear-sightedness, and just judgment, that the Two Ships, which were despatched by

Your Excellency, have arrived safely in Our protected Harbour.*

"When they landed, We interviewed (*lit.* saw) the persons (who arrived by both vessels)—God will bless them, and have treated them well, and with great kindness.

"We questioned them regarding the sale and purchase (of their goods), and offered to pay cash; but could not come to agreement, even after We had communicated with (*lit.* spoken to) them, and tendered (Our) advice. They stayed (here) one month; but after (the disagreement) neither side held converse (with the other).

"Later, they decided to (*lit.* thought of) Trade. As agreed with the Captain (*lit.* him) We had the goods landed and accepted (*lit.* kept) them, delivering (*lit.* sending) to him *Cowries* (*al kuda'u*)—obtained with difficulty and labour—to be handed over to Your Excellency, although the quantity was small.

"We have given them (the Dutch Ships) clearance in preference to all other (Trading) Vessels (here). By God's Grace they will reach Colombo Harbour in safety.

"With the same pleasure (*lit.* As before), We have received in full the valued Presents sent to us by Your Excellency, and have accepted them with prayerful gratitude.

---

* These were the "*Edam*" and "*Africa.*" They were despatched by Governor I. A. Rumpf, with merchandise for disposal, and a Letter to the Sulṭán, on February 27th, 1723.

Specific "Instructions" to the Commanders (as in the case of Dutch vessels occasionally sent across in the previous Century, *e.g.* 1669 "Cocatoo") contain "Secret Price List" of rates fixed for sale, or barter, at the Islands. Here are some:—

Rice. "Rds. 1.13.14 per *parra.* Follow the usual market price, or even let the Rice go at cost price, provided it can be exchanged for *Cowries*; but not otherwise: for this consignment is Fine Coast Rice, which keeps well, whereas what is generally imported there (the Máldives) is Bad Bengal Rice."

Cowries. "All substantial and saleable Cowries may be accepted for the price which Englishmen, and Frenchmen, generally pay, and you also, viz., (as in the year 1669) each *kóṭṭé* of 12,000 shells against Rds. 1 1/5."

'*Sugar*: Rds. 6.9½ per *picul*; *Areka*: Rds. 4½ to 5 at least; *Mace*: Rds. 2.10 per lb.; *Cloves*: Rds. 1.4; *Nutmegs*: Rds. 1.12; *Cinnamon*: Rd. 1.0; *Pepper*: Rds. 38 per *bhár* of 480 lbs.—all prices as fixed by the Batavian Administration."

"By the Almignty God's graciousness, Your Excellency, who cares for Us, will not be forgotten.

Presents.

"Finally (*lit.* After this), We have despatched to (Your Excellency), in love and kindliness, as Presents :—

Mats : Sixty (60).
Cowries (*kuda'u*) : Four (4) Bags
Ornamental Mats : Four (4)
Smaller Mats : Two (2)
Fish-confection : One (1) Jar.
Ambergris : Two (2) Rupees' weight.
Sea-Coconut : Two (2) Rupees' weight.*

"Your Excellency will (We trust) do Us the great favour of accepting these (Presents), and will not disappoint (Us) by declining (to receive) them.

"(Written on) the evening of the 24th day of (the month) Rajab (in the year) 1135 of the *Hijra* Era (April 19th, A.C. 1723.)"

19. THE PORTUGUESE AT THE MALDIVES.

An extract, from what has been placed on record touching the connection between the Portuguese and the Máldive Islands may fitly introduce reference to the Portuguese Missives of Sulṭán Íbráhím Iskandar II to the Dutch :—

Before the end of the Seventeenth Century the Dutch (who had gradually established Factories on the Continent of India, in Ceylon, Sumatra, and the Moluccas (as well as on the Persian Gulf and Red Sea), ruled without rival, and gradually expelled the Portuguese from almost all their territorial possessions.

Pressed by native Rulers upon the land, on the sea they gave way to more vigorous European enterprise.

To this fact the humble and isolated Máldive Islands doubtless owed there escape from further hostile attention by the Portuguese after the rout of their last two attempts to

---

* *Ambergris Sea Coconut*: See Sessional Paper XLIII, 1881, pp. 87, 95, 96; Pyrard (Hak. Soc.) 1887-8, I, pp. 229, 230-2, II, 359; I.

re-capture Mále in A.C. 1631 *circa* and 1650, subsequent to actual sway, (A.C. 1558-1573), falling, as they were, steadily from supreme power in the Orient.

But that sullen hatred and dread of this persistent "Infidel" enemy still continued to exercise the minds of the Islanders, is borne out forcibly by an Arabic Inscription carved in A.H. 1087 (A.C. 1686-7)—nearly forty years after the latest attack—on the Mále Fort, to serve as "a bulwark to repel the accursed *Farángi*."

Time is a mighty soother : before the lapse of a further century from A.C. 1650, all open rancour at least had melted between these once bitterest of foes, so long engaged in internecine conflict at every encounter.

How amicable—superficially at least—had become mutual relations a striking side-light, as interesting as unexpected, was furnished by the discovery in the Colombo Archives in the Eighties of last Century of three Missives from the reigning Máldive Sulṭán (Ībráhím Iskandar II), sent under his Royal Seal, to the Dutch Governors at Colombo.

The Missives (despatched A.C. 1723, 1734, 1735) relate mainly to the reciprocal Trade (Rice and Spices *versus* Cowries) between the Hollanders in Ceylon and the Máldive Islands.

These Letters, strange as it may seem, were indicted—of all foreigners—by *Portuguese* hands,—in all probability, Captains, etc., of vessels trading to Mále.

Indirectly they bring out the erst-while view, diseminated world-wide, prevalent regarding the commercial morality of the Dutch Traders of two centuries back and the ill-concealed disgust of the Máldive Sulṭán, forced to accept, willy-nilly, with obvious reluctance, the hard bargains made by a fresh European race too powerful to resist—grinding terms which may well have driven the above Máldivian Ruler to fraternise even with the Portuguese, once deadly foes of the Islanders.*

No. 2. PORTUGUESE MISSIVE : A.C. 1723.

The Letter (headed by the Seal of Sulṭán Ībráhím Iskandar II) is written on one side only of a single sheet. The Text measures 13 in. by 6 in., covering 28 lines.

* Journal, C.A.S. XXXI, 85, 1931, pp. 35-37.

Its orthography differs appreciably from the standard as shown provisionally by the corrections kindly suggested.

This Missive's contents still further point to the unjustifiable treatment of the Islanders by over-weening behaviour on the part of Hollanders visiting Màle.

Text.

(*Plate II.*)

Transcript.*

(1) SENHOR COMANDOR

(2) FAÇO ESTAS DUAS REGRAS SA(?)PA SABER (3) AS NOUAS DA SUA BOA SAUDE QUE EU DESEJA (DESAJO) PÃ MI (4) EU DEUS DO NADA PIÇO (PEÇÇ) DE SAUDE PRONTO PÃ SERVIR A DEUS A DESPOIS (E DEPOIS) a V.M. (VOSSA MERCE) (5) ASIM (ASSIM) COM SUA VIM (VIERAM) DUAS BERGATIM PÃ MI— (6) NHA TERA (TERRA) EU RESEBI (RECEBI) COM TODA MEO AUTORITADE FIS (FIZ) SUA (SEU) (7) SERVIÇO DA TODA PRECADA (PRESSA) QUE EU PUDIA EU (8) TOMAVA COM OUTRO (OUTROS) MERCADORES OU SEIA COM COM— (9) PANHINHA (COMPANHIA) SEMPRE SUA DEREITO (DIREITO) A COSTOMADO (ACOSTUMADO) NAO (10) FALTAM DE TOMAR : EU P.AMAR (AMOR) QUE TENHO a.V.M.e (11) AQUELE (AQUELA) BOM (BOA) VONTADE TENHO LARGADO TODA (TODO) MINHA (MEU) (12) DEREITO (DIREITO) NEENHU (NENHUMA) COUZA TOMEI. A JENTE (GENTE) DE V.M.FIS (FEZ) (13) BASTANTES

* Transcript and Translation admittedly tentative and venturesome, especially at the end *re* prices.

MALES NA MINHA TERA : EU P VIA DE VOÇE (14) TODA DEI PASAIR (PASSAR) NADA TOMEI MAL : (15) A CAPITAO (O CAPITAO) DE V.M. (16) QUE MANDOU AQUI PERTO DE DU MES (DOIS MESES) NAO QUIZ FAZER (17) CONTRATO EDESPOIS (E DEPOIS) DA SPAR (DE PASSAR) DE DU MES (DOIS MESES) ENTAO COMEÇOU (18) FAZER CONTRATO (CONTRATO) EDESPOIS (E DEPOIS) DE VER QUE IA TODA JENTE (GENTE) (19) DUENTE : EU DEI ORDE (ORDEM) PÃ TOMAR SUA (SEU) FATO (FARDO) (?) ASIM (ASSIM) (20) COMOFORME (COMFORME) PREÇO . . . . . . AMONAO DE—ARECA (21) TOMEI A RAZAO DE TRES COTAS 1/3 EA ARAZ (ARROZ) ? A PREÇO DE (22) 4 COTA E ½ A CANDIH (CANDIL) QUE HE (QUE E) 8 MAO DE BANGALA A (23) 14 PARA DE AQUI TOMEI SATALE (?) 15 P HU CATA (CUSTA) (24) TOMEI CRANO E NOS DE DAVY (?) CASTA (25) 2 RATEL P.2 CATAI TOMEI SUQRE 36 RATEL E ½ P. CATE (26) EMAY QUE DEAS (DEUS) GDE (GUARDE) (S.V.) V.M. MALDIVA HAIE (27) PRO (PRIMEIRO) DE MAIO DE 1723.

Translation.

" Sir Commander,

" We pen these few (*lit.* two) lines in order to ascertain news regarding Your Excellency's welfare (*lit.* good health), that We are desirous of learning (*lit.* which We wish from Your Excellency).

" We pray to God for nothing save soundness of health that We ma serve God as well as Your Excellency's self.

" In this spirit (*lit.* like manner) when Your (Excellency's) vessels (brigs) reached Our country, We received them with full honour; and have helped them to the best of Our power to conclude (*lit.* towards) their business with all expedition.

"From other Merchants, and even from the (Dutch) Company, We have always exacted the Customary Dues; but, on account of the affection and goodwill We bear Your Excellency, We have waived Our right, and recovered absolutely nothing.

"Your Excellency's people have done much evil in Our land; but We have let all pass, and taken nought in ill part.

"During a full month, the Captain, whom Your Excellency has sent here, was not willing to trade; but did so after the solicitations of the people.

"When We saw that all his men were getting sick, We gave orders for his goods to be taken at the prices demanded (by him):

Trade Prices

We have taken :—

"*Areca*: One (1) *amunam*: at $3\frac{1}{3}$ *kóṭṭé* of Cowries.

Rice: at $4\frac{1}{2}$ *kóṭṭé* per *kandi* of eight (8) Bengal *maunds*, viz., four (4) Máldivian *parras*.

Cowries: One (1) *kóṭṭé* at 15 shillings.

Cloves and *Nutmegs*: Two (2) lbs. for two (2) *kóṭṭé* at 15 (? shillings) per *kóṭṭé*.

Sugar: Thirty-six and a half ($36\frac{1}{2}$) lbs. for one (1) *kóṭṭé* at 15 (? shillings).

For the rest, may God Almighty have Your Excellency in His keeping.

Málc (*Máldiva*): 1st May, 1723.

Presents.

"The Presents which We are sending to Your Excellency are :—

Ambergris: One (1) Piece of Rs. 2 in weight.
Sea-coconut: One (1) Piece of Rs. 2 in weight.
Ornamental Mats: Six (6).
Cowries: Sixty (60) *kóṭṭês*
Fish-confection: One (1) Jar.
Dry Fish: One thousand (1,000) Pieces.

REPLY OF DUTCH COUNCIL.

"To the Blessed Sulṭán Íbráhím Iskandar, King of the Máldives.

"We have received the welcome Missives of 1st May and 27th October, of the year now finishing, (brought) by our brigs *Edam* and *Africa*, which have returned, accompanied by Your Highness' vessels.

"With great pleasure, We learnt from these Letters of Your Highness' good health and welfare. We trust that Heaven will grant Your Highness their continuance for many years to come.

"We are deeply obliged, and tender Our thanks to Your Highness, for the kind help and assistance given to the crews of the (above named) two Ships when at the Máldives; as well as for the Presents sent to Us. The latter were delivered here after the demise of the Noble Lord Sir Isaac Augustine Rumpf, Governor of Ceylon.

"In His (Excellency's) place, We expect (the arrival) shortly from the Malabar Coast of the Noble Lord John Hartenberg, as Chief Commander of this Island (Ceylon).*

"If there be anything We can do here, either for the service, or good pleasure, of Your Highness, We trust that kindly intimation will be made to Us.

"Meanwhile, may Your Highness be pleased to accept the little Present herewith sent by the Noble Dutch Company."

H. SHOLL (for the Council).

Colombo, 17th December, 1723.

Presents.

China Plates : Six (6).
Small Medium Paper : Five (5) packets.
Cinnamon : Sixteen (16) lbs.
Cloves : Ten (10) lbs.
Mace : Six (6) lbs.
Nutmegs : Twelve (12) lbs.
Pepper : Thirty (30) lbs.
Persian Rose Water : Three (3) Big Bottles.

---

* Dutch Governors at Colombo: I. A. Rumpf (A.C. 1716-23); J. Hertenberg (A.C. 1724-25).

20. THE FRENCH AT THE MÁLDIVES.

For reasons unknown, the French were, during the whole of the Eighteenth Century, always *personae gratae* at the Máldives. In respect to Sea-borne Trade they easily out-classed their Portuguese and English rivals, and proved themselves specially welcome as Commercial visitors in the first half of that Century, and occasional Allies later.

The "*Tárikh*, or "State Chronicle of the Máldive Sulṭáns," had just cause for its notice of French intervention on behalf of the Islanders, when attacked by their heridi-tary enemy the Ruler of Kanaṇṇúr in mid Eighteenth Century.

A hostile Expedition sent to Mále by Á̤li Rája of Kanaṇṇúr*—ever from the early Sixteenth Century at least a thorn in the Máldive Islanders' side—in A.C. 1752, (at the instigation of a traitarous Máldịvian *Qázi* and *Khatib*, sons-in-law of Sulṭán Ībráhím II) captured "Sulṭáns' Island," and deported Sulṭán Muḥammad Mukar-ram 'Imád-ud-dín III, half-brother of the deceased Sovereign; as well as the latter's only son, who returned to reign (A.C. 1767-1774) at the Máldives—to make the *Ḥajj*, and to be foully done to death on his return.

---

* *Á̤li Rája* ("Sea King"). See Sessional Paper XLỊII, 1881, pp. 46, 47; Journal, C.A.S. XXXII, 84, 1931, p. 44. By con-quest, or otherwise,—in the Sixteenth Century probably (*teste* Pyrard) —the Rájas of Kanaṇṇúr acquired possession of Maliku Island (modern Minicoy)—really the most Northern of the Máldive Archi-pelago, to which it rightly belongs, both racially and by language.

The Kanaṇṇúr Rulers continued, by spasmodic attacks, to make raids on other Northern Máldive Atols, and on Mále itself, until their territory fell to the British in A.C. 1791.

The "*Tárikh*" (Máldivian State Chronicle) records nearly half a dozen Malabar Muslim incursions, or threatened descents, during the Seventeenth and Eighteenth Centuries—all virtually abortive; save those of A.C. 1607, when Sulṭán Ībráhím III was killed; and A.C. 1752, when Sulṭán Muḥammad Mukarram 'Imád-ud-dín III was captured, and Mále held for a few months.

Sulṭán Muḥammad 'Imád-ud-dín III died, still an exile, at Minicoy in A.C. 1757.

Within four months (A.C. 1752) the Máldivians, led by Ḥasan Manikufánu (later Sulṭán Ḥasan 'Izz-ud-dín, A.C. 1759-67) over-powered the Malabars, and re-took Mále.

The following year, a further plundering Expedition from Kanaṇṇúr anchored off Mále.

On the urgent appeal of the Máldive Ministry, bereft of their Sulṭán, Monsieur Le Termellier arrived from Pondicherry, with a portion of Admiral Dupleix' French Squadron, sent to aid the Máldivians against Áḷi Rája's marauders.

The French fleet attacked the Malabars (who had been at the Máldives filibustering for nearly six months) fiercely, defeating them and capturing a *gurábu*; the rest of the vessels fled to Donakuḷi Island (Tiladummatí Atol), followed by the French ; and thence escaped to Kanaṇṇúr.

Subsequently, the French made a Pact with the Máldivian Government ; being allowed to hoist their Flag at "*Ñáne Buruzu*" Bastion of the Fort, and assigned quarters near it on the thoroughfare still styled "*Farangi Magu.*"

In A.C. 1761 a third Malabar incursion of eight vessels reached N. Mále Atol, and occupied Fonadú and Huḷule Islands. The enemy fired on Mále for two days ; but departed on 8th Ramazán, being pursued as far as Ári Atol, where they lost some prisoners.

A Company of French remained in Government service until A.C. 1759 as *Corps de Garde* for a while at Mále, Commander Le Termellier himself ultimately settling down there.*

* Monograph (Máldive Islands), p. 39.

21. WRECK OF THE "RAVENSTEYN."

In May, 1726, the Dutch ship "Ravensteyn" (Captain Antony Klink), conveying a cargo of Gold, had been wrecked on Muḷaku Atol. The survivors who reached Málé, received much kindly treatment, and were subsequently despatched to Ceylon with the gold chests and other cargo recovered from the derelict vessel, as well as a Missive in French.*

The generosity and kindliness exhibited by the Sulṭán, and his people, in most outrageous circumstances due to the intolerable arrogance of the Captain, could not but evoke appreciative acknowledgment even by that fiendish Dutch Governor at Colombo, Petrus Vuyst, (A.C. 1726-29), deservedly executed, in a characteristic Reply to the Sulṭán, rambling into platitudinous matter little relevent to the "Ravensteyn" imbroglio, but obsessed with Western greed for an exclusive Cowry monopoly.

The fiery, long-drawn out, expostulation of Sulṭán Ībráhím doubtless owed its bitter tone—so foreign to all other known Máldivian Official Documents—to being drafted by the French Ship's Captain (mentioned in the Missive), not unnaturally resenting the Dutch Captain's false charge of crimping.

No. 3. FRENCH MISSIVE.

This, in many ways, delightfully piquant Missive contains 144 lines in all, covering three and a half pages of writing, which average from 10 in. to 16 in. by 7 in. to 8 in.

---

* Sulṭán Muḥammad Ghiyás-ud-dín, son of Sulṭán Ībráhím Iskandar II, also employed a French Missive dated A.C. 1769—the only other in that language known—as a medium of communication with the Dutch. See Sessional Paper XLIII, 1881, p. 109, for the French Text and a Translation of this short Missive.

Of the document the orthography is villainously erratic, and much of the sense very involved; indicating a French scribe, poorly educated, whose effusion need hardly surprise.* The style often is trenchant in the extreme.

The Dutch Translation of the Missive (received at Colombo in July, 1726) bears an endorsement of its rendering from the French original by the Attorney of J. Paul Schagen.

Text

(*Plates III—VI*)

Transcript.

" A'MESSIEURS LES GOUVERNEUR | ET CONSEILLE DES VILLE ET FORTS | ET DEPANDANCES DE LA COMPAGNIE | DOLLANDE EN CELON | A COLOMBO

" (*Plate III*, 1) *Messieurs*: par La voy des deux Batiment qui (2) ont partie deCeport Leune Le 8° Et Lautre le 9° de (3) Juin, Vous aure JeCroy Ressus les deux Lettre que (4) Jay Eulhonneur de Vous Ecrire, avec ausi les (5) equipaze duvessaux Le Ravestin, qui Commeje (6) vous ay déja marqué Sestois perdue dans Ces Illes (7) Iey, Le Capitainne duquel vessaux Enuoya tous le de (8) monde, tous fort mal, EnCette Ille, Et mefit (9) demander par le Commandeur quil ausit Enuoyee (10) avec Ces gens des Battaux pr-pouuoir sáuuer, (11) Si Il Estoist posible Les Effait deLa Conpagnie, (12) Sequil ont fait de 9 CaiCe neuf CaiÇe Castée des (13) Seaude La Conpagnie les ql mon Ettée Remie En (14) mon Ille par Mr. Busch, Comme Jay deja Eu (15) lhonneur devous marquer, Les ql. Jaurois Eu deja (16) Lesoin devous Les Enuoyer Si les de Sr Busch y

* A tentative Transcript and Translation of the Missive appeared in Sessional Paper XLIII. 1881, pp. 42-44.

Eut (17) Consenti, mes It mefit Reponce quil ne pouuoit (18) y Consentir, que Le Capitainne ne fusce prejans (19) Sequi na Ettée que Le 13° deCemois Juin, Le de. Capitainne (20) ayant Restée dans Lille de Matteuarié pres landroit (21) ou Sest perdue Le vessaux tous Ce temps Sans auoir (22) Rien fait que je puisce Connettre Estre pr. le seruisce (23) de La Conpagnie, Sepleignant fort des abittans (24) deLade Ille Comme Sil deuoit trauaille Commes des (25) Mattelo durope ne Considerant pas que Sont depauure (26) gens, Les quels Consider le moindre petie Seruice (27) quon exzize, deux pr. vne tres grandre opression (28) Il est assée Messr. a vostre Connessance Seque Ces que les (29) gens des Illes de Maldiue

" (*Plate IV*, 30) Insi Messr vostre Capitainne nauoit aucum droit (31) deSe Seruir desterme, et mounemant dont ilSest Seruie (32) Seruie aSon ariuée a Maldiue deuant tous le (33) Conseille, Deune manier Comme sil venoit fair la (34) guer, Et a son ariuée Jay Ettée plus Informée que (35) tous se temps Il nauoit veritablement Rien fait (36) pr. Leseruiue deLa Conpagnie nayant aportée (37) que des geunille,

" (38) Ousitost que Lede homme fut debarquée Il me fit (39) demander 50 hommes auec 4 grand Battaux pr. (40) Sanuer les Effait de la Conpagnie, scqui me parue (41) si Extraordinair que JeneLuy fit point Reponce (42) Quar Messr. Il faut que vous Sachiez que le vessaux (43) est Essouée dans vne audriot aupres dequel Il ne (44) peut y aller quaneepenne vn petie Battaux (45) Leaux Et le Brigant passant passant par desus (46) Le vessaux, Et dans Cette moisson duv : les mer son (47) affruze dans Cette andriot.

" (48) Si Mr LeCapitoinne auoit voulue sedonner (49) vnpeu peux plus depenne dans le Commancement (50) que Le vessaux at Ettee Essouée on auroit Je (51) Croy Sauuer quelque choze dauantage ; mes Je (52) vous anoue Cette vn Brutalle qui ne prand Conseill (53) depersonne, sequi á fait quil a Resté dans de (54) temp en Cette Ille, Il poura vous

Rander (55) Contte de Cequil ya á fait Jesuie persuadee quil (56) doune tontte lafantte amon gounernement, Ces (57) LaRe-connessance que je Rosoit de Ce Brutalle (58) Lequel Je vous Jur Messr. que si Senestoist (59) Et Lestimme Et Respect que Jay Eu Et moy Et (60) mes entecesseurs pr. La-Conpagnie Je Laurois mie (61) dans vne ȧndroit on Il auroit p'ue a Loizir (62) santir les Insolance de La Brutalittée (63) Je nignor Nullement Messr. que Cede Capitainne (64) ne vous assurrera quil Est possible depouuoir (65) sauuer les effait dela Conpagnie, Et que Indubitablement (66) Il ne vous fasce fair des pance tres Inuttille (*Plate V*, 67) quar Je vous assur de Rechef que dans lasituation (68) ou Est le vessaux, Il Est Impossible deRie fair (69) a moins que lede vessaux ne sonnre ; quoy puisee (70) Sauueer les marchandize qui pouront flotter, sile (71) Le temps permait au Battaux deRestter dehors (72) Et les marchandize pezante que pouront Rester (73) aufont, laConpagnie poura fair les deligence (74) Si elle Juge a propos pr. les Sauuer denuoyer (75) des occazion dans la moisson de-feuuerir Et mars (76) Quant demapart Je vous assur, que sile vessaux (77) Souure, Et quil y est des marchandize qui flotte (78) Comme jevous marque sy deuant, Et que nos (79) Battaux puisce tenir lamer, Jaurie Soin den (80) fair vne exacte Recherche pr. vous les Ranuoyer (81) a La premier occazion.

" (82) Le 18e deCemois desjuin Le de Capitainne (83) en Conpagnie de quelquevn de Ces officiers sout (84) venue ala-porte demon logie auec vnearogance (85) qui ma Je vous assur outré auderniée point, (86) Je vous Le Repette Messr. Si Cenestoist Les (87) Raison que Jay deja Ecrit Sy deuant, Il leurs (88) Seroit ariuée vne tres mauuais affaire Esperant (89) que vous me donnerée la satisfaction qui Est (90) a vn Roy

" (91) Pretendant que Je Lui Eus Remie Cinq hómmes (92) quil dit Luy manquer, Nemayant pas donné (93) Conness-sance dans la partie des 2 premiee vessaux (94) quil manquoit,

Comment pouuoire Scauoir, Si il Estoist (95) partie ou non ou sil auoit Restée dans Lepay, (96) Mes enfin Messr. Jay voulue passer tous sans Bruit a (97) vos Consideration, Je Luy fit fair vne Reponce pr. (98) Luy fair antrer en Luy meme quil deuoit Bien (99) Considerée La mannier dont Il parloit et des Sestte (100) dont Il se seruoit, Sependant Si Ces hommes estois (101) sur Laterre, Je Les ferois Randre, Et de plus que (102) Jauois 3 Batiment en Rade sur leql. Il pouuoit (103) en fair La Cherche, seque sepandant Il na voulue (104) fair Et a Retrouuee Ces gens sur le vessaux de la (105) Conpagnie de france auec le Capitainne duql. Il y (106) a plusr. parolle que Je nay point sceu

"(107) Je vous Ranuoy Messr. Le de Capitainne auec Mr. (*Plate VI*, 108) Busch duql. Je suie tres Contant, pr, estre Veritablemt (109) vne homme fort Brudant, Le Restant des officie (110) vont Jointement auec Les 9 Caice de La Conpagnie (111) qui mauoit Ettee Remie par lede Mr. Busch Le (112) toutte enbarque sur mon Nauir Leql. pr. Cet effait (113) na pas Eu Le temps de dechargée, et suie obligée (114) de Le fair partir dans Cette Ettat pr. au plutot vous (115) donner La satisfaction de Reseuoir et les gens, et (116) Les effiait de La Conpagnie

" (117) Vous mobligerez Sansiblement de procurer au Nacoda (118) de mon vessaux nomme Mamot Safie La vautte (119) de La Cargueson dunauir parseque Luy meme en (120) estoist Chargée des Bingalle, Et pr. vniquement (121) Randre seruisce a La Conpagnie JeLa fait partir (122) dans le meme Ettat pr. y Repasser tons generallemt (123) seque Jay Eu lhonneur de vous marquer sy deuant (124) ausitost que La vautte de son Rie sera finie faites (125) moy La grasce Messr. de Le depesché pr. Bingalle (126) Le plustost q[illegible] fair sepoura pr ne point perdre (127) son passaze Ces Lagr[illegible]e que vous demande (128) Ce Luy qui veritablement soit estre vtille a La (129) Compagnie.

" (130) ET SUIE VERITABLEMENT,
(131) AMY
(132) YBRAIMME CHICONDAR ROY
(133) DELARCHIPELLE DES ILLS
(134) DE MALDIUE."

Translation.

" TO THE GOVERNOR AND COUNCIL AT COLOMBO, OF THE TOWNS, FORTS AND DEPENDENCIES OF THE HOLLAND COMPANY IN CEYLON."

" GENTLEMEN,

" From the opportunity afforded by the two Vessels which left this Port on the 8th and 9th June, respectively, We (*lit.* I) presume that You (Your Excellencies), will have received the two Letters which We have had the honour to address to You together with the equipage of the Vessel " Ravensteyn " that, as We have already mentioned, was lost anon these Islands.

" The Captain of the Vessel despatched the whole of the Ship's Complement, all very ill, to this Island ; and, through the Commander whom he had sent along with these persons, demanded from Us boats to save, if possible, the effects of the Company. This (salvage) they have done in regard to nine Chests, marked with the Company's Seal ; which have been delivered to Us in Our Island by Mr. Busch, as We have already had the honour to inform You.

" We should, ere this, have taken care to send You these, had Mr. Busch consented ; but he told Us that he could not give his assent to it unless the Captain were present. This did not occur until the 13th June, as the said Captain had remained in the Island of *Maduvari* (in Mulaku Atol) near the place where the Vessel was lost, doing nothing the whole time, as far as We can ascertain, of service to the Company, (but) complaining strongly of the inhabitants of the said Island—as if they could (be expected to) work like European sailors—not taking into consideration the fact that they are only wretched creatures, who look upon the smallest service exacted from them as grievous oppression. You (Your Excellencies) are well aware, Gentlemen, of the nature of the Máldive Islanders.

"Your (Excellencie's) Captain, Gentlemen, therefore, had no right on his arrival at Mále to make use of the terms, or to resort to the action, he adopted, in the presence of the whole Council, just as though he had come to wage war.

"We have been further informed, since his arrival, that all the time he has done actually nothing for the Company's benefit, having only brought away some trash.

"As soon as this personage landed, he demanded from Us fifty men and four large boats to salvage the property of the Company—a request which appeared to Us so extraordinary that We gave him no answer. For, Gentlemen, You (Your Excellencies) must understand that the Vessel is cast-away at a spot which a small Boat can reach only with difficulty; as the seas and the surf break incessantly over the Vessel, and, during this Monsoon especially, there is a terrible sea running at the place.

"If, Gentlemen, the Captain had chosen to give himself very little more trouble at first when the vessel was wrecked, some additional property would, We believe, have been saved; but, We assure You, this is a churl who will take advice from nobody, as he showed by staying so long in that Island. He will be able to render You account of what he has done.

"We feel convinced that he lays the whole blame on Our Government. It is all the thanks that We shall receive from this churl; whom, but for the esteem and regard that both We, and Our Predecessors, have borne towards the Company, We should, We swear to you, have placed in a position where he would have had leisure to brood over the insolence of his outrageous conduct.

"We are fully aware, Gentlemen, that the said Captain will assure You (Your Excellencies) of the possibility of being able to save the effects of the Company, and that, doubtless, he will cause You (Your Excellencies) to incur very useless expense ; but We reassert to You that at the place where the Vessel lies it is impossible to do anything, unless she breaks up In that case the cargo which floats might be saved, if the weather allows of the Boats remaining outside (the reef) ; and, as regards the heavy goods, which would sink to the bottom, the Company, should it think fit, might endeavour to send over what suits the occasion, during the Monsoon of February and March, for the purpose of salving them.

"For Our part, You (Your Excellencies) may rest assured that if the Vessel breaks up and any of the cargo floats, as We have notified You before, and (if) our Boats can keep the sea, We shall take care to make a careful search so as to send(whatever is recovered) toYou at the earliest opportunity.

" On the 18th June the said Captain, accompanied by one of his Officers, came to the Gate of Our Palace, displaying a degree of arrogance which We assure You exasperated (Us) to the last limit. We repeat, Gentlemen, that, if it had not been for the reasons We have stated above, the matter would have become very serious. We trust that You (Your Excellencies) will render Us the satisfaction which is due to a Sovereign.

" He alleged that We had sent away five men, whom he said he missed ; without having let Us know at the time the first two Vessels left that they were missing. How could it be known whether they had gone or not, or if they had stayed in the Island ?

" Nathless, Gentlemen, it was Our desire to let all pass without commotion, out of consideration for You (Your Excellencies). We had an answer given him tending to let him see for himself that he ought to consider the manner in which he spoke, and the conduct he displayed ; at the same time (notifying) that, if these men were on shore, We should have them handed over to him ; and, moreover, that We had three Vessels in Harbour which he might search. This he did not choose to do ; and found his men on the Ship of the French Company, with the Captain of which he had many words, unknown to Us.

"We send back, Gentlemen, the said Captain, and Mr. Busch with whom We are greatly pleased as a man possessing undoubtedly much prudence. The rest of the Officers leave also with the nine Chests, belonging to the Company, which had been sent to me by Mr. Busch.

" Everyone has embarked in Our Ship, which, for this reason, has not had time to discharge. We are forced to let her start in this state, the sooner to afford you the satisfaction of receiving the men and the effects of the Company.

" You will materially oblige Us by enabling the *Nákhudá* of Our Vessel, named Maḥmud Sháfa't (*Mamot Safie*) to sell the cargo of the Vessel; because it was loaded from Bengal, and, merely to do a service to the Company, We ordered him to start (even) in the (Ship's) existing condition, to enable all Your (Excellencie's) men, etc., to return together, as We have had the honour of mentioning before.

" As soon as the sale of the (cargo of) Rice is concluded, do Us the kindness, Gentlemen, to despatch him (the *Nákhudá*) to Bengal as early as You (Your Excellencies) possibly can, so that he may not fail to make the passage.

" This is the favour that He who may be of real service to the Company asks from You (Your Excellencies.)

Your Excellencies' Sincere Friend,
" ÎBRÁHÎM ISKANDAR,
King of the Máldive Islands'
Archipelago."

22. REPLY OF GOVERNOR PETRUS VUYST.

" To the Blessed Sulṭán Îbráhím Iskandar, King of the Máldives.

Wreck of the " Ravensteyn."

" The Letter which Your Highness was pleased to write in French to the Governor of Ceylon, and his Council, notifying conveyance of the nine (9) money boxes, brought over by the Captain, the Assistant Merchant and some others of the lost ship " *Ravensteyn* " has been received here; with the boxes mentioned. The Captain with the Assistant Merchant and the other Officers have arrived with the money in good condition.

"The Governor cannot but thank Your Highness in the heartiest way for the help given and the kindness shown not only to these persons, but to the others who have been sent over from Your Realm to Us through the great care of Your Highness. But, instead of making land on this Island, they got ashore in Bengal and on the Coromandel Coast—yet even so, amid people of Our nation—so that they have reached land safely, and Our obligation remains the same.

"This we shall try to prove to Your Highness in every possible way; in as much as We were glad that Your Highness was pleased to take no account of the faults of the said Captain in this and other instances. By this Your Highness has given true proof of Your generous and Royal character; for it behoves Kings more than other men to possess a gentle spirit for the safety of many; and, if every reasonable creature deserves indulgence for its behaviour, so does an unfortunate sailor who has lost everything, as did the said Captain and his crew,—being thereby perhaps somewhat bereft of his senses.

Dutch Vessels to visit Mále for Trade.

"We do not doubt that Your Highness, from Your favour towards the Dutch Company, will be pleased to learn that Our intention is to send to Your Highness a small Ship and a Sloop about the end of next February or the beginning of March.

"These Vessels will come to Trade under Your Highness' powerful protection in Your Kingdom, and they will carry what is known to please Your Highness' subjects; to exchange it there for *Cowries* only; of which there can be no stint when Your Highness is pleased to grant to Us Your Highness' powerful favour; for which We plead with all earnestness and respect.

"This request will be presented, with even more earnestness by the above named Vessels, which go with more substantial proofs of Our gratitude for the kind care bestowed by Your Highness on the Company's money-boxes and servants (of the "Ravensteyn"). For this we shall ever try to make a return to Your Highness' subjects. Some of these who came here again in this Monsoon We have not failed to favour as much as We could. To this fact can also testify Your Highness' Envoy, who carries this Letter, and who handed over to the Governor, with much grace and politeness, the honoured

Missive of Your Highness, so full of expressions and marks of esteem and affection for the Governor and for the illustrious Dutch Company.

" If it were not so, Your Highness would not put such great trust in Us ; and, in truth, Your Highness will never find Yourself deceived, as regards the Dutch : for this nation is good and upright, and has nothing else in view but Peace and Tranquillity, in order to be able to Trade the better. Dutchmen are Traders in their hearts, and, in as much as Your Highness' subjects are also keen Traders, and bold at sea, so is Our esteem for them the greater and We seek nothing more than their welfare. It is for this purpose alone that Our two Vessels will undertake their voyage to the Máldives. Thus Your Highness' subjects will have opportunity to get rid easily of their Cowries ; which can be exchanged for other wares, or for money, as they prefer.

" Why should Our Vessels not be favoured as much as those of other European Nations, that dwell much further from Your Highness' Islands and Kingdom ? For one has much greater interest in the friendship of neighbours than in that of them that live far away, and outside the range of possibility of help in time of need.

" We shall hope, therefore, that it will please Your Highness to commend Our friendship to Your subjects, in order that We may be served with their Cowries in preference to other Nations ; and that We may be thus bound to take an ever growing share in the interests of Your Highness.

The King of Kanaṇṇur

" There will be no need to fear so much a war, or an invasion, by the King (Áḷi Rája) of Kanaṇṇúr ; since, to pay a visit to the domain of Your Highness, one must cross the sea ; and this is not so easy for the people of those lands as to pass on foot over the solid earth.

"Moreover, the King of Kanaṇṇúr will prefer to be at peace, rather than at war, with Your Highness, if Your Highness lives in friendship and good understanding with the illustrious Holland's Company; for that King, in his great wisdom, knows well that it is better to be a friend to the Company's friend, rather than an enemy.

"What We can set on foot, through the power of our Most Noble Lord, The Governor-General, to suppress any evil design of the King of Kanannúr against Your Highness' lands, We shall do ; and provide the first War Ship. Thus all expenses of War materials can be spared to Your Highness.

Presents

"Meanwhile, the Governor thanks Your Highness for the honoured and agreeable Presents which Your Highness was pleased to send Him, along with the Missive. This generosity will be met, so far as possible, by Our (visiting) Vessels. Until that time We shall wait, because Our people desire to have the honour to offer a gift which may please Your Highness.

"We shall not encroach on Your Highness' time any further ; but will conclude this Letter with the hearty wish that Your Highness' Days may be many and Your Treasures over-abundant.

PETRUS VUYST.

In the Castle, Colombo,

January 7th, 1727.

23. MÁLDIVIAN "TANA" ALPHABET.

For particulars of the Máldívian *Tána* Alphabet, (based on Arabic Numeration signs, and almost exclusively adopted throughout the whole of the Archipelago since the Seventeenth Century at least), special reference is invited to Journal, C.A.S. XXVII, Extra Number, 1919.

No. 4. MALDIVIAN MISSIVE

This, the shortest known "*Tána*" Missive despatched by Sulṭán Íbráhím Iskandar II, runs to but twelve and a half (12½) lines of writing, measuring only 7 in. by 4¾ in.

It is doubly dated—*Anno Ḥijrae* 1144, as well as *Anno Christi* 1732.

The form of its script (partly Arabic) may be usefully compared with that of the following Missives, viz. (i) A.C. 1713, of Sulṭán Muḥammad 'Imád-ud-dín II Musaffar (Journal, C.A.S. Vol. XXIX, No. 76, 1923), in interesting contrast to (ii) Missive dated A.H. 1210 (A.C. 1795) from Sulṭán Ḥasan Núr-ud-dín (Sessional Paper XLIII, 1881, pp. 78-81), and Missive of A.H. 1235 (A.C. 1819) received from Sulṭán Muḥammad Múín-ud-dín I. (Journal, C. A. S. Vol. XXIX, No. 76, 1923)

The somewhat unusual type of the consonant "*B*," and the free use of "*Ṇ*" (cerebral), now little employed, will be noted in the present Missive of A.C. 1732.

Text

(*Plate VII.*)

Word for Word Transcript and Translation.

(1) *HIJRA* 1144 *SANAT* MITAVVANA AHARU
of the Hijra Era 1144 Year In this year

AS-SULṬÁN ÍBRÁHÍM ISKANDER (2) RAṆṆAVALÓKA
the Sulṭán Íbráhím Iskandar Lord of War

MAHÁ RADUNGEFÁNU KOḶUBU-GAI WAḌAIGEN INNAWÁ
the Great King at Colombo residing

GORUNUDÓRU (3) KAPPITÁNA(Ṛ) MITEVVIAN E(T)
to the Governor Captain incalculable

FAFFAṚUN *DU'A* SALÁMU MANIKUFÁNUMENÍ
many many prayer-full Saláms (to) Your Excellency

A (4) ḶUGAḌUMENGE VÍ KOMME *HÁJATAKU* ANGAIFÁN
of Our whatsoever wants (to) notify

KAMA HITÁ ṪIBÉ MÍHUA
the fact in (Our) mind Magnate (*lit.* man)

(5) MANIKUFÁNUMEN KIBAA(Ṛ) AḶUGAḌUMEN MI
Your Excellency's to Us this

FAHARU MI ANGÁ BAHÍ MANIKUFÁNU (6) MEN KIBAIN
time this informing word Your Excellency from

MI AHARU MI AI NAU GENAI TAKÉTI
this year here arrived vessel brought goods

IHUN MI VEJJE A (7) HARU GAI VIKUNU AGUN VIKKAI
last this past In the year sold price sold

BOLI HAMAKO(Ṛ) DÍFAI E MÍHUNGE
Cowries adjusting amount after giving Of these persons

TIBI (8) MÍHUNÁI LAIFAI MI MÍHUN DATURU
remaining persons with these men voyage

IMBA KUREVVÍMU AḶUGAḌUMEN
You (Your Excellency) (please) despatch. Us

KI(9)BAIN MI FONUVÁ HAḌIÁ-KOḶA KÍ TIBÁ BEIKALUN
from being sent Present called Your Excellency

ARAIHODÉ LÁHIKU HAḌIÁ (10) E(Ṛ) NÚN VIAS
fitting pleasing Present is not but

HAḌIÁ-KOḶU *QUABÚ* KURABBAIFUN EDI TIBÍMU
the Present's acceptance (We) desire.

MI FA(T) (11) KOḶU TIBÁ BEIKALUN KIBAA(Ṛ)
This Missive Your Excellency to

LIAVVAILÍ FONUVVÍ *ÍSÁ*GEFÁNU HIJU (12) RAIN
written sent Jesus (Christ) in the Ḥijra Era

1732 MITAVVANA AHARU ABURÍLUN SAUVÍS DUVA (13) HU
1732 this year in April the 24th day

KAMU HAḌÁN *WA ALLÁHU A'ALAM*
remember And God knoweth (all)

Translation.

"The *Hijra* (Era) Year One thousand one hundred and forty-four (A.H. 1144).

"In this year, from the Sulṭán Íbráhím Iskandar, the Great King (and) War-Lord, to His Excellency the Governor (and) Commander (*lit.* Captain) residing in Colombo (are proferred), innumerable prayerful greetings (*Du'a Salám*).

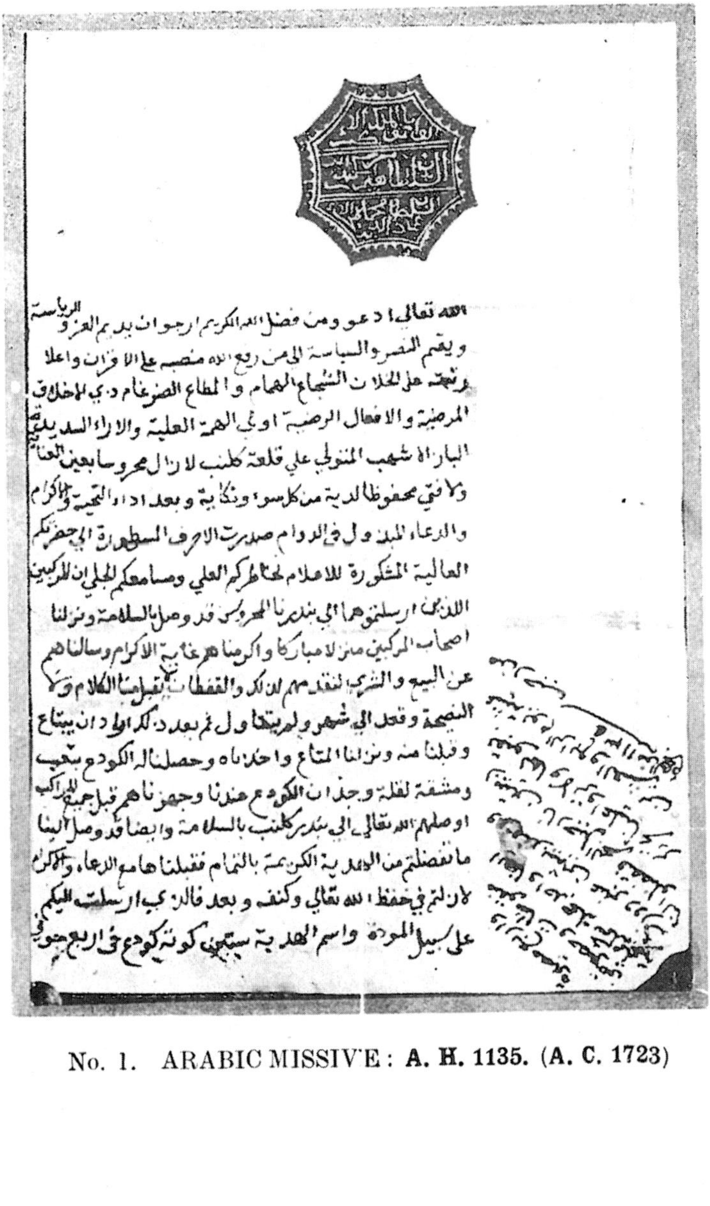

No. 1. ARABIC MISSIVE : **A. H. 1135. (A. C. 1723)**

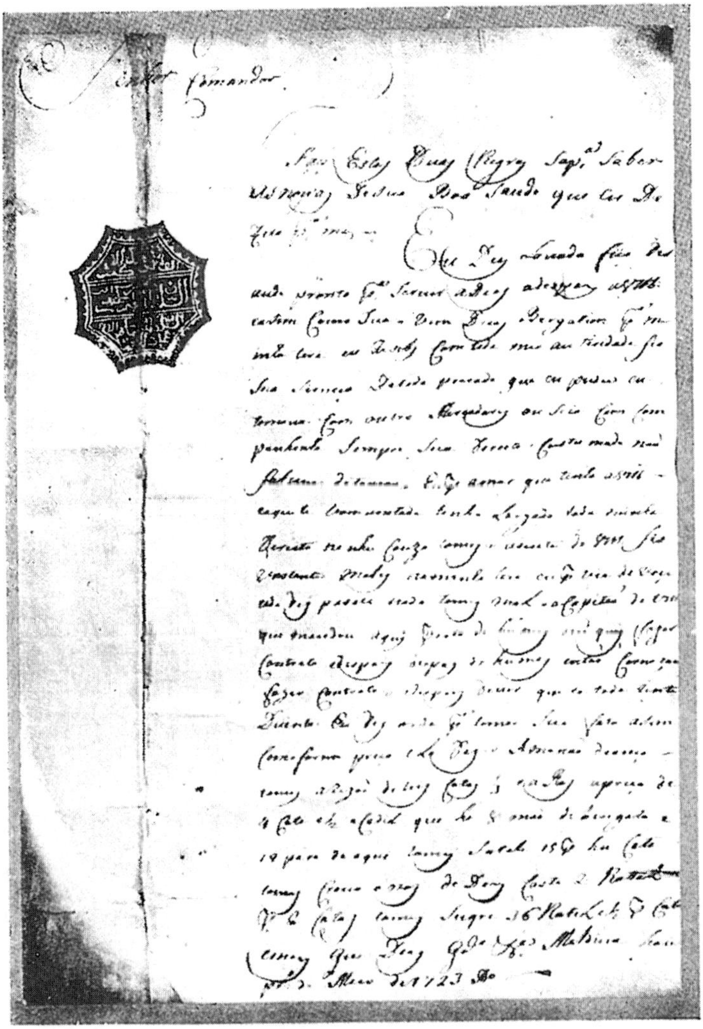

No. 2. PORTUGUESE MISSIVE: **A. C. 1723.**

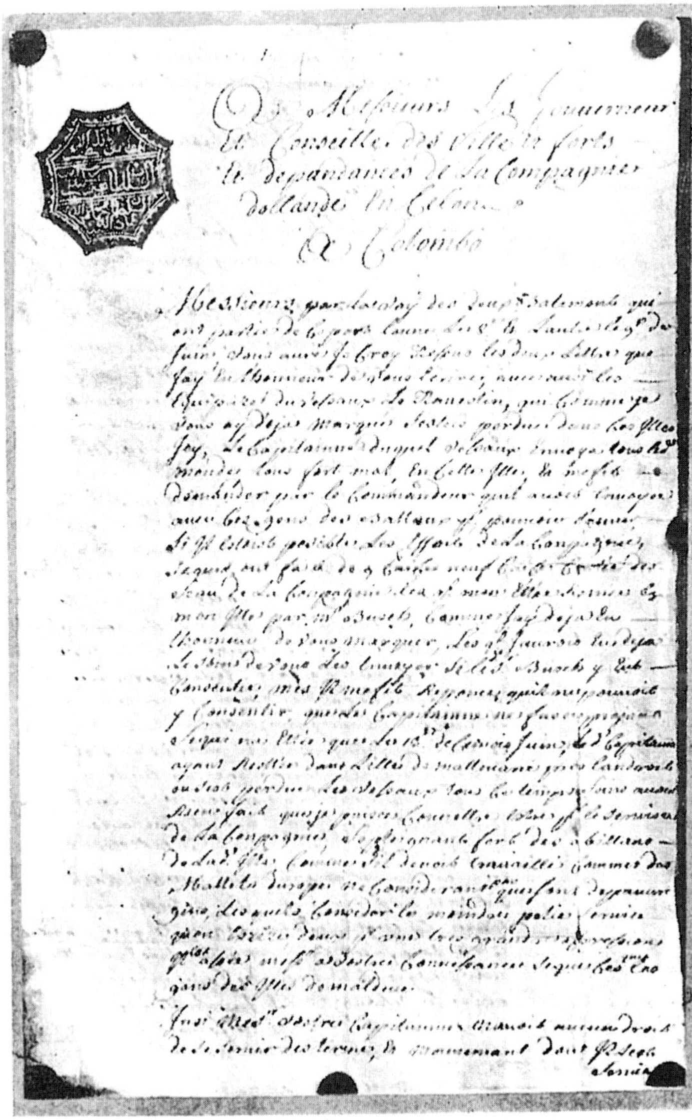

A Messieurs les Gouverneur
et Conseille des Ville et forts
et dependances de la Compagnie
d'ollande en Celan
a Colombo

No. 3. FRENCH MISSIVE : A. C. 1726.

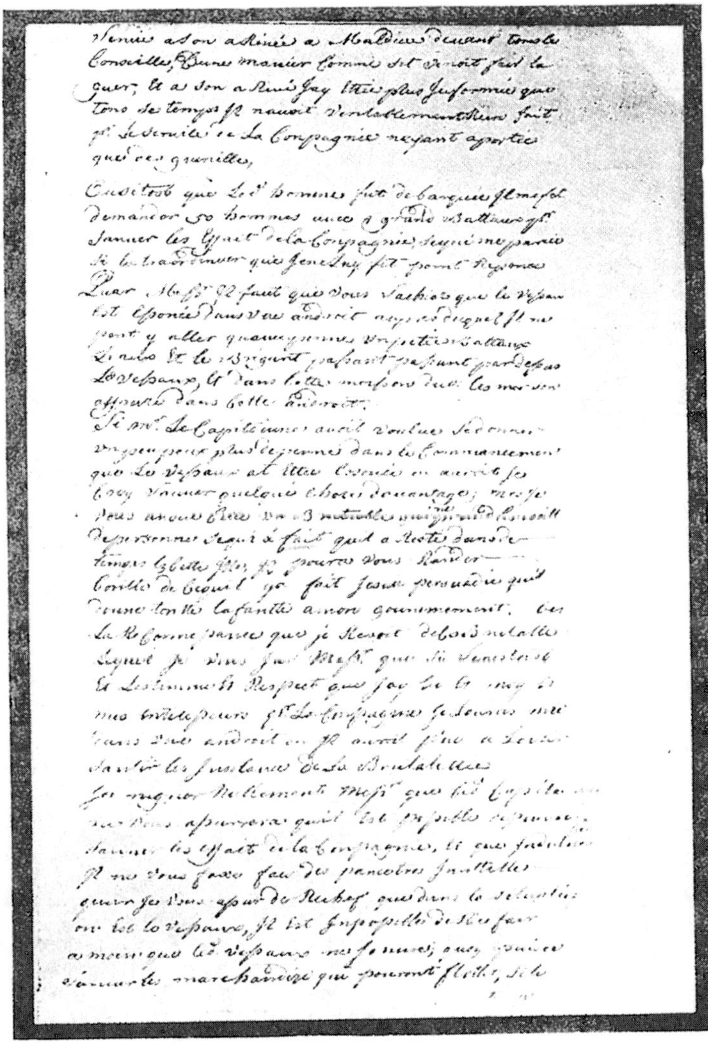

Venüe a son arrivée a Maldive devant tous le
Conseilles, d'une manier Comme sil venoit fair la
guer, et a son arrivé Jay Ettée plus Jnformée que
tous ce temps il navoit veritablement Rien fait
pr. Le service de La Compagnie ne yant aporttée
que ces querelles,

Aussitost que Les hommes fut debarquée il me fit
demander 50 hommes avec 4 grands Battaux pr.
sauver les Effect de la Compagnie, Lequel me parut
si extraordinaire que Je ne Luy fit point Reponce
Car Messr. Il faut que vous Sachiés que le vessau
est Esconcée dans vne androit auprés duquel il ne
peut y aller quavecque nos petites battaux
[illegible] et le brigant pasant pasant par dessus
Le vessaux, et dans cette morsons [illegible] les mer son
afforte dans cette androit.
Si mr. Le Capitaine avoit voulue se donner
vn peu peu plus de peinnes dans le Commancement
que Le vessaux at Ettee Esconcée on auroit pu
[illegible] sauver quelque Choses dauantage; mes je
vous avoue [illegible]
de personnes Lequi a fait quil a Reste dans ce
temps [illegible] pouvoir vous Rendre
[illegible] persuadée quil
donne toutte la facultée a mon gouvernement [illegible]
La Reconnoissance que je Reçoit [illegible]
Lequel je vous [illegible] Messr. que [illegible]
Et [illegible] et Respect que Jay [illegible]
mes [illegible] pr. La Compagnie [illegible]
dans vne androit ou il auroit [illegible]
[illegible] les [illegible] de sa Brutalitée
Je [illegible] Messr. que Led Capitaine
[illegible] vous asseurera quil est Jmpossible [illegible]
sauver les effait de la Compagnie, et que [illegible]
il ne vous [illegible]
[illegible] vous [illegible] de Rechef que dans la situation
ou est le vessaux, il est Jmpossible de Rien fair
a moins que les vessaux ne [illegible]
sauver les marchandise qui pourront flotter, [illegible]

No. 3. FRENCH MISSIVE: A. C. 1726.

No. 3. FRENCH MISSIVE : A. C. 1726.

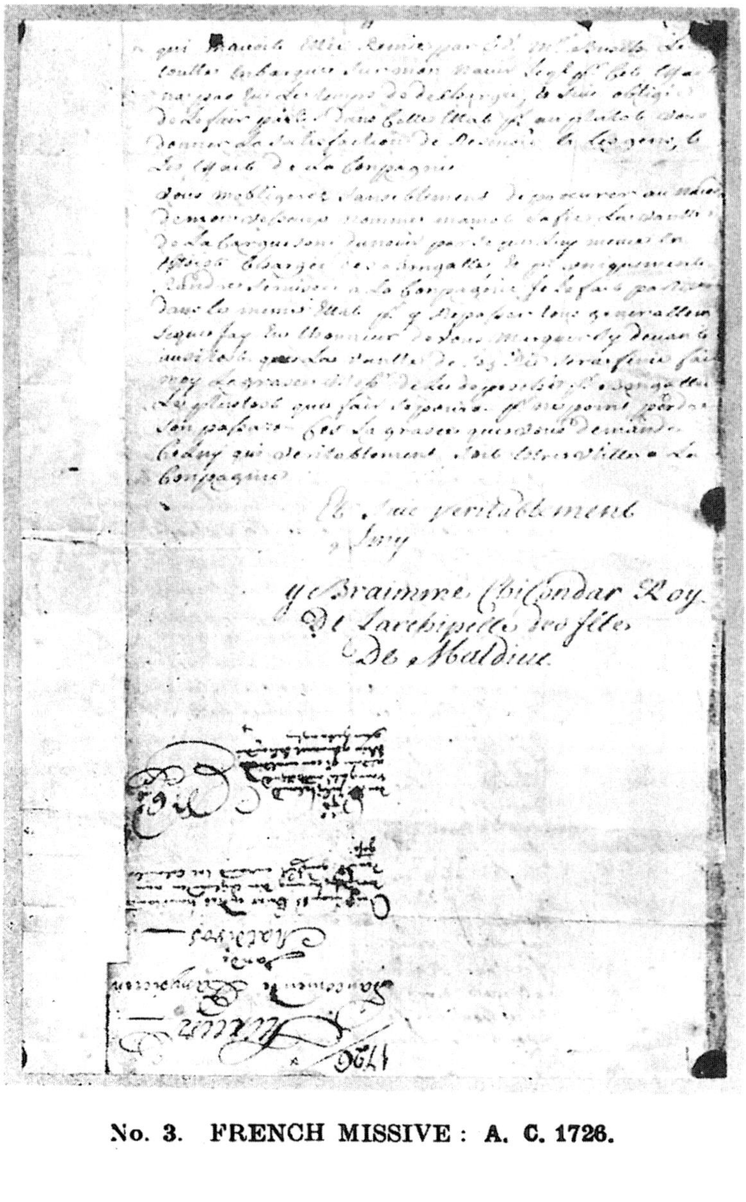

No. 3. FRENCH MISSIVE : A. C. 1726.

No. 4. MÁLDIVIAN MISSIVE : **A. H. 1144 (A. C. 1732).**

"Your Excellency (*Manikufánu*) is the rightful Magnate We deem, whom, it is proper to notify regarding Our every want.

"On this occasion, We inform Your Excellency (that) We are desirous (to secure) from Your Excellency the disposal of the goods taken (to Ceylon) this year by the (Annual) Vessel, at the same prices as they fetched last year—after adjusting the account for Cowries supplied.

"May it please Your Excellency to cause the (early) despatch of these men (Máldivians); so that they may make the return Voyage in company with the men who had (previously) remained (in Colombo).

Presents

"Albeit the Presents, (which are) being sent by Us, are not a befitting, and worthy, gift (*Hadia*) for Your Excellency (*Tibá Beikalun*), We are desirous of their (*lit.* these Presents) acceptance.

"Be it noted that this (Missive) is written, and despatched to Your Excellency, on the 24th day of April (*Aburílun*) in the Christian Year (*Iságefanu Ḥijurain*) (*lit.* *Hijra* of Jesus Christ) 1732.

"God knoweth everything."

APPENDIX A.

TABULATED STATEMENT OF MÁLDIVE SULTÁNS' ORIGINAL MISSIVES : (A.C. 1711-1822-23.)*

No.	Dynasty	Sulṭan	Reign	Missives			
				Arabic	Portuguese	French	Máldivian
1	Diyamigili ..	S. Muḥammad 'Imád-ud-dín II Mûzaffar	1704-1721	—	—	—	2
2	Do ..	S. Íbráhím Ískandar II ..	1721-1750	2	3	1	9
3	Do ..	S. Muḥammad Mukarram 'Imád-ud-dín III	1750-1757	—	—	—	8
4	Muli ..	S. Ḥasan 'Izz-ud-dín I ..	1759-1767	1	—	—	6
5	Diyamigili ..	S. Muḥammad Ghiyás-ud-dín ..	1767-1774	1	—	1	5
6	Muli ..	S. Muḥammad Shams-ud-dín II ..	1774	—	—	—	—
7	Do ..	S. Muḥammad Mu'íz-ud-dín ..	1774-1779	—	—	—	3
8	Do ..	S. Ḥasan Núr-ud-dín ..	1779-1799	—	—	—	19
9	Do ..	S. Muḥammad Mu'in-ud-dín I ..	1799-1823†	—	—	—	11
			Total..	4	3	2	63

* This List of Extant Original Missives ends with the latest *Tana* Missive known of Sulṭán Muḥammad Mu'in-ud-dín I, dated A.H. 1238 (A.C. 1822-23).

† After a hiatus of nine years, the Annual Series continues with a Missive written in *Arabic* ; and, so far as is known, that language, and script, have been exclusively utilised from A.H. 1247 (A.C. 1831-32) onwards up-to-date, for all such communication, during the reigns of the seven Sulṭáns from S. Muḥammad 'Imád-ud-dín IV to the present Ruler S. Ḥasan Núr-ud-dín II.

APPENDIX B.

LETTER OF GOVERNOR I. A. RUMPF.

To the Blessed Sulṭán Íbráhím, King of the Máldives.

"With the arrival of Your Highness' Vessel, We have had also the honour to receive Your Highness' kind Letters accompanied with a Present ; for which We heartily thank you.

Death of Sulṭán Muḥammad 'Imád-ud-din II Muzaffar.

We have learned, with great sorrow, from the Postscript of Your Highness' Missive, and from Your Highness' *Nákhudá*, the death of the Lord Your father, King Muḥammad 'Imád-ud-dín, who always kept up valued friendship with Our illustrious Lords and Masters (Dutch East India Company).

We sympathise with Your Highness most sincerely in this incalculable loss. Concurrently, We express the wish for Your Highness to enjoy all possible blessing and prosperity in Your Highness' succession to, and occupation of, the Máldivian Throne ; on which We pray God Almighty most fervently to establish Your Highness firmly, making Your Highness' reign long and victorious over all enemies, to the joy of Us, who take exceedingly great interest in Your Highness' success

Presents.

We offer through Your Highness' *Nákhudá* a small Present as a token of Our affection and esteem and for the preservation of the mutual friendly relations which Your Highness' welcome Missive above-mentioned requests of Us. This We are fully inclined to show on all occasions, as ever hitherto ; and for this purpose We have been helping the subjects of Your Highness who have come over here ; and supplied them again this year with all they asked which seemed reasonable.

Cowry Supplies.

Already several years in succession We have insisted on a larger importation of *Cowries*. We have increased their price, and have paid for them with such wares and money as Your Highness' subjects require ; and for which other Traders offer here at lowest prices. In spite of all this, the quantity diminishes every year—so much so that at times We have been in the greatest difficulty to find sufficient as ballast for the Ships of the Honourable (East India) Company.

To Our greatest regret We would have been forced, on account of that want, simply to hold them (the Ships) up here, had We not bought from French and other Ships coming from the Máldive Islands a large quantity of Cowries at Rds. 1½ per *cotty*. (*kóṭṭé*). From this We see that these strangers get preference in this trade in the Dominions of Your Highness, and that the subjects of Your Highness are not pressed by Your Highness to bring in good time to this Island greater quantities of Cowries—a commodity which the Honourable Company takes over for good money and a higher price than Your Highness' subjects sell them for in the Máldives to the said nations.

Therefore, once more We press Your Highness, (who has ascended so gloriously the throne of Your Illustrious Forefathers) to pay attention to the difficulty which the Honourable Company undergoes, and to consider such measures with regard to Your Highness' subjects as in Your great wisdom is deemed necessary for a larger and earlier importation of these shells into Ceylon. We are always ready to give for them as much money as Your Highness shall assure Us that Your subjects do receive from others ; so that they, and We ourselves, may then be satisfied.

We have left this matter to be considered in conference with Your Highness' *Nákhudá*. We shall rest satisfied with the Report which he has undertaken to lay before Your Highness.

Dutch Vessels' possible Trading visit to Mále.

If there are no other means to get yearly more Cowries by importation through the Vessels of Your Highness' subjects, the Noble Company might decide to send over to Your Highness' Islands some Vessels to buy, at a reasonable rate, cargoes of Cowries. With regard to this, We desire to be informed of Your Highness' decision, and intentions ; as well as of anything which We could do for the service of Your Highness.

I. A. RUMPF.

Colombo, 10th December, 1721.

EXCERPTA MÁLDIVIANA.

No. 14.—MÁLDIVIAN TABOO OF FREE ENGLISH EDUCATION.

By

H. C. P. Bell, C.C.S. (Retired)

FOREWORD

In a recent Paper,[1] the marked timidity of the Máldive Islanders—that isolated insular race of original Áryan blood, converted from Buddhism by Arabic infiltration to rigid Islámic Faith in A.C. 1153, or nearly eight centuries ago—was asserted to be "gradually diminishing," but hardly less keenly anxious than formerly for the minimum degree of association with foreigners, alien in stock and religion.

This tediously slow, and automatically delayed, advance towards mutual trade intercourse and economic benefit, has covered, roughly speaking, well-nigh a hundred years of Muslim Rule, under in great part the fluctuating reigns of half a dozen Sulṭáns[2] "cabined, cribb'd, confin'd, bound in" to an area one mile by half that limit, varying in their actions, according to the barometrical pressure, under chronic internal civil disturbances, of changing factional origin at Máḷe.

The *fons et origo* to the not unnatural diminution of Máldivian fear of the outside world may, with considerable reason, be attributed to two broad causes, viz., the once prevalent, yearly-growing influx of Indian (Borah) Merchants,[3] invited to settle at Mále as monopolisers of the essential Rice Trade with the Islands; and, secondly, to purely fortuitous circumstances, which virtually forced the continued residence in Ceylon of A. Ali Didi, a disgruntled Máldivian *Bodun*, or Noble, of High Rank and Position, culminating in the protracted domicile in the Island by his descendants to the second or third generation.

Pari pasu with this inevitable, if tardy, lessening of Máldivian temperamental timidity, there has very greatly passed away that co-existing bane of stubborn suspicion and mistrust, exhibited with such comic vividness in the first third of the Nineteenth Century, (fostered by rival Official supporters of obstructive Máldivian Administrative policy), in connection with the British Admiralty Survey of the Máldive Archipelago in A.C. 1835.

As to this entertaining episode, contemporary record can best tell its own quaintly intriguing story.[4]

EXCERPTA MALDIVIANA : No. 14.

1. BRITISH SURVEY OF THE MÁLDIVE ISLANDS.

A Survey of the Máldive Islands, lying in the direct track of Trade to India, had been for many years considered of the greatest importance to Navigation in these Seas.

"After the completion of other Marine Surveys in the Indian Ocean, Captain Moresby was ordered to proceed to the Islands in the *Benares*, with the *Royal Tiger* and the *Maldiva* as tenders. He carried Special Letters to the Sultán from the Governments of Bombay and Ceylon, clearly setting forth the object of his mission.

"The *Benares* arrived at Mále on the 15th November, 1834; but her appearance excited among the natives such apprehensions as augured ill for friendly intercourse.

"Natural timidity of character, and recent political circumstances, combined to induce this feeling.

"The mal-administration of the reigning Sovereign (Sulṭán Muḥammad Mu'in-ud-dín I A.C. 1799-1835), and the egotistical interests of his Ministers had, two years previously, provoked a bloodless " Rebellion " headed by the Sulṭán's brother-in-law H. Aḥmad Dídí *Doṛiméná Kilége-fánu.*[5]

"The insurgents were successful, and secured the person, and threatened the life, of their Ruler; who procured his safety and release by promising satisfaction of their demands.

"Aḥmad Dídí, mistrustful of the Royal word, left the Máldives secretly for Arábia. Returning for a while to Cochin, he watched the course of events at home; being supposed at Mále to be meditating the exploitation of a Malabar Invasion—the dread effects of which had been more than once felt in former days by the Islanders.

"Captain Moresby was supposed, not unnaturally, to be the agent of Aḥmad Dídí's scheming.

"As soon as the Survey Vessels anchored off Mále, a boat was sent off to demand the cause of the visit. The Máldivians' uneasiness was not dispelled by the request for permission to carry out a Survey of the Group.

"An interview with the Sulṭán being proposed, His Ministers at length came on board, apologising for the delay on account of His Highness' ill-health; but were very careful not to commit themselves by answering questions. No information could be obtained from them for many days: at length the Sulṭán's health suddenly improved, and a further interview was fixed; but on the appointed day His Highness had a relapse.

"Ultimately, Captain Moresby was compelled to state definitely that he would commence the Survey on a specified date with, or without, consent. On that day operations commenced without permission.

"The Máldivians were additionally alarmed at the time by a Letter from the Bengal Government regarding the

Establishment of a Coal Depôt on the Islands. To this proposal the Sulṭán excused himself from acceding, on the grounds of "indifferent anchorage, and the bad disposition of his subjects."

"Gradually, the natives grew somewhat more easy in mind, although by no means free from all apprehensions; for the "spell" of the British Surveying Flags was fatuously objected to until they were allowed to set up their own also."

The chief obstacles in the way of friendly intercourse were eventually removed by events consequent on the death of Sulṭán Muḥammad Mu'in-ud-dín I in January, 1835, and the accession, at the age of 17, of his second son, under the title of Sulṭán Muḥammad 'Imád-ud-dín IV.[6]

Distress among the Islanders was increasing; and the public voice demanded the recall of Ahmad Dídí. The young Ruler, therefore, invited his uncle to join the State Council; on which he became the most influential personage and adviser, although declining any Official Portfolio.

2. H. AHMAD DÍDÍ KILÉGEFÁNU AND DESCENDANTS.

Always favourable to the British, Aḥmad Dídí used the advantage of his position to pay a debt of gratitude for chance rescue at sea in a Man-of-war, by forwarding the early completion of the Admiralty Survey, convincing the Islanders of the folly of opposing so powerful a Government from whose Dominions was almost exclusively derived their staple food (Rice), and endeavouring generally to remove any bad impressions which the unsophisticated actions of his countrymen might have given.

He even obtained permission for Naval Lieutenants I. A. Young and W. Christopher to remain at Mále after the departure of the *Benares*.

The value of these services may be gauged by assessing the elusive character of the Máldivians, so tenaciously displayed.

Aḥmad Dídí, endowed with far more enlightened views than the majority of his fellow-Chieftains, remained steadfast in his predilection for the English ; and continued to exercise at Mále marked beneficial control in political affairs for some years.

Much of his ability was inherited by his son 'Ali Dídí[7] (commended by the Sulṭán in 1850 to the notice of Lord Torrington, Governor of Ceylon), who, as stated above, became a domiciled Ceylon subject, and resided at Galle until his death. Through keeping up his commercial intercourse with the Islands, and India, he acquired considerable wealth.

At one time serving at Mále as *Boḍu Baḍéri*, or Treasurer. certain intolerable embarrassments connected with State Finance falling unduly on his personal estate, are rumoured to have led to permanent estrangement with Sulṭán 'Imád-ud-dín, his cousin, and driven him to seek relief by definitely settling in this Island.

His son Íbráhím Dídí *Doṛiméná Kilégefánu,*[8] Prime Minister to several Royal occupiers of the *Masnad*, received an English education in Ceylon ; as did his three able sons, and some of their children—virtually all of whom have held, in due course, the highest State Offices of trust in the Máldive Administration.[9]

3. MÁLDIVIAN REJECTION OF FREE ENGLISH EDUCATION.

The warped mantle of Sulṭán Muḥammad Mu'in-ud-dín I, in regard to closer intercourse between Máldive Islanders and the British in Ceylon fell, as said. on his hardly less prejudised, and unprogressive, son, Sulṭán Muḥammad

Imád-ud-dín IV, who occupied the throne from A.C. 1835 to 1882, or over forty-six years.

His narrow-minded attitude was to be exceptionally exhibited within four years of accession, on the unique occasion of a special liberal offer by the Governor of Ceylon to the Máldivian Ruler.

4. LETTER OF GOVERNOR SIR J. A. STEWART MACKENZIE: A.C. 1838.

On November 6th, 1838, Sir J. A. Stewart Mackenzie, then Governor of this Island, addressed the following exceptionally generous Letter of invitation to His Highness the Sultan Muhammad 'Imád-ud-dín IV:

The Governor's Letter

The Queen's House,
Colombo, 26th November, 1838.

His Highness Sultán Muhammad 'Imád-ud-dín,
Máldive Islands.

"I have received, by Your Highness's Ambassador. Your Highness's very friendly Letter, and I much rejoice to hear of Your health and Your continued friendship for the British Government and for myself.

"I shall do everything in my power to promote the good understanding which exists between us, and I am confident that, should any British Vessels touch at the Máldive Islands, Your Highness will afford them protection and furnish them with such articles as they may require.

"Your Ambassador Ibráhím *Nákuda* has conducted himself in a very proper manner, and much to my satisfaction. I have sent by him some Presents, which I beg Your Highness to receive as tokens of the friendship of the British Government.

"Having understood that it is the wish of Your Royal Highness, as well as that of many of Your subjects to be taught the English Language, I am prepared to give them the opportunity of acquiring that language, without any cost to themselves ; and I invite two of Your Royal Highness's subjects, not exceeding 16 years of age, whom You may be pleased to select and send to Colombo.

"I would also propose that those youths should be accompanied by two Members of their own family, who will be kindly received, on a temporary visit. They will have the means of seeing where the scholars are to be settled, and of being satisfied as to the place and situation where the two youths reside while they remain in Ceylon to learn the English Language.

"May Your Highness continue to enjoy a prosperous and happy reign.

(Sgd.) J. A. STEWART MACKENZIE."[10]

The name of the Governor's informant remains unknown ; but, if he was still alive, could hardly have been other than that stout supporter of British interests, Ahmad Dídí *Doriménú Kilégefánu*, who figured so prominently in the British Admiralty's Survey transaction of 1835.

But, be that as it may, it is evident that even Ahmad Dídí's advocacy of the far-reaching action of the English Government could not prevail against the counter factional influence brought to bear on their weak Sovereign by other Members of the Máldivian Administration and Aristocracy, bent on a selfish policy of crass folly, which would nullify inevitably the wise prophetic vision of British enlightenment.

The fatuous result is painfully shown up by the sequel.

5. REPLY OF SULTAN MUHAMMAD 'IMAD-UD-DIN : A.H. 1255 (A.C. 1839[11])

The Arabic Missive, dated in the month Sh'abán A.H. 1255 (A.C.1839) despatched in answer to the Governor

Sir Stewart Mackenzie's Letter by Sulṭán Muḥammad 'Imád-ud-dín IV, (A.C. 1835-1882), though couched in terms of strict courtesy and friendliness, declines unequivocally Sir Stewart Mackenzie's tentative effort towards initiating for the Máldive Race sure means of steady emergence from semi-darkness into continuous enlightened advancement, by association with the world at large.

The Sultán's Missive

" His Royal Highness Muḥammad 'Imád-ud-dín, the Sulṭán of the Máldive Islands, wishes many (*sic*) prosperity and success, to His Excellency the Right Honourable the Governor of Ceylon.

" We have received Your esteemed Letter, and kind Presents.

" From the perusal of Your Letter, We were fully convinced of the great inclination (*sic*) Your Excellency bears towards Us.

" Your Excellency has been pleased to desire (*sic*) Us to send from Our Dominion two youths, below 16 years of age, to Your Island, for the purpose of being Educated in Your Language, without any expense to Us, either for their education or boarding ; and, moreover, that two of Our people may be sent thither to see if those youths are settled and comfortably kept there.

" This proposal We are conscious, has emanated from Your Excellency with a view of promoting and perpetuating the good understanding existing between Us.

" But We regret that Our Religious Principles do not allow Us to avail Ourselves of the benefit of the kind offer thus made by Your Excellency : because Our Religious Tenets prohibit Our children being so instructed in their youth.

Please to accept Our respects and compliments

Sanat 1255, in the month of Shawwan."

The above represents the Official English version of the Sulṭán's Missive, as turned out in the Colombo Secretariat of the day, by an obviously incompetent or dishonest Translator—not improbably minded himself personally to strengthen the Máldive policy through deliberate misrepresentation.

Such a catagorical rejection (accepted Officially, without any question, solely on its bare misstated English face verbiage) of an ultra generous offer. naturally left the Ceylon Governor no option but to bow—doubtless with unfeigned regret—to the wholly uncompromising attitude of an semi-independent, friendly Ruler of however lowly, Islanders, be they never so unadvanced, owing to sea-girt isolation limiting them inevitably to extremely restricted outlook, and heavy disabilities against progress in cosmopolitan culture.

For diplomatic, no less than friendly, reasons the matter of the Educational topic was then allowed to drop incontinently ; and has never been resuscitated.

Sulṭán 'Imád-ud-dín's Reply, once accepted as decisive against all further attempt to provide the Máldivians gratuitously with an over-sea English Education, has resulted in the Máldive Administration following out to the present time, its own independent policy, untrammelled by outside interference of an embarrassing, albeit well-intentioned, nature.

6. MISTRANSLATION OF THE SULṬÁN'S MISSIVE

But mark. So far as ascertained, no effort seems to have been made by the British Authorities at Colombo to check the in part lamentable—not to say culpable—effusion quoted above ; foisted on the Ceylon Government, by a charlatan—may be venal—Ceylon Government "Máldive Translator," as professing to reproduce undistortedly the *ipsissima verba* of the Sulṭán's Arabic Letter.

For virtually a century, therefore, it has continued to discredit the Ceylon Archives by a sad blot on the Máldivian Government's fair name. in a deplorable travesty of the true wording—particular of the salient clauses—figuring in an important State Document, which unaccountably passed Official scrutiny in Ceylon, reflecting, sadly on British Clerical supervision of a past period.

The Translations of the Sulṭán's Missive, given below in the *Appendix*, will be welcomed as exculpating, (if far too belatedly) Sulṭán Muhammad 'Imád-ud-dín IV from the astoundingly unjust stigma under which His Highness has lain for a hundred years, thanks to down-right misrepresentation, totally unjustified, of the true motive for His Highness' rejection of an English " gift horse " so generously proffered for acceptance.

For, it is patent, in order to excuse Himself, as does the Sulṭán, for non-compliance with Sir Steuart Mackenzie's exceptional offer, puts forward the actual plea, *primâ facie* reasonable, of implied prohibitory Máldive Custom, or regulations. against Máldivian youths' inability to avail themselves of it.

" It is not possible for the boys of the Máldives," records His Highness emphatically—a Royal ruling to be regarded as absolutely sound as manifestly final. Such a simple plea would in itself have been sufficiently unchallengeable.

Sulṭán 'Imád-ud-dín was fully within his rights in employing, an he chose, a clear effective reason, had it but been duly represented even in an English garb as plainly stated in Arabic.

But it was not to be. The brazen assertion credited to His Highness in the garbled Translation of His Missive, submitted to the Ceylon Government for consideration, viz., that " Our (Máldivian) Religious Principles do not allow Us to avail Ourselves of the benefit of the kind offer . . . . because Our Religious Tenets prohibit Our children being so instructed in their youth", basely attributed to the Muhammadan Ruler, displays either crass inexcusable ignorance, or deliberate suppression, of Muslim tolerance universally adopted the world over in regard to the acquisition of other Tongues, *quâ* Secular Education, pure and simple as divorced from all Religious incorporation.

It is conceded openly by Muslims as a body that neither the *Qurán*. *Hadiz*, nor other recognized Religious Islamic Treatise, contain anywhere, either directly, or by fair inference, the slightest form of prohibition against any orthodox Followers of the Muhammadan Faith becoming acquainted, to the full, with various branches of Secular knowledge, whether derived from English, or other foreign sources.

7. BIBLE EPISODE.

Should it ever transpire that there still existed in the Forties of the Nineteenth Century at the Máldives an anti-British attitude, its continued prevalence may not impossibly have survived from the fiction during the Admiralty Survey of 1835, further increased by tradition of a chance incident, no less tactless than discourteous to the British, which occurred seemingly, it is rumoured, during early years of the reign of Sulṭán Muhammad Mu'in-ud-din I, who ascended the Máldive Throne in A.C. 1799.

To this well-meaning but unfortunate episode, which ended abortively for the particular Non-Conformist Religious Body, by prompt and drastic Máldivian Official action, the Indian Navy have a short reference in the Memoir of 1836.[12]

"So averse are the Island Authorities to anything like emigration that an attempt to Translate the New Testament, by means of a Hindustani *Munshi*, failed at Bengal.

"The man engaged was recalled by the Sultán to Mále, before the Gospel of St. Matthew had been gone through.

"We have seen and conversed with the Máldivian above referred to (he is now venerably gray), and he spoke of his engagement under the Rev. Mr. Brown with readiness and evident self-gratulation.

"This Translation as far as it goes, is, We believe, in the hands of the Serampore Missionaries."[13]

8. PROGRESS OF EDUCATION AT THE MÁLDIVES

Muslim Education has been authoritatively summed up in a pithy paragraph :—[14]

"Education without Religion is to the Muḥammadan mind an anomaly. In all Books of Traditions there are Sections specially devoted to the consideration of Knowledge ; but only as far as it relates to a knowledge of God, and of "God's Book"—the *Quran*.

"The outstanding aim and object of Education in Islám is to obtain a knowledge of the Religion of their Prophet; and anything beyond this is considered superfluous, and has been even held to be dangerous."

MUHAMMADAN CONVERSION : A.C. 1153.

The Conversion of the Máldivians to Muḥammadanism is definitely fixed by their *Tárikh*, or "State Chronicle of the Máldive Sulṭáns," as having occurred in the mid-Twelfth Century (A.H. 548 ; A.C. 1153), and—owing to the long-continued isolation of the Islanders for a period running nearly to eight centuries in its broad general form—has made comparatively little advance up to this day, in spite of intercourse inevitably growing, however slowly, decade by decade, with the outside World.

Of this markedly conservative progress, one or two brief glimpses may be casually got, here and there, from the all too short references afforded in haphazard notices in the *Tárikh*, and by the visits (only two so far as known) by Europeans, who had the opportunity,—ample in one case, very limited in the other—of studying, at first hand, the

Educational System in vogue at Mále, during the earliest years of the Seventeenth, and in the first half of the Nineteenth, Century.

9. FRANCOIS PYRARD: A. C. 1602-7.

The Purser of the *Corbin* (one of the first two French Vessels which voyaged to the East), wrecked on the Máldive Atols, spent five years of captivity at Mále, A.C. 1602-07.

In his lengthy and intriguing account of the Islands[15] François Pyrard used most regrettably scimped and tantalising brevity in his bare notice of Máldivian youths early-years' in education—outside the purely Religious branch of compulsory Muslim training, ruling on the Islands at the time.

What little the Frenchman puts on record goes to confirm the rigid persistence of the Islámic Code of Religious and Secular Instruction alike, imbibed for four and a half centuries since the Royal imposition of Muslim Proselitism at the Máldives.

His notice (exclusive of strictly Islámic Studies and Ceremonials) is limited to what follows :—

"Their studies are to read and write, and to learn their *Alcoran*, and so to know how they have to live.

"They write their lessons on little tablets of wood, which are whitened ; and when they have learned their lesson they efface what they have written, and whiten them afresh, unless the writing is required to be preserved.

"In that case, they write upon parchment made of the leaves of the tree *Macore queau*,[16] whose leaf is a fathom and a half long and a foot broad. They made books of it, which last as long or longer than ours, without decaying.

"In teaching their children to write, they use wooden boards made on purpose, well polished and joined, and spread thereon some fine, powdered sand ; then they make the letters with a bodkin and bid them imitate them, effacing betimes what they have written, and using no paper for this purpose.

"They all treat their Masters with the same respect and honour as their own fathers, by reason whereof they may not contract marriage together as though related in affinity.

"Among them are men who make a pursuit of Study, and are esteemed vastly learned in their knowledge of the *Alcoran*, and *Catibes*, or *Naybees*. These two offices are compatible; the *Catibe* may be a *Naybee*, and the *Naybee* a *Catibe*.[17]

"Mathematics are taught and much cultivated, especially Astrology, which is studied by many, seeing that the Astrologers are consulted at every turn."

Two hundred years later Lieut. Young and Christopher, of the Indian Navy Survey,[18] (who remained by permission at Mále for not many weeks after the completion of the British Admiralty Survey of the Máldives, till the dread "Mále Fever"[19] forced them to leave), were able as their quota to afford virtually no further details supplementing Pyrard's inadequate information touching youthful training.

10. I. N. LIEUTS. YOUNG AND CHRISTOPHER: A.C. 1835.

The Indian Navy Officers statement is equally brief:—

"Children of both sexes are required to read the *Koran* through under the tuition of priests of the inferior order; and their lesson is begun very early—at three years of age.

"To be able to read is all that appears to be thought necessary, and it is not pretended that more is attempted to be taught.

"When once through the *Koran*, the children receive no further instructions, except being initiated in the Ceremonials of Religion.

"As to a knowledge of writing, the children are left to acquire it themselves, if they feel inclined, in the best way they can; and hence arises the great difficulty experienced in determining either the true sound of letters, or the orthography of words."

Happily the course of events during the latter half of the Nineteenth, and the first third of this, Century, has opened up a very different outlook. Several Máldivians of gentle blood—Nobles and even scions of Royalty, during the past three-quarters of a century or more, have received a sound English Education at British Colleges in India and Ceylon.

This encouraging fact cannot but, in due time, bear still more satisfactory fruit than that already produced, and lead to the sure, if not as rapid as desirable, spread of greater general enlightenment at the Máldives ; with the introduction to *Arabic* and *Urdu*, at Mále of *English* as a welcome sister language, already adopted of a Tri-lingual group in lieu of the present day well-founded Bi-lingual limitation as now practised at the "Caffooria College," Colombo, with *Arabic* and *Tamil*.

11. MÁLDIVIAN EDUCATION : TWENTIETH CENTURY.

After the efflux of a further period of hundred years since the unhappily curtailed stay at Mále of Lieutenants Young and Christopher, the present writer was enabled (whilst specially engaged on the Archaeology of the Group) to jot down incidentally a thumb nail partial sketch of the position of Education (apart from its exclusive Muslim concomitants, in force at Mále in A.C. 1922.

The Notes then made is given below :—

"The Government Administration has long entered more than creditably for the Religious instruction of Máldive children, male and female, from about the age of six years.

"Throughout the Atols teaching devolves usually on the *Khaṭibs* and *Mudins*.

"At Mále children of Royalty, and the well-to-do higher classes, are taught at the Palace and their residences.

"For those who cannot afford private tuition, the Government subsidizes School Masters (M. *Eduru Míhun*) for the four Wards (M. *Avaru*).

"The Government further provides free copies of the *Qurán* in Sections for the use of children too poor to purchase them.

" Hours of attendance: 6.30 to 9.30 a.m. and 12.30 to 2.30 p.m. for young boys and girls; older and more advanced children may also come voluntarily at night from 6.30 to 8 p.m.

" Returns of the daily attendance have to be furnished every month by the *Eduru Míhun* to the *Bodu Baḍéri-Gé* (Secretariat and Treasury).

" In addition to learning to read the *Qurán*, all the daily prayers (M. *Namádu*) with the *Solavat* (Adoration of the Prophet) have to be got by heart.

" Children learn to write both *Tána* (current Máldivian Script) and *Arabic* on boards (M. *fila*).which are smeared with liquid lime allowed to dry. On this surface the letters are applied with a bamboo pen (M. *galan*), the ink (M. *davadu*) being made from burnt coconut-shell powdered.

" All pupils are expected to be able at least to read the whole of the *Qurán* before obtaining a Certificate of Efficiency.

" When scholars are considered qualified, a Report to that effect is made to the *Boḍu Baḍéri-Gé* by the Teachers; but they may continue to attend for further tuition in Religion.

" Arithmetic is not taught in the schools, but learnt from teachers or parents at home.

" In addition to regular Religious instruction at *Qurán Schools*, there are schools for Navigation, and others where the *Arabic*, *Urdu* and English languages and a deeper knowledge of Muslim Theology, can be acquired.

" From the Higher Schools, students may rise to be *Álims* (*Uluma*), and so become themselves qualified to teach at their own houses.

" A substantial building, bearing the appropriate superscription " *Madrasa* " (College) intended for such Advanced Students was built a few years ago in Henvéru Ward.

These curt sporadic notes may possibly adumbrate, if nothing more, faint signs of some ultimate substantial potential progress towards provision for the advancement of Education, both high and low, where—in fullness of time, be it never so delayed—the Complete Curriculum of Studies at the Máldive Islands will embrace a virile knowledge of the *English Language*, imparted in one or more " Colleges," as an essential part of the mental equipment of leading

Máldivians with whom the future advance of the Islands is inevitably bound up.

APPENDIX

SULTÁN'S MISSIVE : A.H. 1255

Missive in Arabic, dated Sh'abán, A.H. 1255, despatched by Sulṭán Muḥammad 'Imád-ud-dín IV, in reply to a Letter from His Excellency Sir J. A. Stewart Mackenzie, Governor of Ceylon.

This special Missive runs to twenty (20) lines of script in all—55 written vertically. 5 diagonally in the right-side margin.

The larger portion measures perpendicularly 8 in. by 2 in. crossways ; the concluding diagonal lines penned, 4½ in. by 3¼ in. respectively.

The Seal die of the Sulṭán, bearing the title (1) " *As-Sulṭán*, (2) *Muḥammad 'Imad*-(3)*ud-dín* " appears within a small Oval Frame, as adopted by this Ruler. In dimensions 7/8 in., by 5/8 in., it is placed well above the Text towards the right.

The Arabic words are inserted in brackets immediately after their respective English equivalents, and embrace the entire contents inclusive of its Muslim Religious Benediction.

As universally with Royal Máldivian documents. the Missive is inscribed in a neat hand.

Mr. A. Muḥammad Amin Dídí, son of Ahmad Dídí, Doriméná Kilégefánu, in his ever-ungrudging generosity, has most kindly favoured the writer with an admirably expressed Running Translation couched in Official Style.

The writer has also been kindly supplied no less kindly with another such Translation by Mr. E. 'Abdul Hamid Dídí, much on the lines of his nephew Muḥammad Amin Dídí's version here printed.

In addition to the above, a meticulous Word for Word Transcript and Translation, as made by Mr. M. T. Amír, the learned Khaṭíb of Vékanda Mosque, Colombo, is offered as of additional value.

AS-SULTÁN MUHAMMÁD 'IMÁD-UD-DÍN

Transcript

1. MIN SULṬÁN DÍBAT MUḤAMMAD 'IMÁD-UD-DÍN ILÁ HAZARAT AL-'ALÍYAT
2. VA AD-DAULAT AS-SANÍYAT. VA AL-MARÁTIB AL-BAHÍYAT A'ANI BIZALIKA ÍLÁ
3. MAḤBŪBIHI AL-MUBÍN AL-MUTADAUMATI ḤUBBU-NÁ VA ḤUBBU-HUM MIN QADÍM
4. AZ-ZAMÁN ILÁ AL-ÁN FÍ AL-UMARA AL-MAZÍN MAN KÁNA RAISAN
5. FÍ QIL'ATI SAILÁN AL-ḤAṢÍN KHAÍYARA ALLÁHU HÁLAHU MIN AḤSANI
6. AHWÁLI AS-SALÁṬÍN VA KAṢṢARA AMVÁLAHU VA A'IYÁLAHU VA ABṬÁLAHU
7. BILÁ ḤISÁB WALÁ TABIYÍN ṢUMMA AL-'ILÁMU ANNA KITÁBAKUM
8. VA HADIYATKUM AR-RAḤÍM AL-MUSTAHAB ATTARHÍM VÁRIDUN 'ALAINÁ
9. FAQA BILNÁ VA QARANÁ VA FAHIMNÁ MÁ FÍHÁ MIN AQVÁL AL-MAWÁDDATI VA AL-MURAHMATI
10. FA WAJADNÁ FÍHÁ ANNAKUM TUḤIBŪNA AN-NURSILA ILAIKUM GHULÁMAINI
11. MAFHŪMAINI MIN GHILMÁNINÁ VA 'UMRUHUMÁ TAḤTA SITTATI 'ASHRA SANAT
12. LITU 'ALLIMUHUMÁ ḤARFAKUM VA AQVÁLAKUM BILÁ SHAIIN MINNÁ VA LITHUSSINU LAHUMÁ IHSÁNAN
13. KAṢÍRÁ FÁ AḤASNA LIZALIKA GHAYAT ATTAḤABÍB VA AḤRÁ FÍ
14. QULUBINÁ 'ALAIKUM MÁ YAJRI FÍ QALB AL-MAḤBŪB LILḤABÍB WALAKIN
15. TARAKNÁ ZALIKA LIKAUNIHÁ LAMYUMKIN LIṢIBIYÁNI AD-DÍB
16. VA HAZA VA AS-SALÁMU 'ALAIKUM BILÁ MIQDÁR
17. WALÁ TAḤSÍB HURRIRA BI TÁRÍKH SHAHRI SH'ABÁN
18. SANAT 1255 MIN HIJRAT AN-NABIYI RASŪL AKHIRI
19. AZ-ZAMÁN SALL-ALLÁHU 'ALAHI VA 'ALÁ ÁLIHI VA AṢHÁBIHI
20. MÁ IKHTALAFA AL-JADIDÁN VA ṬAL'A AN-NIRÁN.

APPENDIX

Text

MÁLDIVE ISLANDS.

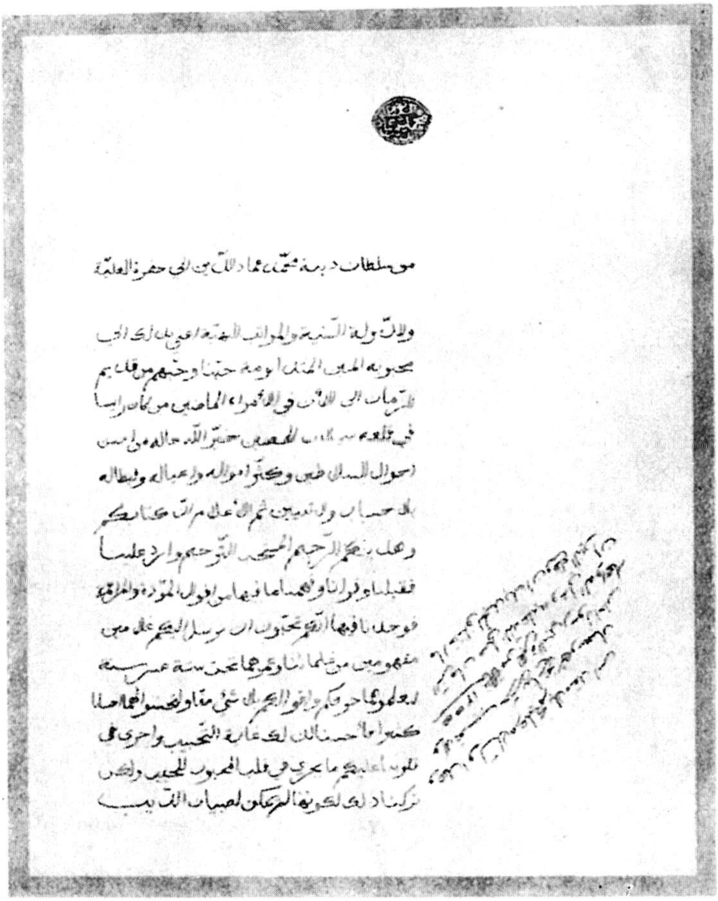

SULṬÁN'S MISSIVE : A. H. 1255.

Translation.

From the Sultán Muhammad 'Imád-ud-dín, the Sultán of the Máldives, to the Distinguished Presence His Excellency the Governor of Ceylon, (to wit. the Officer Administering the Noble Government of the protected Fortress of Ceylon), the friendship between Whom and Ourselves has been continuing from (the time of) the friendship of past Governors of Ceylon and Our Ancestors.

May God make His (the Governor's) State the choicest of States, and bless Him with wealth, descendants and army in numberless fold.

We have the honour to inform Your Excellency that We have received Your Excellency's loving and esteemed Letter and Presents We have read, and understood, the contents of the Letter, and have accepted the Presents (with pleasure). We (much) appreciate the words of love and mutual friendship expressed therein.

We note that it has pleased Your Excellency to invite Us to send two intelligent boys (of Our Nation), under sixteen years of age, to Ceylon, to be educated in Your Language and Script, and that they will be treated well, without any charges falling upon Us. We appreciate Your Excellency's good intention (for the Máldive Islands), and in Our heart We are grateful to the full for Your Excellency's offer, so friendly made; Nevertheless (We regret that) such action will not be suitable for the boys of the Máldive Islands.

May Peace be upon You.

Written in the month of Sh'abán in the year 1255 of the Hijr of the Last of the Prophets (Muhammad). May the blessings of God be (bestowed) upon Him and His family, as long as Day changes into Night and Sun and Moon appear.

Word for Word Transcript and Translation.

From (the) Sultán (*min Sultan*) of the Máldive Islands (*Díbat Muhammad 'Imád-ud-dín* to (His Excellency) (*lit.* the Exalted Presence, *ilá Hażarat al-Aliyat*), (the Governor) of the Government (*ad-Daulat*) noble (*as-saniyat*), renowned (*va al-marátib*), and pre-eminent (*al-bahiyat*) to wit: (*lit* whereby We mean) (*a'ani bi zalika*), to the well-beloved (Government) (*ilá maḥbubihi al mubín*) whose friendship (*ḥubbu-hum*) and Our friendship (*ḥubbu-ná*) have continued (*al-mutadaumati*) from olden time to the present (*min quadím az-zamán ilá al-án*).

Among the past (*Fi al mazín*) Governors (*al-umra*). (He) is the Paladin (*raisan*) who ruled (*lit* were *man kána*) in the protected (*al-ḥasín*) Fortresses of Ceylon (*Qil'ati Sailán*). May Allah ensure (*khaiyara Alláhu*) to Him the standing (*ḥálahu*) of the high estate (*min aḥwáli*) of the best (*aḥsani*) *Sulṭáns* (*As-Salátín*), and multiply (*va kaṣṣara*) His wealth (*amwála-hu*), and family (*va aiyálahu*), and soldiery (*va abṭálahu*) beyond limit (*bilá ḥisáb*) and description (*valátabiyn*).

Moreover (*Ṣumma*), We notify (*lit.* it is informed) (*al-ilámu*) that Your (Excellency's) Letter (*kitába-kum*) and Your pleasing (*ar-raḥím*), and praiseworthy (*al-mustahab attaraḥím*). Presents (*Hadiyat-kum*) have reached Us (*wáridun 'alai-na*). We have accepted (*faqabil-na*), and read, and understood (*va Qara-na va fahim-na*) what expressions of congeniality and friendship (*Má aqwálfiha va al-muráḥamati*).

Then, therein We found (*Fí há fa wajadná*) that You (Your Excellency), *anna kum*) (graciously) desires Us (*tuḥibú-na*) to send (*annursila*) to You (*ilaī-kum*) two of Our intelligent (*mafhúmaini*) boys (*ghilmáni-ná*) under the age of 16 years (*va umruhumá taḥta sittati 'ashra sannat*) to be instructed (*litu 'allimiuhuma*) in Your writing (*ḥarfa-kum*) and Your language (*va aqvála-kum*) without any expense (*lit.* anything) (*bilá shayin*) from Us (*min-ná*) and to treat them (*lituḥsinu lahumá*) with much kindness (*kaṣira ihsánan*).

Therefore, We felt (*Fa aḥas-na*) extremely touched (*lit.* deep love, *ghayat attaḥabíb*) for that (*lizalika*) (offer): and it is impressed upon Our hearts (*ahra fí qulubi-ná*) (in regard) to You (*alai-kum*) (like) that which fills (*lit.* will be *má yajrí*) in the heart (*fí qalb*) of the beloved (*al mahbúb*) towards the lover (*lil-habíb*).

But (*valakin*) We did not comply (*lit.* We put that off *tarak-ná zalika*), because it is (*likaunihá*) not possible (*lam yumkim*) for the boys (*liṣibiyáni*) of the Máldive Islands (*ad Díb*).

And this (*va haza*) (in conclusion) Peace be on You (*v'as salámu alai-kum*) without measure and without count (*bilá miqdar valá taḥsib*).

Written (*hurrira*) on (this) date (*bi tárikh*) in the month (*shahri*) of Sh'ban in the year (*Sanat*) 1255 of the Hijra (*Hijrat*) of the Prophet (*an-Nabiyi*)—the Messenger (*Rasúl*) for the last period (*akhiri az-zamán*).

May Allah bestow blessing (*ṣall-Allâhu*) on Him (*alaihi*) and His descendants (*va'ala álihi*) and followers (*va as-ḥábihi*), so long as (*má*) the two new things (Day and Night) (*al-jadidán*) change (*ikhtalafa*), and the Sun and Moon (*lit.* the luminous bodies *an-nirán*) rise (*va ṭal'a*).

FOOTNOTES

1. (P. 169) Journal, C.A.S., Vol. XXXIII, 87. 1934.

2. (P. 169) Sulṭán Muḥammad 'Imád-ud-dín IV (1835-1882); S. Íbráhím Núr-ud-dìn (1882-1886); S. Muḥammad Mu'in-ud-dín II (1886-1888); S. Íbráhím Núr-ud-dín (1888-1892); S. Muḥammad 'Imád-ud-dín V (1893); S. Muḥammad Shams-ud-dín III (1893); S. Muḥammad 'Imád-ud-dín VI (1893-1903); S. Muḥammad Shams-ud-dín III (1903-1934); S. Ḥasan Núr-ud-dín II (1934. reigning).

3. (P. 169) Borah Merchants (Shiah Muslims) of Northern India began to trade at the Máldives spasmodically from about the Sixties at last Century; and were gradually allowed to remain at Mále as their numbers slowly increased. A few firms still exist there, trading mainly in Rice, which the Islands do not produce to any appreciable degree.

4. (P. 170) "Memoir on the Inhabitants of the Máldiva Islands" (Transactions, Bombay Branch, Geographical Society) by Lieutenants I. A. Young and W. Christopher, of the Indian Navy, 1836-38, p. 50.

5. (P. 171) Aḥmad Dídí *Doriméná Kilégefánu*, son of Ḥusain *Fámudéri Kilégefánu*, and descended, through collateral branches from one common ancestor (Don Maraduru Fandi Kalégefánu of 'Hurá) as the Muli Dynasty of Sulṭáns still reigning. See Sessional Paper XV, 1921; Appendix D.

6. (P. 172) Sulṭán Muḥammad Mu'in-ud-dín I (A.C. 1799-1835) had married Burunigé Dídí, a sister of Aḥmad Dídí *Doriménú Kilégefánu*. Aḥmad Dídí, as Prime Minister, had the confidence of the British Governors of Ceylon, and did not fail at times to play "Gaházi" to the Sulṭán's "Elisha." See C.A.S. Journal for amusing confirmation.

7. (P. 173) 'Ali Dídí, son of Ḥ. Aḥmad Dídí *Doriméná Kilégefánu*, held the post of *Bodu Baḍéri* (Treasurer) at Mále for a while, prior to settling definitely at Galle in Ceylon, where he died.

8. (P. 173) Íbráhím Dídí *Doriméná Kilégefánu*, eldest son of A. Ali Dídí, born in Mále, lived in Ceylon before returning to the Máldives in 1884, where he held official charge of the Revenue and Customs Departments under both S. Muḥammad 'Imád-ud-dín IV and his son S. Íbráhím Nùr-ud-dín. He was virtually Prime Minister as those Sulṭáns' Chief Adviser, and later, he occupied the full substantive post under other Sulṭáns. He died at Mále in A.C. 1929 greatly regretted. *Multis ille flebilis occidit.*

9. (P. 173) I. Ahmad Dídí *Doriméná Kilégefánu*: Ámir 'Abdul Majid Dídí. *Ranna Badéri Kilégefánu*; 'Abdul Hamid Dídí Effendi, long Máldivian Government Representative in Ceylon (sons of Íbráhím Dídí *Doriméná Kilégefánu*), A. Muḥammad Amín Dídí (son of Ahmad Dídí), A. M. Muḥammad Farid, A. M. Ḥasan Farid (sons of Amir 'Abdul Majid Dídí).

10. (P. 175) Máldivian State Records, Colombo, 1838.

11. (P. 175) History has repeated itself. All Missives issued by Sultáns of the Máldives, from A.C. 1825 at least to 1933, were written at Mále in Arabic, and their English Translations made in Colombo. These were apparently unchecked by competent Interpreters, and the scandal of mistranslation naturally grew, until repeated travesties in distorted and incomplete rendering of Missives from the Island Rulers became at length so marked and intolerable as to force the Máldivian Administration to the necessity of reverting to the older time system of despatching Royal Documents almost invariably written in Máldivian language and Character (*Tána*), accompanied further at the present day by English Translations made at Mále itself. This reversion to the former practice, with this added security came into adoption at the date of the Institution of the Máldivian Administration of the New Constitution for the Máldive Islands promulgated in 1934.

12. (P. 179) "Memoir on the Inhabitants of the Máldiva Islands."

13. (P. 180) The unsuccessful quest by careful enquiry regarding the fate of this Translation into the Máldive Language of St. Matthew's Gospel will be found set-out in full in the Ceylon "Times" and "Observer" of January 14, 1925.

14. (P. 180) "Dictionary of Islám" (Hughes) p. 18.

15. (P. 181) Voyage of François Pyrard, 1619, (Hak. Soc.), Vol. I, pp. 184-186.

16. (P. 181) Máldivian *Má-karikeyo* (Sinhalese *Vetakeyiyá*), *Pandanus odoratissimus*. See C.A.S. Journal. Vol. XXVII, Extra No. 1,919, pp. 161-2.

17. (P. 182) Regarding Máldivian *Khatibs*, *Naibus*, etc. See Pyrard, Vol. I, pp. 123-150 ; Sessional Paper, XIX, 1821, pp.

18. (P. 182) "Memoir on the Inhabitants of the Máldiva Islands."

19. (P. 182) *Mále Fever.* (M. *Mále huma*). This likely Máldive synonym for the modern deadly "*Malaria*" scourge, known so fatally in Ceylon and elsewhere, seems to attack all Europeans who make a prolonged stay at Mále. It well-nigh killed the Captive Pyrard in 1602-07 ; obliged Lieutenants Young and Christopher to hasten their departure from the Islands in 1835, and has not spared later visitors to the Máldives.